Urban Transport and the Environment
for the 21st Century

FIRST INTERNATIONAL CONFERENCE ON URBAN TRANSPORT AND THE ENVIRONMENT (URBAN TRANSPORT 95)

Conference Chairmen

L.J. Sucharov and C.A. Brebbia
Wessex Institute of Technology, Southampton, UK

International Scientific Advisory Committee

P. Bly (UK)
R.D. Bornstein (USA)
D.E. Boyce (USA)
T. de la Barra (Venezuela)
F. Filippi (Italy)
T.C. Giras (USA)
C.A. Guillen (Brazil)
Y. Hayashi (Japan)
R. Howell (UK)
B. Hutchinson (Canada)
L. Lundqvist (Sweden)
M. McDonald (UK)
I. Masser (UK)
G. Mattrisch (Germany)
K. Miyamoto (Italy)
D.J. Palmer (UK)
N. Papola (Italy)
C. Peters (UK)
G. Sciutto (Italy)
P. Segretain (France)
M.A.P. Taylor (Australia)
A. Yeh (Hong Kong)

Organized by:

Wessex Institute of Technology

Sponsored by:

American Society of Civil Engineers (UK Chapter)
and
The Institution of Highways and Transportation

Urban Transport and the Environment
for the 21st Century

Editor:

L.J. Sucharov

Wessex Institute of Technology, Southampton, UK

Computational Mechanics Publications

Southampton Boston

L.J. Sucharov
Wessex Institute of Technology
Ashurst Lodge, Ashurst
Southampton, SO40 7AA
UK

Published by

Computational Mechanics Publications
Ashurst Lodge, Ashurst, Southampton SO40 7AA, UK
Tel: 44 (0)1703 293223, Fax: 44 (0)1703 292853

For USA, Canada and Mexico

Computational Mechanics Inc
25 Bridge Street, Billerica, MA 01821, USA
Tel: 508 667 5841, Fax: 508 667 7582

British Library Cataloguing-in-Publication Data

A Catalogue record for this book is available
from the British Library

ISBN 1-85312-323-4 Computational Mechanics Publications, Southampton
ISBN 1-56252-247-7 Computational Mechanics Publications, Boston

Library of Congress Catalog Card Number 95-67484

*The texts of the various papers in this volume were set
individually by the authors or under their supervision*

PREFACE

One of the greatest challenges facing the next millennium is to effect a well integrated and environmentally acceptable solution for urban transportation. The First International Conference on Urban Transport and the Environment, held in Southampton in June 1995, enabled planners and engineers from around the world to address the problems of urban transportation. In spite of many decades of studies, involving research and experiments, success has often been elusive and more importantly, there is still a lack of consensus of what constitutes an acceptable integrated transport policy within the urban fabric and its impact on the environment.

This book presents over fifty papers from researchers and planners worldwide in all aspects of urban transport systems: future vision, environmental aspects, planning and design, urban safety, and emerging technologies.

Our thanks are due to all those who have contributed to the Conference, with special thanks to the International Scientific Advisory Committee who have helped in refereeing the papers and thus have assisted in the success of the meeting.

In fact the success of the meeting has been somewhat anticipated by our European colleagues in that the Universitat Politécnica de Catalunya have offered to host the second Conference. This offer has been accepted, and consequently the meeting will be reconvened in Barcelona on 2-4 October 1996.

Lance J. Sucharov
Southampton, June 1995

CONTENTS

SECTION 3: ENVIRONMENTAL ASPECTS

SECTION 4: PLANNING AND DESIGN

SECTION 1:
URBAN TRANSPORT SYSTEMS

Railways as an urban transport system: roles, technologies and analysis tools

M. Galaverna, A. Imovilli, G. Sciutto
Dipartimento di Ingegneria Elettrica, Università degli Studi di Genova, Via all'Opera Pia, 11a, I-16145 Genova, Italy

1. Introduction

Railway is the most effective, safest and most economical mode of transport that allows large amounts of people to travel inside urban areas. Moreover, the use of electric traction makes the railway an urban transport system that is "clean" in terms of the severe problem of air pollution. Unfortunately, building new metrorail systems is often unfeasible, due to huge obstacles of economic and environmental nature. In view of these considerations, there is currently a growing interest in the possibility of utilizing the existing railway lines, both state-owned and licensed.

Actually, in most cases, railway lines go through medium and large Italian cities; however, only in few cities do railway lines play a key role in urban transport.

2. The role of railway in urban transport: the Italian situation

The exploitation of railway lines as a support for city traffic, at least in the main directions of traffic, is encountering many difficulties.

Although each city must face specific problems, nevertheless, it is possible to define some situations typical for many Italian cities. An important factor is represented by the dependence of the direction of railway lines on the shapes of the urban areas they go through. In this context, it is possible to distinguish three types of cities:

a) coastal cities with a linear expansion, through which railway lines are in the direction of length, with many stations inside urban areas (e.g. Genoa, Bari, Naples, Reggio Calabria);

b) cities about circular in shape, tangent to railway lines, with one or two stations in urban areas (e.g. Bologna and many cities of medium dimensions);

c)   cities of various shapes, with terminal stations in central areas and some transit stations in urban areas (e.g. Turin, Milan, Florence, Rome, Palermo).

Type a) cities are of course the most suited for the use of existing railway lines as support lines for urban traffic. At present, in all the aforesaid cities of this type, trains of Italian Railways are already utilized for urban services. In these cities, the requirements for the development of train services concern the addition of new stations and an increase in the traffic capacity of railway lines, along which goods trains and passenger trains of all categories run according to daily schedules.

In type b) cities, the development of regular urban railways services is difficult, as railway lines are located in fringe areas with respect to urban areas. In such cities, there is a greater interest in regional-metrorail projects. Significant examples of such undergrounds are in the Emilia and Veneto regions.

In type c) cities, the presence of terminal stations favours the penetration of railways lines into central areas. On the other hand, the development of urban services imposes constraints on train traffic and requires connections among the various transit stations. Such connections are currently under construction in Turin, Milan and Rome.

In order to contribute effectively to solving urban-traffic problems, railways services should exhibit particularly attractive characteristics for potential users. In more detail, they should offer [1]:
- a high frequency of runs, as for metrorail systems; otherwise if such a frequency is impossible or unsuitable due to traffic requirements, it is at least necessary that, during the different daily periods, trains should follow one another at constant intervals so that users are not obliged to consult railway timetable or to remember train schedules;
- capillarity on the territory, that is, several stops are required, at short distances (typically, 1 km long); moreover, urban-service trains should always stop at all stations;
- particular fares (i.e., different from those specific for usual railway services), with the possibility of integrating the fares for the different urban-transport systems.

It is useful to compare the characteristics of urban railway services in Italy versus the afore aid standard requirements. The existing services can be classified as follows:

1) Underground-like services of Italian State Railways.

The train schedule of Italian Railways (FS) includes 16 lines officially used for underground-like urban services. Both urban-services trains and trains of other types (even long-route ones) run on these lines. Urban-service trains are classified as metro-trains, with particular fares. Such lines are described in Table 1.In addition to these lines, Italian Railways offer, on the lines Genoa Voltri - Genoa Brignole and Fiumicino Aereoporto - Rome Tiburtina-Monterotondo , services at exactly 15 min. and 20 min. intervals, respectively. Though these services are not included in the official 1993-1994 train schedule as underground-like services, nevertheless, they exhibit many characteristics of such services.

Table 1 - Underground-like services of Italian State Railways

	L	T	(a)	(b)	H
Napoli Gianturco - Pozzuoli	17	27'-29'	yes	yes	7'-9'
Palermo Centrale - Giachery	10	19'	yes	no	-
Palermo Not. - S.Tommaso N.	10	12'-20'	yes	no	-
Venezia S.L. - Mestre	8	10'-11'	no	no	-
Enziteto C. - Torre a mare	25	(+)	no	no	-
(*) Ciampino - Roma Termini	14	12'-18'	no	no	-
S.Maria delle Mole - Roma Termini	18	17'-23'	no	no	-
Cesano di Roma - Roma Ost.	27	30'-45'	no	no	-
Monterotondo - Roma Tib.	21	25'	yes	yes	20'
Lunghezza - Roma Tib.	15	21'-32'	yes	no	-
(*) Colle Mattia - Roma	26	20'-23'	no	no	-
Pomezia - Roma Term.	24	14'-25'	no	no	-
Ponte Galeria - Roma Tusc.	19	26'	yes	yes	20'
Torre in Pietra - Roma Term.	41	35'-45'	no	no	-
Pantanella - Roma Term.	19	20'-28'	no	no	-

(*) *In the council of Rome there is an integrated fare system.*
L   =   *section lenght in km;*
T   =   *time to cover the whole section in minutes;*
(a)   =   *regular stops for all trains at all stations;*
(b)   =   *constant headways between underground-like trains;*
H   =   *headway time;*
(+)   =   *no links for the whole section.*

2) Urban services of Italian Railways

In addition to the previous sections, there exist sections of Italian Railways (typically shared by several lines) that connect various stations in the same city. On these sections, services are more or less frequent, and trains have heterogeneous characteristics, come from different places, and fall into different categories. Intervals between trains are not constant, event though they are quite short at some times of day. All these characteristics are typical for the following sections:

• Milan Certosa - Milan Porta Garibaldi, terminal section of the Milan Rho line: it is shared by the lines towards Turin, Arona, Luino e Varese;
• Milan Greco Pirelli - Milan Porta Garibaldi, terminal section of the Monza - Milan line: it is shared by the lines towards Como, Lecco, Bergamo;
• La Storta - Rome Tiburtina, terminal section of the line towards Viterbo;
• Reggio Calabria Catona - Reggio Calabria Pellaro, urban section shared by the Tyrrhenian and Ionian Lines.

Similar services, with intermediate characteristics between urban and suburban services, are offered on the sections Turin - Chivasso and round Florence.

3) Urban services not belonging to Italian Railways

Various licensed railway lines or those managed by a State government official offer urban services [2]. They are indicated in Table 2. In the cases of the Perugia P.S.G. - Perugia S. Anna and Cosenza FS - Cosenza Centro lines, trains run mainly on urban sections; in the other cases, trains run on the terminal sections of wide-range railway lines.

Overall, the conditions that should make a railway service meet the standards typical for undergrounds (i.e., constant headways, uniformity of schedule times) are fulfilled only in very few cases. Nevertheless, on some lines, the frequencies of train-runs are very high (in Naples and Milan, trains run at intervals of only 3 minutes).

Table 2 - Urban services not belonging to Italian Railways

	L	T	(a)	(b)	H
Napoli Gianturco - Pozzuoli S.	17	27'-28'	yes	yes	7'-8'
Cesano di Roma - Roma Tiburtina	40	50'-60'	no	no	-
Palermo Centrale - Giachery	10	19'	yes	yes	25'
Palermo Notarbartolo - Tommaso N.	9	9'-15'	yes	no	-
Venezia S.Lucia - Mestre	8	9'-11'	no	no	-
Bari S.Spirito - Bari Parco Sud	15	20'-30'	no	yes	30'

L   =   *section lenght in km;*
T   =   *time to cover the whole section in minutes;*
(a) =   *regular stops for all trains at all stations;*
(b) =   *constant headways between underground-like trains;*
H   =   *headway time.*

3.   Limitations related to railway-line potentialities

To analyse the difficulties concerning the use of existing railway lines as underground-like lines, it is necessary to divide railway lines into two categories:
1)   under-utilised (or even closed to regular traffic) railway lines;
2)   over-utilized railway lines.

The former are represented by terminal sections of branch lines and by side-tracks (either industrial or harbour ones) present in various cities, even in central areas, and often little utilized, as compared with traffic capacity. The recent recoveries, in Genoa and Palermo, of tracks previously used for harbour traffic and now utilized for the development of underground-like services are quite significant. Moreover, in various cities of medium dimensions, limited changes might allow suburban sections of branch lines to become suited for a passenger service of the underground type. As they are mostly single-track railway lines, the frequency of train-runs is mainly linked to the number and the positions of passing points. Possible changes concern a partial track doubling (which is suitable where no urban restrictions nor natural obstacles exist), the building of new passing points, the applications of an electric axle-counter block and of a remote-control system.

The use of underground-like trains on high-traffic lines seems more critical. Studies on traffic capacity show how the presence of slower trains (stopping at all stations) and of fast trains on the same line leads to a non-optimal utilization of the traffic capacity of the line [3]. It is often difficult to add new trains because the existing ones utilize the line to its capacity limits; therefore, the residual traffic capacity is zero or insufficient.

The insufficiency of residual traffic capacity, can be faced by two different approaches, which can be defined as an infrastructural solution and a technological solution. The former consist in the building of new infrastructures (new lines, doubling of existing lines). This solution is in conflict with notable territorial restrictions. In many cases, the narrow space between existing railways lines and the surrounding urban space does not allow the laying of parallel tracks. Even in the absence of urban restrictions, the cost of new railway structures in urban areas is very high and the realization times are very long. This holds true for underground structures, too.

An alternative (though partial) to the realization of new infrastructures is represented by the application of technological measures to existing lines, for the purpose of increasing traffic capacity. Such measures concern the rolling stock and traffic control systems. As to the former, it is worth noting that underground-like trains of Italian Railways and of some licensed railway lines have already been built with specific material. Moreover, new trains will be added. Therefore, local trains are becoming more and more similar to those of actual undergrounds. By contrast, concerning traffic control systems, the presence of trains with different characteristics has so far prevented the application of specific control systems for underground-like traffic to ordinary railway lines.

4.   Technological solutions to increase traffic capacity

The traffic capacity of a double-track railway line depends on the systems used in the stations and on the signalling system, which determines the minimum distance between two trains running one after the other in the same direction. Some underground-like or *people mover* systems use sophisticated signalling systems, at high automation level, that allow very reduced headways (1 minute long) between trains, while meeting all safety and time requirements.

It seems reasonable to wonder whether the use of such signalling systems on an existing railway line may allow so reduced headways also in the presence of other trains. This possibility would lead to an extremely efficient utilization of existing infrastructures, at a lower installation cost than the one required by an infrastructural solution. Moreover, it is interesting to analyze the conditions that make a technological solution preferable to an infrastructural one.

The difficulties that oppose the transfer of signalling technologies from undergrounds and *people mover* to urban sections of ordinary railway lines are linked to the presence of trains (both passenger and goods ones) that are not used for an underground-like service.

Replacing, on urban sections, common signalling systems of Italian Railways with different systems, typical for undergrounds and suitable for shorter headways between trains, poses the following problems:

- Unless they are limited, headway reductions for long-route trains, in accordance with train speeds or train compositions, might turn out to be unsafe.
- The benefits, in term of traffic capacity, resulting from shortened headways might be nullified by lower traffic capacities inside station areas; such capacities are related to the number of platforming tracks and to the arrangement of station layout.
- A replacement involves modifications to the station-plan regulations not only of underground-like trains (for which specific regulations might be accepted) but also of long-route trains running on urban sections.

In general, the possibility of modifying operation regulations encounters obstacles and difficulties that increase with the number of elements that are in contrast to current regulations. Neglecting such conflicts is not a sound design philosophy because it involves the risk of specific, though very accurate, investigations that are not likely to lead to short-term practical applications.

Therefore, it seems more advisable to associate a new signalling system (aimed at reaching a higher frequency of trains) with the existing one, without need for replacing it. Moreover, a new system should not influence the running of trains not used for urban services; such trains could even ignore the new signalling system. For instance, this can be accomplished by using the technique of coded-current track circuits, that is, by adding codes that may be picked up only by underground-like trains provided with suitable cab-signal devices.

To sum up, to obtain the increase in traffic capacity, required for an increase in urban services, some technological solutions can be adopted, which can be applied, in the long term, to urban sections of high-traffic railway lines provided with automatic block systems.

Such solutions are:

- shortening of headways;
- modifications to station layout;
- adding to existing track circuits new special-frequency circuits and/or colour-light signals only for underground-like trains (as an alternative cab-signal system based on electromagnetic transmission points).

Moreover, it is necessary to explore the possibility of predicting the traffic of underground-like trains with free schedules. Such trains might better exploit the intervals of time between long-route trains by adapting themselves to the various schedules in a dynamic way. If free-schedule traffic, already present on urban railway sections to meet service requirements (e.g., isolated locomotives), might be combined with a high frequency of trains runs, it would make a railway service (from the user's stand point) entirely similar to an underground service.

5. Computer simulation as an analysis tool

In general, the construction of new infrastructures ensures a greater increase in traffic capacity than technological modifications to existing railway lines. The availability of four tracks instead of two allows different traffic flows to be separated, hence it also allows a high traffic capacity, even when technologically simple traffic-control systems are used. However, a comparison between the two situations should be made in terms of a cost/benefit analysis. A technological solution offers a smaller increase in traffic capacity, but the cost and time requirements may be much smaller. Therefore, if the benefit-to-cost ratio is considered, a technological solution may turn out to be preferable in many cases.

To make sound investments, it is important to use, in addition to usual tools for an economic analysis, a specific tool able to predict, in technical terms, the benefits resulting from alternative solutions, typically, in forms of traffic capacity (i.e., number of passengers carried in the unit time).

Traffic capacity does not depend only on the headway system on a line but also on layout conditions and on station systems. The complexity of station yards and the related restrictions may impose long headways. Due to the large number of factors involved, it is difficult to evaluate by analytic methods the traffic capacity that might be obtained, for instance, by innovative signalling system, or by utilizing free-schedule trains. For traffic-capacity evaluations, the use of computer programs specific for the simulation of train running is much more effective than analytic approaches (necessarily simplified), as it combines a good precision with high flexibility [6]. In other words, many running situations or design alternatives may be simulated by simply inserting new input data, with a notable saving in time, as compared with analytic methods.

6. Conclusions

The paper has pointed out that, in many cities, suitable structural or technological modifications (sometimes of limited cost) can make existing railway lines suitable for being utilized for urban transport. This has already been achieved in some Italian cities, but further evolutions, both quantitative and qualitative, of underground-like urban services are possible. Moreover, the article has stressed the usefulness of computer simulation, which represents an analysis tool that can be employed as an aid to decisions concerning the choice of investment targets.

7.   References

[1] AA.VV. *Trasporti pubblici urbani. Valutazione delle prestazioni*, Quaderno OCSE n° 42, 1980.

[2] Jane's Urban Transport Systems, 1992

[3] Vicuna, G. *Organizzazione e tecnica ferroviaria*, CIFI, 1989.

[4] Menafoglio, G.M. *Sistemi innovativi: sviluppo, situazione e prospettive*, Rivista Trasporti e Trazione, 1/1989

[5] Godard, X. *Mèthodologie de l'analyse multicritère appliquèe aux transports urbains*, INRETS, 1973.

[6] Galaverna, M., Savio, S. and Sciutto, G. A *Railway Operation Simulator for Line Traffic Capacity Evaluation*, COMPRAIL '92, Washington, 1992.

Goods distribution in historical city areas by electric vehicles. Case study

M. Galaverna,[a] S. Migliaccio,[b] E. Musso[c]
a Dipartimento di Ingegneria Elettrica, b Istituto di Geografia ed Economia dei Trasporti, c Istituto di Urbanistica, Università degli Studi di Genova, Genova, Italy

Abstract

This paper describes a methodology for facing the problem of goods distribution in historical city centres, while taking into account the particular infrastructural restrictions and especially the narrow streets to which such areas are subject. Research has focused on the transportation supply and demand in Genoa's historical area, starting from a statistical investigation that has allowed to quantify the flow of goods traffic and to know the origin and destination of goods, the organization of supply and the requirements of the traders operating in this area. The paper proposes a new transport system that would organize and rationalize the distribution of goods (gathered in a storage area) to and from the historical area. To this end, the system could employ electric vehicles whose dimensions, in terms of both carrying capacity and power, are suitable for the traffic level in the area considered.

1 Introduction

Historical centres raise considerable problems with regard to social and environmental degradation and to the mobility of people and goods, because of their position with respect to subsequent urban expansion. The lack of information and data which could support decision makers is one of the main difficulties that public authorities must face when trying to tackle such problems. The present study aims at achieving functional, organizational, and technical solutions in order to obtain:

- greater efficiency of the goods distribution system;
- rationalization of vehicle traffic, and the consequent reduction in congestion level, air pollution, and noise level;
- conversion of the problem of accessibility and inside mobility into a potential factor for increasing the value of the area: a first step towards the urban and architectural recovery of this important cultural heritage of the old towns;
- improvement of traffic condition in areas which give access to historical centres.

Genoa's historical centre is the largest in Europe after Venice; it cover 113 hectares and it has a high density of tertiary activity.There are about 22300 inhabitants and some 8600 people work in the area. Currently, about 140 commercial and service vehicles enter the historical centre every day; these vehicles traverse the 5 access points and the few inside routes, causing disturbance and congestion. The streets along which commercial vehicles can pass are so narrow that 2 or 3 vehicles can render the street unusable. These data outline the particular commercial use of Genoa's historical centre. The research has included an analysis of the supply and demand of goods transportation. The transportation demand has been investigated through a questionnaire addressed to a representative sample of those economically and commercially involved in the area under consideration; the transportation supply has also been investigated by interviewing carriers who work in historical centre of Genoa.

2 Reference Universe and Sample

Information about the economic parameters of the area being considered has been found in the Register of Firms at the Chamber of Commerce of Genoa. By using this data base and by using selecting the traders, office and workers in the area, we have been able to define the "universe of reference". In March 1994, there were 3569 activities operating in Genoa's historical centre; these may be subdivided into 11 categories: banks, offices, clothing shops, grocers' shops, chemists'shops, supermarkets, craftsmen's laboratories, restaurants, home services, other small or large-size activities.

It has been necessary to refer to a statistically representative sample in order to perform the analysis. Random selection is a method that allows one to obtain a representatative sample of the population, with respect to every variable, defined a priori or after the selection. A good coherence of the sample can be obtained by using both objective choice criteria (according to the principle of pure casuality) and subjective criteria (based on the processing of the available data), which allow the selection process to be checked in compliance with the principle of casuality and highlight the most significat sets of units with regard to the analysis being performed.

For this study, a multi-phase (two-step) sampling method has been used: a first sample is extracted from the files and the incorrect units, i.e., the units that do not belong to the reference universe, are eliminated. The sample so far obtained is then submitted to the second selection. The sample relevant to agents working in the considered area has been built, on the basis of the above-mentioned universe, by means of a selection performed in accordance with the principle of casuality and the composition of the primary universe. The composition of the sample is shown in Fig.1.

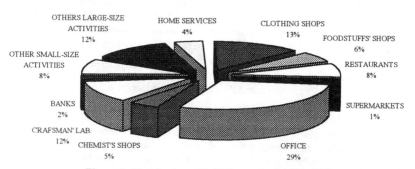

Figure 1: Distribution of initial sample (100%=357)

The selected traders, office and workers have been sent a questionnaire in order to:
- outline the main problems in the area under consideration;
- evaluate the demand for transportation;
- describe the parameters of the commercial activities;
- investigate the origin/destination points of goods and people and the flow of traffic.

226 questionnaires have been answered, corresponding to a percentage of 63%, which is quite high. The answers are still representative of the universe being considered, because their composition is very similar to that of the primary universe, as Fig.2 shows.

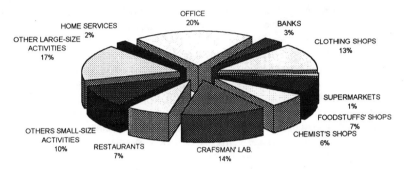

Figure 2: Distribution of the sample collected (100%=226)

3 Main problems for people working in historical areas

Those interviewed were asked to express their opinion about the problems specific to the historical centre. Figure 3 shows the topics which resulted from the interviews in order of importance; accessibility as the most serious problem 80% saw, followed by environmental degradation (69%).

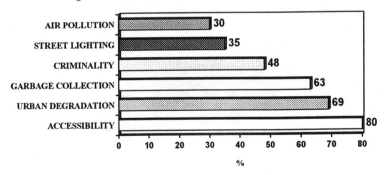

Figure 3: Survey of main problems (in %)

The lack of availability of loading and unloading areas represents the most serious difficulty as far as goods distribution is concerned: more than 64% of those interviewed mentioned this problem. This situation is also confirmed by the fact that more than 63% stated that loadind and unloading activities are performed in places where parking is forbidden.

4 Goods transportation demand

Two main components form the demand for goods transportation: supplies, i.e., the flow of goods directed to traders working in historical centre, and deliveries, i.e., flow of goods that originates from historical area. An analysis of goods supplied allows us to estimate transportation demand as a number of items of luggage and provides information which is important when a reorganization of the goods distribution system in historical centres is being planned. Most of traders stated that they receive goods throughout the day, although local regulations forbid drivers of delivery vans to enter the historical centre after 11 a.m. Interviews have indicated that large vehicles are used, in spite of the narrowness of roads; vans (64.5%) and lorries (23.5%) are used in most cases. In consideration of the average content of a single delivery (5 or 6 items corresponding to a total weight of less than 15 kg), the present goods distribution system seems to leave room for improvement; a large percentage of goods are delivered by using vehicles which are too large with respect to the carrying capacity which is really needed. The research has also indicated that 46% of traders are supplied by professional carriers, 19% use their own vehicles, 35% use both their own vehicles and professional carriers. Only 35% of traders interviewed need of rapid supplies (within 24 or 36 hours); 24% do not need rapidity, 41% only on some occasions.

The traders whose goods are delivered to their customers are 40% of the total. Goods are delivered all day; only 11.3% of deliveries take place before 11 a.m.. As for supplies, goods are delivered by vehicles which are too large in regard to the carrying capacity which is really needed, even if disproportion is less evident.

The total goods transportation demand in historical centre of Genoa is evaluated about 10242 items per day; as Fig. 4 shows, 75% of the demand is formed by supplies (entering flows) and 25% by deliveries (outgoing flows). Drivers who carry goods into historical centre (7836 est. items per day) do not usually collect the goods that are to be delivered to customers (2406 est. items per day). As a consequence, a rationalization of the distribution system would permit a reduction of the number of vehicles circulating in the area being considered if the same vehicles which carry goods to historical centre were utilized to carry the outgoing flow of items to be delivered to respective customers; theorically, the number of circulating vehicle might be reduced by 25%.

SUPPLIES (ENTERING
FLOW) 7836

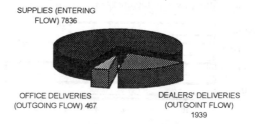

OFFICE DELIVERIES   DEALERS' DELIVERIES
(OUTGOING FLOW) 467   (OUTGOINT FLOW)
                                              1939

Figure 4: Total goods transportation demand (100%=10242 items/day)

5 Goods transportation supply

The analysis of the goods transportation supply system, with regard to available infrastructures and carriers who supply transportation services to and from the area being considered, is essential to discover how the distribution system can be improved.

The main problems that have emerged in this analysis linked to the peculiar features of the infrastructures in the historical centre, are:
- carrying capacity of roads, which is very low;
- road improvement is not possible because of town-planning and architectural constraints;
- parking areas are insufficient;
- the historical centre can be reached through a few access roads, and the circulation inside is restricted to a few routes.

Other negative factors concern the cheracteristics of the market:
- competition among carriers is intense;
- goods to be transported are heterogeneous;
- delivery time is often long, due to the above-mentioned infrastructural constraints, transfers between different vehicles, risk of theft and the fact that transportation demand is scattered.

Infrastructural constraints and the particular features of the market cause a loss of productivity in transportation activity and a consequent increase in costs. According to most of the carriers interviewed, the average cost of a delivery in urban area is about 4500 Italian liras (about 2,8 US dollars), while the cost of a delivery to the historical centre of Genoa can be 30% to 50% higher. To a great extent, this extra cost does not burden professional carriers since it falls on the retail carriers who usually receive a fixed extra payment when the historical centre is the destination of a delivery; nevertheless, in such cases the extra payment may not cover the increased expenses.

Transportation supply in the historical centre is performed by traditional carriers (72%), who also transport bulky items, by express carriers (15%), specialized in the transportation of packers, documents, small parcels to be delivered quickly and by other carriers (13%) such as postal services and bank-carriers. It is estimated that daily about 6315 items are transported by professional carriers and 3927 by traders personally. Every day 60-70 goods vehicles and another 80-90 public service vehicles (Telecom, Gas, Electricity and other sevices) enter the historical centre. Private vehicles, frequently used for delivery services or, less frequently, for supplied, are to be added to the above-mentioned 140-160 public service vehicles per day. Consequently, these factors increase traffic congestion, decrease the effectiveness of the goods distribution system and damage the quality of life in the area being considered.

6 Possible solutions and their evaluation

On the basis of the information obtained, four possible programmes have been studied in order to reorganize distribution of goods. These plans have been submitted to the judgment of the traders directly affected by the proposed solutions (see Figures 5, 6, and 7). They are:
a) restriction of times in which goods transportation in historical centre is allowed, for instance, before 9 a.m., during lunch-time, after closing;
b) separation of the flows of goods traffic, having regard to the different kinds or dimensions or destination/origin of the transported items;
c) realization of a inter-exchange centre operated by one local agency; a unified administration of goods transportation in historical centre might be created through an association of carriers, with the possible partecipation of public authorities. In this case, the employment of electric vehicles might be envisaged togheter with the enforcement of the current traffic limitations.

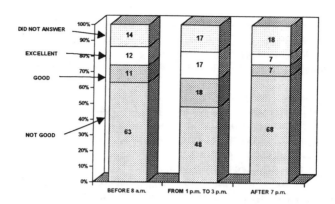

Figure 5: Deliveries during closing time (100%=226)

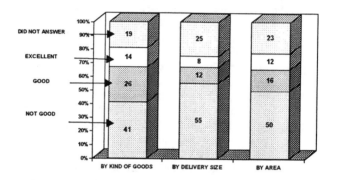

Figure 6: Differentiated deliveries (100%=226)

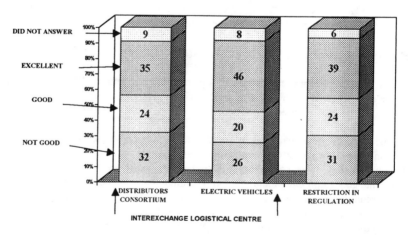

Figure 7: Other possible solutions (100%=226)

As the above-mentioned figures show, the traders involved in this study have not approved the solutions a) and b); such measures would probably be disregarded, as the current traffic limitations are. However most of the traders interviewed would support innovative solutions, as Fig. 7 shows; 66% of traders approve the creation of an agency for local goods distribution by means of electric vehicles, 63% approve the enforcement of traffic limitations, which is considered necessary to put innovative solutions into effect, and 59% would encourage an association of carriers. The opinions of the traders interviewed are in accordance with some relevant indications shown by the transportation demand analysis. By relating the need of rapidity in relation to the traders' habit of transporting their goods by their own vehicles, the matrix shown in Table 1 has been obtained. Table 2 represents a possible aggregation of the data contained in the previous matrix. As Table 2 shows, the reorganization of the distribution system on the basis of a centre for goods interchange, to be built close to the historical centre would not introduce any appreciable variation with respect to the present activities of 48.2% of the traders interviewed (hence should be acceptable). For two other groups of traders (respectively 31.4% and 16% of the total) it is advisable to plan some solutions which would take into account their specific requirements. The proposed reorganization should be strongly disapproved of 3.6% of traders; for this group, a particular derogation might be foreseen.

Table 1: Need for direct supplies and for fast deliveries (100%=166)

DIRECT SUPPLIES

	%	YES	SOMETIMES	NO
	YES	3.6	16.9	14.5
FAST DELIVERIES	SOMETIMES	6	9.6	8.4
	NO	10.8	12.1	18.1

Table 2: Evaluation of consensus on interchange logistical area (in %)

NO (3.6)	"FAST CORRIDOR" NEEDED (31.4%)
COULD BE PERSUADED (16.8)	OK (48.2)

The carriers' opinion about the proposed reorganization of goods distribution system in the historical centre of Genoa can be synthesized as follows:
- they would support the creation of a interchange goods centre in order to rationalize and unite goods distribution activities on condition that this solution did not cause an increase in costs;
- they think that the creation of an association among the carriers in order to manage the goods distribution system is unlikely, because the competition among them is too strong;
- further restrictions to vehicle circulation is a matter of indifference forcarriers.

7 Availability of electric vehicles

Electric minivans have been developed by Ansaldo Research in partnership with other companies, such as FIAT, and Sheffield University, as part of the EEC/BRITE European research project. The electrical drive of the minivan developed by Ansaldo is characterized by the presence of an induction motor and an IGBT DC/AC converter; battery voltage is 216 V, rated power is 35 kVA and maximum power is 72 kVA. The converter can be used both for induction motors and for permanent-magnet motors; the efficiency of the converter is 0.95. Other electric vans have been developed by Ansaldo in co-operation with CESI; a DC drive with 18 kW IGBT chopper was built for the first prototype, while an AC drive with water-cooled 20 kVA IGBT inverter has been developed for the final prototype.

Furthermore, the italian company Piaggio developed an electric minivan, which was produced until 1994; it was obtained from a four-wheel versionof the "Poker", the widely used "Ape" three-wheeler. This manufacturer currently produces a bimodal motor-scooter, equipped with both an electric and internal-combustion motor, which is suitable for the transportation of small-size packages; a new electric van is being designed.

8. Conclusions

This paper has shown that there are different solutions to solve the problems of the goods distribution in historical centres; some of these solutions have the approval of people who work and live in the area. In order to reach the optimal solution for each hystorical centre, it is important, on the demand side, to assess the flows of goods distribution, and, on the supply side, the topology of the area case study, and its physical characteristics.

References

1.   Bobbio, A. *Lo sviluppo di sistemi innovativi nel settore dei veicoli ibridi e bimodali*. Rapporto interno Ansaldo Ricerche 1993
2.   Fabbris, L. *L'indagine campionaria*. Roma. Nuova Italia Scientifica, 1989.

Feasibility of potential radial corridors for guided urban transport technologies in Greater Belfast

J.D. Ferguson,[a] J.M. McEldowney,[a] A. Smyth[b]

[a] *The Queen's University of Belfast, Belfast BT7 1NN, Northern Ireland*

[b] *University of Ulster, Jordanstown Campus, BT37 0QB, Northern Ireland*

Abstract

This case study reviews part of a 15 month evaluation of guided urban transit for the Greater Belfast area carried out by a joint Universities land-use transportation unit (JULUTU) from the two universities named above.

The existing transport scene is set by considering some basic parameters such as current public transport ridership, car ownership and central area parking in the private and public domain. Recent and future short term infrastructure changes in transportation are described and the effects on transportation patterns of changing land use within the Laganside city river development are forecast. Three radial corridors were screened positive for guided transit from the first stage of the economic and ridership evaluation. The methodology for establishing these three potential guided transit corridors is considered and discussed in the light of the changing political climate.

1 Background

The joint Universities research team was appointed by the Northern Ireland Transport Holding Company in April 1991 to consider alternative urban transport technologies, and in particular, guided transit for the Belfast Metropolitan area. Publication of the final report took place in December 1993 [1].

However, transport policy is now poised to alter course since the publication of the Royal Commission's report in October 1994 [2]. Although the

Government has as yet not officially responded, it is apparent that it is not totally convinced by the Commission's report. Para. 11.47 of the report states:

"We recommend that the government make more reserves available for new light-rail systems so that they can be built within a reasonable time in those conurbations for which they are an integral part of an overall transport strategy".

Despite the lack of response, there has already been a rethink on the UK committed roads programme with cutbacks in expenditure in the November 1994 budget.

Recently within the Belfast area, a new planning vision report on the City Centre has been published [3], the £89m Cross Harbour Road and Rail Link approaches and bridges have opened to traffic and a major urban dual carriageway road scheme in the south east of the city through an environmentally sensitive area has been abandoned by the Department. In the authors' view, with changes in the political and transport policy climate, the stage is now set to consider once again alternative technologies as an integral part of any new transportation strategy.

Although this paper looks at the engineering and environmental factors affecting potential urban radial corridors, a brief discussion of the existing transport patterns in the greater Belfast area is initially considered.

2 Urban Structure and Transport

The Belfast Urban Area is best characterised as a medium density settlement based on axial lines with outlying sub-centres, most notable of which are Lisburn, Bangor, Comber, Newtownards, Carryduff and Carrickfergus. This is the area defined as the Belfast Metropolitan Area in the current study (see Fig. 1).

Within the time horizon of the study to the year 2030, the opportunity presented itself for an alternative public transport to provide a focus for urban growth and support desired land-use patterns. However, the basic form of the Belfast Urban Area BUA surrounded by green-belt is more or less established, and there is likely to be a   stabilisation of the population by 2030 at approximately its current level. Therefore radical changes to the existing land-use pattern are unlikely. Hence, while urban structure as a whole might be marginally altered by light rail in a more sustainable direction (encouraging denser development and thus limiting sprawl and dispersal), the major impact of light rail or other technologies on sustainability would have to occur within the present urban structure.

The most recent review of transportation within the Greater Belfast Area commenced in August 1985 for the period up to the year 2001 [4]. A further review is scheduled to be commissioned and will have to include major changes of cityscape within the area. The most notable recent change is on a 14.5 acre site within Laganside where a £15m 200 bedroom hotel, a £20m concert hall, a parks marina and a multi-storey car park along with office and shop developments are under construction. These projects coupled with the river Lagan clean-up scheme and major regeneration of the city's dockside will have repercussions on the city's transportation requirements.

3   Car dependency and the future for public transport in Belfast

Notwithstanding the rural nature of Northern Ireland, the Province exhibits substantially greater expenditure on private transport than other rural areas of the United Kingdom or the Republic of Ireland. The private vehicle fleet is younger in age terms while car ownership overall is only marginally less than the United Kingdom figure. Expenditure on public transport is extremely low at around 5% of transport expenditure. Belfast itself, however, enjoys a low level of car ownership [0.24 cars/person in 1989] similar to the more disadvantaged industrial cities of Great Britain. On the other hand, the supply of road and parking space is among the most generous.

In marked contrast, public transport use is the lowest per capita in the United Kingdom for peer group urban areas. In this respect, the city has witnessed an unparalleled decline in bus use since the late 1960's. Until the last few years the stringent funding had forced a reduction in in-vehicle comfort level while the limited availability of shelters contributed to a decline in the image of bus travel. As a result, the 'transit habit' in Belfast had been broken and the car/taxi based life-style firmly established.

In contrast, rail has benefited from the dispersal of population and a government policy in recent years which has provided unprecedented levels of capital investment as well as retaining a substantial subvention towards recurrent costs. The opening of the cross river rail link and a new proposed station in central Belfast are example of this. Nevertheless, until rail achieves adequate penetration of the Central Business District its potential in-vehicle time advantages are negated while the limited size of the network, the large costs of extending heavy rail systems and the current absence of coordination with the much larger bus network also limits the use made of an infrastructure capable of serving substantially larger number of users.   There are now proposals to set up a combined bus and rail authority which could change the public transport network considerably.

4   Preliminary identification of corridors and the technologies

Corridor screening criteria were developed from previous studies both within the United Kingdom and abroad and thence applied to Belfast conditions.

From the assessment of theoretical and operational characteristics of various transport modes, a number of conclusions were drawn:

- The capacity of most operational systems tend to be found in the lower end of the potential capacity for each mode as specified by manufacturers' figures.
- In the majority of UK cities, the issue does not appear to be one of capacity but realising a minimum viable level of demand.
- In most cases, appraisal of Light Rail Transport (LRT) is undertaken in comparison with the conventional bus system currently obtaining in the city in question (and existing rail service if this exists).

There are a number of factors which influence the quantifiable elements of screening criteria for alternative public transport technologies. Minimum viable ridership for any technology will reflect for instance availability or otherwise of suitable rights of way including the opportunity to exploit the use of existing infrastructure. The local unit costs associated with construction and operation of transport facilities, site conditions, the length of the proposed system and the degree of peaking in the area served are other factors. The availability of 'additional' supra-national funds could also affect the threshold obtained. The ability of any proposed technology to achieve such thresholds in a particular locality will in turn reflect the existing base market for public transport, the improvement in the relative attractiveness of public transport potentially afforded by the alternative technology and restraint whether passive or active of car use in areas served by the proposed technology. In turn, these conditions will reflect land use considerations including residential densities and degree of concentration of commercial activities and employment in downtown areas.

5   Alignment opportunities

The following corridors (see Fig. 1) met the agreed base patronage and potential journey time criteria defined under this process:

Eastern Approaches (A) - Bangor

Eastern Approaches (B) - Dundonald/Comber
Southern Approaches (A) - Ormeau/Saintfield Road
Southern Approaches (B) - Lisburn
Western Approaches - West Belfast
Northern Approaches (A) - Antrim Road
Northern Approaches (B) - Shore Road

The overview of opportunities consisted of three elements:

1. Operations : including existing carriageway or other alignment considerations.
2. Capital Costs (fixed infrastructure).
3. Environmental Planning Issues.

From previous work, it was apparent that the assessment of opportunities should be restricted to Light Rail Transit (LRT), Guided Light Transport (GLT) and Busway (Guided and Unguided). This decision was taken on the basis of capacity/demand considerations and unit costs of construction for alternatives. Conventional bus priority measures were excluded from consideration as they were regarded as being sub-strategic measures.

In the case of the environmental planning assessment, this was based on a check-list of criteria drawn from the literature. Fieldwork involved site investigations of the alignment options to obtain information on the basis of which each would be scored against the relevant criteria.

6 Operations and capital costs

Where entirely new alignments were identified, additional assessment involved the suitability and impact of new infrastructure, the opportunities for and impact of tunnelling, where necessary, and the integration of new infrastructure with existing transportation networks. An initial objective for the engineering section of the project was to obtain suitable mapping at 1:1250 or 1:2500 scale of all the potential corridors within the Belfast area. However, this objective was refined to consider coarser 1:10,000 scale mapping of the area supplemented by large aerial photograph mosaics due to the extent and cost of the work involved. Where areas were considered to be particularly sensitive, 1:1250 scale mapping of the corridors was evaluated. Existing transport corridors were used wherever they were available. In the preliminary assessment, corridors were considered on five radial approaches to the City Centre. In particular, the Southern Approaches (A) covered a corridor width of at least half its length which produced seven preliminary lines for evaluation.

Typical cross-sections for shared surface and segregated on-street running of LRT or guided bus were prepared to determine minimum operational widths and swept path alignments on different classes of urban road [5]. In the more sensitive areas, horizontal geometric parameters were checked to ensure that they were within the appropriate design standards. As far as vertical control was concerned, it was generally considered that most routes were within the maximum gradients specified by the technologies [6].

For the costing of each alternative, lengths of routes were categorised as being at grade, elevated or in tunnel and whether they were on street or segregated. Unit costs were derived for different types of LRT and guided bus running, allowing for track and formation, stations or stops, and signal control [7].

7   Environmental planning assessment

All potential corridors were subjected to a broad environmental assessment sieve, drawing on recent transportation studies in Britain. Fieldwork was generally based upon a check-list drawn from the literature.

It was found that, in general terms, environmental considerations (defined as visual effects, severance and impacts on townscape, property and amenity) do not constitute an overriding constraint along the corridors investigated (Fig. 2) as compared with the potential impact of road improvements required to accommodate a car-based transport provision over the study period. The overall environmental quality of the potential corridors is mostly of a type which would absorb the environmental impact of LRT or bus-based systems, provided that individual sensitive buildings or small areas were protected at the detailed design stage. In fact, in some cases, the introduction of a consistent linear design element would prove an environmental benefit.

Segregated running on median strips is precluded among many major radial routes in Belfast because of the restricted carriageway widths. Therefore, in environmental terms, segregated running along current and former railway lines or sub-surface operations, wherever possible, offers the best solution for operation in environmental terms. Notable exceptions are pedestrianised or traffic calmed areas in which LRT, or other electrified modes can contribute to the environmental quality.

8   A basis for a refined corridor assessment

Notwithstanding the improvements currently being or recently made to public transport infrastructure serving Belfast the study team consideration of improvements which are warranted in a number of travel corridors within the Belfast Metropolitan Area. The proposals are based on the premise that public transport can offer a realistic alternative to the private car for many trips to/from the city centre providing certain requirements are met. These encompass both general criteria as well as conditions specific to individual corridors. In general terms, the following conditions are required to be met:

1.   Full penetration of the Central Business District.
2.   Operations free from the congestion generated by other vehicles, where possible by a separate facility (busway or guideway) to ensure a running speed competitive with the private car.
3.   A quality image in keeping with self-esteem of car users.
4.   Good quality of travelling and waiting environments.
5.   High levels of frequency.
6.   High levels of information provision including real time information.
7.   Coordination of timetables between services on a corridor basis and through ticketing.

The use of these criteria as a sieve in the process of selecting the most promising corridors and technologies underpins the recommended strategy.

In relation to mode image, it is now generally recognised that LRT enjoys a superior image to conventional bus operations. The major question mark relates to the performance of guided buses and express coach operations. In relation not the latter, the evidence does indicate that such operations marked professionally, with a separate identity from the ordinary bus and in conjunction with a package of traffic management measures, high quality waiting facilities and information provision can enjoy an enhanced image compared to the bus. However, it will be unlikely to match the performance of LRT in this regard. Image in part reflects perceived levels of comfort including general ambience of the travelling environment. In this regard, the bus even in guided mode has not shown itself to be capable of matching the best levels achieved by modern Light Rail Vehicles (LRVs).

Recent interest in guided buses in the UK has stemmed from a bus industry feeling threatened by the possibility of large numbers of LRT systems. In part, this is due to the legal and regulatory frameworks attaining in Great Britain. Absence of operations on the ground in the UK generally forces reliance on hypothetical responses by the market to the mode.

9   Conclusions

Three radial corridors Eastern Approaches (B), Southern Approaches (A) and Western Approaches were selected for the recommended strategy. Refinement of the 'long list' of alignments to produce a systems concept which could prove cost-effective in an individual corridor, depends on a number of conditions. Such conditions fall into five main areas;

(i)   a substantial actual or potential market for public transport,
(ii)   right of way opportunities which permit any technology to demonstrate a substantial improvement over existing conditions both by public and private modes,
(iii) environmental pressures emanating from existing patterns of travel demand, and
(iv)   land use characteristics and development pressures,
(v)   security of the system for both users and the public.

Fulfilment of these 'conditions' does not necessarily demonstrate that a case does exist for alternative technologies. Nevertheless, it does provide a basis for now focusing further analytical work leading to strategic recommendations, which may result from incoming investment through the peace process. Also, the fifth condition is not now so critical.

10   References

[1]   JULUTU Alternative Urban Transport Technologies for the Belfast Metropolitan Area. Final Report to the NI Transport Holding Company, Belfast, 1993.

[2]   The Royal Commission on Environmental Pollution, "Transport and the Environment", 18th Report, CM 2674, HMSO, 1994.

[3]   Department of the Environment for Northern Ireland, "Belfast City Centre Vision for the Future", HMSO, Belfast, 1994.

[4]   Halcrow Fox & Associates, "A Review of Transportation Strategy for Belfast (1986-2001)", Final report to Department of the Environment (NI), 1987.

[5]   Saffer, H., " Traffic management design for Light Rail", paper presented at seminar on the Civil Engineering aspects of street running light railways, Manchester, Infrarail, 1994.

[6]   Boak, J.G., "South Yorkshire Supertram : route and civil works", Proc. of Institution of Civil Engineers, Transportation, 1995, 111, 24-32.

[7]   Umney, A.R. & Miller, D., "Study of costs of cut and cover tunnel construction", Transport Research Laboratory, Contractor Report 252, 1991.

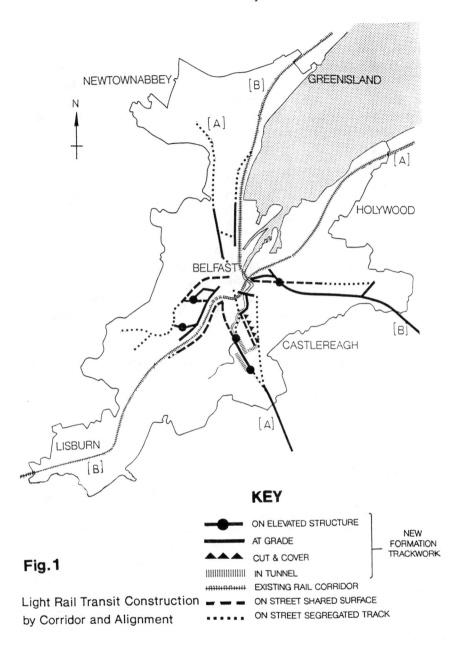

Fig.1

Light Rail Transit Construction
by Corridor and Alignment

KEY

●━━━● ON ELEVATED STRUCTURE		
━━━ AT GRADE		NEW FORMATION TRACKWORK
▲▲▲ CUT & COVER		
‖‖‖‖‖‖‖ IN TUNNEL		
╫╫╫╫╫ EXISTING RAIL CORRIDOR		
━ ━ ━ ON STREET SHARED SURFACE		
• • • • • • ON STREET SEGREGATED TRACK		

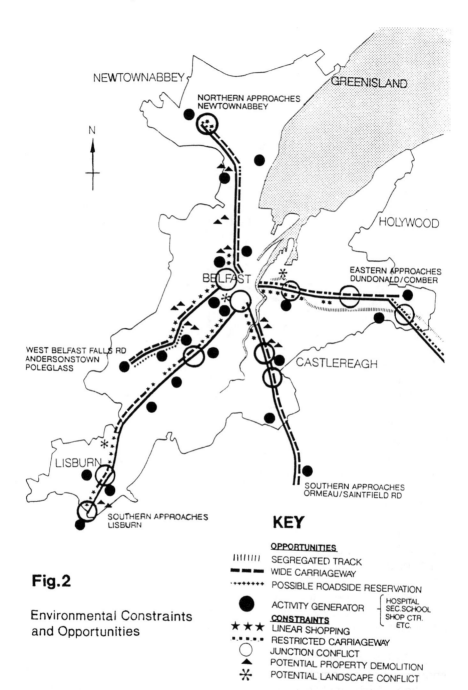

Fig.2

Environmental Constraints
and Opportunities

KEY

OPPORTUNITIES

‖‖‖‖‖‖	SEGREGATED TRACK
▬ ▬ ▬	WIDE CARRIAGEWAY
··········	POSSIBLE ROADSIDE RESERVATION
●	ACTIVITY GENERATOR

HOSPITAL
SEC.SCHOOL
SHOP CTR.
ETC.

CONSTRAINTS

★ ★ ★	LINEAR SHOPPING
·■·■·■·	RESTRICTED CARRIAGEWAY
◯	JUNCTION CONFLICT
▲	POTENTIAL PROPERTY DEMOLITION
✳	POTENTIAL LANDSCAPE CONFLICT

Light rail transit system of Karlsruhe

R. Schneider

Verkehrs-Consult Karlsruhe GmbH, D-76131 Karlsruhe, Germany

1 Introduction

In congested urban areas problems caused by transportation have increased continuously for many years. This is evident due to the increasing noise and air pollution as well as an overloaded road network. To decrease the negative effect of road transport on the environment and to maintain the functionality of road networks, alternatives to the motorised individual are necessary. For these reasons the greatest emphasis is placed on regional public passenger transport, as the demands of the private car are more likely to be met by selectional service of public transport. The alternatives "on foot" and "bicycle" are of great importance for short distance travelling and for bringing passengers to public transport vehicles. Amongst the different regional transport systems, rail transport is at the centre of attention. When considering the amount of motorised individuals today, it is evident that a lot needs to be done to decrease them. As the financial situation of the public sector is very strained, solutions, obtained by reasonable effort and lasting improvements, must be found. A new solution has been found to combine urban and regional traffic so that the advantages of both systems are used. Light rail transit (LRT) vehicles coming from the regional areas use existing rail lines and are subsequently tied up with the urban traffic at existing junctions or junctions that have still to be developed. This enables the passenger to save time and reach the city without having to change vehicles.

This is a considerable solution as it provides a service improvement in public transport and a gain in market value, whilst the value of the private car is hard to recede. As a comparatively smaller financial burden is achieved, this is the solution for the future. This solution also meets the political demands of the communities and regions. Because it was developed for the city and region of Karlsruhe, it has been given the name "Karlsruhe Model".

In the following elaborations, the Karlsruhe Model is discussed shortly, whereas emphasis is placed on a description of the initial situation which applies to many other cities and regions. The main objective of the presentation is to give an insight view of potentials to combine urban and regional traffic by applying the Karlsruhe Model. The effects of this advanced solution will be assessed by travel demand and costs. Lastly, the potentials from the political side and regionalisation will be discussed.

2 The Karlsruhe Model

The city Karlsruhe with its 280 000 inhabitants is the main centre for the middle upper Rhine region. More than often it is the rule that the railway stations of the DB lie far away from the city centre. Shuttling passengers between the regions and the city centre, specifically business people and students, are forced to change from the DB train to the LRT vehicle (figure 1). For the passenger this costs time, money and a loss in the quality of transport. To lure inhabitants of a region with an attractive public transport system, the service is gradually extended into the region. For a number of years city LRT vehicles are already travelling on the previous DB lines to Bad Herrenalb and Ittersbach in the south as well as to Linkenheim-Hochstetten in the north. On these lines the LRT vehicles fall under the Eisenbahn-Bau- und Betriebsordnung (EBO): a German act for railway construction and service. These lines were built up for the use of LRT vehicles as they had been closed to passenger transport of the DB and some of these lines were only occasionally used for goods transport. The advantage of not having to change vehicles at junctions between the region and the city of Karlsruhe brought forward the idea of using the DB lines for a city passenger service with a direct tie up to the city centre.

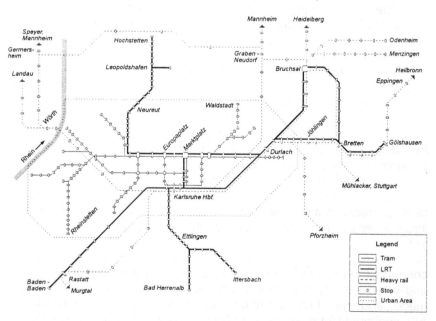

Figure 1: Public transport area of Karlsruhe

The initial situation was difficult to master as the demands of the DB service on DB lines and the LRT service on city lines had to be fulfilled. Demands of the passenger, the transport services and simply general demands are summarised in a catalogue of criteria as follows:

-   The user would like to reach his destination quickly, comfortably and affordably.

-   The passenger transport service would like cost-saving vehicles, a railway infrastructure and running methods that reduce fixed and variable costs as well as providing a good quality of service to improve its income.

-   It is in everybody´s interest to get a functional transformation from car traffic to pollution-free transport methods as well as an economical public passenger transport system.

The biggest problem was finding a vehicle that could be used on the DB and LRT lines and that could use different energy systems. The LRT vehicle of Karlsruhe was transformed so that it could use the DB lines in the region (figure 2). Their outer appearance changed only slightly, but from a technical point of view they are a new development under the following aspects:

-   The vehicle functions in the LRT (750 V Direct Current) as well as in the DB (15.000 V Alternating Current) electrical net.

-   The wheel profile is a mix profile and allows for the use of switches on LRT and DB lines.

-   The vehicle, in the contrary to the vehicles used in Karlsruhe until now, can now operate on a two directional basis.

Because the boarding height of platforms on DB lines differs considerably from that of the city centre, compromises had to be found.

In a test period the vehicle was put into DB service between the railways stations of Karlsruhe and Pforzheim during the autumn of 1992. A regular city service could be started after the tie up of the DB line, Karlsruhe-Bretten, with the LRT lines at the railway station Karlsruhe-Durlach had been constructed. The new LRT line S4 connects the city of Bretten to the main railway station of Karlsruhe in that when the city area is approached, a turn-off from the DB line is made and the LRT continues on LRT lines and reaches the Albtalbahnhof (A LRT stop in close proximity to the main railway station of Karlsruhe).

The LRT connection between Karlsruhe and Bretten fulfils only the first stage in the implementation of the "Karlsruhe Model". In the coming years further stages will follow:

-   During the summer of 1994 a LRT service was started between the main railway station of Karlsruhe and the cities of Bruchsal and Rastatt as well as on the DB line between Bruchsal an Bretten.

-   A LRT connection from Pforzheim through the city centre of Karlsruhe is planned in the next two years.

-   During this same period a new LRT line will be started between Wörth and Karlsruhe. In the city district of Knielingen a tie up will be made with the LRT net.

Figure 2: Bimodal LRT vehicle of Karlsruhe

3 Effects of the Karlsruhe Model

The LRT lines have become very popular and all the new LRT lines have experienced a considerable increase in passenger numbers. This development is due to a number of measures that were implemented simultaneously:
The not having to change vehicles, the reduction in travelling time and the modern look of the vehicles play a role. A uniform fare system was developed that in most cases made travelling cheaper for the passenger. In the outlying regions a tie up by bus was made with the LRT stops as well as providing parking facilities for bicycles and cars at these stops. A concentrated timetable was introduced for daytimes and an extension was made to after midnight.

To illustrate the effects which come with the implementation of the Karlsruhe Model, the Karlsruhe-Bretten line is taken as an example here.

Constructional changes

The city line Karlsruhe-Bretten runs from the main station of Karlsruhe on LRT lines through the city centre (pedestrian zone) and is tied up with the DB lines at the station of Durlach. In order to achieve the tie up a ramp was necessary at the station. There it is possible to change to the long distance trains of the DB on the same platform. To continue in the direction of Bretten, the LRT line runs over the DB railway line that heads for Heidelberg on bridges built for this purpose and turns into the DB line to Bretten. The main constructional changes that took place were the tie up at the Durlach station and the building of a new 2.4 km connecting line. In addition to these, 7 new stops were constructed so that more areas could benefit from the line.

Servicing program

A considerable change in the services offered results from the dual system. The following table shows important numbers:

Table 1: Time Table Change

	before	after
Amount of trains per workday and direction	19	38
- of the DB direct service to the main station	19	9
- of the LRT service to the city centre	0	29
Rhythmic timetable	no	yes
Start of last trip in Karlsruhe on workdays	8:00 p.m.	0:53 a.m.
Start of last trip in Karlsruhe on weekend	8:00 p.m.	1:53 a.m.

Fares

With the introduction of the LRT line to Bretten, the regional fare system was applied to it. This means that the trains of the DB and the LRT vehicles could be used with one single ticket. Furthermore, this ticket enables the user to change vehicles as often as he/she likes as well as to use the connecting bus lines.

Table 2: Fare Change

	before	after
Monthly ticket Bretten-Karlsruhe/City Centre	200 DM	105 DM
Regio ticket (2 adults, 2 children) for 24 hours	---	12 DM

Demand

The implementation of the LRT service on the Bretten line led to extensive changes in demands. This is primarily due to changes in the selection of transport means offered.

Table 3: Demand Change

	before	after	today
Number of passengers per workday	2200	7500	10 340
- of the DB service	2200		1840
- of the LRT service	0		8500

Costs

Investment in the constructional changes amounted to 80 million DM. Service costs are made up of costs attributed to the vehicles (depreciation, servicing, energy), staff and track usage. The variable costs per kilometre are about 12 DM for the LRT vehicle (in double traction), 18 DM for the Light Rail Vehicle of the DB and 25 DM for the electric or diesel units of the DB. At least 80% of the costs are covered. At the moment a loss of 700.000 DM per year is made.

4 Investigations in other regional transport areas

LRT systems are presently experiencing a global renaissance. It should however be noted that the new LRT systems have little in common with the conventional systems of the past. The vehicles, the carefully designed transport facilities and the study of traffic flows offer a far more attractive alternative. The direct tie up of a LRT system with the DB is however not appropriate for all cities. Because there is a lack of experience in this field and because conditions in the area may be unsuitable, the decision of how and in which combination regional traffic is to be financed, must be done individually. Competitive systems must be compared critically, as for example the tram system and the regional main line system.

Previous experience has shown that investment in the successful implementation of a Karlsruhe Model on a city should be justified. Sometimes a transport system for bigger masses, like the S-Bahn in Germany or rapid transit in the UK is a more efficient alternative. Furthermore, the existence of infrastructure with expansion possibilities and financing are necessary.

The principle initial situation of the region Karlsruhe can be found in many other urban areas. For this reason, the VCK, which is a subsidiary of the Karlsruhe transport services, is active throughout Germany and also internationally.

Cities and regional areas, that are considering the tie up of a LRT system with main lines are Saarbrücken and Aachen (cross border services), Heilbronn, Ulm, Wiesbaden, Osnabrück, Rostock, Halle and Dessau in Germany, Graz and St. Pölten in Austria, Ljubljana in Slovenia, Kent in the UK and L'Ile de France. In many of these cities the old tramway system had been shut down and now an introduction of the old system into the new LRT system is being considered.

5 Transference by taking into consideration regionalisation

Regionalisation of rail passenger transport will bring considerable changes into the structure of public transport. Regionalisation means that authorities in the fields of planning, organisation and finance will be passed from a national level to the federal states and districts. Apart from road and LRT services, the regional passenger rail transport is almost completely in the hands of the Deutsche Bahn AG (DB). Only in a few cases the federal states or districts have authority. Examples here are the regional railways of the federal state of Baden-Württemberg (AVG, SWEG, HZL, WEG) and also the district railway of Düren.

Furthermore, regionalisation means that communities and regional districts express their wishes at a regional transport service.

Regionalisation offers big changes for a customer friendly and economical functioning of regional traffic, but may also contain unforeseen risks. The service that the DB offers for regional traffic today is only indirectly influenced by communities and districts. This is achieved by holding time table conferences regularly at which representatives for the respective regions are present. However, the final design for services to be offered, for all components (rail line network, time table, vehicle, stops, etc.), lies in the hands of the DB. It must also be mentioned that the end product is not paid for by the communities and regional districts.

Because local and regional authorities only have a slight influence in deciding which services should be offered, the result is a lack of interest for collaborating work. The lack of financial support is also a reason. Only with the start of proceedings for the closing down of a rail line, regional authorities were made aware of their responsibilities in their area. The DB is primarily interested in feeder traffic to the main lines and local and regional needs have only secondary priority.

Regionalisation gets the regional authorities involved in the design for services to be offered. They are also interested in doing this economically. A positive aspect is that conflicts in the politics of transport are discussed in the respective area.

Dangers may also come with regionalisation. The new person in authority must develop structures to avoid these. They must also make sure that capital is used efficiently for regional passenger rail transport. The balancing of this capital will be problematic on the credit as well on the debit side of the balance sheet. It must also be noted that DB enterprises have a uniform fare structure and passenger information which can be put to good use. The big variety in service and information structures for busses and deregulation in Great Britain are an excellent example.

Regionalisation should therefore be implemented very carefully so that institutions of authority, users and operators achieve optimum results.

Maritime transport of people in urban areas

E. Musso, C. Migliaro
Transport Economics, University of Genova, Via A.
Bertani, 16125 Genova, Italy

Abstract

This study is intended to examine the setting up of alternative sea transport services for passangers in coastal metropolitan areas.

Comparison between land and sea transport will be carried on the basis of:

• production costs (for the whole community and not for the individual user) in each different transport mode;

• fares, speed and comfort offered to users.

Particular attention will be focused on the relationship between the cost to the community and the cost to consumers, since different levels of subsidization and/or of externalities may cause a non optimal modal split.

1 Introduction

High congestion levels and growing pollution rates draw attention to the ever increasing problem of finding new solutions for urban mobility.

In coastal metropolitan areas the transport system development is furthermore constrained by sea, which is likely to cause a state of general structural congestion. In these areas the distance by sea between two coastal centers is often shorter than by land, or, if congestion of road networks occurs, it might be covered in less time than that required for cars which, otherwise, are more adaptable and comfortable.[1]

The study of an alternative high speed maritime transport, therefore, is justified if the sea means captures public and private road transport users so to contribute towards resolving congestion and pollution problems in town centers (which represent externality costs substained by a good part of the community).

Research has been organized in the following phases:

• study of the effect of high speed in passenger transport;

- analysis of supply and cost functions in urban transit for each transport mode;
- analysis of supply and cost functions of high speed maritime transport;
- comparison between different transport modes, namely regarding costs (investments and overheads) and efficacy of the supplied service (costs to users, time and comfort);
- development of a modal split model to evaluate the probability of choice of maritime transport, related to cost, speed and comfort performances;
- intermodal utilities in landing points.

2 High speed urban transport: innovations and effects

The high economic development and the growing importance of comunications in productions process and in social relationships have led, in the last 25 years, to a strong increase of mobility. This has led to the creation of a more complex transport network which makes transport nodes more attractive for the users (transport and comunication network, harbours and aerports, commercial services, medical centers and universities, ...).

Metropolitan areas, especially monocentric area, in the past characterized by high congestion levels and growing pollution rates, have developed towards suburban areas (see: metropolitan cycle).[2]

The metropolitan area improvement needs increasing decentralization levels and a new land use without giving up a high degree of internal cohesion.

There is a need for the improvement of the internal urban accessibility based on a quicker and more efficient transport network (with speed performances of about 60-90 minutes, due to the recent technological innovations, i.e. 100-150 km distances) and on the economical specialization of metropolitan region and area centers.The strong ties between economical activities, high rank services, social life and land caracteristics need replanning and a requalification of the economical, social and transport structures of urban areas (giving particular evidence to the public urban transport).

High speed transport systems may lead to a change in the relations between the different economical and land subjects (segments).As regards sea transport in urban or subregional areas (such as high speed railway transport between metropolitan areas), high speed may contribute, through a product and process innovation of the vehicle (particularly hull and engine), of the port terminal, of the services organization, to the ridefinition of interactions between different subjects of the economic and land system.

The improvement, following the introduction of high speed transport systems (both qualitative as growing comfort, and quantitative, especially for 60 mile distances, as reduction of the travel time), involves an increase of activity in sea transport mode under one condition. The consequent average total unit cost growth, due to the introduction of the necessary technological innovations, must not be higher than that of the transport demand curve, which is fairly sensitive to the offered service best quality.

This only happens when high speed vehicles are used, whereas traditional means don't seem able to be economically competitive and to offer the same service standard.[3]

3 Costs Of Production And Transport Supply Characteristics

The research shows a comparative production cost analysis for each passanger transport mode in urban or suburban areas. Supply is related to a transport network which is split in ways corresponding to each route and transport mode (ways are, generally monodirectional and radial).[4]

Demand transport function attributes for each distance a settled traffic volume, a travel time and a generalized transport cost (see §4).

The analysis of the infrastructure endowment and of the vehicles used is made relative to the different transport modes (sea and railways, public and private road transport). It has to do with structural transport ways, offered capacity and possible structural lack causing congestion.

In particular, a survey of ordinary transport condition (trunk roads, main roads following the coastal transport ways and connecting the hinterland) must be made, of motorway infrastructures (tollgates and their placing in urban centers), of railway infrastructures (harbour landing, dock conditions, the draught and the length of passanger wharves).

As far as the offered service level is concerned, the analysis will deal with: frequency of transport means per hour (and its variance), offered seats, covered routes, actual travel times for the users, also keeping in mind the possible slackenings caused by urban traffic congestion and intermodality time (for example: between bus and train).

This research, because of lack of space, briefly mentions the technical characteristics of means and the cost structure of high speed sea transport, in order to choose the most suitable vehicle for the hypothesised line service.

The analysis of technical characteristics (sea keeping, wave standing, propulsion power), structural ones (capacity offered, draft, beam and lenght) and economic ones (cost of capital, fuel consumption per hour) of high speed vehicles (s.e.s., a.c.v., s.w.a.t.h., catamarans and hydrofoils) has led to the choice of surface effect ship.[5]

Infact, through the analysis and evaluation, with help of graphic and statistic regressions, of functional relations between the considred structural variables, it was established that the s.e.s. has a real conformity with the global needs of this study (high sea keeping and wave standing, limited draft and fuel consumption).[6]

The analysis of technical and economic characteristics and the transport supply function, are established in spite of different levels of subsidization by the public administration which causes repercussions on the rate system.

Figure 1 compares the production costs of the different public transport modes for equal routes (60 mile).Table 1 shows an example of the production structural cost for sea transport service with a distance of 60 miles (data 1992).

Figure 1 points out that the values of the dependent variable (costs) are influenced by those attributed to the independent variable (covered kms). Moreover, the note is of particular interest, the respective position of the three curves remains similar to the one shown for the different compositions of "seats-km" product.

Hypotheses of table 1:
- 50 knots average speed
- 350 operating days
- 12 years ship cost depreciation at costant rate
- 2 travels per day

Table 1 - *Example of a maritime transport travel cost, at high speed, for a 60 mile route (data in italian £, 1992).*

capacity\ncosts	250 passengers	500 passengers	750 passengers
fuel	227.000	350.000	416.000
port charges	100.000	100.000	100.000
investment pss/trav.	800.000	1.000.000	1.450.000
crew	400.000	400.000	400.000
insurance	1.450.000	1.750.000	2.050.000
maintenance	230.000	350.000	400.000
general expenses	100.000	130.000	150.000

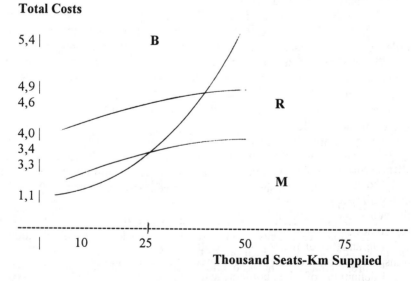

Total Costs

Figure 1 - Transport cost production curves (for 60 mile routes; italian milions £, 1992)

B: bus transport; **R**: rail transport; **M**:maritime transport.

The compared analysis of costs structures related to the transport supply, implies some particularly interesting conclusions.

Firstly, in the sphere of inland transport, bus transport is competitive for contained supply levels. On the contrary, for high supply levels (about forty thousand seats-km per day, figure 1), the total production cost of a rail transport service is always below the corresponding cost capable of satisfying the same urban road transport supply.

As regards bus transport, an increase of supply involves a rapid growth of vehicle numbers and, consequently, a rise more than proportional of the costs.

Secondly, the rail transport production cost function is always above that of sea transport. This suggests that maritime transport is better than rail transport because of the costs for the community, if sea transport is technologically feasable and if the its interconnection with other transport modes at the beginning and/or the end of the transport cycle (lack of intermodal parking, an impossible connection with urban transport network) doesn't involve an increase of generalized costs.

It must be remembered that the results of this comparison consider the total production cost of the examined services, considering that there are differences in the cover of these costs.

Therefore, the proposed notes may be made up for an excessive and economical injustified level of public subsidies of some transport modes compared to others.

Thirdly, the critical level of competitiveness of sea transport with public bus transport is for lower supply levels (about twentyfive-twentysix thousand seats-kms in the example) than those of rail transport. This is able to widen the potential use area of non-road transport (that causes greater congestion and pollution costs) and, finally, to widen the use area of public transport if we think of the low competitiveness level of urban public transport compared to private road transport.

4 Transport Demand

In metropolitan regions, a wide range of centrality factors of different origin (work services, the use of service supply, commodities buy, transport intermodality, market intermediations,...) causes one or more focal centers to attract remarkable mobility flows, both sistematic or non.[7]

The study of mobility demand potentially obtainable by sea transport will deal with sistematic flows (surveyed by the National Institute for Statistics) and the non sistematic and not chance mobility flows (obtainable through market researches).

The analysis of the region interested in the introduction of the maritime transport service, is concerned with three fundamental aspects:

1.definition of the borders and of the administrative competences (municipal, provincial and regional);

2.quantification of the demografic indexes (population trend) and economic ones (perhead income, number of companies member of Chambers of Commerce, employment rate, banking credits and deposits, the number of students registered at University);

3.the survey and classification of data relevant to urban mobility flows (raiway and motorway) in appropriate matrices origin/destination.

The distribution of mobility between the considered transport modes - apart from the fundamental problem of subsidization of different mode production costs - depends on the monetary costs (rates) and the non monetary ones (travel time and discomfort) for the transport service users.

5 Transport Modal Split

The distribution of mobility between the different transport modes will follow from the choice made by a great number of users and its real consistency, all thing being equal, depends on predictable and unpredictable facts connected to these choices. The variations of these facts are often added in an unclear way.

Therefore, for the planning or the testing of any transport demand system data, the real demand surveyed through a market research linked, moreover, with high operation times and high management costs should be known.

In reality, the study is limited to considering the real mobility average value relating to the more significant interval for the problem examined. A demand model is represented by a mathematical function which associates a determined activity system and transport supply to the average value of demand during a determined interval.

The behaviour models, usually used for modelling the transport demand, are of the "chance utility" kind. The basis of the logical procedure is the hypothesis for which the user is rational decision maker (who maximizes his utility) and that it's only possible to calculate the chance that the user will make a certain choice.[4]

In particular, the common user utility can be splitted in: a non chance utility (costant for each user given the same travel characteristics) and an aleatory residue. Considering different hypotheses on the connected distribution of aleatory residue, different models are generated , among which are Logit and Probit models.[4]

The first easier one considers the aleatory residue of the different alternatives distributed according to a determined law (for example: Weibull Gumble aleatory variable).

The latter, unlike the previous one, lets us compare transport alternatives with partially added parameters (for example: two public transports with a partially common way); nevertheless its application leads to high management costs and to an analytic complessity.[8]

The chosen statistic model, Logit or Probit, considering a preset mobility level, gives us the chance percentage which a common user has of choosing a transport mode. The choice is made considering three foundamental parameters, transport time, rate and comfort (reliability, punctuality, ...).

It's clear that a simple variation of even one of the parameters (low production costs, shorter travel time, higher mode reliability, comfort and punctuality) can vary the chance of choosing a transport mode and so to deplace mobility from one to another transport mode.

6 Research outcome

The outlined methodology has been proved by an application hypothesis of high speed sea transport in the eastern Ligurian "Riviera" between Genoa and some coastal centers, so as to create a line service which satisfies an increasing sistematic mobility towards the Genoa node.

As regards the obtained results, it seems that, given the actual metropolitan mobility level (rather low for the hypothesised routes), a maritime transport, in the eastern Ligurian "Riviera", is applicable only between Genoa and a few centers obtaining a total cover of investment and overhead costs.

This result, yet, is affected by the considering that a great part of investments and overhead costs of other transport modes aren't covered by the users: in particular, the infrastructural costs (both in rail and in road transport), a good part of rail transport overheads, the road transport externalities (pollution).

The total production costs analysis of different transport services shows, on the contrary, that, if transport mode subsidization were on equal terms, the users modal split should be more favourable to sea transport, so as to allow the cover of the costs.

It rises, therefore, the correct allocation costs problem in order to prevent that the different subsidization levels to cause users' non optimal transport mode choice.

Besides, the increasing financial straits of the central and local public administration, rise the same problem: in fact, the current situation, for which public administration finances a great part of public transport costs and a part of private transport costs, can't keep on.

If public subsidizations for transport services were on equal terms, the high speed maritime transport, in metropolitan and regional areas, should be, sometimes, more competitive than other transport modes.

References

[1].Petriccione, S., *Trasporti Urbani nelle Città di Mare*, 1987.

[2].Musso, E., *Trasporti e Movimenti Ciclici nelle Aree Metropolitane*, Ecig, 1990.

[3].Marchese, U., *Innovazioni, Alte Velocità, Trasporti Marittimi*, II Symposium on High Speed Marine Vehicles, Napoli, 25-26 March 1993.

[4].Cascetta, E., *Metodi Quantitativi per la Pianificazione dei Sistemi di Trasporto*, Cedam, 1990.

[5].Jane's, *High Speed Marine Craft*, Ed. Robert L. Trillo, 1992.

[6].Polydorou, G., *Veicoli Avanzati ad Alta Velocità*, Rapporto 3952, CeTeNa, 1990.

[7].Marchese, U., *Aree Metropolitane in Italia, Anni '80*, Cedam, 1989.

[8].Kanafani, A., *Transportation Demand Analysis*, Mc Graw-Hill Book Company, 1983.

Vehicle drive modelling for metrorail integrated system simulators

P. Firpo, S. Savio
Dipartimento di Ingegneria Elettrica, Università di Genova, Via all'Opera Pia, 11a - 16145 Genova, Italy

Abstract

The traffic related analysis of the electrical behaviour of a metrorail transit system may be today successfully performed thanks to integrated system simulators able to solve the network electrical equations taking into account the movement of the scheduled trains. The correctness of the simulation results are strictly connected with the implemented models, as far as, particularly, on-board electrical drives are concerned. In this paper the authors present different vehicle macromodels, to be utilized for system analysis, and related to both chopper and inverter fed electrical drives. The results of simulations performed by SISTEC, the integrated system simulation software developed by the authors, are then presented and discussed.

1 Introduction

During the top-level design of a modern metrorail, system engineering studies play a fundamental role, as the detailed design is developed on the basis of the choices performed in such phase: as far as system electrical analysis of the combined operation of power supplies, traction equipments and train controllers is concerned, the only conceivable mean of carrying out such studies is by using computer simulation techniques.

The main advantage related to the use of system simulators is that such software codes, thanks to the high speed and computational potentiality of computers, enable complex models to be utilized, avoiding the overestimation of electromechanical parameters, which derives from the use of simplified calculations, with a consequent increase in the usefulness and accuracy of the predictions, compared with the results obtained with traditional procedures.

In integrated system simulators, it is to say software packages able to evaluate, during the movement of the vehicles along the track, the electrical status of the system (energy delivered by the electrical substations, electrical substations current and voltage, trains pantograph current and voltage), it assumes fundamental importance the modelling of on-board electrical drives: in fact, being the electrical behaviour of the system a function of the power absorbed during tractioning phases, or delivered in braking operations, it depends on the mechanical status of the vehicles, but the mechanical characteristics of trains and the relevant movement is a function of pantograph voltage.

In this paper the authors present four different drive models: the first two models simulate each vehicle on the basis of its rated tractive and braking effort, with and without a maximum limit of pantograph current; the second two models simulate, in a more detailed way, a chopper and an inverter drive.

Thanks to the simulations performed on a metrorail track by means of SISTEC, the integrated system simulation software developed by the authors, the models are compared and discussed.

2 Vehicle simplified models

To analyze the traffic related electrical behaviour of a DC fed metrorail system it is mandatory to have at disposal vehicle models which allow to compute, at each integration step, the tractioning or braking efforts: the pantograph absorbed or delivered power, if regenerative braking is present, will be therefore calculated on the basis of the mechanical power, once known the overall train efficiency.

Being trains the loads, either passive or active, of the electrical network, once known their actual electrical power, it is possible to solve the non-linear equations which characterize the electrical network, thanks to linearization procedures commonly utilized in DC *load-flow* problems.

In this paragraph, two simplified models, able to represent the mechanical behaviour of the vehicles, are presented.

The first model, commonly utilized in system simulators, represents the vehicle without taking into account the relation between motors torque and pantograph voltage: whatever is the on-board electrical drive, the vehiche is modelled on the basis of the rated mechanical characteristics, it is to say thanks to the rated torque versus speed characteristics.

For this reason, the model is not able to simulate the torque decrease which, during tractioning phases, might be caused by pantograph voltage drops.

This modelling may be therefore utilized only when the electrical configuration of the network (number and position of the Electrical Substations, rectifier groups rated powers, section of the catenary, etc.) and, above all, the traffic conditions guarantee a minimum pantograph voltage which, according to the manufacturer specifications, allows the electrical drive to furnish its rated mechanical characteristics.

During minimum headway system operations or when a fault occurs in one of the Electrical Substation rectifier groups, the pantograph voltage profile is often far from the rated one and therefore the use of this model may cause errors for both the electrical and mechanical quantities evaluation.

In fact, the hypothesis of vehicle rated characteristics means that, for a given speed, the vehicle tractioning phase is always performed with the rated effort whatever is the pantograph voltage, and therefore with the maximum electrical power absorption: this may lead to an underestimation of train running times, an overestimation of the power delivered by the Electrical Substations and, if the model is utilized during system design, an oversizing of the power network.

The second simplified model represents again the vehicle on the basis of the rated mechanical characteristics, but with the introduction, during tractioning phases, of a maximum pantograph current limit.

Thanks to this new modelling, it is possible to simulate the tractioning effort as a function of the pantograph voltage according to a direct proportionality law.

The results of the simulations performed with the last model are obviously more accurate, compared with the results related to the previous one, but not at all satisfying, as the motor torque is a linear, but not direct proportional, function of train pantograph voltage, and in particular operating conditions only. For this reason the authors present, in the following paragraph, two detailed macromodels of the on-board electrical drives able to solve the above mentioned problems.

3 Vehicle detailed models

In this paragraph the authors present two detailed models able to describe the mechanical behaviour of the vehicles as a function of the pantograph voltage, for both a chopper fed DC motor drive and an inverter fed asynchronous motor drive. Starting from the electrical configuration of the two drives and taking into account the control operations usually adopted in metrorail applications, the authors have defined a set of simple equations which may be implemented in an integrated system simulator to overcome the problems related to simplified models, it is to say to eliminate the errors which may occurr during system electrical and mechanical analysis.

Chopper DC drive

The electrical power scheme analyzed in this section consists of a chopper and a separately excited DC motor; the DC-DC converter is directly fed by the pantograph. Being the integration step usually adopted in system simulators equal to 1 second, the analysis of the DC motor may be performed thanks to its steady-state equations:

$$\begin{cases} V_a = R_a I_a + L_{af} I_f \, \omega \\ V_f = R_f I_f \\ T_m = L_{af} I_f I_a \end{cases} \tag{1}$$

where V_a, I_a, R_a are the armature voltage, current and resistance respectively, V_f, I_f, R_f are the field voltage, current and resistance respectively, T_m is the motor torque, ω the angular speed and L_{af} is a fictitious coupling inductance.

Furthermore, the relationship between the armature voltage V_a and the pantograph voltage V_p may be expressed as follows, being $\alpha(\omega, V_p)$ the chopper duty cicle:

$$V_a = \alpha(\omega, V_p) \, V_p \qquad (2)$$

Once fixed the pantograph voltage to its rated value V_{pr}, it is possible to determine the motor torque characteristic, during tractioning phases; according to the regulation usually adopted in metrorail applications, the characteristic may be subdivided into the following three zones.

Zone 1 $\qquad 0 \leq \omega \leq \omega_{1r}$
The armature voltage, thanks to chopper duty cicle regulation, is increased till its rated value and the field current is kept constant; as a consequence the armature current and the motor torque are constant and equal to their rated values I_{ar} and T_{mr} respectively. The speed limit ω_{1r} and the motor torque may be calculated on the basis of equations system (1):

$$\omega_{1r} = \left(\alpha_r V_{pr} - R_a I_{ar} \right) \Big/ L_{af} I_{fr} \qquad (3)$$

$$T_m = T_{mr} = L_{af} I_{fr} I_{ar} \qquad (4)$$

where I_{fr} is the rated field current and α_r is the rated duty cicle.

Zone 2 $\qquad \omega_{1r} < \omega \leq \omega_{2r}$
The armature voltage is kept constant at its rated value and the field current is decreased till its minimum value I_{fmin}. As a consequence the motor current is constant and equal to its rated value while the motor torque decreases as $1/\omega$. The speed limit ω_{2r} and the motor torque may be calculated on the basis of equations system (1):

$$\omega_{2r} = \left(\alpha_r V_{pr} - R_a I_{ar} \right) \Big/ L_{af} I_{fmin} \qquad (5)$$

$$T_m = (\alpha_r V_{pr} \, I_{ar} - R_a \, I_{ar}^2) \, / \, \omega \qquad (6)$$

Zone 3 $\qquad \omega > \omega_{2r}$
No regulation is performed, the armature voltage and field current are kept constant and equal to their rated and minimum values respectively; as a consequence, both the armature current and torque decrease according to motor natural characteristic.

It is clear that the above relations, written for the rated value of the pantograph voltage, may be applied to model the vehicle electromechanical behaviour in any condition.

If the rated duty cicle is smaller than 1, the chopper may partially recover pantograph voltage drops, allowing the vehicle to furnish its rated performances. Otherwise, the effect of the decrease of train pantograph voltage is the decrease of the speed limits ω_{1r} and ω_{2r}; the new pantograph voltage related speed limits may be calculated by means of relations (3) and (5) and the relevant torque characteristic evaluated. It also evident that the second simplified model of paragraph 2 is not able to simulate the real operation of the vehicle as the motor torque is neither directly proportional nor, in particular circumstances, a linear function of pantograph voltage.

Inverter AC drive

The electrical power scheme analyzed in this section consists of a voltage source inverter and a squirrel cage induction motor; the DC-AC converter is directly fed by the pantograph. As previously mentioned, being the integration step usually adopted in system simulators equal to 1 second, the analysis of the 3-phase AC motor may be performed thanks to its simplified steady-state equations:

$$\begin{cases} I_2' = \dfrac{V_1}{\sqrt{\left(R_1 + \dfrac{R_2'}{s}\right)^2 + \left(\omega_{el} L_e'\right)^2}} \\[4ex] T_m = \dfrac{3\,p}{\omega_{el}} \dfrac{R_2'}{s} I_2'^{\,2} \\[3ex] s = \dfrac{\omega_{el} - p\omega}{\omega_{el}} \end{cases} \qquad (7)$$

where V_1 is the RMS value of the first harmonic of the motor phase voltage, I_2' is the RMS value of the stator related rotor current, R_1 is the stator resistance, R_2' is the stator related rotor resistance, L_e' is the stator related overall leakage inductance, ω_{el} is the feeding angular frequency, ω is the motor angular speed, p is the number of polar pairs and s is the slip.

Once fixed the pantograph voltage to its rated value V_{pr} and with the hypothesis that the motor rated voltage is obtained with the inverter square wave operation, it is possible to determine the motor torque characteristic, during tractioning phases; according to the regulation usually adopted in metrorail applications, the characteristic may be subdivided into the following three zones.

Zone 1 $0 \leq \omega \leq \omega_{1r}$

Neglecting the problems related to motor low speed, the stator voltage and the feeding angular frequency are proportionally increased till their rated values,

V_{1r} and ω_{elr} respectively, thanks to inverter PWM regulation, in order to keep the slip angular frequency s . ω_{el} constant and equal to its rated value; as a consequence the motor torque is constant and equal to its rated value T_{mr}. The speed limit ω_{1r} is the motor rated speed, and therefore a known term, while the motor torque may be calculated on the basis of equations system (7), which may be written also as a function of V_{pr}, utilizing the relation between the pantograph voltage and the motor phase voltage:

$$V_{1r} = V_{pr} \frac{\sqrt{2}}{\pi} \qquad (8)$$

Zone 2 $\omega_{1r} < \omega \le \omega_{2r}$

The stator voltage is kept constant at its rated value and the feeding angular frequency is increased in order to keep constant the mechanical power: as a consequence the motor torque decreases as $1/\omega$ till the motor reaches the speed limit ω_{2r} which corresponds to the intersection between the constant power curve and the maximum torques envelope; the motor torque may be expressed as:

$$T_m = T_{mr} \frac{\omega_{1r}}{\omega} \qquad (9)$$

while the speed limit ω_{2r} may be calculated by solving the following system:

$$
\begin{cases}
T_{mr} \dfrac{\omega_{1r}}{\omega_{2r}} = \dfrac{3\,p}{\omega_{el}^*} \dfrac{R_2'}{s^*} \dfrac{V_{1r}^2}{\left(R_1 + \dfrac{R_2'}{s^*}\right)^2 + \left(\omega_{el}^* \, L_e'\right)^2} \\[4ex]
s^* = \dfrac{R_2'}{\sqrt{R_1 + \left(\omega_{el}^* \, L_e'\right)^2}} \\[3ex]
s^* = \dfrac{\omega_{el}^* - p\omega_{2r}}{\omega_{el}^*}
\end{cases}
\qquad (10)
$$

Zone 3 $\omega > \omega_{2r}$

The stator voltage is kept constant at its rated value and the feeding angular frequency is increased in order to keep constant the slip angular frequency which during the operation in zone 2 has reached, starting from the rated value, the value corresponding to the relevant maximum torque. As a consequence the mechanical characteristics is represented by the maximum torques envelope and may be expressed as:

$$C_m = \frac{3\,p}{\omega_{el}} \cdot V_{lr}^2 \cdot \frac{\sqrt{R_1^2 + \left(\omega_{el}L_e'\right)^2}}{\left(R_1 + \sqrt{R_1^2 + \left(\omega_{el}L_e'\right)^2}\right)^2 + \left(\omega_{el}L_e'\right)^2} \tag{11}$$

The above described relations may be applied to model the vehicle electromechanical behaviour in any condition. The effect of the decrease of train pantograph voltage is the decrease of the speed limits ω_{1r} and ω_{2r}; the new pantograph voltage V_p related speed limit ω_1 may be calculated as follows:

$$\frac{V_{pr}}{\omega_{1r}} = \frac{V_p}{\omega_1} \tag{12}$$

while the new pantograph voltage related speed limit ω_2 may be evaluated by solving the equations system (10). Finally the zone 2 and 3 torque characteristic may be determined thanks to relations (9) and (11) respectively.

It is clear that, also in this case, the second simplified model of paragraph 2 is not able to simulate the real operation of the vehicle as the motor torque decrease may be a non-linear function of pantograph voltage drop.

Also the hypothesis that the motor rated voltage is obtained with the inverter square wave operation, may be removed by introducing in equation (8) a corrective factor $\gamma(V_p)$ smaller than 1 in rated operations and able to be increased for a decrease of Vp, in order to simulate that the DC-AC converter may partially recover pantograph voltage drops, allowing the vehicle to furnish its rated performances.

4 Simulation results

In this paragraph the authors present the comparison between the chopper detailed model and the simplified models, performed by means of SISTEC, an integrated system simulator able to analyze the electrical behaviour of the power network and the running performances of the vehicles, during power supply normal operations and fault conditions.

On a track of about 1.2 km, without curves and grades, a complete running diagram, composed of a start-up, a cruising and a braking phase, is considered for each model; the vehicle weighs 100 tons and is equipped with two DC motors, each of them characterized by a rated voltage of 750 V and a rated current of 500 A. The simulations have been performed assuming a constant pantograph voltage equal to 600 V, in order to analyze the behaviour of the three models in conditions far from the rated one.

In Figures 1 and 2 the train running diagrams and the pantograph currents, related to the simplified model (curve a), the current limited simplified model (curve b) and the chopper detailed model (curve c) respectively, are shown.

Finally, in Table I, the pantograph average electrical powers together with the train running times are presented.

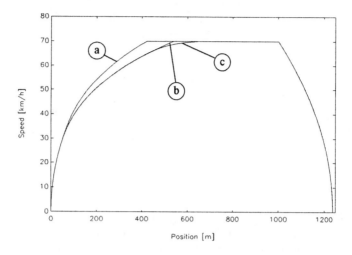

Figure 1 - Train running curves

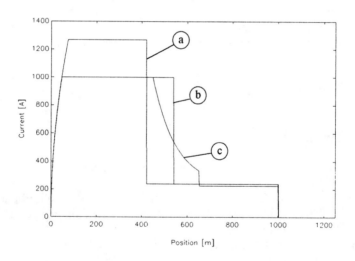

Figure 2 - Train pantograph currents

The results show, in these particular operating conditions, a similar behaviour, as far as the running times are concerned, for the following reasons:

- the torque differences between the current limited simplified model and the chopper detailed model mainly occur at high speed;
- the effects of torque difference between the three models are smoothed by system inertia.

In spite of this, great differences are present in both the pantograph current behaviour and the average electrical power absorbed by the trains; in particular, the increase of the average power related to the first simplified model is about 13%, compared with the power absorbed by the detailed model, but also the limited current simplified model causes an overestimation of the pantograph power of about 10%.

Table I

	Simplified Model	Current Limited Model	Chopper Detailed Model
Running time	91.9 s	93.5	93.7
Average Power	295.6 kW	288.9 kW	261.8 kW

5 Conclusions

The electrical design of a metrorail transit system may be successfully performed thanks to integrated system simulators: being the phenomena, which influence system electrical behaviour, non-linear and mutually coupled, a classical approach may be utilized only with the introduction of heavy simplifications which may determine an oversizing. In order to achieve correct results from the simulation process, mandatory is the accurate modelling of the system, expecially as far as vehicles are concerned. In this paper the authors propose detailed models, for both chopper and inverter fed electrical drives, and, by means of simulation results, show the relevant differences with simplified models.

6 References

1.   B. Mellit, C.J. Goodman, R.I.M. Arthurton: *Simulation studies of energy saving with chopper control on the Jubilee Line*. IEE Proc., Vol. 125, n.4, April, 1978.

2.   R.A. Uher, D.R. Disk: *A train operations computer model*. Int. Conf. Comprail '87, Frankfurt, July, 1987.

3.   N.B. Rambukwella, B. Mellit, C.J. Goodman, Z.S. Muniene: *Traction equipment modelling and the power network solution for DC supplied rapid transit power system studies*. IEE Int. Conf. on Electric Railway Systems for a new Century, London, September, 1987.

4.   S.R. McKay, V.I. John, G.E. Dawson: *Rapid transit performance studies with an interactive train operations simulator*. Int. Conf. Comprail '92, Washington D.C., August, 1992.

5.   J.G. Yu, R.W. sturland, L.R. Denning: *A general motor modelling for transit system simulation studies*. Int. Conf. Comprail '94, Madrid, September, 1994.

6.   R. Miciardi, S. Savio, G. Sciutto: *Models and tools for simulation and analysis of metrorail transit systems*. Int. Conf. Comprail '94, Madrid, September, 1994.

Flexible method of operation of guided systems

V. Stölting,[a] V. Klahn[b]

[a] *Institute for Transportation, Railway Construction and Operation, University of Hannover, D-30167 Hannover, Germany*

[b] *Engineering Office for Railway Operation Systems*

Abstract

In the last years the light rail or trolley has had a renaissance in the world. In every western country cities upgrade their systems (e.g. Hannover) or create new networks (e.g. Manchester and Sheffield). Traffic and environmental problems in urban areas caused this development. However, it is very expensive to build up these lines completely new. So it is necessary to find possibilities of using existing tracks and upgrade the capacity, or if there is no passenger traffic today to use these lines for different traffic modes, for example railbuses, light rail or guided buses. There are three aspects that are interesting, first regulations and laws, second the economical question whether such a traffic system is more efficent than a railway system or not, and third aspect are the technical problems and the infrastructure.

1   Introduction

Because of ecological problems in our cities all over the world people in most of the industrialized countries think about alternatives to the individual traffic. The automobile causes noise and polution in our congested city centers. The living quality in the residential areas is not very good and the children do not have the possibilities to play in the streets. So it is necessary to think about more ecological transport modes for our urban areas. One possibility is the mass transportation sytems like railway, light rail and buses, especially the trolley bus.

In these fields we started our research work at the Institut of Transportation, Railway Constrution and Operation at the University of Hannover. Especially for Hannover we designed a regional light rail network that uses the existing infrastucture of the German National Railway (DB AG) in the city centre and it's own tracks in the suburban area and the villages.

2   Guidelines and Regulations

2.1   General

In Germany we have different laws and regulations for the different modes of transport. It is for example not possible to drive with a tram on railway tracks even they have both the same gauge and the same electric systems. In the next paragraph I want to point out a few important subjects of this topic.

2.2   Definition Railway and Tram

In the German Law of Passenger Transport (PbefG) a tram is defined as a railway that

- uses streets and the way of operation is adapted to the road traffic, or
- uses a special formation subgrade with the way of operation is similiar to the railway of No. 1 above

while these railways are exclusively for the transportion of people in cities and and their suburban areas. On the other side the conventional railways have their definition in the General-Railway-Law (AEG) of Germany.

" Conventional railways are all kind of railways except the tramways"

2.3   Operation Guidelines and Regulations

Based on these definitions both systems have their own operation guidelines and regulations. In Germany the conventional railway has its **Eisenbahnbau und Betriebsordnung (EBO)** and the tramway the light rail the **Straßenbahn-Bau und Beriebsordnung (BOStrab)**. These two regulations determine the operation, the construction of the vehicles and formation-subgrade and the signalsystems. But in most cases they are quiet different. I will describe this with an example, the vehicle clearance profile. Figure 1 shows a profile of a light rail and a conventional railway. The profile of a conventional railcar is much bigger than a light rail. For example at a platform height of 760 mm the difference between both profiles is 375 mm. So it is not possible to drive with a conventional railcar on light rail. On the other side you have a large gap between a light rail and a levitated platform.

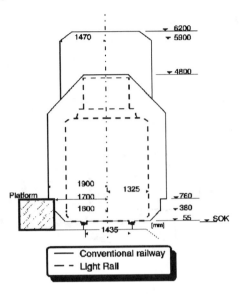

Figure 1: Vehicle Clearence Profile

This was only one example for the differences and problems when light rail and conventional rail use same tracks. But in general it is easier to drive with a light rail car on the conventional rail. The best example is the light rail system of Karlsruhe, where light rail cars run on their own tracks in the city of Karlsruhe and on DB AG tracks further outside in the country (Figure 3). The light rail car of Karlsruhe is a two system traction unit that allows the operation on the light rail net of Karlsruhe (600 V AC) and the DB AG net (15 kV DC). The vehicle has all necessary installations for driving on railway tracks. However such a vehicle is very expensive, it costs between 3.5 and 4 million DM. The power pack in the middle section of the light railcar costs nearly 0.3 - 0.5 million DM (Figure 2) itself.

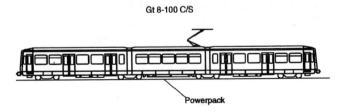

Figure 2: Light Rail Car GT8-100C/S

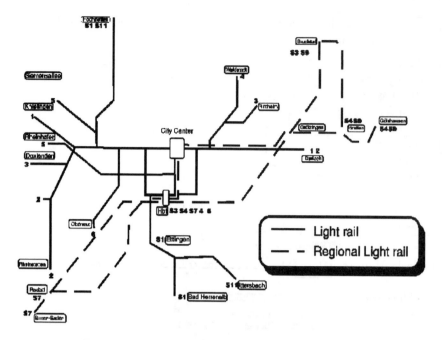

Figure 3: Light Rail Network of Karlsruhe (1994)

3   Field of Application

After a most impressive start of the light rail system in Karlsruhe a lot
of authorities wish to install such a system in their areas. On the one
hand the installation in Karlsruhe appears to be simple, with no major
difficulties which made the authorities think that this system is a cheap
alternative to a conventional rail or bus system. But they forget that
such a system requires large investments and that you cannot copy a
transportion system without adapting it for the behavior in your city.
This leads us to the question: When is which system suitable? I want to
mention four systems: a conventional railsystem with a electrical powered
motorcoach train, a light rail, a railbus and a bus system. Table 1 contains
the main technical data.

	electrial powered motorcoach	light-rail two car unit/ three-car unit	railbus	bus
speed [km/h]	120-140	90-100	90-100	80
passenger capacity unit	448	249	ca. 160	ca. 100
passenger capacity longest version	1344	498/747	480	ca .150
maximum capacity passenger/h	16128	6976/8964	5760	1800

Table 1: Main technical datas of different transportation systems

The electrical motorcoach is the system with the highest capacity, but in comparison it needs the most expensive infrastracture. The other two rail systems both nearly have the same capacity, because a light rail can only drive with a two car unit inside the city. For this reason the capacity is smaller than it could be. In Germany it is not permitted to drive on streets with vehicles that are longer than 75 m. But on the other side, that is the advantage of the light rail. You have the option to drive in both networks.

On a highly frequented conventional railway line it would not seemwise to install an additional system, but if there are railway lines in the region or in less populated areas it would make sense to introduce a light rail line or a railbus line. The choice between the two systems depends on what kind of system exists in the area or whether the authority plans to lead the vehicles into the city centre, for example the pedestrian areas, or into the villages. In this case vehicles must be limited to a width of 2.65 m. The bus is the best choice for a feeder system. It's advantages are flexibility and small units. The only possibility to increase the capacity with a bus system is to install a guided bus line on the main routes, but the problem is that such a system is unsuitable for pedestrian or residential areas.

4   Example for a Regional Light Rail System

In the last years our institute investigated how to install a regional rail system in the greater Hannover area. The greater Hannover area is formed by the city of Hannover with 500.000 inhabitants and some smaller cities within a range of 40 km. Public transportion consists of five conventional railway lines, which operate every hour in the peak hour, a light rail network in Hannover with 11 lines operating nearly every 8 minutes and a bus-net as a feeder system. Figure 4 shows a modified rail network in this area for the World Exposition EXPO in the year 2000 and the proposed regional light rail network.

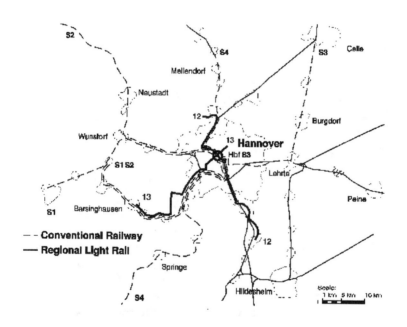

Figure 4: Proposed Railway Network for the Greater Hannover Area

The regional light rail line should serve the less densely populated areas within the region to the North and the Southwest. With such a system it is possible to link villages directly to the city centre, which adds the attractiveness for using the public transport. On some relations the travel time will cut by half of today's travel time and there will be no change of the transport mode. Another advantage is that it is possible to run through the centre of a village. Figure 5 gives the impression of a proposed light rail line in a small village near Hannover.

Figure 5: A proposed passage through a small village

5   Conclusion

Because of the ecological problems in our cities and the intention to improve the living conditions we have to think about alternatives to the individual traffic. Considering the budget restriction we have to develop systems that use the existing and upgraded infrastructure. The Regional Light Rail is such a system. It has the possibility to use conventional railway tracks on one part of the line and it can run as a tramway on the streets or as in Karlsuhe, in pedestrian areas. With this system we can pick up the traveller near his home and carry him directly to his destination, shopping or working, without using to many different traffic modes.

References

[1] Hein, C & Stölting, V.: " Untersuchung über die flexible Anwendung von Bau- und Betriebsvorschriften für eine S-Bahn-Strecke im Raum Laatzen/Messe" Institut für Verkehrswesen, Eisenbahnbau und -betrieb, 1992

[2] Sporbeck, J., Steinwede, F. & Stölting, V.: " Regionalstadtbahn Hannover, Strecke Bennemühlen/Flughafen - Sarstedt", TransTeC Hannover & Institut für Verkehrswesen, Eisenbahnbau und -betrieb, 1993

[3] Stölting, V. "Untersuchung zur Nachnutzung der EXPO-Ausbaumassnahmen zwischen Bismarckstr. und Laatzen durch die Regionalstadtbahn", Institut für Verkehrswesen, Eisenbahnbau und -betrieb, 1994

[4] Straßburger, G., & Stölting, V. "Reisezeitverbesserung auf Stadtbahnstrecken durch Einführung von Expresszugkonzepten", Institut für Verkehrswesen, Eisenbahnbau und -betrieb, 1994

[5] Habich, G., Straßburger, G. & Stölting, V. "Betriebsimulation der Stadtbahnlinie C-Ost im Bereich der Pferdeturmkreuzung", Hannoversche Verkehrsbetriebe AG ÜSTRA & Institut für Verkehrswesen, Eisenbahnbau und -betrieb, 1994

Supply system of Warsaw Tram Company – present state and outlook for a new century

L. Mierzejewski,[a] A. Szelag,[a] J. Wrzesień[b]

[a] Warsaw University of Technology, Institute of Electrical Machines, Electric Traction Group, Pl. Politechniki 1, 00-661 Warsaw, Poland

[b] Warsaw Tram Company, Senatorska 27, Warsaw, Poland

Abstract

The main means of mass transport in Warsaw are trams. Warsaw Tram Company operates the largest urban electric transport network in Poland. Six hundred fifty street cars are on service every day (from nine hundred being on stock) on one hundred sixty kilometres of lines. A commercial speed reaches 20 km/h and maximum traffic capacity of a single route in rush hours is ninety cars per hour.

Fortunately in Warsaw tram lines were intensively used in sixties and seventies, even so it was an opposite to a general trend in the world, where trams were abandoned and changed by buses or cars. So nowadays it is easier to revitalize its role in the city mass transport system.

The paper presents the present state of the supply system of the Warsaw Tram Company and the perspectives, as changes in economic system in Poland creates new demands for electric transport system in Warsaw. Problems with financing new projects to expand the tram lines, buy new cars and equip the substations with new devices (low-current fault detectors, remote control etc.) become evident. But, from the other way now it is an easy access to new high more efficient technology from different foreign companies. The outlook for the supply system improvement, with taking into account the results of study work which were carried out with co-operation of Warsaw University of Technology Electric Traction Group is enclosed. Some results of the study works (measurements, simulation experiments) are presented [1-8]. The modification of the system is treated as a long term investment in Warsaw, where strong needs for better, safe and environment friendly service of electric urban transport has to be fulfilled by a widely spread network of trams, one line of trolley-buses, suburban railway and the first line of underground. The last one will be put into service from the beginning of 1995.

1. Warsaw trams supply system history and the present

In 1905 year Warsaw Tram Construction Committee was established, which decided to build their own power station for supplying energy to the constructed new lines of trams. The decision was undertaken after taking into considerations an alternative:
- supplying energy from Warsaw Power Station (owned by Electrical Society) and then converting a.c. voltage to 0.6kV DC in tram traction substation using rotary converters (mercuric rectifiers weren't known yet);
- building new power station for straight supply of DC 0.6kV energy (its rated power by 1939 year reached 10,5 MW).

Quite apart from this power station between the First and the Second World War there were three mercuric rectifier traction substations built (with total rated power of 16,7 MW) supplied from Warsaw power station. First trams were energized from the power station 26th of March 1908. After the destruction during the Second World War the supply system of Warsaw Tram Company have been being intensively reconstructed, developed and used for increasing number of street cars and traffic. It was rather against the general trend in the world, where tram lines were liquidated.

Nowadays it is opposite, due to revitalisation of trams as environmental friendly means of transport, interest in street cars is world-wide increasing.

The present electric transport system in Warsaw, the capital city of Poland with the population over 2 millions consists of (Fig. 1):
- tram lines,
- trolley-buses (one 14km long line, 3 traction substations),
- suburban tram (EKD),
- first line of underground (in construction),
- suburban railway lines.

However, the main means of electric transport in town is street-car, which overhead catenary supplying energy to trams is spread through Warsaw and is characterised as follow:
- 81 km of flat and 192 km of multiple contact line,
- 7000 overhead catenary posts,
- 41 traction substations equipped with 151 (3-4 at each substation) 6- and 12-pulse diode rectifiers have total rated power of 120.8 MW, which makes 75% of tram cars' rated power during rush hours,
- 432 km of feeder cables, total number of feeders - 320, usually 8 feeders in each substation, an average section of the catenary supplied by one feeder has 1.2km, the feeder cables are connected to the overhead catenary in 324 points (typical feeding scheme: an unipolar supply),
- 360 km of return cables, which are connected to running rails in 214 points.

A failure frequency of different supply system equipment in 1994 is set in Table 1.

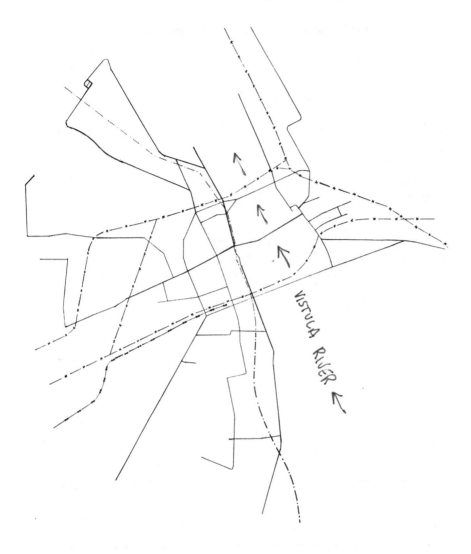

Figure 1: A scheme of electric transport system in Warsaw.

——————— tram lines

——·——· first line of underground (operating from 1995)

——·——· underground line under construction

—••—••— suburban tram (EKD)

—×— suburban railway

Table 1   Failure frequency of the tram supply system.

	overhead catenary	supply system			
	on line	crossings, switches, insulators	cables	substation a.c. equipment	high speed circuit breakers
number of failures	40	27	5	24	11
time of failures [minutes]	1672	1472	214	1750	263

It should be pointed out, that the tram track in 80% is separated from the streets. But the fact, that running rails, used as a return conductor, have low resistance to the ground, creates problems with the stray current protection.. The problem was profoundly examined in the project [5], where stress was put on decreasing voltage drops in running rails by uniform reconstruction of the return cables network and the points of connection the return cables to the running rails, and proper maintenance of rails and their parallel bonding. The specialized software, allowing simulation of the whole supply system with taking into account the rail-earth resistance was used.

The feeders are equipped with high speed breakers Wse and BWs (nominal current 3kA and braking current 40 kA) with asbestos-free extinguishing chambers manufactured by Apena (Poland).

Due to the fact, that the feeding sections and the feeder cables are not very long, the short-circuit resistance for long-distance faults in overhead catenary is low enough to allow high speed breakers to identify properly short-circuits currents from loads (Fig. 2- two short-circuit currents recorded in the traction substation feeder). Electric Traction Group invented a short-circuit detector [2], but as a result from the analysis of supply system parameters and load of feeders it appeared that there is now no need for installing that kind of device.

Power to the traction substations is supplied via 15 kV AC (mainly cable) lines with an average short-circuit power at the point of common coupling 100 MVA. It is well enough not to influence any other energy receivers connected to the same AC busbars by harmonics and quick current changes produced by substations' rectifiers.

In order to keep the supply system functioning there are 11 tower wagons and one fitting wagon in service with the total number of 240 staff working on power supply system operation.

The technical parameters of the supply system of Warsaw Trams were analyzed in the project [5]. The objective of the study was to check operating conditions of the supply system, the load of substations, voltage drops and energy losses in the contact line, the level of the stray currents impedance, breaking short-circuits and finding weak points in the supply system, which could limit the traffic capacity of lines. The results of the project were used to upgrade the supply the system and improve its reliability and efficiency.

2. Rolling stock

The rolling stock operating in streets in Warsaw is rather old-fashioned and a typical street-car is in service for over eighteen years, while the normative age is about seventeen. There are three models used: 13N (the oldest), 105N and 106N cars (manufactured by Konstal, Poland) connected in two-car trains. Body of all wagons are based on PCC type construction, with doors on one side. Further technical data of 105N car are as follow:

arrangement of axles:	4 motored axles on two boogies, BoBo
length:	13500mm
floor height	890mm
tare weight	16,5 t
seated capacity:	20
standing capacity	63 (4 persons/1 m2)
motor power	4 x 40 kW
maximum speed	72 km/h
maximum acceleration	1,4 m/s2
noise inside (outside)	75 (85) dB

Type 13N cars (with a barrel starter) and 105N (with a switching starter) are equipped with rheostatic control during starting and a switch-over of motors' groups while 106N car has chopper control unit and ability to regenerate energy during a deceleration. A typical recorded regenerate cycle of 106N wagon is presented in Fig.3. During the research project undertaken by Electric Traction Group of Warsaw University of Technology [1,5,6] quite apart from measurements on board of trams, energy consumption of tram cars for different traffic conditions were analyzed with simulation methods. Exemplary results of the study - a curve of unitary energy consumption as a function of distance between tram stops, with taking into account street lights, are shown in Fig. 4.

3. Energy consumption

The present technical status of the supply system fulfils all the requirements for energy supply to the trams. The voltage drops don't exceed 10% (equivalent) and the loads of the substations are below their load capacity. The ordered histograms of the instantaneous load of the traction substations according to their load capacity are shown in Fig. 5.

The traction substations are a great energy consumer and in 1994 they used 129 GWh energy with tg fi 0.15 to 0.38. An average cost of 1 kWh of energy in 1994 was 0.04 $. The receipts from tickets covered 65% of expenses for functioning of the Company. Energy losses in the each of the traction substation supply section didn't exceed 5% (in the case with the largest supply sections). The total traffic service supplied by the trams was 42,3 Mln car km. These figures spread into the months are shown in Fig. 6. An average unitary energy consumption (calculated from the global energy consumption and the traffic service) for 13N cars was 2,8 kWh/car km while 3,45 kWh/car km for 105N wagons.

4. Outlook for the new century

From the beginning of the 1995 there is a revolution in mass transport in Warsaw expected as the first part of the first line of the underground is to be put into service with the whole line finished by 2000. Next line of underground will cross the Vistula river (planned to operate by 2010) and will be oriented parallel to existing suburban railway lines. So in next 5-15 years in the city centre, in main transport routes, trams will still be used as main means of transport. In the outskirts of the city the trams will be used as well as the buses, trolley-buses and suburban railway. Strategic plans to extend the role of trams in the peripheral parts of the town exists, while in the city centre the underground will take over the role of mass transit leader from the trams.

Modernization of trams in Warsaw will include firstly the rolling stock, among them ordering new articulated and low-floor wagons with DC motors and choppers, AC drive or modernization of existing wagons will be reviewed. The price of a new articulated low floor tram manufactured in Poland is several times cheaper then the price of wagons built by the leading manufacturers in Europe. The new trams should be equipped with a high speed circuit breaker on board, as some failures were caused by short-circuits originated in the rolling stock main circuit. The use of cars with regenerative energy equipment will give significant energy savings, but the efficiency of the regenerative braking will be higher when inverters are installed in traction substations. As it is known from the experience in other traction systems, it is a very costly solution and its effectiveness strictly depends on the crossection of the overhead catenary and the feeder cables. The introduction of bilateral feeding, examined during the project [8], will give in some sections another energy saving due to lower losses and longer sections for regenerative energy between the trams. In the traction substations 6-pulse diode rectifiers will be gradually changed by 12-pulse ones. 20 traction substations are now equipped with an old type remote control system and there was warding contract by tenders undertaken in 1994 for supplying equipment to build a new load-dispatching unit with monitoring and remote control of power supply to the all traction substations. The introducing this project will give significant economic results (all the substations will operate without staff) and improve the reliability of the supply system. Due to the high costs of this investment it will take about ten years to finish the project. For purposes of proper maintenance of the overhead catenary specialized equipment (diagnostic and measurement wagons etc.) is needed and using new catenary fittings and insulators will lower the failures in this, nowadays the most vulnerable to damages part of the supply system.

All above mentioned aspects, undertaken very difficult circumstances of an economic transformation era, will warrant that Warsaw trams will be revitalized to the role of main means of mass transport in the twenty first century.

Acknowledgements

The authors wish to thank the Warsaw Tram Company for supplying information used in this paper.

Bibliography

1. Mierzejewski L., et al, Reliability, availability and energy saving in electric traction systems for urban agglomerations. *Grant KBN 8S 502 03005*, 1993-95

2. Analysis of short-circuits in supply system of Warsaw Tram Company *Research work (not published)*, Warsaw, 1994.

3. Analysis of proposed solutions of remote control and monitoring of tram power supply system of Warsaw Tram Company. (not published),Warsaw 1994.

4. Mierzejewski L., Szeląg A., Strawiński W. - Implementation of simulation for calculations of trams supply system. (in Polish), *Transport Miejski,* 8/1987.

5.Mierzejewski L., Szeląg A., Drążek Z.-.Analysis of functioning and recommendations for modernization of DC tram supply system of the Warsaw City Transport Company. *(work for the Warsaw Tram Company)*. 1985-1987.

6.Mierzejewski L., Szeląg A., Drążek Z.-New methods of DC tram supply system design.(not published). *Research work of Electric Traction Group*, Warsaw University of Technology. 1986-1990.

7.Mierzejewski L., Szeląg A., Drążek Z.- Analysis of functioning and recommendations for modernization of DC tram supply system of the Elblag City Transport Company ,*(work for the Elblag City Transport Company)*, 1987.

8. Mierzejewski L., Szeląg A., Drążek Z. -Principles of bilateral DC supplying network for trams and trolley buses in Poland. *Research work of Electric Traction Group, Warsaw University of Technology*, (not published), Warsaw, 1989.

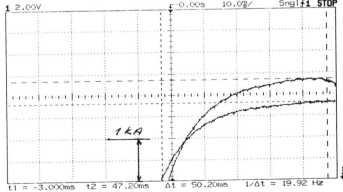

Figure 2: Two short-circuit currents of a feeder
(two different positions of a fault point).

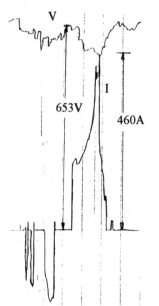

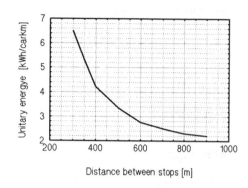

Figure 4: Unitary energy consumption of a tram car
as a function of distance between stops.

Figure 3: Regenerative braking current I and
voltage V of a 106N car.

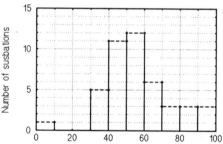

Figure 5: Ordered histogram of a number of substations
according to their instantaneous load.

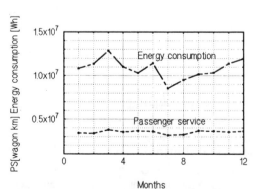

Figure 6. Tram passenger traffic service and energy consumption in 1994.

Intelligent marine transportation system: SMARTT

C. Berkowitz,[a] C. Bragdon,[a] M. Reardon,[b] S. Yahalom[c]

[a] *School of Aviation & Transportation, Dowling College, Oakdale, New York 11769, USA*

[b] *Harbor Consultancy International, Hingham, Massachusetts 02043, USA*

[c] *SUNY Maritime College, Ft. Schuyler, New York 10465, USA*

Abstract

This paper addresses the need to develop a High-Speed Marine Vehicle (HSMV) which is designed for commercial urban applications as an alternative to land-based vehicle travel and to provide an economic stimulant for the U.S. maritime industry, merging intermodal issues with technology.

This paper addresses the marine transit problem which is to increase the market for and construction of high-speed marine vehicles for commercial use in the U.S. and to develop, design and prepare specifications for a prototype vehicle through an international collaborative effort to serve the high-speed transportation markets, and additional markets in the world.

This paper proposes bringing together a unique consortium which would be positioned to develop construction activity in shipyards and an integrated intermodal marine vehicle system (SMARTT: Swift Marine Advanced Response Transport Technology) which would reinvigorate the state-of-the-art in innovative high-speed marine design and applications for the 21st century.

1 SMARTT Consortium

The SMARTT (Swift Marine Advanced Response Transport Technology) Consortium is structured to advance the development of HSMV design and construction technology for current and future owner/operators and shipyards interested in building in the U.S. The consortium would research, develop, design a prototype HSMV, through an international collaborative effort to serve high-speed marine transportation markets in the U.S. and abroad. This would be accomplished by identifying markets and developing a new vehicle design for the U.S. and export markets.

Consortium members would include, ferry operators and potential ferry operators, shipbuilders, technologists, educators, research centers, local and state governments, federal agencies, foreign experts, investment specialists, trade associations, consultants, naval architects and marine engineers, business leaders, marketing experts, economists, planners, engineers and designers. The consortium would represent the latest thinking on available innovative technology application for HSMV.

2 Background

A major portion of the world's urban development is associated with waterways including human settlements found along rivers, bays, harbors and oceans. There are more people carried over the water each day by every type of vehicle from the long-tail boats of Bangkok to the 6,000-passenger Staten Island Ferry, and the sophisticated Hong Kong Jetfoil, then there are air travelers. Ferries are an integral part of the world's intermodal transportation system, but play a minor role in the U.S.

In 1971 the U.S. Department of Transportation identified the potential for HSMV. This study estimated that 500,000 people (1970 census) in 30 cities could be expected to use HSMVs daily as their principal mode of transportation (based on the 1990 census and urban growth, this figure would double). Another 50 cities were identified as long-range markets. It also pointed out that the U.S. had led the way in the development of high-speed marine technology but that the developments had been oriented toward military application. In 1984 a follow-up study was conducted by the U.S. Department of Transportation. The study focused on the potential for high-speed service in Boston, Hawaii, Lake Michigan, New York City, Providence, Ft. Lauderdale, San Francisco, Seattle, Virgin Islands and Washington, DC. At that time, only four HSMVs operated in the U.S.

Current Situation
By better utilizing the potential capabilities of the nation's waterways, the urban centers would be better able to provide convenient and cost-effective urban transportation service and, at the same time, help to relieve some of the major gridlock on the overcrowded highways, bridges, tunnels and transit systems, all of which impairs our economic development potential.

Vehicular traffic entering the urban area is choking the highway networks, and the central business district access and parking has become impossible; private vehicular subsidies have added to the problem; public transportation is barely able to hold its own and air quality countermeasures have failed to contain high pollution levels. Added to these environmental concerns, active community groups have caused the delay and, in some cases, the abandonment of key congestion-relieving projects including highway, bridge, airport and transit improvements.

To turn things around, the urban centers have been involved in a process of reevaluating their transportation networks and capital investments in order to find better ways of meeting growing transportation demands and changes in travel patterns while meeting Federal Clean Air requirements.   With these overwhelming multidirectional pressures, it has become absolutely essential to find and support alternate ways to maintain and improve access within the urban centers.   Time and time again, high-speed marine transportation systems with special emphasis on the passenger mode have been proposed.

Despite this interest in marine transportation, it has experienced very slow growth.   There are many reasons for this, including: continued advances in land-based transport technology, government fiscal policies and transportation programs, failure to utilize available and developing technologies, lack of a clear understanding of actual costs of development and operation and a lack of vision, and the absence of a national HSMV policy and direction.

Domestically, ferries are being reintroduced and considered as alternatives to congested bridges and tunnels, highways under construction and airport access problems, as well as avenues to coastal recreation, as a method of meeting Clear Air mandated goals as a more energy-efficient transit vehicle, and as environmentally-sound high occupancy vehicle which can travel on "self-healing roadways," the waterways.   Additionally, the focus of private investment in 1,000 waterfronts as part of urban revitalization across the US has brought new interest in HSMV links to these areas.   Clearly water-based transportation can bring relief to the already overtaxed land-based transportation network therefore offering a strategic method of expansion without spatial conflict

Market Potential
In 1995, it is estimated that there are about 350 ferry systems in the U.S. and several thousand vessels. Of these, there are only 55 high-speed vessels operating. Approximately 150,000 persons travel by ferry in the U.S. each day. This is less than half of the 350,000 passengers who

travel each day by ferry in Istanbul and only a small fraction of the 1971 U.S. Department of Transportation projections.

Most of the high-speed vessels in the U.S. are based on Australian and Norwegian designs, with the U.S. designed vessels principally high-speed planing monohulls. These vehicles are built in the U.S. Although there have been three or four U.S. monohull, amphibious and surface effect designs put into service in the U.S., this country is still dependent on the technology of other countries for this market.

Worldwide, the fleet of HSMV is about 1,000 (excluding the former Soviet Union fleet, estimated at 1,000). The annual delivery of new HSMVs now exceeds 100 vessels, as contrasted to 1988, when 56 vessels were delivered each year. The principal builders and designers of the world's fast ferry fleet are the Norwegians, Australians, with a significant increase in building activity and markets in Japan and China.

In the slower-speed North American ferry market in 1993, over $1 billion in passenger and car ferries were under construction. The bulk of these were for large car ferry systems. A few small U.S. shipyards were even exporting vessels, which demonstrates that price and quality already offer the marine client the best product.

Meanwhile, in San Francisco Bay, Washington State, New York Harbor, Jacksonville and Rhode Island, transportation planners are identifying new markets for HSMVs. San Francisco's ferry program anticipates $75 million in investments in shore facilities and HSMVs. New York has committed $32 million in waterfront investments, and negotiated for new services to be provided by seven to ten new vehicles, for a tentative program of $80 million. Staten Island Ferry is considering introduction of HSMVs to replace or supplement the existing operation, requiring at least 10 new vehicles. The New York City Council has approved a 12-year lease for a private company to operate HSMVs from Staten Island to midtown Manhattan. Rhode Island is investigating the potential market for HSMVs to Long Island, Newport and Martha's Vineyard. On Long Island, a $40 million car-carrying high-speed ferry is in the development stage and the Long Island Association working with the State of Connecticut are finalizing plans for a ten to fifteen HSMV service across the Long Island Sound. In the Caribbean operators are finding great success with new high-speed car-carrying Scandinavian catamarans.

With the passing of the Intermodal Surface Transportation Efficiency Act of 1991 (ISTEA), $100 million was provided for ferries, along with discretionary funds for San Francisco, New York City and Alaska. Ferries are also eligible for general ISTEA funds ($6 billion), should governmental agencies designate their ferry program as a candidate. There is at least a market for 20 fast ferries under existing funded programs which would be most likely built using Australian and Norwegian technology.

Other Markets
Most marine transport experts and operators have concluded that there is a large world market for HSMVs for: commuting, city links, emergency response (police, fire, customs, emergency services, local regulatory agencies, medical), airport shuttles, coastal refrigerated cargo, river service, rural development, oil pollution cleanup, recreation, express package delivery, island community service where automobiles are prohibited or inaccessible, rough water areas, offshore oil platforms, fishing boat and cargo ship crew transfers, drug interdiction, humanitarian efforts, stabilized platforms for deep ocean research, trans-ocean traffic, transport to off-shore incineration facilities and the short-haul cruise market. Part of the consortium's work would be a world-wide marketing study to define specific HSMV opportunities on a country-by-country basis. HSMVs clearly fill a transportation niche in many market areas, with their total number representing a significant quantity.

3 Design and Construction

To establish a design program that promotes the sale and construction of HSMVs in the U.S., the consortium would develop a data base on national and international activities and technologies, conduct technology assessments, participate in technology transfer and finally design a new generation of HSMV.

The consortium would evaluate the financial feasibility of potential operations and develop the parameters for providing satisfactory service, that has low initial costs and is economical to operate and maintain; develop a program for public and private financing alternatives; set standards for intermodal terminals, intermodal connections, safety and operations, labor needs and licensing, environmental standards and conflict resolution.

4 Management

The consortium would be managed by an executive board. The management would oversee the consortium's performance through working groups that would be chaired by an executive board member. The latest operation management techniques would be applied throughout the process. The consortium would remove all obstacles to constructing an HSMV prototype in a U.S. shipyard and to promote expansion of this market; to use the interactive information highway, include establishing an international HSMV electronic forum to provide state-of-the-art products and information sharing.

The first priority of SMARTT would be the design and construction of a HSMV prototype and to make U.S. shipyards internationally competitive and efficient in this market. All working groups would utilize state-of-the-art technology and management techniques.

5 Work Groups

The consortium would establish work groups chaired by a member of the consortium's executive board in the areas of international activities, Research and technology transfer and system design and operation.

International
This group would serve as liaison to foreign participants. Determine foreign needs, relationships with foreign equipment suppliers and shipyards. Consult with foreign team members who are willing to support the concept of building HSMV in the U.S. market. Determine if the foreign market would be served as a combination of U.S. production and overseas production for hulls, components and subsystems with most of the electronics, propulsion and electromechanical components coming from U.S. sourcing or subcontracted to local suppliers.

Research and Technology Transfer
This group would seek and obtain the most recent innovative research and technological knowledge from all over the globe; seek the most appropriate engine and system packages to accommodate variation in speed requirements and other equipment needs; and obtain the best shipyard construction methods through international cooperation and implementation.

System Design and Operation
This group would design a vehicle to accommodate specific answers to specific needs and will use simulations to evaluate research and design options to determine their potential success.

6 Technical Approach

The consortium technical approach would explore the application of available technologies for the HSMV. The consortium goal would be to develop a state-of-the-art multipurpose marine vehicle. The vehicle would be designed with the flexibility of being used in various environments and configurations including passenger, vehicle, cargo, etc. The consortium will investigate hull design options on a flexible HSMV design, displacement and planning hulls, hydrofoil vessels, semi-planing, catamaran hulls and surface effect platforms will be investigated. The ranges of applicability of each configuration will be evaluated. Factors such as hydrodynamics, hull strength, propulsion, seakeeping, survivability, passenger comfort, interface with terminal facilities, environmental impact, and construction and operating economics will be studied. The analysis of propulsion factors will include propulsors such as fixed pitch propellers, controllable pitch propellers, ducted propellers, vertical-axis propellers and water jets. Propulsion and auxiliary prime-mover investigations will include high-and medium-speed diesels, gas turbines and fuel-cells. The use of electric transmissions will be considered.

The vehicle would utilize human-centered technology. Access and egress, controls, machinery and seating would be optimized. Lighting, monitors, information displays, as well as other sensor systems would be integrated into the design. The cockpit would be evaluated for its reliability and user ability afloat. Control and display design would incorporate human-machine interface considerations to facilitate the crew's ability to perform vehicle systems operations. Crew workload would be based on the human-centered approach. The vehicle would be designed around the operator, crew and passenger needs and requirements using a client/customer satisfaction model. This HSMV is a natural off-shoot of the intelligent vehicle concepts and transfer of military technology. The maritime industry would greatly enhance its standing by emphasizing technology and human performance.

The HSMV would also enjoy the following characteristics: multi-use/multi-purpose platform, flexible design elements, designed to operate in a three-dimensional environment, employ GPS, collision-avoidance, night-vision, bridge automation, stabilization, cargo handling systems, human centered ergonomics, state-of-the-art materials, fuel efficient, advanced communications, fiber optics wiring, on-board MIS, interior and exterior custom display technology, advanced safety systems, surveillance systems, environmental restraint systems, fail-safe fire safety, joint use of external systems, innovative financing, focus groups for user input, advanced and automated maintenance systems, advanced electronic and on-board computer applications. Clearly SMARTT would represent proactive technology based leadership that is economically feasible.

7 Financing

The consortium would give special emphasis to funding with the objective of finding new sources of financial support, and minimizing owner/operator and shipyard overhead costs. The consortium will research and study the financial needs of participants and potential participants in the program; financial analysis of the products vis-à-vis market conditions and financial incentives; performance evaluation and recommendations for improvements in the areas of construction; and identification of financial support. In this area, low-cost business loans, transit subsidies, financial incentives for construction of vehicles from equipment manufacturers and others, multi-financing innovations, cost-sharing proposals, minority program assistance, replacement alternatives, improved management of paying and billing methods and others would be identified and offered.

The consortium would be creative in determining the financial needs and sources of funds. Consideration would be given to low-cost loans, small business loans, subsidy to transit operators, financial incentives, multi-financing innovations, minority program assistance, cost sharing, replacement alternatives, improved management of paying and billing methods and others will be identified and offered.

8 International Cooperation

The consortium would initiate fast-track joint applied research with US., Russia, Ukraine, China, Australia, Scandinavia, Britain and Hong Kong, the centers for HSMV vehicles and construction, in order to explore collaborative technology development. For example, the Russians have developed high-speed passenger hull technology which can be matched with U.S. superior high-value elector-mechanical systems and propulsion systems. Working in partnership with Russian, Chinese, Australian, Scandinavian, British and Hong Kong researchers in a cooperative effort can help rebuild U.S. shipbuilding capabilities and redeploy personnel from defense to commercial activities. Overall administration and organizational leadership would remain with the U.S. representatives.

9 Training

Because of the application of new and advance technologies systems, controls and displays, the consortium would include shipyard construction management. The training would include maximum practical use of simulation and learner-centered training technologies and practices for construction.

10 Conclusion

The consortium would have a long-term impact on developing and expanding the market for U.S.-built HSMVs world-wide by positioning the U.S. shipbuilding industry and selected ports to be the center for active economic growth and proactive leadership in this market niche by the 21st century.

Computerized level crossing system of urban commuter line

A. Taguchi

Technical Research and Development Division, Central Japan Railway Company, 1-6-6, Yaesu, Chuo-ku, Tokyo 103, Japan

Abstract

Central Japan Railway operates urban commuter lines and have approximately 1800 level crossings. In the urban area, at the most busiest level crossing, 400 or more cars pass through the level crossing in one hour. Furthermore 20 trains or more train traffic passes in one track only in one hour. Hence if the level crossing protects double track, 40 or more train traffic passes the level crossing in one hour. This naturally demands high reliability of level crossing protection. This paper explains its system configuration, philisophy of system designing, its configuration and short distance track circuit for level crossing.

1 Introduction

With the help of the technological progress, the number of railway accidents is decreasing, especailly in the urban commuting railway, we Japan Railway operate many trains that the effect of the technological progress appears very easily. So that the number of the railway accidents is decreasing tremendously. We are proud of the decrease. Unfortunately the number of the level crossing accidents is not decreasing tremendously. It have been decreasing a little. The level crossing accident becomes severe accident easily that this is a big problem of Japan Railway.

Level crossing, this is the interface between road traffic and railway traffic. This means that level crossing is the contact point of two systems, road traffic system and railway traffic system. So that we do not have any effective methods to reduce the number of the level crossing accidents. The biggest reason of it is that road traffic is controlled by people in general. As a natural result of this, the safety education is not perfect. On the other hand, the number of the railway traffic and train speed become more severe condition. For example, the number of the train traffic becomes two times as many as that of five years ago.

In consequence of this, the level crossing environment becomes more and more worse. To reduce the number of the level crossing accidents, many kinds of countermeasures have been performed now.

We, Japan Railway, the railway operator, the most important countermeasure is to increase the reliability of the level crossing protection and control. With the help of the computer technological progress, now the computerized level crossing protects many important level crossings.

2 Philosophy

The most important point to make and construct new system is its philosophy. To decide its designing philosophy, we have analized the level crossing accidents. On the other hand, we have gathered information of abroad level crossing system and accidents. After these analisys, the philosophy had decided.

The problem of the level crossing accidents of Japan Railway are as follows.

1) The number of the level crossing accidents is decreasing a little. Nevertheless this is the weakest point of the railway. 60% of the railway accidents are level crossing accidents. Furthermore 200 people die in the level crossing accidents in one year.

2) The number of the train traffic is increasing and the train speed becomes more higher. In despite of this, the road traffic increases extremely and the average weight of the car increases, especially the freight carreer becomes very heavy. In contrast to this, the level crossing protection and control technology is not changed basically. The flyover construction needs a lot of money that the number of the level crossings does not decrease extremely. As the result of it, long time protection of the level crossing causes a social problem. Furthermore, light weight trains are introduced to save the electricity, and the result of it, accident of the light weight train is more severe.

3) Level crossing obstacles are difficult to be detected by the track circuit, that normally the obstacles are found by train operator. Accordingly it is difficult to detect the obstacles on time, and the recognition of the level crossing sometimes delays and this phenomanon causes an accident.

4) Many train traffic causes a long level crossing protection and it causes a lot of rash passes. In addition, the level crossing barrier is made of bamboo that it is easy to be destroied and difficult to protect from the heavy freight carrier.

5) The existence of the level crossing is not recognized occasionally. The man—machine system should be improved.

The condition of the overseas level crossings are as follows.

1) In the urban area, both in Europe and USA, almost all of the level crossings are disappeared and become flyover system.

2) Many countries do not have the stop duty, when a car passes the level crossing.

3) The level crossing barriers are made of metals.

4) Train detection is performed by axle counter (there are two types, one is electrical system, and the other is mechanical system.), and short distance track circuit.

5) Overhang level crossing signals are used. (In USA, many overhang signals are existed.)

6) In Europe, their level crossings do not recognize train speed and kind. So that railways of Europa do not have any system, which averages the level crossing protection time. However USA has several level crossings, which measures the train shunt impedance of the track circuit. It controls the protection time of the level crossing with the measurement of the impedance.

7) The level crossing accidents ratio is almost similar to all over the world. The ratio is 1−3 accident(s)/100 level crossings/year. Every countries have the problem of rash passes. In USA, 700 people die in level crossing accidents in one year.

8) In USA, there is a system which informs the rash passing, which is monitored by camera near by level crossing, to the police office by digital data transmission.

9) In UK and Germany, there are several level crossings which are controlled by dispatching centre. They are dispatched with the help of visual monitoring system.

10) Computerized level crossing is realized in Germany, and it can be jointed to the road traffic control system.

We have been aiming to construct the best level crossing system. However we have a lot of level crossings that our investment is limited to a certain part. To realize the best system, we decided to invest to the most important part, level crossing controller. The reason of it is that the system exchange of level crossing controller needs a long time and man−power. Time and man−power are the most important factors and it is impossible to get them easily. After the decision, we decided the sort of the control system. We had chosen a computerized system. This is mainly because it is cheap and standardized easily. With the analisys and survey described above, we had determined the philosophy of the new system as follows.

1) Fail−safe

This is the most important factor of signalling system. If one of the kind of trouble happens, the system have to stay in the fail−safe side. To realize this fail−safe character, specialized computer operation method is needed. This philosophy was decided before analisys.

2) High reliability

To endure several checks before investment, the computerized level crossing have to have higher reliability than old type level crossing. We regard that the old type level crossing has enough reliability. Nevertheless to introduce new type computerized level crossing, we demanded higher reliability.

3) Easy construction and maintenance

The old type level crossing controller is consisted of relays. When the level crossing control logic was exchanged, for example the train speed−up, each level crossing controller should be changed their wiring individually. Sometimes this individual wiring exchange causes a fatal accident, because it is unstable. To avoid such an occasion, we had to make a new system, which is easy to be constructed and maintained.

According to the philosophy, which was described above, system configuration was decided.

3 System configuration

Before the determination of the system configuration, system premises condition have to be decided. The system premises conditions are described as follows.

1) Simplified replacement character

The old type level crossing controller have to be replaced easily by new system. It is very important factor.

2) Standardized hardware and software

The standardized hardware and software mean easy construction and maintenance.

3) Simplified designing system

Each level crossing has its own control condition, for example double track or single track? there is a turnout or not? and so on. So that the old type controller have to decide its own wiring, because it has many relays and each relays are wired and finally control logic is obtained. New type computerized level crossing controller does not have such relays, so that there is not any wiring. Instead of the wiring, level crossing data input installs the level crossing system. As the result of this, mistakes of wiring are disappeared and level crossing control system installation time had become very short.

4) Improved safety

With the memory of the computer, the system memorize the action of every machines, for example barrier, track circuit and so on. Naturally the reason of any kind of troubles are found very easily. Furthermore this system recovers unstable equipment's troubles, and pursuits each train traffic by the information of track circuits. From this, the safety of the system is improved extremely.

These four premises are important, because they decide the size of the system. Then naturally cost of the system is determined. On the other hand, to desigen the level crossing control logic, the method of the train detection and its premises are determined as follows.

1) Trains are detected by short distance track circuits

Short distance track circuits are used in Japanese level crossing system. So that Japanese short distance track circuit has very high reliability. Unfortunately we use very few axle counters that we avoided the axle counter.

2) Short distance track circuit sometimes fails 1−2 second(s)

The length of the short distance track circuit is too short that the train axle shunt is usually unstable. As the result of it, sometimes it fails 1−2 sec. or shorter.

3) Train headway exceeds 30 seconds

Now we operate 30 trains/hour in the most busiest lines. So that this premise satisfies the severe train traffic operation.

4) Short distance track circuit sometimes troubles, but it is fail—safe trouble

Track circuits detects train by "relay". The important character of the relay is that when it is broken, it stays one side. With the usage of this relay character, the trouble of the track circuit is fail—safe. Of course we use relay in our short distance track circuit system.

5) A certain train is not detected by two short distance track circuits at the same time

This means that the train is not so long and it does not shunt two track circuits in the same time. This is natural specification in Japan.

6) A certain short distance track circuit is not shunted by two trains at the same time

The length of the short distance track circuit is 15—30m that this is natural specification.

7) Two or more train can exist between two short distance track circuits

Sometimes the short distance track circuits are separated 500m or more, that this is natural premise.

With these premises, system configuration was decided. Fig—1 shows the configuration.

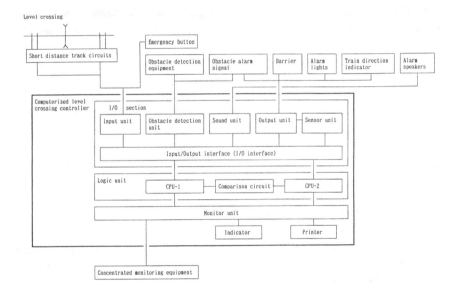

Fig.−1 Computerized level crossing system configuration

The explanation of each unit are described as follows.

Logic unit: Logic unit is the most important part. It is fail—safe computer system and 2 CPU's compare with each other. This is the traditional usage of CPU for fail—safe system.

Input unit: Train detection information and obstacle information are input via this input unit.

Obstacle detection unit: The obstacle information is signalled and alarmed to the train driver.

Sound unit: Level crossing signal sound is transmitted from this sound unit.

Output unit: Level crossing alarm electricity is sent from this output unit.

Sensor unit: Level crossing alarm condition is sensed at this sensor unit.

I/O interface: Interface between CPU and each equipment, moreover it protects the CPU unit from thunder.

Monitor unit: The movement of the CPU's and its I/O information are monitored in this monitor unit.

Concentrated monitoring equipment: This equipment transmits trouble information to the dispatching centre automatically.

Short distance track circuit: It is explained in the Chapter 4.

Emergency button: Push button for emergency.

Obstacle detection equipment: With infrared rays, obstacles are detected by this obstacle detection unit.

Obstacle alarm signal: Obstacle alarm is signalled to the train driver.

All of the interfaces are designed to be applied to the old system that replacement is very easy. Also it can endure high voltage from thunder and so on. Furthermore it is fail−safe system design and the system reliability is very high, because it is difficult to rewrite the information of the CPU's.

4 Short distance track circuit

Remember that the train detection method and its condition are very important to control the level crossing. This is mainly because the level crossing control system controls the level crossing with the premise that train detection information is absolutely correct. So that stable operation of the short distance track circuit is necessary. We needed to prove that its stableness. Also we have checked that short distance track circuit does not influence to the computerized level crossing controller.

4.1 Short distance track circuit operation stableness

Fig.−2 shows the circuit of the short distance track circuit. Fig.−3 shows the block diagram of the short distance track circuit. Fig.−2 and 3 show that the circuit is feed back oscilation circuit. Hence the transistor amplification ratio (hFE) indicates its stableness. Therefore hFE was measured in the field. The frequency is 20kHz. The characters of this track circuit is described as follows.

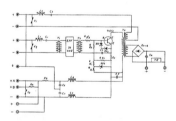

Fig.−2 Short distance track circuit

1) Track is the constant distributed circuit. The model of the constant distribution of the rail track is

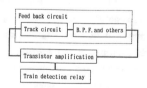

Fig.−3 Block diagram

shown in Fig.−4. The value of the
constant Z (Series impedance)/km and
Y (Parallel admittance)/km are
expressed as follows.

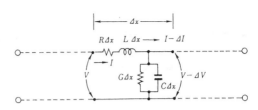

$$Z = 0.204 + j\ 0.031$$
$$Y = 0.035 - j\ 0.100$$

Real number is resistance(Z) and
conductance(Y), and imaginary number
is inductance(Z) and susceptance(Y).
Short distance track circuit
length is 15−30m that they have to
be changed according to its length.

Fig.−4 Constant distributed
model of the rail track

By the way, in Japan, there is rainy season in the early summer. At that time, on the
railway track near coast, the parallel admittance, especially the real part, sometimes becomes
0.5 or 0.7. This means that parallel admitance changes extremely by weather and the
season, and several countermeasures are needed. Fortunately short distance track circuit is
short that the influence from the parallel admittance exchange is not so big. We had done
field experiment and were enlightened that even in the worst parallel admittance, the short
distance track circuit does not stop its oscilation.

2) The stableness of such an oscilation circuit is determined by the amplifier hFE. hFE is the
symbol of current amplifier ratio between base−emitter. At a glance of this circuit, collector
current is not changed easily that hFE is very stable. As the result of it, the impedance
between base−emitter is stable. The impedance value is 80 Ω and the reason is

Z=26/ i × hFE. Constant 26 is decided
by the 2SD111NO transistor
pecification. The result of this is
that stable oscilation of short distance
track circuit is expected and realized.
Fig.−5 shows frequency−hFE character
measured.

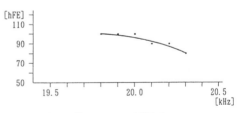

Fig.−5 Frequency−hFE character

3) Frequency−train detection length charactor
is shown in Fig.−6. This shows that
train detection length and train detection
sensitivity is controlled by its frequency.
This is natural because oscilation circuit
stableness is determined by its frequency.
We used several inductance to exchange
the circuit oscilation frequency, and
decided the most stable frequency.
These measurement are checked by theoretical
calculation, four terminals network,

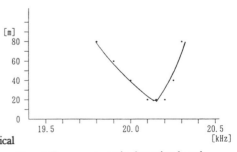

Fig.−6 Frequency−train detection length

and agreeded. With the help of these measurement and calculation, we have confirmed that short distance track circuit is suitable for computerized level crossing system.

4.2 Interface between computerized level crossing controller and short distance track circuit
The interface between short distance track circuit and computerized level crossing controller is important. Suppose that even if the short distance track circuit detects train and inform to the computerized level crossing controller, but accuracy information does not arrive to the level crossing controller. So that arrester is equipped to the interface, because almost all of the mistake information is appeared by thunder that arrester is the best method to solve this problem. In Japan, many thunder appear and make a lot of troubles to the electrical railway equipment. Fig.−7 shows the interface ciecuit.

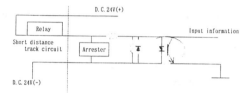

Fig.−7 Interface between short distance track circuit and computerized level crossing controller

With the help of the arrester, heavy voltage from thunder is not appeared to the computerized level crossing controller. Same interfaces are adopted all of the interface.

5 C o n c l u s i o n

Now Central Japan Railway uses 200 computerized level crossing systems and these are mainly used in the urban area. We beleive that the computerization of the level crossing control is the best way to get high reliability of level crossing control. We plan to replace all of the level crossings to the computerized level crossing controller and hope to reduce the accidents.

SECTION 2:
FUTURE VISION

Urban travel demand: a growing business, but can it last?

P.H. Bly, M. Dasgupta
Transport Research Laboratory, Crowthorne, Berkshire RG11 6AU, UK

Abstract

This paper provides an overview of trends in urban travel demand, and examines the consequences of future travel trends for environmental degradation (congestion, CO_2 emissions and other urban problems), and considers the extent to which behavioural responses, technological developments and the adoption of new policies might ameliorate the future problems. The paper uses the results from modelling studies to examine the likely impacts of possible transport measures such as car restraint, public transport improvement, traffic management etc., as well as land-use policies aimed at reducing the need to travel and encouraging modal transfer to energy efficient modes.

1   Introduction

In the UK, road traffic (vehicle-kms) is growing at over 3 percent per year, and is forecast to double by 2030 or 2050, depending on the rate of economic growth. It is widely accepted that, unless there is specific action to contain the growth, the outturn is likely to be closer to the higher forecast than the lower.

Road transport has caused problems of congestion, safety and environmental damage since before the internal combustion engine was invented. But the seemingly insatiable demand for the go-anywhere mobility of the private car, and in particular the less obvious effects of exhaust emissions, has raised a concern which questions the sustainability of present transport trends in a much more serious and consensual way than ever before.

This paper discusses the extent to which it will be possible to cater for these trends in the longer term future, the power of technology to reduce transport problems, and the use of a range of transport policies to modify them.

2.   PAST TRENDS AND POSSIBLE FUTURES

Car ownership continues to grow strongly in a number of countries (Figure 1)[1]. In relation to GDP per head, the absolute trends are very similar in different countries, and without any constraint on car ownership there is no reason to believe that we shall not continue to follow where the USA leads, with little saturation in road traffic growth in the foreseeable future. The phenomenal success of the car, and the consequent fall in public transport use, particularly bus, is clearly demonstrated by past trends in travel in the UK (Figure 2)[2].

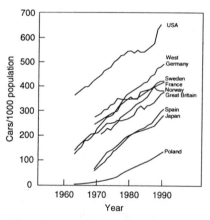

Fig. 1 Trends in car ownership in several different countries

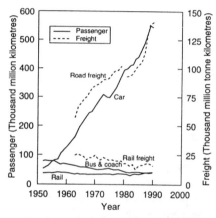

Fig. 2 Trends in use of different transport modes in UK

The domination of the car is less marked for travel to the centre of cities, to be sure. For the largest cities, it is generally public transport which dominates: in London, car takes only 14% of peak-period trips to the central area, and it is rail (mainline and underground) which takes the lion's share (90%) of the rest[2], but for travel in the Greater London area as a whole, private transport (mainly car) takes 73 percent of passenger-kms travelled[3], excluding walk and cycle, which account for a relatively small proportion of distance travelled. Thus even in a very large city, with congestion severe in many areas, car use is little lower than the national average of 86 percent of passenger-kms.

The same general trends are seen in all developed countries. Figure 3 shows that car takes a dominant and still growing share of all mechanised trips in the built-up areas of 52 cities which provided this data to a joint ECMT/-

OECD study[4]. Nevertheless, it is interesting that some cities show low car modal shares even though they have relatively high car ownership (notably Genoa, Vienna, Bern, Dusseldorf, and even Edinburgh). There may be questions about comparability of definition here, but it raises the question of to what extent urban car use may be influenced by prevailing transport policies.

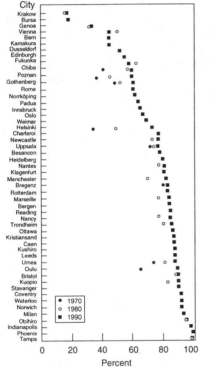

Fig. 3 Car's share of all mechanised trips in the built-up areas of 52 cities in the OECD study

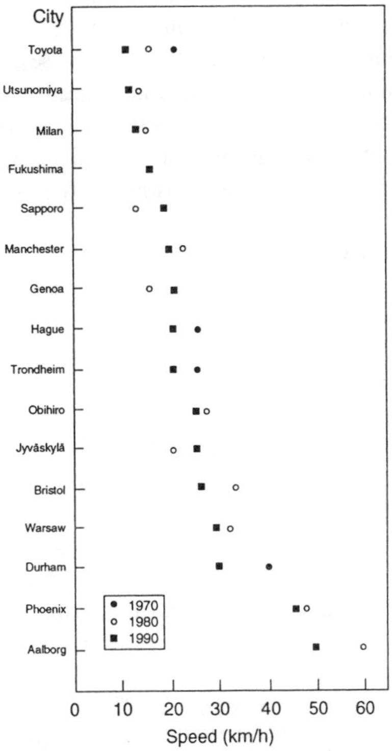

Fig. 4 Average morning-peak traffic speed in the CBDs of 16 cities in the OECD study

3.   URBAN PROBLEMS

Growing road traffic causes problems of congestion, accidents and environmental damage. Of these, we have achieved considerable success in improving safety (deaths and serious injuries halved since 1963, despite traffic growth of 170 percent), and this problem will not be considered further here. By contrast, problems of congestion and environmental damage have become more marked and widespread as traffic has grown, and some of the less obvious environmental effects have become clearer with greater scientific knowledge.

The CBI has estimated that congestion delays cost the UK about £15 billion per year.   Figure 4 shows that average road speeds (morning peak in the Central Business District) have deteriorated over the last decade in threequarters of the 16 OECD cities for which data were available[4].   Note also that speeds are 20 kph or lower in almost half, suggesting that, given the indirect routeing of road traffic and access times, road travel is probably not much quicker door-to-door than walking within the CBD.   In the UK, total road length has increased by 5.4% since 1980, compared with traffic growth of 50%, so the density of vehicles on the network has increased by 45% on average.   This does not imply a comensurate increase in congestion, partly because road construction and improvement is targeted to increase capacity where it is most needed, but also because land-use development and the parallel adjustment of activity and travel patterns has spread the growth in traffic away from the main urban areas, while peak periods of traffic demand have lengthened.

Environmental problems are less easily summarised than congestion, since they cover a very wide range of aspects.   Most recent concern has lain with air pollution, however, especially with the health effects of particulates, and with the effect of carbon dioxide (CO_2) from burnt fuel on global warming. Tightening regulation on exhaust emissions and noise will ease some problems, as Figure 5 shows for the regulated pollutants carbon monoxide (CO), volatile organic compounds (VOC) and nitrogen oxides (NOx), though not, importantly, for particulates or the "greenhouse" gas CO_2.   Much of the fall in the regulated pollutants comes from the fitting of three-way-catalysts to the exhausts of petrol-engined vehicles, but this will be overtaken by traffic growth in 2010 or so, with air pollution increasing thereafter under present regulation.   However, it should be noted that further reductions are already under consideration for 1996, and these would delay the upturn.   Emissions of particulates and NOx from diesels remains a problem.   Greenhouse emissions will tend to increase in line with traffic, unless vehicles become more fuel-efficient.

Environmental problems go beyond air pollution, however, and the spreading of traffic out from the urban areas will increase the exposure of wider sections of the population to local air pollution, dirt and dust, noise, severance, and land-take.   Indeed, our car-based lifestyle raises wider social questions of whether it might be less desirable overall than patterns of living based on more restrained transport habits, despite the undoubted advantages of easy mobility.

4.   TECHNOLOGICAL SOLUTIONS

Technology has already contributed substantially to improving safety and reducing both congestion and environmental damage.   But, for the latter two problems, road traffic growth has outstripped the individual improvement.   In part, at least, this is because society has yet to place a sufficiently high cost on these issues to secure the best that technology can do.

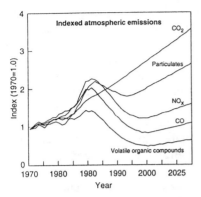

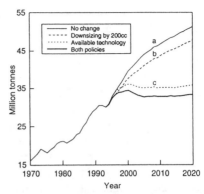

Fig. 5 **Predicted future trends in total traffic emissions of regulated pollutants and carbon dioxide**

Fig. 6 **Predicted future emissions of carbon dioxide from car traffic, under "High" economic growth, if smaller-engined cars are used and the best of foreseeable energy-efficiency technologies are adopted**

Some road-building will still be desirable, and technology is making this quicker and cheaper, but the disadvantages in terms of land-take, intrusion and severance attract more widespread opposition than they used to, and pressure to make better use of the existing capacity has increased. Much has already been done to increase capacity on both urban and interurban roads, in terms of junction layout and road design, traffic-responsive signals, roundabouts and traffic management systems, and general traffic and parking control. More will undoubtedly be done, since we are on the verge of radical innovations in advanced traffic electronics and information systems (transport telematics). These will provide drivers and public transport passengers alike with more comprehensive information about all aspects of the transport system, so that drivers can be guided to take the most efficient routes, and congestion can be minimised across the network, junction control will become still more sophisticated and integrated, and incidents such as breakdowns, accidents and small roadworks detected and traffic redirected quickly and efficiently. Even so, it seems unlikely that these techniques can increase network capacity by more than a few year's growth in traffic demand (Bly et al[5]).

Ultimately, but still decades away despite the existence of impressive prototypes, there is likely to be some practical implementation of the "automated road", in which vehicles steer, accelerate and brake themselves, and can operate safely and reliably at very small headways. This can potentially increase road capacities enormously, but is much more likely for intercity roads than urban roads. Without careful planning, this raises the danger that urban areas will be left to cope with much higher inflows of traffic from each feeder road than at present, exacerbating urban congestion rather than decreasing it.

There is still appreciable scope for further reductions in exhaust emissions from both diesel and petrol engines, and in the meantime it is likely that California will lead the way into low-emissions vehicles running on different fuels and with different powerplants, with the use of electricity in some form (whether by batteries, flywheels, fuelcells, or hydrogen is as yet unclear), which will at least remove the emitted pollution from the urban area. Use of petroleum fuels too, and therefore emissions of CO_2, could be cut drastically, even with internal combustion engines. Figure 6 shows predictions made by Wootton and Poulton[6] of future CO_2 emissions from the UK car fleet, (a) assuming the higher level of growth in the NRT forecasts with only minor fuel efficiency improvements, (b) assuming the same vehicle fuel efficiencies but with a shift in demand to rather smaller engines, and (c) assuming adoption over a twenty-five-year period of currently-available technologies to reduce fuel consumption (lower weight, better aerodynamics, more efficient transmissions, better engine management, reduction of cold-start effects) by, ultimately, about 50% for petrol engines and 40% for diesels[7]. This suggests that, if this perhaps extreme level of efficiency can be achieved in mass production and normal use, total CO_2 emissions could be held only slightly above present levels until about 2020. By then, there may be little prospect of further improvements in spark-ignition engines, but their domination is likely to have been substantially eroded by more environmentally-friendly substitutes.

Technology has also done much to reduce noise: heavy lorries, for example, are now little noisier than were cars twenty years ago, and further noise reduction is possible. Technological improvements in tunnelling may also remove more traffic from sensitive places altogether by taking it underground. But in general, technology can do little to reduce the general nuisance that the physical presence of traffic causes to the people who have to live, work or shop in its proximity, or, as we have seen, to remove congestion delays from places with a particularly high demand.

It is possible that sophisticated telecommunications can create electronic access to activities which is almost as acceptable as physical presence, and we are now on the threshold of such "virtual reality". At the least it will have a substantial effect on the distribution of physical travel in time and space. It is conceivable that it will be so successful that it reduces the demand for physical travel to the point where congestion is no longer a problem. If not, however, we will have to turn to transport policy, rather than technology, to solve some of the problems.

5.   POLICY SOLUTIONS

It is more efficient in terms of fuel use (and therefore emissions), noise and general disruption, and use of road capacity, to transport people in a dense urban area by public transport, rather than by private car. Technology will make public transport more attractive and easier to use, but it will probably be still more effective in enhancing car travel, so there will be little voluntary transfer, except to the extent that congestion and parking problems worsen.

It is important, therefore, to examine possible policies to reduce car use. Dasgupta et al[8] have applied a two-zone single-link model to five medium-sized UK cities to explore the likely effects of a number of different policies aimed at encouraging transfer to public transport. The model embodied a mechanism to redistribute trips between different destination areas, and replicates our current knowledge on demand elasticities and speed-flow relationships.

The policies tested were to reduce bus fares by half, to increase all fuel costs by 50 percent, to double central area public parking charges, to halve both public and private central area parking places, and to impose a charge of £2 peak and £1 off-peak on all cars crossing a cordon around the central area. The model predicted the changes in modal split, distance travelled, average road speeds, costs of travel and emissions. All these policies made public transport more attractive relative to car, causing a reduction in total vehicle-kms, an increase in average road speeds, and a reduction in emissions. The parking and cordon policies discourage travel to the central area and displaced some traffic to the outer areas, where speeds fell slightly.

Table 1 summarises these effects on total vehicle kilometres travelled, as a proxy for both congestion and environmental nuisance. There are substantial differences between the cities which Dasgupta et al were able to relate fairly convincingly to the prevailing transport conditions of the cities, but the general pattern is clear. Cheaper public transport (or better services, since this would give much the same result) on its own seems unlikely to attract a large proportion of travellers from car. Making car travel more expensive is more effective, though both approaches in combination would have a still greater effect.

Table 1 Modelled effects of urban transport policies on total vehicle-km[8]

Test	Leeds	Bristol	Sheffield	Derby	Reading
Fares x 0.5	-1.5	-0.7	-1.2	-1.3	-1.7
Fuel cost x 1.5	-3.7	-3.7	-3.2	-2.6	-3.8
Parking charges x 2	-1.2	-2.8	-2.3	-1.5	-3.1
Parking places x 0.5	-4.0	-3.6	-4.8	-2.9	-3.0
Cordon charge £2/£1	-4.0	-3.4	-5.1	-4.7	-4.2

It is especially difficult to attract people from the car because our way of life is closely tied to its go-anywhere mobility, and patterns of both travel and land use reflect this dispersion in a way which collective transport cannot adequately serve. It is often suggested that the key to this problem is to plan land use to reduce the need for travel by, for example, bringing workplaces closer to homes. This is a very difficult thesis to test, but again modelling work using the interactive transport and land-use models of the International Study Group on Land Use and Transport Interaction (ISGLUTI)[9] suggested that, if travel choices remain as unrestricted as they presently are, even large shifts in land use patterns are likely to have only a marginal effect on either car use or total travel. Table 2 (based on Dasgupta and Webster[10]) summarises the effects of three tests: in two, the overall urban population density is increased by 2% per year over twenty years, with new building development left free to locate anywhere in the urban area in one case, but prohibited in the outer areas in the other;   the third policy redistributed the existing manufacturing employment evenly in proportion to the population resident in each zone of the city.   The results in the Table are the averages obtained from running four models (CALUTAS, DORTMUND, LILT and MEPLAN) on 4 cities (Bilbao, Dortmund, Leeds and Tokyo).   It can be seen that even the very substantial reversal of the prevailing trends towards lower urban population densities has only a modest effect on modal split, travel distance, road speed and emissions. The redistribution of employment has a smaller effect still, because workers prefer the greater choice offered by greater distance, rather than accepting the nearest suitable workplace. Of course, if travel were restricted, by making it much more expensive for example, people would choose workplaces closer to home, and in that case there would be advantage in a land use pattern which provided workplaces more closely integrated with residential development. But our present land use patterns have been formed by the widespread availability of the car, and they can be reversed only on a long timescale. Moreover, the ISGLUTI study also suggested that restriction of car use in a limited area could have adverse effects by encouraging travellers to use their cars to different, unrestricted, destinations, rather than using a different mode to the original one.

Table 2   Modelled effects of land-use policies on transport[10]

	Urban density grows 2% pa		Manufacturing jobs spread evenly among population
	Unrestricted development	Outer Area restrictions	
Car trips	-2.0	-3.3	-0.1
Public transport	+3.7	+2.7	-0.4
Walk trips	-3.3	+4.8	+0.0
Trip length	-4.6	-7.9	-0.3
PCU-km	-1.8	-3.1	-0.1
Speed	+1.2	+2.1	+0.1
CO_2	-2.1	-3.9	-0.1

6.   IN CONCLUSION

Despite the widespread view that we will be unable to cope with the predicted doubling of road traffic over the next thirty years, in the absence of any specific active discouragement it seems likely that it will happen, and that even without substantial road construction the country will absorb it without catastrophic congestion bringing the transport system to a grinding halt. The extra traffic, primarily by car but with road freight contributing appreciaby, will manifest itself largely as a spreading of the peak periods, and faster growth rates in periurban and rural areas.   Nevertheless, this will represent a considerable spreading and worsening of traffic delay, nuisance and environmental damage.

Technology will be more able to reduce the environmental damage than the congestion.   There remains considerable potential to reduce the emission of harmful pollutants and greenhouse gases, though beyond the next twentyfive years petroleum-fuelled vehicles will have to be replaced by less polluting types of motive power and energy if greenhouse emissions are not to grow.   On this timescale, too, automatically operated road vehicles may have been introduced on some roads, but this may merely exacerbate congestion and parking problems in urban areas.   Conceivably, demand for physical travel might be reduced by advanced telecommunications, but as yet there is no evidence.

For improvements beyond these advances of technology, changes in present travel behaviour brought about by policy will be required.   Better, cheaper public transport would help, but on its own the effect is likely to be small. Reorganisation of land use in an attempt to reduce the need for travel may also have only a small effect if pursued in isolation.   Making car travel more expensive in towns is likely to be more effective, but would need to be planned and coordinated carefully with land-use and wider policies if individual towns are not to be disadvantaged by a discouragement of economic activity.

Acknowledgement   Crown Copyright 1995. The contents of this paper do not necessarily represent the views or policies of the Department of Transport.

REFERENCES
1. International Road Federation. *World Road Statistics*. IRF, Geneva.
2. Department of Transport. *Transport Statistics GB*, 1991. HMSO, London.
3. Department of Transport. *National Travel Survey 1989/91*.HMSO, London.
4. Dasgupta M. Urban problems and urban policies: OECD/ECMT study of 132 cities. *Proceedings of the Conference on "Travel in the City: Making it Sustainable"*. Dusseldorf, June 1993.
5. Bly P H, Hunt P B, Maycock G M, Mitchell C G B, Porter J and Allsop R E. Future scenarios for inland surface transport. *TRL Report 130*, 1995.
6. Wootton H J and Poulson M L. Reducing carbon dioxide emissions from passenger cars to 1990 levels. *TRL Report PA3016*, 1993.
7. OECD/IEA. Low consumption/low emission automobile. *Proceedings of an Expert Panel*, Rome, February 1990. OECD, Paris.
8. Dasgupta M, Oldfield R H, Sharman K and Webster F V. Impact of transport policies in five cities. *TRL Report PR107*.
9. Webster F V, Bly P H and Paulley N J, editors. *Urban Land-use and Transport Interaction*. Avebury, Aldershot, 1988.
10 Dasgupta M and Webster F V. Land use/transport interaction: policy relevance of the ISGLUTI Study. *Proceedings of the Sixth World Conference on Transport Research*, Lyon, June 1992.

Solving the problems caused by traffic saturation of cities – new approaches to mobility

D.J. Martin

AEA Technology, Harwell, Oxon OX11 0RA, UK

Abstract

Growth in transport demand over recent years has caused environmental degredation in many urban areas. Particular challenges arise when a city's transport system is operating close to saturation. A wide range of techniques is being examined by local authorities to help solve these problems. This paper puts forward a performance assessment methodology of the effectiveness, the costs and the benefits available from these techniques.

1 Introduction

The key trends in urban transport during the last few years have been an overall growth in transport demand and a growth in the modal shares of private cars and road freight vehicles. Along with these growth patterns have emerged problems of environmental degredation. Congestion, noise, pollutant emissions and accidents are all of concern to local authorities and the general public alike. The consequent cost of the European economy is estimated to be at least 50 billion ECU per year for road transport.

In many city areas, there are also signs that the transport system is operating close to saturation. Under these conditions, instability can occur, and this has been observed for example, in "grid-lock" situations or in "very poor" air quality episodes. There is a need, therefore, for effective solutions to these problems and for new approaches to the mobility requirements of urban transport users to be developed.

Saturation problems result not only from transport demand within the city, but also from extra-urban pressures.   Therefore measures are needed to define and control the urban: extra-urban interface.   Potential solutions include the provision of modal interchanges for passengers (such as park-and-ride), and the use of peripheral warehousing for freight.   Such warehousing could be used to combine loads for efficient local distribution by a minimum fleet of purpose-built urban delivery vehicles.

Planning controls are an important tool in the longer-term transition to a better city environment.   A key objective would be to reverse the current trend towards excessive specialisation of sectors of urban space.   Such controls can be made more acceptable in a market economy if they are linked to a strategy for infrastructure renewal and urban regeneration.   For example, investment in efficient freight and passenger transport arteries and networks can foster the city as a centre for wealth production and human creativity.

Innovative technologies will be vital in facilitating human-centred solutions to urban transport needs.   These technologies include enabling systems, such as road transport informatics for road pricing and better logistical control of transport fleets, as well as new vehicle designs and concepts.   The latter area encompasses solutions such as:

- self-service electric cars;
- pelletted automated systems, in which small vehicles have flexible routing options on a mass transit network;
- segregated bus systems;
- hybrid or gas-powered low-floor buses;
- light rail and guided bus systems.

Fiscal measures for the management of transport demand make use of the intrinsic dynamics of city transport.   For example, congestion charging is effective, since user charges increase rapidly as the traffic density edges closer to capacity.   Emissions charging can be deployed in a similar way.   Such measures require underpinning technologies such as roadside sensors and intelligent tags for vehicles.

Another human-centred solution is the preferential treatment of citizens of the city.   Parking controls and zone access controls can be used to favour local residents.

Similar measures relate to the promotion of social integration and an enhanced quality of life.   For example, pedestrian zones, better cycling facilities and good access for urban public transport can all contribute in making the city centre an attractive, vibrant hub of social activity.

Clearly, transport measures need to be efficient as well as human-centred, and these two objectives can be achieved in a compatible way. Urban public transport can provide good access in an energy-efficient manner: light rail and advanced bus technologies have proved both attractive and environment-friendly. Similarly, efficient strategies for urban freight distribution can be tailored to human needs: for example, through the introduction of appropriate vehicle technologies, zone access controls and logistical systems.

2 Policy Options

A wide range of options has been developed and implemented by local authorities and others to help solve these problems. Many of these options are motivated by objectives other than the management of saturation issues. Nevertheless, they have some potential in attempts to overcome or reduce the environmental impact of transport. The spectrum of broad options for tackling urban transport problems includes:

- transport demand management, using information systems and fiscal methods;
- transport supply and traffic management, using operational and traffic control techniques;
- improved service quality and efficient public transport, including new vehicle and fuel technologies;
- improved facilities for inter-modal transfer;
- optimisation of urban space and infrastructure, including long-term land-use planning;
- promotion and support of urban public transport.

These can implemented by a combination of local initiatives and national policies. The key tools for the implementation are:

- fiscal policies;
- regulatory policies;
- planning policies;
- infrastructure investment;
- research and technological development;
- promotional initiatives.

The level at which each of these policy tools can be implemented in the most effective manner is subject to debate. The most useful level to consider here is that of local authority competance because considerable progress is being made at this level, both in the UK and in other Member States of the European Community.

3 Case Study Examples

Small and medium-sized cities have experienced the most significant changes in mobility patterns because these areas have had to deal with problems that had previously been typical only of larger urban areas. The experience of many cities which have undertaken urban traffic management policies is that barriers to their implementation arise from a variety of sources. The most obvious of these barriers is the public hostility to prohibitions and restrictions on access. Individual members of the public need time to assimilate improvements which may have been advocated for the public benefit but which, when the time comes for implementation, turn out to be in conflict with their other interests and deep-rooted habits. Nevertheless, several small and medium-sized cities can point to successful traffic management schemes which have brought about at least some or all of the desired improvements. An important characteristic of such schemes is that they have been introduced as part of an urban transport strategy.

For example, in York the city council developed a transport policy with the following main strategies:

- **access management and restructuring of public spaces** - this involved a major pedestrianisation scheme and vehicle restrictions in the city centre;
- **the promotion of soft modes** - this involved the improvement of pedestrian and cycle facilities with new pedestrian/cycle routes and cycle parking facilities;
- **synergy of modes** with the use of park-and-ride schemes and bike-and-ride schemes;
- **tariff schemes** for parking to penalise long-stay parking near the city centre;
- **traffic management** in and around the city centre using an Urban Traffic Control (UTC) system to improve traffic flows;
- **traffic management** using traffic calming techniques to reduce vehicle speeds in residential areas.

In Bristol, an integrated approach has been adopted with three main elements:

- **land-use and development strategies** - with a combination of re-orientation of land-use and a revised parking policy;
- **improved transport supply** - including modernisation and improvement of public transport, promotion of soft modes and synergy of modes such as park-and-ride;

- **managing travel demand** by means of traffic management and access management together with information and publicity on alternatives to the car.

In Chester, the main strategies have been:

- **access management** - by extending the existing pedestrian zones and building an inner city by-pass;
- **synergy of modes** - by introducing urban traffic control on the inner ring road;
- **modernisation of public transport** - by providing bus priority measures;
- **promoting of soft modes** - by providing more facilities for cyclists;
- **tariffs** - by introducing charges for on-street parking.

Many more examples of traffic management initiatives can be found, which utilise a combination of approaches on the lines given in these three examples. Wilkins [1] has collated case studies from the UK and Ireland as part of a larger European Commission study programme [2].

A general conclusion from these case studies is that different problems are being addressed in different ways. Due consideration is given by the local authorities involved to the impact which the traffic management strategy will have on the traditions and expectations of each individual city. This clearly makes comparisons between cities somewhat difficult. The difficulties are further compounded because there are no readily apparent measures by which the successes or failures in these strategies can be judged. Hence, for the present, the transport community can only rely on what is effectively anecdotal evidence for assessing the value of transport demand management technologies and methods.

4 Evaluating the Effectiveness

It will be important for decision makers in local authorities and elsewhere to have reliable and well-based information on which they can make choices regarding the most suitable combination of traffic management strategies. Of prime interest are the costs, the benefits and the effectiveness of the measures adopted. There remain powerful public pressures for innovation in ways which will enhance urban quality of life, road safety and environmental protection while still delivering a viable transport system for the city at reasonable cost.

A noticeable barrier to efficient use of resources is the tendency for management and regulation of these issues to focus on established "prescriptions" for related features and activities, as opposed to the performance output improvements which those features and activities help to achieve.   A performance-oriented, rather than a prescriptive, methodology for evaluation is needed for alleviating traffic-generated problems in cities.

The performance-oriented approach has four main stages:

- identifying relevant activities, the public and private costs and what benefits they are expected to provide;
- identifying suitable yardsticks of performance against which to judge what these activities help to achieve;
- developing alternative proposals to achieve equivalent or improved performance at reduced cost; and
- securing commitment from transport operators, the relevant regulators and other parties on the basis for evaluating changes and on the proposed changes themselves.

Some useful progress has been made in establishing suitable performance measures and in carrying out the necessary evaluations. Table 1 lists some examples of measures which have either been used or are part of the traffic management strategies in a number of UK cities.   The performance measures can be conveniently grouped into those related to safety, environment and congestion.   As can be seen from the Table, safety measures are the most easily identifiable and quantified, whilst both environmental and congestion measures do not have a commonly accepted basis.

5 A Performance Assessment of "Mobility"

The definition of mobility - whether it is "sustainable" or otherwise - is subject to considerable discussion. In the absence of an agreed description of what is meant by mobility, it seems preferable to concentrate on those features of urban transport which can be measured and quantified, and to seek improvements in them. Quality of service provision can they be assessed against suitable performance indicators.

The performance indicators which are most relevant include:

- for safety performance:
  - accident rates,
  - casualty rates,

  Both of these should be expressed in terms of pedestrian and car occupants per vehicle - km in the specified urban area;

Table 1   Examples of Measures Used to Evaluate the Performance of Traffic Management

Location	Safety	Environment	Congestion
Bristol	Reduce casualities by 33% by the year 2000 and by 50% compared with 1987	CO_2 emissions in 2000 to be no greater than in 1990	Reduce car share of total city journeys to less 50%
Leicester	Accidents rates reduced by 50% in traffic calmed areas	600,000 car trips per year substituted by re-opened Ivanhoe rail line	Journey times reduced by between 10% and 20% due to UTC
Liverpool	-	Energy saving of 29 GJ per year	-
York	Reduction of 30% in the number of road casualties	-	Journey times reduced by 20% due to the inner ring road

- for environmental performance:
    - energy consumption rates,
    - air quality,
    - traffic-induced noise and vibration exposure;
- for congestion:
    - city centre journey times.
    - modal share of public transport,
    - pedestrian journey times.

Separate indices need to be developed for each of these performance measures. All can be quantified for "before" and "after" the introduction of traffic management strategies in an urban area. All can be used as targets for achievement. The challenge facing urban planners, transport operators and local authorities is to select the most appropriate set of targets which will meet the objectives of improved traffic management without incurring excessive cost.

6 References

1.   Wilkins, G.T. *Efficient solutions for improvement of urban transport*, A Thermie Programme Action, ETSU, Harwell, 1993.

2.   European Commission, Directorate-General for Energy *European medium-sized cities: the urban mobility management*, A Thermie Programme Actions, Brussels, 1994.

The implementation of city transportation strategies – a planning perspective

C.A. Brook

Clive Brook Associates (Town Planning and Development Consultants) Limited, 2, Northwest Business Park, Northwest Road, Leeds LS6 2QH, UK

1   Introduction

When I commenced my professional planning career in 1966 with Essex County Council, Land Use Transportation Studies had very recently come into vogue and a number of the major planning authorities had established specialist teams. These teams produced studies and plans utilising, what were then, fairly new modelling and survey techniques, but the studies followed the basic survey-analysis-plan approach. The scale and nature of the studies was such that they all too rarely resulted in a comprehensive and coherent plan capable of implementation, let alone integrated implementation where the various strands of a strategy are taken forward together.

Transport strategies for cities in the U.K. are now usually presented in a comprehensive fashion but rarely are the means of implementation and phasing-in of the strategy dealt with on a comprehensive and integrated basis. This paper examines the problems of achieving the integrated implementation of transport strategies and their relationship to the city-planning process, which should be so central to their realisation. The basic reasons behind these problems lie in the following areas:-

A)   The lack of full integration of city planning with transportation planning.

B)   The funding and bidding mechanisms which are used.

C)   Local Government structures and administrative capabilities.

D)   An absence of experience of the integrated implementation of strategies.

In "Urban Public Transport Today" Simpson [1] refers to the "rise and fall of integrated land use/transportation planning". Such integrated planning occurred in the late 1960's and early 1970's in the U.K. in selected areas where Passenger Transport Executives and Metropolitan County Councils were enabled to operate integrated land use/transportation planning. While this gave some hope for the future the system was substantially dismembered in the 1980's, particularly with the abolition of the Metropolitan County Councils. Yet the need for integrated land use/transportation planning has never been greater, and grows year on year due to increasing road traffic congestion in our cities and the resulting environmental problems. The relatively weak position of public transport as a result of declining bus passenger-miles, bus de-regulation and a lack of investment in local rail services exacerbates the problems.

The emergence of recent Government Guidance in Planning Policy Guidance Note 13 [2], in the Government's Sustainable Development Strategy [3] and in the Royal Commission on Environmental Pollution's recent report on Transport and the Environment [4] at last give serious recognition to the core problems and the need to tackle them. Prior to examining more closely the integrated implementation of transportation strategies I briefly look back to earlier metropolitan transportation strategies in order to assess the extent to which they have been successful. I use the Leeds Metropolitan area as a case example.

2   Transport Planning in Leeds - A Brief Historical Perspective

The City of Leeds forms part of the West Yorkshire conurbation which is a grouping of large urban areas and smaller towns located along the spine of the M62 Trans-Pennine Motorway. While Leeds is the dominant City it is not centrally located within the conurbation, by contrast for example with Manchester's location at the core of the Greater Manchester conurbation . The location of the dominant city and the form of a conurbation are of fundamental importance to past and future travel patterns.

The first relevant study was that undertaken by Sir Colin Buchanan and his team when they produced their report "Traffic in Towns" in 1963 [5]. Leeds was selected as one of three case studies and the Study had three main objectives:-

i)   examining the number and character of vehicular movements that would arise as vehicle ownership or use approach the potential maximum.

ii)   to indicate the scale and pattern of alternative distributor road networks required to meet varying proportions of the potential demand for vehicular movement.

iii)   to indicate the impact of increased traffic on the town centre and the scale of the changes that would be required.

There was a recognition, as stated in paragraph 26 of the introduction , that "the commuter cannot be forced back onto public transport". While the expansion of public transport was seen as making a large contribution to reducing car commuting this was not to be regarded as a solution in its own right but as one arm of a co-ordinated policy (paragraph 27).

The main Buchanan proposals for Central Leeds were :-

i)   The creation of an extensive traffic free shopping area.

ii)   A new district distributor road to the east of Vicar Lane.

iii)   Redevelopment of 48% of the Central Area to facilitate the rear servicing of those buildings which front onto the pedestrianised area.

iv)   The re-grouping of uses to form environmental areas.

v)   A circulation system of primary and district distributor roads.

Following the Buchanan Report the City Council produced their own City Centre Transport Strategy in the late 1960's under the direction of the City Engineer and Planning Officer, Geoffrey Thirlwell.   This approach by an integrated professional department under a strong chief officer enabled the production of a fairly comprehensive strategy, which included a new inner ring road, four major quadrant multi-storey car parks, extensive pedestrianisation of the shopping core with high level pedestrian links from the shopping centre to the commercial office area to the west. A new bus service was to link the four quadrant car parks and take passengers into the heart of the centre.   The costs of this Strategy were extensive and only parts were implemented.   Some 25 years on two phases of the seven phase inner ring road await completion, and only one of the four quadrant car parks has been built.   An extensive pedestrian area has been completed but only a small portion of the upper level walkway was built and the linking bus service was removed following only a short period of operation.

These earlier transport strategies had a heavy bias towards the central area of the City.   In 1977 WytConsult [6] produced a study of the detailed traffic patterns and demands throughout the West Yorkshire metropolitan area.   The recommended strategy for Leeds identified the primary problem as being that of catering for travel demands in peak periods.   The proposals were to cater for a modest growth in car usage and to provide as attractive a public transport system as possible, within the limited funds seen to be available.   The recommended Strategy is set out on page 255 of the report and includes commuter parking restraint in the central area. The potential need for cordon pricing and a future light rail system are highlighted. Cordon pricing is today still not on the policy agenda and only the first phase of a light tramway system has achieved Government approval in principle. The most current transport policy document for the City is the Leeds Transport Strategy [7] and this forms one of a group of related, but separately produced strategies (Economic Strategy, the Unitary Development Plan, the Green Strategy). This document was based upon a strategic study and public consultation carried out in 1990. The existing congestion problems of the City are mapped and the most congested areas are on, or outside the inner ring road. It is predicted that the number of vehicles entering the city centre during the peak is likely to rise by 30% by 2010. The Study findings also noted the high level of usage of train services by commuters and that peak period commuting by train is largely by people from car owning households. However it is my view that the propensity for other household members currently commuting by car to switch modes to rail is lessened by the high levels of present occupancy of trains and the current lack of platform capacity at the main station. The Study found that bus usage levels were declining at a rate of 1.7% per annum, due to cost, unreliability and unattractiveness of he service. Consequently the scope to attract commuter journeys to public transport in the short to medium term is exceedingly limited and dependent on major investment.

The number of parking spaces in the central business area (based on surveys in 1987/1988) was some 24,000 and some 38% of short stay spaces were occupied by long- stay users, yet there was still some spare short-stay capacity off-street. There is significant commuter car parking pressure and with a projected city centre job growth of 15,000 to 2001, due to new business allocations in the Unitary Development Plan this pressure can only increase. The City Council's solution in their Unitary Development Plan is to reduce the availability of long-stay car parking with almost immediate effect, yet in the absence of other counter balancing policies in their Transport Strategy. The shortcomings of this approach were recognised in the 1963 Buchanan Report [5] .

The Transport Strategy document [7] at paragraph 5.53 states that **"any restraint of city centre private vehicle traffic can only be expected to be successful provided that it does not damage economic prosperity , and an attractive alternative is offered".**

This paragraph continues **"it is judged feasible to adopt a policy of improving public transport combined with expanding city centre pedestrianisation and limiting the growth of private car travel to the city centre without adverse consequences on the city centre's economic status. "**The Transport Strategy proposals are to implement extended pedestrianisation in the centre, together with a "public transport box" and a new loop one way gyratory for car traffic around the City Centre and just beyond the "public transport box". The Strategy recommends that parking restraints should only be used when park-and-ride proposals and improvements to public transport have been introduced whereas the Unitary Development Plan policies, already being introduced in advance of the adoption of the Plan, seek to enforce strong control over long-stay parking before these other measures are implemented.

These transportation strategies for Leeds have varied in the extent to which their approach can be described as comprehensive, but without exception their implementation has been limited in many respects. Public transport improvements have not been progressed and the need/demand for central area parking has increased. The planning and transportation policies have not been prepared in concert with one another and their implementation has been essentially disparate.

3   Government Policy and the Future Development and Implementation of Transport Strategies

There is no doubt that Government policy is changing with regard to the future planning and funding of transport in U.K. cities. Guidance in PPG 13 [2] seeks to bring land use and transportation planning closer together than it has been for several years. One of the key objectives of this Guidance is to reduce journeys by private car both in terms of length and numbers and over a period of time to achieve a redistribution of land uses via the development plan and development control systems which will bring homes, jobs and services into closer proximity with one another. Such a redistribution of development is clearly one of the main ways of influencing future patterns of movement in a sustainable way . It will take many years for this challenging new Guidance to have a major impact on travel patterns and modes and yet there is a recognition by central and local government that it is necessary to start somewhere.

Some local planning authorities have fully embraced this new Guidance in the reviews of their Development Plans. It can be argued that some of them have embraced the principles too enthusiastically in their revised plans, given the need for realistically phased strategies. Humberside County Council in reviewing their Structure Plan have proposed that virtually all new development should be located within the major urban areas and the main towns, whereas the existing settlement strategy emphasises the importance of channelling some development towards selected settlements, including for example villages with a good range of services and a railway station connecting them to the main urban areas.

There is a clear emphasis in PPG 13 and other PPG's (in particular the recently proposed revision of PPG 6 [8] on retailing) of a return to an emphasis on development within urban areas where services and employment tend to be concentrated together with transport foci. A clear word of warning is however necessary as an over concentration on development within urban areas will in many instances lead to a loss of amenity for those already living there and to what has been referred to as town cramming. The development of new satellites including new settlements and new mixed use developments on the edge of urban areas can be used to encourage counter flows on public transport corridors which is highly beneficial to the revenue funding of services, particularly newly introduced light rapid transit systems. Great care is needed in the selection of the types of developments which should be linked to a city centre. For example the Sheffield Supertram route linking the Meadowhall out-of-town regional shopping centre to the city centre has led to further losses of trade for the city centre.

Funding and Transport Strategies

Long term policy guidance and transport and planning strategies are linked to short term plans and programmes by the bidding system for Government funding of transport infrastructure. Until very recently the main annual bid document was the Transport Policy and Programme (TPP). These are submitted by metropolitan and county highway authorities and they have largely concentrated on bids for schemes within the bidding authority's area. The new "Package Bid" approach for transport capital funding introduced by the Department of Transport enables a more integrated approach to investment in transport infrastructure and a better balance between investment in highways and public transport schemes. It also enables a group of authorities to work together with a Passenger Transport Executive to plan for transport investment , short and long term, within an area or areas which have close relationships in trip origins and destinations, rather than planning transport investment within constrained administrative boundaries.

The Association of Greater Manchester Authorities working together with the Greater Manchester Passenger Transport Authority have presented a joint package bid for the Greater Manchester Conurbation [9] the foreword of which refers to the wish to "see a more integrated approach to the investment in transport infrastructure with a better balance between investment in highway and public transport schemes". The ability to co-ordinate the spending on highways and public transport year on year, within the context of a longer term strategy, presents, for the first time, the opportunity of the integrated implementation of these strategies. In their first Package bid document the Manchester Authorities emphasise the importance of greater co-ordination with the regional offices of the Departments of the Environment and Transport in "relation to national, regional and local transport strategies". This further necessary ingredient of integrated implementation has not to date been realised in a sufficiently comprehensive manner.

4   The Relationship Between Development Plans and Transportation Strategies

My experience to date has been that Development Plans (Structure Plans, Unitary Development Plans and Local Plans) have not been prepared in concert with

Transportation Strategies nor have development proposals been adequately assessed in transportation terms. Consequently there is a lack of co-ordination which greatly inhibits integrated implementation of the Transport Strategy.

The Unitary Development Plans prepared for the cities of Leeds and Manchester both exhibit examples of development proposals which pay scant regard to good transportation planning . The final drafts of these Unitary development plans were produced in advance of PPG 13 [2] which encourages a greater level of co-ordination. In Leeds allocations are proposed for park-and-ride sites which bear little or no relationship to good existing or proposed public transport routes and therefore the issue of their successful implementation is very much in question. It has become clear from our involvement in two of these park-and ride site proposals that no thought has been given to the funding possibilities or the timing of their implementation .

In Leeds our studies have included an analysis of long-stay commuter car parking provision, future requirements and the restraint policies proposed in the Unitary Development Plan on future provision. These policies are promoted alongside policies for the expansion of city centre office provision. In the Transport Strategy, and reflected in the Unitary Development Plan, there are proposals for public transport improvements including the first phase of a new LRT system, and new rail and station capacity which cannot be introduced prior to 1999 at the earliest. Yet a parking restraint policy is proposed, and being implemented, without the means to divert large numbers of commuters onto public transport. In the circumstances we have proposed an interim parking policy which would allow additional long term parking spaces until the public transport improvements are implemented. The City Council's transport consultants have estimated that at best only an 8% diversion of car trips to public transport will occur with the first phase of the Leeds Supertram in place. Our studies and those of the Council's consultants have demonstrated that without the implementation of major public transport improvements, more cross town trips will take place in search of peripheral parking spaces, there will be an extension of on street parking into residential areas and greater congestion on the highway radials leading to the perimeter of the City Centre. Major public transport investment must proceed hand in hand with the progressive implementation of parking restraints.

A further example of the lack of integration between Development and transportation plans are proposals for new railway stations in Development Plans where extra stopping points cannot actually be serviced by the current line capacity, and the investment for the required extra capacity has not been considered in either of the relevant plans.

5   Concluding Statement

PPG13 [2] and associated Government guidance and research are beginning to recognise the need for the greater integration of Development Plans and Transport strategies. Similarly the package bid funding system for the first time allows for both a balanced bid between highway schemes and public transport and a much sounder base for the integrated implementation of proposals. I consider that there is a need for appropriate interim policies to cushion the adverse effects arising from the lack of integrated policies and integrated implementation. Current and historic experience of the production of transportation Strategies suggests that there is a long way to go in achieving integrated implementation at the local level.

References

[1]   Simpson B. J., Urban Public Transport Today, Chapter 6, *Land Use & Public Transport Planning* E. & F. N. Spon, 1994.

[2]   Department of the Environment - *PPG13 - Planning Policy Guidance, Transport*, March 1994.

[3]   Sustainable Development - *The U. K. Strategy*, HMSO Cmnd 2426, Januuary 1994.

[4]   Royal Commission on Environmental Pollution (Eighteenth Report) - *Transport and the Environment*, HMSO - October 1994.

[5]   Buchanan Colin, *Traffic in Towns*, 1963.

[6]   WytConsult, *The West Yorkshire Transportation Strategy*, October 1977.

[7]   Steer Davies Gleeve, *The Leeds Tranport Strategy*, February 1991.

[8]   Department of the Environment, *PPG 6 - Town Centres and Retail Developments*.

[9]   Association of Greater Manchester Metropolitan Authorities and the Greater Manchester Passenger Transport Authority - *Greater Manchester Package Bid*, 1995/1996.

Alternative urban transport technologies for the Belfast Metropolitan Area in the period to 2030 AD: the research design and its implications for study recommendations and policy outcome

A.W. Smyth,[a] J. Douglas Ferguson,[b]
J. Malachy McEldowney[b]

[a] *Transport Research Group, University of Ulster at Jordanstown, BT37 0QB, Northern Ireland*
[b] *Queens University of Belfast, Belfast BT7 1NN, Northern Ireland*

Abstract

The study of Alternative Urban Transport Technologies for the Belfast Metropolitan Area 1991/92 commissioned by the Northern Ireland Transport Holding Company Ltd/D.O.E.
(N.I.) had three main goals:

1 The development of guidelines for assessing the potential technologies for Belfast based on a review of conditions in other sites.

2 Review of 'candidate' technologies and the development of systems concepts to meet the long term transportation needs of the concurbation.

3 Assessment of the efficacy of the systems concepts including their operational, economic and financial performance and implications for the environment and the local economy.

This paper provides an overview of the research design employed and considers the implications of the approach adopted for the study recommendations together with the likely policy response from the government body which commissioned the study.

1 Introduction

At present Belfast is served by conventional buses, a limited network of railway lines operated with diesel multiple units and a 'black-taxi' paratransit service. The majority of areas are dependent on buses and these have suffered from a dramatic decline in passenger numbers in recent decades. Such a scenario of declining public transport is not unique to Belfast and in other cities similar problems have stimulated the examination and implementation of alternative transport technologies.

The **Belfast Urban Area Plan: 2001 (BUAP)** Adoption Statement [1] published in 1989 committed Government to the improvement of public transport in support of urban region goals for industry, commerce and housing. For the longer term Government recognised that demands placed on the total transport system by economic development and social economic and demographic trends required that alternative technologies should be assessed for their potential to contribute to local land use, economic and environmental goals.

It was in this context that the Northern Ireland Transport Holding Company (N.I.T.H.Co.) commissioned the Transport Research Group, (T.R.G.) University of Ulster and the Departments of Environmental Planning and Civil Engineering at the Queen's University of Belfast to undertake an assessment of the potential for Alternative Urban Transport Technologies (A.U.T.T.) in the Belfast Metropolitan Area [2]. The research goals set for the A.U.T.T. study called for:

1. The development of guidelines for assessing the potential of alternative urban transport technologies for Belfast based on a review of conditions in other cities.
2. A review of candidate technologies and the development of systems concepts to meet the long term transport needs of the conurbation.
3. Assessment of the efficacy of the systems concepts including their operational, economic and financial performance and implications for the environment and the local economy.

The study was to be characterised by a number of particular features:

- recognition of the two way relationship between land use and transport
- study not to be technology driven and to avoid preconceived ideas for the future development
- 40-year time horizon to reflect durability and longevity of many of the technologies under consideration
- elicitation of 'lessons' from the experience of other cities
- study area to encompass urban area and city region

2 The Preferred Strategy

The recommendations which emerged from the study can be summarised under three main headings as follows:

Transport Infrastructure

Proposals which may be ultimtely inplemented will reflect a tradeoff albeit implicit in the relative importance attributed to the implications of alternative strategies for the various impact groups/objectives. Because it is apparent from the pattern of impacts that in general substantial accessibility, environmental and economic development potential benefits would accrue from investment in a network of Light Rail Transit (LRT) lines. Moreover the analysis demonstrated that assuming the availability of supra-intra funding, on the basis of the efficiency indicator, NPV, the scheme performs well.   The investment would generate some 2000 man years of direct employment much of it local during implementation both through construction of fixed infrastructure and rolling stock under Alternative A, a four line network covering two corridors eastward from the city centre, one in the south encompassing the controversial Annadale-Grahamholm/Ormeau corridor and a route intended to serve West Belfast.

In the case of the busway proposals (Alternative C) the accessibility, environmental and development potential benefits would be much more modest particularly with respect to the environment and development potential. At the same time the NPV value was much smaller. Conversely the gross capital costs would be less than 40% of the figure of £143 million required to implement for Alternative A.

Overall Alternative A provided the greatest value for money on the basis of efficiency, accessibility, environmental and economic development potential benefits and assuming coordination between public transport modes and availability of EU Funding. The choice therefore ultimately rests on the relative importance which society, as reflected in the decisions of its elected representatives and public officials place on these impacts. In the absence of EU Funding LRT Alternative A could not be justified on efficiency grounds alone. Moreover, the absence of coordination would tend to rule out any substantial LRT network.

Complementary Transport Measures

Legislation current in 1992, the year the study was completed, required both rail and bus companies to compete in the market place and to operate on a commercial basis. However, a fundamental prerequisite for the introduction of alternative public transport technologies study area is co-ordination of services between operations in the relevant corridors. A number of alternative innovative structures through which such co-ordination could be achieved were put forward. The study also made recommendations concerning a range of bus priority measures including with flow bus lanes and Selective Bus Detection (SBD) equipment installed at certain light controlled junctions. These would provide the basis for a network of high quality commuter services.

It was evident from the study that travellers to Belfast City Centre are generously provided for in terms of parking space. The work highlighted the unusually high propensity for free and subsidised parking for commuters working in the public sector. Together with the involvement of this sector in the financing and construction of multi-storey carparks this is clearly undermining the relative competitiveness of public transport. The study made recommendations on the general direction of future policy on parking including park 'n' ride at peripheral sites.

Complementary Land Use Measures

Belfast (like most UK cities) is in the final stages of 'decentralisation'. In future it will tend to stabilise rather than 'recentralise' with regard to residential land use but some recentralisation - particularly focused on the city centre - may occur with regard to employment. Land availability and topography are unchanging stabilising factors and the current policy of containment will continue for the foreseeable future. All of these 'stabilising' factors point to the conclusion that any new public transport would have to maximise the existing potential - high density, low car ownership, compact form, centre orientated axial pattern - rather than relying on additional growth. A compact, centralised pattern of development would also favour the inner city given that all the routes envisaged pass through these areas which have the highest residential densities and the lowest car ownership. The acceptance of higher residential densities along transport lines generally would provide opportunities for thinning-out elsewhere providing open space or recreation facilities. The preference for traditional two-storey housing could be accommodated within the density recommendations made in the study.

In the city centre the key planning policy should be the control of parking provision - which Belfast has hitherto been more reluctant to undertake than most UK cities. Allied to this urban design policies, which specifically earmark transport modes for 'high-building location', a common policy in many cities could provide developers with an incentive to propose integrated station/commercial schemes in selected areas and could divert high-building schemes from more sensitive townscapes.

The study conclusions appear to contradict those drawn by the Belfast Transportation Strategy Review (BTSR) [3] as summarised in the BUAP [4] and the subsequent Belfast City Centre Local Plan (B.C.C.P.) [5] which in both cases rejected any case for LRT. Given that all these studies were initiated within a six year time span how can such widely divergent conclusions be reached? It can be argued that the factors likely to influence the conclusions reached include the demand forecasting models and assessment frameworks employed, the assumptions concerning the regulatory framework and the sourcing of funding, and the planning horizon. Together these form the core of a study research design and it is our contention that differences in research design have played a major part in producing the different conclusions concerning the efficacy of introducing alternative urban transport technology into the Belfast Metropolitan Area reached by these studies.

3 Research Approach

The research design for this study while adopting many of the conventional guidelines set out for strategic urban transportation planning also sought to extend they methodology and at the same time simplify the process. The former was to be achieved by an attempt to integrate land use and transportation elements permitting feedback effect between travel demand, transport supply and the spatial distribution of population and commercial activity (Fig. 1). At the same time a proposed review of conditions in other cities was seen as offering an approach whereby screening criteria might be developed to reduce the number of systems concepts alternatives and candidate technologies to be assessed at a detailed modelling level without introducing unnecessary bias into the process. The research design can be characterised as consisting of three main phases or stages as follows:

In Stage 1 a review of conditions in other UK cities and abroad provided for screening criteria reflecting viable ridership thresholds for a range of technologies under different site/alignment condition and broadly consistent with output from Section 56 based appraisals to be developed and applied to facilitate identification of the most promising corridors in the study area for further investigation. Stage 1 also addressed the issue of the appropriateness of the various alternative urban transport technologies to the market conditions likely to obtain in any medium size city with a similar spatial structure to that of Belfast. Additionally, the cost implication of various technologies and consideration of the likely maximum ceiling on funding (from public sources) were taken into account. These pointed to restricting analysis of alignment opportunities and constraints to medium and low capacity modes such as LRT, Guided Busways and Guided Light Transit. Various automated systems in this capacity range were also excluded either on grounds of cost (underground) or environment (elevated systems). The possibility of unguided busways and High Occupancy Vehicle (HOV) lanes was kept under review.

Stage 2 focused on the opportunities and constraints facing any decision to introduce a number of alternative urban transport technologies into the existing

Alternative Urban Transport Technologies Project

Fig. 1

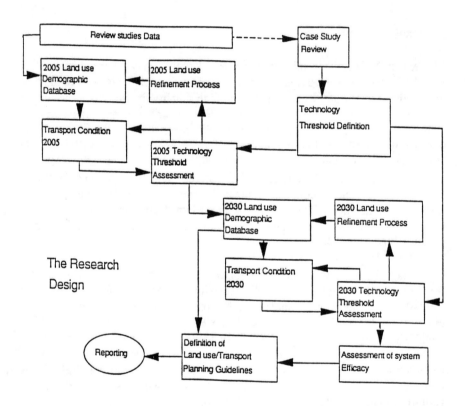

The Research Design

urban fabric and surrounding commuter hinterland making up the Belfast Metropolitan Area. The overview of opportunities carried out in Stage 2 consisted of three elements:

1. Operations: alignment availability including the practicality of on-street operation.
2. Associated Capital Costs (fixed infrastructure only).
3. Environmental Planning Issues associated with individual alignments.

Each of the corridors selected as a result of Stage 1 was assessed individually producing potential routes and in some instances more from one route option. Analysis was based on current civil engineering practice while particular attention was given to the suitability of road junction design and traffic control where on street operation was implied. More details are given in Ferguson, McEldowney and Smyth [6]. Stage 2 also involved a screening of this set of corridor alignment options as a precursor to definition of a number of systems concepts which would be subject to detailed analysis using the full transportation model. In contrast to the AUTT research both the other studies referred to undertook little analysis of specific corridor and alignment conditions.

Stage 3 involved the detailed modelling of systems concepts and the application of a formal and comprehensive assessment of options. This provided the basis for the development of the preferred strategy recommendations. In this instance forecasts of travel behaviour were obtained from the B.T.S.R. model with amendments made to it. In addition certain sensitivities were employed to reflect elements not explicitly addressed in that model structure. Estimates of demand were made for the do minimum public transport and highway network and for the various systems concepts. Forecasts were derived for both coordinated networks and those employing continued competition between public transport modes including any new technology and existing bus services. In the case of the BUAP/BTSR study the analysis of alternative transport technologies was completed in advance of the BTSR transportation model becoming fully operational while for the BCCP an updated version of the model assuming a competitive regulatory framework was employed.

In the case of the AUTT study a distinction needs to be drawn between the forecast of demand for travel <u>within</u> the study area covered by the BTSR model in full, namely the Belfast Urban Area, from external locations for which the BTSR model in effect assumed no modal shift in travel behaviour. Forecasts of internal demand were made using the BTSR model. For external travel use was made of the stated preference models developed by Transecon International [7] for use in assessing various railway projects in the Belfast area in the case of corridors currently served by rail, while for others it was assumed that the BTSR modal split model would apply beyond the internal zone boundary.

In Stage 3 a comprehensive assessment framework was required compatible with the output from detailed modelling of schemes. Such a framework should reflect the planning goal and the values underlying same for the study area. Consideration was given to relationships between urban structure and transport and the further consequences of different urban forms for energy efficiency, the environment generally and the concept of sustainability. These were translated into a number of objectives.

- Efficiency (Quantifiable Benefits/Costs)
- Accessibility
- Environmental Compatibility
- Economic Development Potential
- Feasibility

Assessment involves examining the extent to which the various systems concepts and related measures meet the objectives   defined within the assessment framework.   While the importance of these various objectives is recognised conventionally, emphasis is placed on the efficiency objectives as well as funding to the detriment of consideration being given to the other objectives. Increasing use is being made of more comprehensive assessment frameworks by the European Community following practice standard in many Continental countries. In this study no attempt was made to explicitly identify either the absolute or relative importance of each of the objectives. Instead the objectives and the performance of the systems concepts in relation to them were ultimately presented in a multi criteria format goals achievement matrix. This facilitated identification of the 'trade-offs' implied by implementation or indeed non implementation of proposals.

For the case of the BUAP/BTSR study the assessment framework was less comprehensive following conventional UK practice as of the late 1980's while for the BCCP a more comprehensive approach to assessment was invoked. Unlike the BUAP/BTSR study the AUTT study assessment framework provided for the possibility of supra national funding contributing to the costs of introducing a new system.

In relation to the planning horizon both the BUAP/BTSR and the BCCP studies employed forecast years some 15 years after the base year. In contrast the AUTT study incorporated two forecast years, one approximately 15 years and the second some 40 years after the base year.

4 Government Response to the AUTT Study Findings

The study was completed in 1992 and submitted to NITHCo.,which subsequently handed the work over to the Department of the Environment (NI).

There has been no response to the study by government to date. However, in the intervening period the delayed BCCP report rejected arguments in favour of Alternative Public Transport Technologies. A realistic conclusion to draw concerning the AUTT study is that its findings have been rejected. Nevertheless, Government did announce one major policy change in February 1995, involving a switch to coordination between public transport modes. Such a policy shift was recommmened by the AUTT study as a prerequisite to the introduction of radical improvements to the public transport system in the Belfast Metropolitan Area.

References

1. Department of the Environment for Northern Ireland. Belfast Urban Area Plan 2001 Adoption Statement December 1989, Belfast

2. Transport Research Group, University of Ulster and The Department of Environmental Planning and Civil Engineering, The Queens University of Belfast. Alternative Urban Transport Technology for the Belfast Metropolitan Area. 5 Volumes, 1992 (Unpublished)

3. Halcrow Fox and Associates with Steer Davies〈Leave. A Review of Transportation Strategy for Belfast 1986-2001. Volume 1. Final Report. Executive Summary. Belfast, April 1987.

4. Department of the Environment for Northern Ireland. Belfast Urban Area Plan 2001. H.M.S.O. 1987 and 1990

5. Department of the Environment for Northern Ireland. Belfast City Centre Local Plan. Belfast 1994.

6. Ferguson, J.D., McEldowney, J.M. and Smyth A. Feasibility of potential Radial Corridors for guided urban transport technologies in Greater Belfast. Proceedings of Urban Transport and the Environment in the 21st Century, Southampton, 1995.

7. Transmark/Transecon International. Northern Ireland Railways Corporate Plan 1987-1992 Technical Report 4 (Belfast) Cross City Links Options Appraisal. London, September 1986 (Unpublished)

Future aspects of acceptable transportation and mobility concepts – the industrial researcher's view

G. Mattrisch, C. Neuhaus

DaimlerBenz Research 'Technology and Society',
12274 Berlin, Germany

0. Preliminaries: Looking globally at trends in urban transport, the overall attitude is negative, mainly because it is just "too much". Presupposing an essential increase in urban traffic, we have to expect both severe functional deficits and severe acceptability problems. Some elements of potential solutions are described.

Putting these premises at the beginning of this paper means implicitly focusing on industrialized or nearly industrialized agglomerations. For any other case functionality of the urban transportation system under tolerable economic and ecological conditions is a 'must'. (Fig.1)

Anyway, future transportation approaches for industrialized urban areas have to be assessed with similar criteria: How do they work? How do they affect the quality of life? How expensive are they? Additionally, what might be a good solution let's say for Southampton, might not be appropriate for Stuttgart, Dresden, Bologna etc.

All these statements are not new. The tasks are evident for a quarter of a century, as one might find proof in Colin Buchanan's famous "Traffic in Towns". Approaching the start of the 21st century, there are three emerging qualities, on which we shall to comment:

1. A higher degree of integration of transportation aspects into any other field of human activities, especially scenarios of urban development (Chapter 1)

2. A new willingness in focusing the planning process more on the communicative than on the technical/methodological aspects (Chapter 2)

3. New technological options:
   - Information/Communication (Chapter 3)
   - Energy and Emission Control (Chapter 4)

1.   **Scenarios of urban developments. One needs to have an integrated view of urban/spatial developments instead of debating isolated traffic means. Two scenarios of mobility and communication in agglomerations of today and tomorrow - (1)"Planned Urbanity" and (2)"Cities in the Process of Self-Regulation"are illustrated as examples for potential common goals and as a token for the basic assumption: the future is open.**

The interdisciplinary research group "Future Urban Living" adopted two scenarios describing the future of urban agglomerations. Both scenarios help to stimulate the discussion on two issues : (1) where the possible development of today´s agglomerations could lead to and (2) how this development could be influenced to achieve a desired result. (Fig. 2)

The first concept "city of planned urbanity" describes a densely populated area with a remarkable mixture of the functions living, working, shopping and recreation. In this city of density, many people do not need a car since distances are short and public transport is efficient. Many of the daily journeys can be made by foot or by bicycle. Relatively strong governmental planning, as well as a change in the attitude of the citizens, is necessary for a development specified in this concept.

On the other hand, there is the "City in the Process of Self-Regulation". In continuation of the tendencies of the last decades, the unchanged desire and the individual decisions of private households and business actors are the main driving forces here. As a result, the city can be described as "urban sprawl". As large, monofunctional zones, spacious residential areas and big commercial centres along intersecting highways surround the former city centre. Shopping malls and specialised retail stores in the outskirts of the city even supply the citizens of the inner districts. Due to their competitive pricing, these stores dominate the retail business in the entire region. The structure of the city forces the residents to cover long distances on their daily trips. As a consequence, the car is indispensable as a personal item. Traffic activities far exceed those of the other scenario and outnumber even those of today. But, although looking for a parking space or waiting in traffic has become a time consuming day-to-day occupation for the residents of this city, they consider having a private car as a symbol of individual freedom.

The main issue of both of these scenarios is the fundamental interdependency between mobility and territorial structure - i.e. allocation and density of the origins and destinations of the daily trips. Looking at the two scenarios, one is free to decide which scenario one prefers, or which one could be useful. This remains a normative or political decision. In every case, however, one has to see a fundamental reduction in traffic activity - or even freezing of it at the present level - which requires a "U-turn" of the strong current trends of territorial development in western countries. If present developments continue, the *individual* mass-mobility will inevitably increase.

2.   **The Planning Process: It can be observed, that, as a basket of instruments to anticipate future developments, every field of application planning is radically changing - away from the technocratic approach of mastering and control, towards a more communicative, option-generating process. What could that mean for future urban transport policies?**

The main field in which this change phenomena can be observed is strategic planning of companies. However, especially in Germany, tendencies of privatization of public tasks and the requirements of an aspired "lean administration" foster these fundamental changes in the dominant planning approach in the fields of transportation planning or 'City Management' in general.

What is the new quality of planning activities? The main feature seems to be the diminishing relevance of data and information as success factors for the planning process (see fig.3). Instead, the communicative qualities and the ability and willingness to form a consensus of issues and objectives of the planning process are highlighted. The new purpose of planning is to generate options and to evaluate expenditures and benefits of these options.

One consequence for the corporate planning process is to work mainly with scenarios as an integrated part of strategic planning. Once the organization has learned to use this instrument effectively, the planning process becomes open and dynamic, with the main effect being comprehensive strategic learning. There is no basic argument why this orientation towards options and scenarios should not find its way into urban transport policies or city management.

The experience of DaimlerBenz in founding strategic planning activities on scenarios of possible developments is very positive. The first quality is the comprehensive view of a defined situation by considering more than one direction, and the second new property is constituted by the visionary power and the communicative aspects of the instrument, so that an essential diffusion into different areas of application can be forecast.

3.   **Integrated Infrastructure: The most essential objective might be to reduce unnecessary traffic and, at the same time, to improve conditions for necessary traffic. Intelligent infrastructure measures are prerequisites for that purpose. Promising approaches of the PROMETHEUS research program are outlined.**

Prometheus started in 1986. It is part of the EUREKA initiative and stands for "*Pro gram* for a *E*uropean *T*raffic with *H*ighest *E*fficiency and *U*nprecedented *S*afety". All the major European automobile companies, their suppliers and numerous research institutes have been participating in this unique precompetitive research venture, which resulted from an initiative on the part of Daimler-Benz, and transcends normal market rivalries. The project's goals are to markedly improve the safety, performance and environmental compatibility of road traffic by utilizing state-of-the-art information and communication systems.

Some of the results can be demonstrated. As they are to be integrated into mass products within the next years, one can expect marked effects on traffic conditions.

1.   Communication via satellite: Keeping in contact - the antenna on the roof of a PROMETHEUS truck allows the driver to communicate with the dispatcher at headquarters. (fig.4)

2.   Information: The individual route guidance system helps the driver to find the best route in any city. Based on a digital road map and together with up-to-date traffic information the on-board computer keeps the driver informed via verbal messages and a display. (fig.5)

3.   Cruise control: the slots beside the headlamps of this PROMETHEUS demonstrator are scarcely noticable. Located inside are the infra-red sensors, which measure the distance to the vehicles in front. (fig.6)

4. Obstacle detection: The on-board computer in the Daimler-Benz research vehicle VITA (Vision Technology Application) scans road markings and vehicle contours in the camera image. Road curvature and obstacles are detected so that the vehicle can be steered automatically. (fig.7)

5. Driver assistance: the Daimler-Benz research vehicle VITA (Vision Technology Application) has a real autopilot that can brake, accelerate and steer. The driver can rely on the system while using his mobile telephone or taking notes. (fig.8)

These are some selected examples of on-going research activities to improve traffic conditions.

4. **Transport-relevant technologies: An important task remains in reducing negative impacts of transport - i. e. pollution, noise, energy consumption etc. - by application of advanced technologies. Main areas of R&D are energy conversion, energy storage, pollution and noise control, integration of information and communication technologies into the transport system.**

Nearly 100 % of the existing car fleet is based either on Otto or on Diesel technology - i.e. different concepts of fuel combustion. Both concepts lead to emission problems, even though modern emission control technologies can be quite effective. The question is why Otto/Diesel have not yet been replaced by other, less emissionary technologies. The main answer to this question is the enormous advantage in energy storage. Fig.9 demonstrates the relative energy density of different concepts. One can see that even the most advanced battery concept requires nearly 100 times more weight than the classical Diesel.

Illustrated in Fig.10 is the fuel cell technology, which is a most promising approach in terms of energy demand and storage capacity. At the moment this data is not yet realistic for mass products, because fuel cell application in cars is still in the R+D-phase, and there is no serious forecast as to when this approach would be mature for mass application. Once it is invented, it will affect the transport sector enormously.

A comment about emissions (Fig.11) - one has to accept that those technologies which play a major role in the current debate - i.e. electricity and hydrogen - are not suitable for solving the CO_2-problem. Once again, fuel cell technology offers the best progress.

5.   **Conclusions/Research Outlook: Essential progress can only be produced by co-ordinated and consistent R&D work within and between the four mentioned fields, especially on an international level. Joint programs including industry, academics, transportation consultants and experts from local, national, and supra-national administration should be fostered.**

We have to assume that the need for transport and mobility will not diminish, rather it may increase. Without major efforts, an essential acceptability gap of the transport sector as a whole has to be forecast. Some future-orientated approaches in different regions of action were sketched: scenarios of urban development, advanced planning methodologies, PROMETHEUS, and current trends in automotive R+D. One basic message that can be read into these examples, is that Daimler-Benz has built up a unique awareness about future developments and a high competence in transferring these scenarios into R+D-projects and products.

Due to limited space and time, we focused mainly on road transport - reflecting the assumption that we have to expect essential acceptability problems in this sector more than anywhere else. It does not at all mean that the examples shown could be understood as solutions: our view is that these are necessary elements of future oriented mobility concepts and have to be combined with other concepted approaches in an intelligent way.

Comprehensive solutions of complex future problems require additional co-ordinated R+D work of many actors. Furthermore, isolated solutions and sectoral optimization approaches can be dysfunctional in the overall system, so careful and serious analyses of mobility issues are needed, but maybe a courageous design of possible developments and acceptable options is needed even more.

Forschung Technik und Gesellschaft

Today´s Traffic Conditions

DAIMLERBENZ
Forschung und Technik

LI/Ma-Scan Zukunftslabor   03.03.95

UrbanLiving in 2020
Two Scenarios

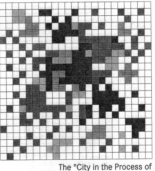

The "City in the Process of Self-Regulation"?

The "City of the Planned Urbanity"?

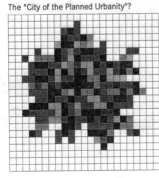

■ e. g. Working
■ e. g. Dwelling
■ e. g. Shopping
■ e. g. Recreation (sports, cinema etc.)

②

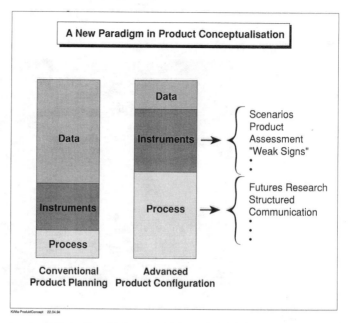

Forschung Technik
und Gesellschaft

Product
Conceptualisation

③

DAIMLERBENZ

Forschung und Technik

Forschung Technik
und Gesellschaft

Communication via
Satellite
(PROMETHEUS)

④

DAIMLERBENZ
Forschung und Technik

Forschung Technik
und Gesellschaft

Route Guidance
(PROMETHEUS)

DAIMLERBENZ
Forschung und Technik

Forschung Technik
und Gesellschaft

Cruise Control
(PROMETHEUS)

DAIMLERBENZ
Forschung und Technik

Forschung Technik
und Gesellschaft

Obstacle Detection
(PROMETHEUS)

DAIMLERBENZ
Forschung und Technik

Forschung Technik
und Gesellschaft

Driver Assistance
(PROMETHEUS)

Forschung und Technik

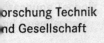

⑨

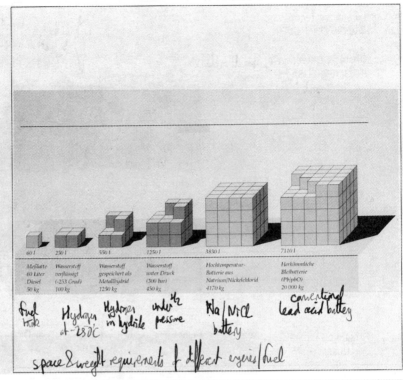

Meßlatte	Wasserstoff	Wasserstoff	Wasserstoff	Hochtemperatur-	Herkömmliche
60 Liter	verflüssigt	gespeichert als	unter Druck	Batterie aus	Bleibatterie
Diesel	(-253 Grad)	Metallhydrid	(300 bar)	Natrium/Nickelchlorid	(Pb/pbO)
50 kg	100 kg	1250 kg	450 kg	4170 kg	20 000 kg

60 l   250 l   550 l   1250 l   3830 l   7110 l

fuel tank   Hydrogen at -250°C   Hydrogen in hydride   under H2 pressure   Na/NiCl battery   conventional lead acid battery

space & weight requirements of different engines/fuel

⑩

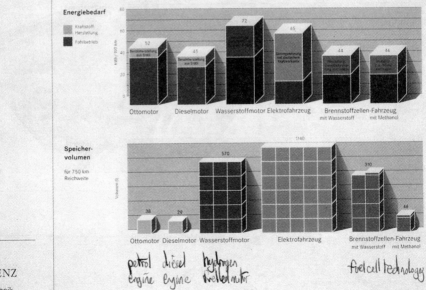

Energiebedarf
Kraftstoff-Herstellung
Fahrbetrieb

kWh / 100 km

52   45   72   65   44   44

Ottomotor   Dieselmotor   Wasserstoffmotor   Elektrofahrzeug   Brennstoffzellen-Fahrzeug
mit Wasserstoff   mit Methanol

Speicher-volumen

für 750 km
Reichweite

Volumen (l)

1140
570   310
38   29   46

Ottomotor   Dieselmotor   Wasserstoffmotor   Elektrofahrzeug   Brennstoffzellen-Fahrzeug
mit Wasserstoff   mit Methanol

petrol engine   diesel engine   hydrogen fuelled motor   fuel cell technology

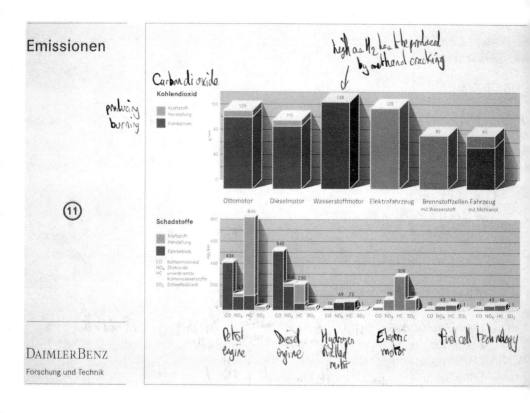

Emissionen

producing
burning

(11)

Carbon dioxide

Kohlendioxid

light as H₂ has t be produced
by methanol cracking

Kraftstoff-
Herstellung
Fahrbetrieb

Ottomotor   Dieselmotor   Wasserstoffmotor   Elektrofahrzeug   Brennstoffzellen-Fahrzeug
mit Wasserstoff   mit Methanol

Schadstoffe

Kraftstoff
Herstellung
Fahrbetrieb

CO Kohlenmonoxid
NOₓ Stickoxide
HC unverbrannte
Kohlenwasserstoffe
SO₂ Schwefeldioxid

Petrol   Diesel   Hydrogen   Electric   Fuel cell technology
engine   engine   fuelled   motor
              motor

DAIMLERBENZ
Forschung und Technik

Threshold values for compatible load-bearing capacities of roads and urban areas

H.-J. Collin
ARGUS – Arbeitsgruppe unabhänagiger Stadt- und Verkehrsplaner, D-38106 Braunschweig, Germany

Abstract

In the solution of problems in urban traffic planning, it is mainly the demands for services in moving and stationary traffic resulting from the urban benefits, and rarely the load-bearing capacity and availability of traffic areas on roads and parcing spaces that is used as a basic.

One important reason for this is the lack of corresponding methods and standards, with the help of which the setting of threshold values in urban traffic planning can be considered.

The LADIR-method is based upon derivation of threshold values for town-compatible motorized traffic. The starting point is the state of affairs that the existing loads of motorized traffic are incompatible, that a necessary road traffic is indispensable for the functionality of a town and that the order of magnitude "town-compatible road traffic" is to be placed between these two figures.

1 The situation

Mainly urban traffic planning is oriented along already existing or precalculated car traffic and the need for parking spaces. Rarely the planning is based on availability and load-bearing capacity of traffic areas on roads and parking spaces. Resulting from this are problems and contradictions of the traffic colliding with non-traffic demands. These contradictions have an effect on the town-compatibility of the road traffic. The functioning of as well as the living in the town are threatened.

The aim of traffic planning must be to produce town-compatibility of the urban road traffic. A threshold of the load-bearing capacity can be placed between maximum possible traffic and minimum traffic which is absolutely necessary for the functionality of a town.

Communities react very slowly to creating compatibility standards for their traffic planning. One of the reasons for this is that so far methods and standards for traffic development planning which can be applied easily do not exist.

Whithin a research project a method has now been developed for determining the town-compatible load-bearing capacity through road traffic.

The aim of the LADIR-method is the determination of a town-compatible (reasonable) load-bearing capacity through the road traffic of a certain planning area. A planning area can either be just one part of the town or the whole town. Then the respective threshold value can be estimated depending on the valuation criteria in relation to the town planning situation as well as the compatibility demands which are to be defined.

2   The contents and structure of the LADIR-method

Usually urban traffic planning proceeds from the demand for traffic services of moving road traffic and parking vehicles resulting from urban usage. In contrast to this the stucture of the LADIR-method refers to the availability and the load-bearing capacity of traffic areas. Therefore the road traffic which is to be considered "town-compatible" is defined according to its form of appearance and quantity depending on function and usage demands in the respective town planning situation.

There are basically two different town planning situations:

- The Main Traffic Arteries network (MTA network).
  This network includes the economic traffic required for the functioning of the town and the overall traffic. The effects of the moving traffic and its road infra-structure play the most important role (load-bearing capacity of the roads).

- The urban areas situated in between the MTA network.
  In these areas the parking vehicles play the most important role in determining the area load-bearing capacity.

The load-bearing capacity of the roads is determined by means of the traffic load-bearing capacity and the town planning compatibility. The traffic load-bearing capacity results directly from the traffic (noise, accident danger). Therefore the threshold values can be indicated in traffic related units (vehicles/h). In contrast, the town planning compatibility is not primarily depending on the quantity of moving vehicles. To quantity these threshold values different units ie dimensions have been introduced to describe the town planning situation.

Special emphasis has been put on filtering out simple-to-use criteria which show the spectrum of town-compatibility sufficiently and which can also be used as a basis for calculation methods.

Therefore town-compatibility is marked by three different areas with each having two criteria:

- Environment:
  Exhaust and noise;
- Surrounds:
  Accident danger and separation effect;
- Urban development:
  Area and urban character.

All of the criteria can have standards or threshold values for the load-bearing capacity of the traffic and for the town planning compatibility; keeping ie exceeding these determines the extent of traffic- (in)compatibility.

The load-bearing capacities which are united in certain types of town planning situations can be spatially combined. The result is a statement for a certain planning area for the overall load-bearing capacity of the traffic which is just about town-compatible (figure 1).

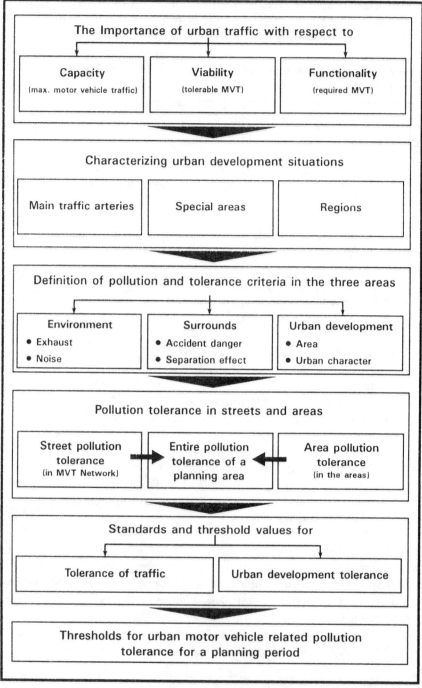

Figure 1: Research structure overview

The load-bearing capacity of roads in the MTA network

It is assumed that different town planning situations have different "sensitivities" ie different demand levels. Therefore a standardization of the urban areas has been made. Five town planning criteria classify the MTA network (figure 2).

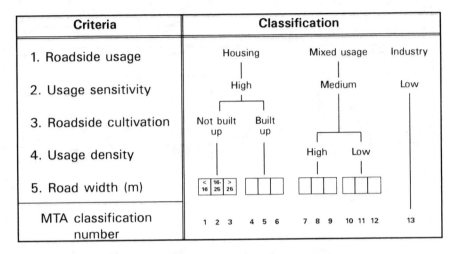

Figure 2: Classification-framework for the MTA network

Proceeding from the three above mentioned load-bearing areas the respective six criteria for determining the load-bearing capacity of roads in the LADIR-method are specified as follows:

■ **Town planning compatibility**

- Threshold values for pavement width,
- Road area proportions,
- Admissible maximum speed,
- Separation effect.

■ **Traffic-compatibility**

- Noise,
- Safety.

Simultaneously, recommendations are made for the respective compatibility thresholds. These are values which have a normative character. That means that these threshold values can not be uniquely defined. Therefore three different demand levels are defined for the overall estimation of the compatibility:

■ Level 1: High demand
■ Level 2: Medium demand
■ Level 3: Low demand

Figure 3 shows the suggested compatibility threshold for the determination of the town compatible load-bearing capacity of the roads.

Load-bearing capacity of roads			
	Level 1 (high demand)	Level 2 (Medium demand)	Level 3 (Low demand)
Town planning compatibility			
• Threshold values for pavement widths [m]	2,50	2,00	1,50
• Road area proportions (minimum percentage for mobility residential and green areas) [%]	40	30	20
• Vehicle maximum speed [km/h]	30	40	50
• Crossing quality of the road area (required medium distance of crossing aids) [m]	100	250	500
Traffic compatibility			
• Threshold value for noise (day) [dB (A)]	50	60	70
• Save crossing ability for pedestrians (maximum traffic per traffic direction) [vehicle/h]	600	800	1000

Figure 3: Compatibility thresholds for the MTA network derived from respective literature

Area load-bearing capacity for urban areas

According to the building regulations different demand levels for different area types can also be established for urban areas:

- Area type 1: High demand,
- Area type 2: Medium demand,
- Area type 3: Low demand.

Criteria for determining the area load-bearing capacity are:

- **Minimum conditions**

  - Minimum pavement width,
  - Driving lane width.

- **Town planning compatibility**

  - Road area proportion,
  - Maximum driving lane width.

Figure 4 shows the recommended compatibility thresholds for urban areas.

Area load-bearing capacity									
	Area type 1 (high demand)			Area type 2 (Medium demand)			Area type 3 (Low demand)		
Minimum conditions									
a) Threshold values for pavement width per roadside [m]	2,50			2,00			1,50		
b) Threshold values for driving lane widths [m]	3,50			4,50			5,50		
• Required minimum widths (sum 2 x (a) + (b)) [m]	8,50			8,50			8,50		
Town planning compatibility									
	Road width [m]								
• Road area proportions	<16	16-25	>25	<16	16-25	>25	<16	16-25	>25
Mobility, residential and green area proportion [%]	33	35	35	27	30	30	23	25	25
Proportion of parking traffic [%]	34	35	40	35	35	40	34	35	40
Proportion of driving lane [%]	33	30	25	38	35	30	43	40	35
• Maximum driving lane width [m]	5,50			6,50			7,00		

Figure 4: Compatibility thresholds for urban areas derived from respective literature

3   The application of the LADIR-method

The **LADIR**-method used to calculate the town compatible load-bearing capacity through road traffic is an open method. It has a fixed methodical application and the contextual form is eligible within certain limits. Therefore the basis is given to determine the compatibility by considering the respective environmental objectives within a community and by considering the knowledge of the latest findings. This "openness" of the method is necessary because the determination of compatibility tends to be rather normative. It can not be based on clearly, provable threshold values.

■ The first step of the LADIR-method is the determination of the compatibility limits.

■ The second step is the calculation of the load-bearing capacity of the road or of the area.

Carrying out this calculation for a whole town or just certain parts of a town allows a third step, ie to determine for the respective area the maximum compatible number of vehicles moving in the road network and to determine at the same time the number of vehicles to be parked in public road areas of housing areas.

Moreover the analysis of exceeding threshold values shows which measures can be taken to make the road or the urban area more compatible, and it shows the urgent need for such measures. However, it is not dealt with strategies and measures with which the determined threshold load-bearing capacity can be achieved.

4   The outlook

From traffic development planning to the analysis of town-compatible traffic

In order to solve the problems resulting from the traffic effectively, an implementation and realization of a new kind of integrative and all-embracing development of traffic concepts is necessary. This also includes a new structure of traffic development planning.

An initial fact is that only based on threshold values aimed at a town-compatible traffic load-bearing capacity, the ranking of road traffic can be relativated and be defined more precise. Resulting from this strategies and concepts can be developed for traffic avoidance, and alternative traffic types (walking, cycling, public transport) can be further advanced in a more precise way.

Therefore it seems - also for ecological reasons - necessary as well as possible to apply the existing LADIR-method to further traffic development planning, consisting of five work phases in local practice:

    I.   Main conditions and situation analysis,
    II. Determination of the town load-bearing capacity and of the reasonable load-bearing capacity,
    III. Valuation of necessary changes; comparison of actual and desired values (priority list),
    IV. Concept development and valuation of effects,
    V. Aspects of feasibility.

Partial results of these phases can be used in order to influence the traffic conditions strongly in discussions with people concerned, the population and others. This way, more effective and more reasonable ideas than before can be achieved in traffic politics.

Moving forward beyond 2000

R.L. Williams

Transportation Department, Lothian Regional Council, Edinburgh EH1 1BL, UK

Abstract

Between 1981 and 1991 car ownership in Lothian increased by 45% and national projections to 2001 indicate a further 20-33% increase. The Council does not wish to build more roads simply to cater for increased traffic. Instead there is a long term aim of giving the streets of Lothian back to people.

Since it was formed it has worked for economic development with improvements in road safety and a healthier environment . The more vulnerable transport users have been aided in part by increasing their degree of segregation from others.

This paper looks at measures:
1) which have led to an increase in numbers of local train travellers
2) which it is hoped will stablise the decline in use of local bus services.

In town centres some streets are being pedestrianised, in others footways are being widened by reducing space for motor vehicles. Lothianwide there are now 600km of facilities for cyclists, most also available to pedestrians and segregated from general traffic. This paper looks at:
3) measures to assist pedestrians in residential neighbourhoods and in some shopping areas
4) ways to promote cycling for recreational and essential journeys so that the 40% increase between 1981 and 1991 continues beyond 2000.

1 Introduction

This paper looks at aspects of four policy areas where alternatives to the use of the car are being implemented:
railways   buses   pedestrian routes   bicycle ways

Over the past 15 years the infrastructure has been adapted to improve road safety, achieve a healthier environment yet still encourage economic development. Edinburgh now has a bypass enabling people and goods to travel between East or Midlothian and West Lothian. But schemes for inner and suburban ring roads were withdrawn over 15 years ago. Most large communities elsewhere on major roads are by-passed and many inter-urban public transport links have been improved.

As part of a review of the Structure Plan (Lothian Region[1]), that Council together with Edinburgh District Council and the Scottish Office commissioned a transport and environmental study by MVA et al[2]. This showed that Edinburgh's transport problems will worsen unless action is taken requiring substantial investment. Titled *"moving FORWARD"* Lothian Region[3] has launched a new strategy. Concerns about the role of cars and environmental damage are requiring a reassessment of travel habits and policies so we anticipate and respond to change. Can a transport system be developed to meet needs in a way which provides choice and is sustainable?

Table 1 Travel to work in Edinburgh

	1971 Census	1981 results	1991 [4]	2000 Target	2010 [3]
car,m/c	29.1%	38.2%	45.8%	47%	36%
pub.transport	46.5%	41.3%	32.1%	34%	41%
walk	19.9%	16.9%	14.5%	16%	18%
bicycle	0.7%	1.4%	1.8%	3%	5%
other	3.8%	2.2%	5.8%	-	-

Table 1 shows that journeys to work made in Edinburgh between 1971 and 1991 saw an increase of 50% in the percentage of people using a car. Using cars more often and for longer journeys causes more:
accidents   acute traffic congestion
noise and air pollution   pressure on parking places
costs for businesses   consumption of limited fuel
Greater reliance on cars also causes public transport problems, reduced mobility for people without access to a car and less pleasant and less safe conditions for pedestrians and cyclists.

2 Lothian backs ScotRail

In 1979 the Regional Council [5] issued a Discussion Paper which identified the rail network as being capable of carrying more passengers on local journeys. As a result 6 stations have been built on 3 lines radiating from Edinburgh Waverley and a 4th, freight, line was reopened to passengers with 3 stations at Uphall Station, Livingston North and Bathgate. The Regional Council paid for a branch line to be electrified in conjunction with electrification of the East Coast Main Inter-City Line, and for the provision of refurbished electric multiple units to replace ageing diesel multiple units. New cycle racks and car parks have been provided, and existing ones extended at most of the 25 passenger stations in the region. Several stations have bus feeders.

Rail measures incorporated in the 1985 Structure Plan issued by Lothian Region[6] have now been implemented; the Regional Council's[i] 1995 Structure Plan therefore proposes a further 2 stations in West Edinburgh and 2 stations in West Lothian on existing rail lines. Fife Regional Council, which administers the area on the other side of the Firth of Forth, has been given permission to finance the provision of additional stations and extra rolling stock. This will help Fife residents commuting into Edinburgh.

In 1971 the Registrar General for Scotland[4] recorded 2610 persons resident within what is now Lothian as travelling to work by train. The 1981 figure was 2960. By 1991 this figure had reached 4780 persons. That is 1.5% of all working residents. Since 1986 the Regional Council[7] has been sampling the number of morning peak hour travellers crossing the boundary of Central Edinburgh. A one day rail count varies from year to year but is usually in the range 5000-6000 persons. However the 1994 figure has fallen by 10 percent perhaps as a consequence of the rail strike in the summer of 1994. ScotRail are taking a number of initiatives to win their passengers back.

Traditionally city centres are where public transport can have a dominant role. On the western edge of Edinburgh there is however an area of former marshland which is being developed for shopping, industry and office uses. Known as South Gyle or Edinburgh Park, eventually over 20000 people may be employed there. Currently one rail station on its eastern boundary attracts 8% of morning peak travellers to the area from central Edinburgh or Fife. There are proposals for another station to be built

on a different rail line to serve people living in
W.Lothian and points further west. Should developers
be asked to fund this? Can the new Edinburgh council
afford it? Would trains stop there? Would they have
any spare seats for extra passengers wishing to
exploit rail's advantage of being segregated from
road congestion to travel to this new destination?

3 Lothian loves the bus

Outside the London area the residents of Lothian make
the greatest use of public transport in the UK with
an average of over 300 journeys per person per year.
Most of the journeys are made by bus. In order to
improve the reliability of buses some 10 km of bus
lane were designated 20 years ago and there have been
minor additions since then. There are also a number
of 'bus gates' which provide special access for buses
to several residential areas, shopping centres etc.

While between 1981 and 1991 bus use measured by
the Registrar General for Scotland[4] for the journey
to work in Edinburgh declined by 10%, bus journeys in
central Edinburgh declined at a slightly slower rate.
The morning peak cordon survey yielded 35400 bus
passenger crossings in 1994 compared with 38200 in
1986, a reduction of 7.1% over 8 years. This is less
than the decline in bus use in Scotland which, for
the 8 years ending in 1992/93 shows a decline of 20%.
This decline cannot be attributed to fewer buses as
Scottish Office figures [8] show bus-kilometres
increasing by 20% over the same period.

As approximately 90% of bus journeys in Lothian
are provided commercially, the Region's influence in
ensuring a good quality, attractive bus service is
limited to specifications for tendered services and
provision of the road infrastructure. There are 29
bus operators in Lothian and since deregulation in
1986 most of Edinburgh's bus stops have had details
of all services added to the bus stop flags. Some
300 of the stops also display timetable information.

My department also took over responsibility for
a motley collection of bus shelters. Maintenance
policies and procedures were clarified and a programme for installing new shelters was extended. Some
have had seating installed.

The Regional Planning Department are also looking into bus stop displays of real time information
about approaching bus(es). There are examples of this
in London, Southampton and a number of other cities.

While it is good that prospective pasengers can be advised that their bus is 8 minutes late, both they and the bus company would prefer the service to be less susceptible to traffic delays. Proposals by the Regional Council[9] for GREENWAYS have therefore been devised for speeding the flow of buses and other road users. The initial Regulations for GREENWAYS were sent to the Secretary of State for Scotland and in January 1995 he indicated he was minded to approve the Order, subject to a few modifications.

The proposals are similar to the Red Route schemes in London. Lanes segregating buses from other traffic are to be marked out with a green slurry seal. On the main road certain areas are to be marked out for loading or short term parking. More signalled crossings are proposed for pedestrians and cyclists and traffic calming measures are being installed on residential side roads to deter extraneous movements by traffic which ought to be using the main road.

The City of Edinburgh Rapid Transit (CERT) system is another measure being promoted by Lothian Region[10] to further upgrade public transport by increasing the frequency of service and greatly reducing bus journey times in the west of Edinburgh. The system is planned to provide a largely segregated reliable, high quality, high speed, purpose built route for buses only between the airport and the City Centre via the expanding development of Edinburgh Park. It will link suburban bus services to the north and south of the route and will interchange with rail at two proposed stations on the edges of Edinburgh Park. It is hoped that proposals can be lodged in Parliament in November 1995.

Table 2 Pedestrian flows

Weekday Two-way flows	13-14 h	09-18h
Princes St, n-side, Edinburgh	10 200	42 600
Waverley Bridge, Edinburgh	-	22 158
George IV Bridge, Edinburgh	-	12 620
High St, Old Town, Edinburgh	-	9 570
Rose Street, Edinburgh	-	8 460
Northumberland St,w-side,Ncastle	5 900	35 000
Church Street, Liverpool	11 605	-
Strøget, Copenhagen	7 060	49 700
Longe Viestraat, Amsterdam	6 350	47 960
Kaufingerstr, Munich (before)	-	72 000
Kaufingerstr, Munich (after ped scheme)	-	175 000

Refs:E & T P[11], City of Newcastle[12], Ramsay[13], Lothian Region et al[14]

4 A Walk around Lothian

Princes Street, Edinburgh is one of the busiest shopping streets in Europe as shown in Table 2. About 7 years ago the footway on the busy northern side was widened at the expense of one traffic lane. Despite this, a sample of shoppers questioned by E & T P[11] still complained about congestion on the footway, too many people, too much traffic and air pollution.

Consultation is continuing on proposals to make most of Princes St one-way for general traffic (but 2-way for buses and cyclists) and enable the footway to be widened further. As part of a renewal scheme, footways in the High St of Edinburgh's Old Town were widened to improve its environment and E & TP's proposal[11] for improving a pedestrian route between the university, the Old Town and Princes Street is in progress. This benefits residents going to work/college, tourists, shoppers who are also pedestrians.

Some residential areas have a poor pedestrian accident rate. A number of other residential areas are also used as through routes by persons outside the area. A variety of traffic calming measures are being implemented to reduce the speed of traffic and discourage through use. In addition to speed humps, cushions, tables, carriageway narrowings, chicanes and footway build-outs are being employed. If traffic speeds have been reduced to nearer 20mph considera-tion can be given to a Traffic Regulation Order which would formally designate a 20mph zone in accord with Scottish Office [15] regulations.

In the first five areas where calming schemes have been implemented 9% of people interviewed by Scotinform[16] asked for more humps to be installed, 8% asked for other speed reducing measures to be added and 5% asked for their road to be stopped up for through traffic. In this way pedestrians, be they young or old, will feel and be safer in their street. 2% of respondents asked for the humps to be removed.

5 Lothian leads in cycling

Lothian has over 600km of facilities available for cyclists. How has this come about and what effect has this had on cycle use? At the time of the previous local government reorganisation in 1975 Regional and District authorities in Lothian agreed to a policy of purchasing disused railways as they became available, with the Region purchasing those that might have some long term transport use. In the meantime they could be laid out as walkways for people to walk or cycle along. After requests from the local cycling campaign organisation, SPOKES, the Council commissioned a report from John Grimshaw & associates[17] on how better cycling facilties might be provided. The result, a 30 year programme, was accepted in principle by the Region's Transportation Committee in 1985.

Table 3 Lengths of cycle facility in Lothian
(completed or in progress as of 31 March 1994)

	East Lothian	Mid-Lothian	West Lothian,inc Livingston	Edinburgh
Off-road routes managed by LRC,km	7.5	6.6	391.9	36.2
Off-road routes managed by others (inc Districts)km	23.2	17.3	2.7	39.0
Shared-use footway, km	10.8	3.2	7.8	15.1
Cycle or bus & cycle lane, km	7.0	0.0	0.0	38.7
Total	48.5	27.1	402.4	129.0

During the last few years a capital expenditure programme averaging approximately $£^1/_2$M pa has been implemented on cycle schemes to create the size of network shown in Table 3. It is likely that the percentage of capital resources deployed on cycling will increase to 3% of the roads & transport budget.

Councils in Lothian have provided some off-road routes along rivers/burns, along parts of the coast and through a few of their parks. Families particularly like the safety of such routes. Where there is a break in a route traffic signals can be provided to reduce conflicts with motorised traffic.

There are two ways in which some degree of segregation from traffic can be offered when establishing longer links between off-road routes:
    a) by redesignating footways for shared-use by pedestrians and cyclists
    b) by marking out part of the carriageway for use by cyclists
Generally in Lothian, where cyclists are sharing with pedestrians there is no line marked out to segregate them. Where there is segregation it is pedestrians who invade the cyclists' area. All bus lanes, with and contra-flow, are available for cyclists and on some radial routes without bus lanes cyclists benefit from provision of cycle lanes. This was reported by

Williams[18] as also being done at a few roundabouts with histories of cycle accidents where other measures to assist cyclists have not been possible.

Livingston is a new town in West Lothian which has a segregated footpath system. In 1987 this network was formally made available for shared-use by cyclists and pedestrians. Since then there has been a programme of improving the existing network, extending it to connect with neighbouring communities, and signing the main grid routes.

Table 4 shows a number of ways in which changes in the use of cycles can be measured for the Edinburgh area. Du Feu[19] reports the 1994 increase in SPOKES membership as being partly due to substantial completion of a segregated cycle network in north Edinburgh which was marketed by signing, a household drop of leaflets showing where the routes led, and by an action day in a local park. Pedestrians comprise 70-80% of users on this network using it for going to work, school, shopping and recreation. This reinforces the view that routes should be segregated from traffic, and not just for reasons of road safety.

Table 4 Indicators for growth in cycling

Census:Travel to work	1971	1981			1991	
Edinburgh,No.cyclists	1520	2680			3460	

Edin. central	1968	1977		1984	1987	1991	1994
cordon survey,							
inbound cyclists	203	330		511	680	583	636

SPOKES		1979	1981	1984	1987	1991	1994
members		283	520	500	512	661	990

Refs. Registrar General for Scotland[4], Lothian Region[7], De Feu[19]

6 Conclusions

Lothian's investment in transport systems such as railways and off-road cycle tracks for shared-use by pedestrians and cyclists has been shown to be a good policy by their increasing use. Until further funds become available for the CERT rapid transit system the Region's *moving* FORWARD strategy is looking towards GREENWAYS, a sophisticated form of bus lanes, as one means of improving the attractiveness of buses and so stabilise their slow decline in patronage. Many people start or end their daily journeys on foot. Lothian has not forgotten them and is providing more space for their movement, sometimes by reducing areas allocated to motorised traffic both where they live and in town and suburban centres.

7 References

1. Lothian Region, *Structure Plan 1995*, Lothian Regional Council, Edinburgh, 1995.
2. MVA, Peida, Turnbull Jeffrey Partnership, *Joint Authorities Transportation and Environmental Study- Final Report*, Edinburgh, 1991.
3. Lothian Region, *2000 moving FORWARD*, Lothian Regional Council,Edinburgh, 1994.
4. General Register Office, Scotland, *National Censi for 1971, 1981, 1991*, HMSO, Edinburgh.
5. Lothian Region, *Transportation in the Edinburgh area*, Lothian Regional Council, Edinburgh, 1979.
6. Lothian Region, *Structure Plan 1985*, Lothian Regional Council, Edinburgh, 1985.
7. Director of Highways, Morning Peak Travel into central Edinburgh, meeting dated 9 Aug 1993, *Transportation Committee Reports, Minutes 1993/94* Edinburgh,1993,Lothian Reg. Co.,Edinburgh, 1994
8. Scottish Office, *Scottish Transport Statistics, No. 14, 1992/93*, HMSO, Edinburgh, 1994
9. Director of Highways, Greenways: Summary Report, Consultation, traffic regulation, capital finance, traffic calming, meeting dated 5 April 1993, *Transportation Committee Reports, Minutes 1992/93*, Edinburgh,1993,Lothian Reg. Co.,Edinburgh, 1993.
10. Lothian Region, *CERT: Tackling traffic congestion in Edinburgh*, Lothian Reg. Co., Edinburgh, 1994.
11. Environmental & Transport Planning, *Pedestrian routes in central Edinburgh, a report for Lothian Region*, E & T P, Brighton, 1992.
12. City of Newcastle Planning Department, *Report of the Pedestrian Survey*, Newcastle upon Tyne, 1963.
13. Ramsay, A., *Scope and criteria for pedestrianisation*, MA thesis,Manchester University Dept.of Town & Country Planning, Manchester, 1967.
14. Lothian Region,City of Edinburgh,Edinburgh Chamber of Commerce & Manufactures, *Lothian Region shopping study*, Lothian Reg. Co., Edinburgh, 1986.
15. Scottish Office, Department of Transport, *Traffic Advisory Leaflet 11/94:Traffic Calming Regulations (Scotland)*, Scottish Office, Edinburgh, 1994.
16. Scotinform, *Traffic Calming*, Lothian Region, Edinburgh, 1994.
17. John Grimshaw & Associates, *Lothian Region Cycle Project Report*, Lothian Reg. Co., Edinburgh, 1985.
18. Williams, R.L, Are roundabouts dangerous for cyclists?, in The Bicycle:Global Perspectives,(ed R Boivin, J F Pronovost), pp280-3,*Proceedings of Conference Vélo-Mondiale*, Montreal, Canada, 1992, Vélo-Québec, 1992.
19. Du Feu, D, *Spokes membership trends*, personal communication, SPOKES, Edinburgh, 1995.

The development of transport and changing attitudes

C.M. Peters

Department of Civil Engineering, University of Portsmouth, Portsmouth, UK

Abstract

The development of transport is inextricably linked to the general development of civilisation as we understand it today, and this paper examines these connections through a review of the development of transport. The review specifically investigates transport with regard to trade, land-use, the development of the car and the transport infrastructure and their impact on the environment.

1 Introduction

The Twentieth Century: in 1916 Henri Dieterding[1] of Royal Dutch Shell anticipated *'A Century of Travel'*, in 1973 Galbraith[2] identified *'An Age of Uncertainty'*, in 1992 Yergin[1] described *'The Century of Oil'*, more recently Hobsbawm[3] reflected upon *'An Age of Extremes'*. The twentieth century has indeed been all of these. The quest for travel and the power to do it has dominated the century. The results of this appear to be bringing the world of the 21st century to the brink of possible destruction, but in a very different way to the military threat at the beginning of the twentieth century.

. Whether the current environmental debate is seen as exaggerated by mass media and vociferous minorities or as a problem of truly global proportions, there can be little doubt that despite all the widespread efforts the overall pollution problems are getting worse, and calls for action are quite justified.

This paper presents a personal view of the development of travel and transport with respect to the political, economic, social and cultural changes of modern civilisation from before the industrial revolution to the present time.

2 Civilisation, Early Land Use Development and Trade

Ever since the beginning of civilisation mankind has learned to take advantage of his environment by changing or modifying its use to develop its potential. The early stages of civilisation entailed the transformation from a 'hunter-gatherer' lifestyle to a nomadic and then settled existence. Bronowski[4] identifies that "early nomadic peoples would have needed to follow the natural migration of wild herds - but that sheep and goats (the first animals to be domesticated) have no natural migrations". He thus suggests that "when man domesticated the animals he assumed the responsibility of nature for them". This would imply that it is important how society transports and cares for its domestic animals. Early development of agriculture in some areas was also accompanied with mineral and timber development.

As populations became more settled and less warlike their numbers grew, villages grew to towns and towns developed to cities. This settled form of existence also encouraged the development of specialisation skills (e.g the blacksmith, carpenter), so that individual households would be no longer independent and self sufficient but more inter-dependent upon each other.

Towards the end of the dark ages of European history (circa 1300-1400) there emerged two main centres of industry and trade. To the south were the Mediterranean ports and city states (dominated by Barcelona, Genoa and Venice) - and in Northern Europe the Hanseatic League, dominated by Lübeck, Hamburg and Cologne[5]. Both these trading centres reached out to much of the then known world, but there also existed considerable north-south trade between the two areas. In 1453 the fall of Constantinople (now Istanbul) to the Ottoman Empire effectively closed off access to the east for the Mediterranean city states. This stimulated the western Europeans (particularly Spain and Portugal) to investigate alternative routes to the east. It was mainly those countries with an Atlantic seaboard which had developed the larger ships capable of venturing across the deep oceans. As history records the Americas were discovered in 1492, and following the circumnavigation of the world, thereafter the main trade routes were to be east-west rather than north-south.

In Great Britain through the first phase of the industrial revolution (1760-1870), the location of industry revolved around location of natural resources, for example textile mills were located near water power, with housing constructed locally by mill owners and the population moved in. The canals were the prime movers of both raw materials 'in' and the shipment of manufactured goods 'out' to towns and ports for sale and export. At this time overseas interests by Europeans was more a trading and missionary venture.

As the industrial revolution spread across western Europe towards the east and to North America it brought dramatic land-use changes together with many investment and employment opportunities. Clearly there was a general tacit acceptance to this industrial development. After some two hundred years, and at the peak of industrial output of the 1960s-1970s it was inconceivable to those involved that the *sunset* of many of these traditional industries was to be just two decades away.

3 Trade and Transport

The opportunities for our forebears to travel were obviously much less than today, however in reality the extent of travel in medieval times is generally underestimated. England in the middle ages had many markets and fairs - people would often travel 10 to 20 miles to take their goods to market[6]. Both water and land transport were extensively used. England had many navigable rivers which were used for travel (and unlike on mainland Europe travellers were not deterred by tolls), but the use of weirs to control water levels did hinder navigation.

In the fifteenth century most roads were merely tracks over the existing ground, it was not until the seventeenth century that the designated turnpike routes appeared, and the properly constructed roads by Engineers came a century later. It was particularly during the rainy season that carts became bogged down and travelling between towns was particularly hazardous.

The key point about transport and trade prior to the twentieth century was the load carrying capacities of the horse[6]:-

One horse could carry up to 150 kg on pannier or 2 tonnes by cart

A horse drawn canal barge could carry 100 tonnes (or more)

A coastal ship (of the day) would carry 300-400 tonnes

The major factors which would affect trade through the transport developments of the industrial revolution were:-

changes in cost and speed of travel, and extensions of markets

Following the opening of Bridgewater's canal (Worsley to Manchester) in 1761 the cost per tonne of transporting coal was reduced from £2 (by road) to 30 pence (by canal)[7].

With regard to the transportation of bulk goods of low value (coal, ores, clay etc) where the transport costs are a significant portion of the overall commodity costs - **then cost of transport is vital.**

For the transportation of high value goods (e.g silks, gemstones, woollens) where the transport costs are relatively low - **then speed of transport is vital.**

It is significant to note that the steam railways introduced in the early nineteenth century were able to cater for both high value and low value goods, and that up until that time all land transport was relatively very expensive.

4 The Era of Motor Transport and the New Century

The machine that is most commonly acknowledged as the first motor car is the Benz three-wheeler built in 1883. This was far from the earliest attempt at a form of mechanised road transport; in the nineteenth century many steam driven road vehicles were demonstrated[5][8] - but they tended to be big and cumbersome, noisy and emitted clouds of black smoke. The Benz machine was much more compact but still had all the other liabilities. However the single factor which gave it distinct advantage that was to maintain its dominance through independent use, was the power source: a compact liquid fuel which to this day (bar nuclear fuels) contains more energy per unit mass than any alternative, and it did not require a large copper boiler or a concrete jacket!

As these contraptions were noisy, slow, unreliable and emitted clouds of noxious fumes it was difficult to see how they would catch on. They were however the playthings of the wealthy and as such over the next two decades gradual improvements were made, not the least of which was the invention of the pneumatic tyre patented by Dunlop in 1888[9]. This allowed for improved suspensions which gave a much more comfortable ride and allowed higher speeds, (but not in the UK as higher speeds were illegal[8]), this in turn gave added impetus to further improvements and developments.

Early in the new century two significant events were to happen - a war started in Europe in 1914 and Henry Ford was building cars for a new generation of farmers in the USA.

The war swept away or changed the old European Imperial dynasties which allowed a greater prosperity for the masses and Ford showed how to make cheaper cars for ordinary people. However the political changes were not fully effected until after the Great Depression and World War Two[3]. But by the end of 1945 there was a more determined spirit to build a better future - this time for both vanquished and victor. There was a real *spirit of freedom*, and in all the chaos of war torn Europe nothing epitomised this freedom more than the *freedom of the open road* - which was to be especially significant in western Europe and North America. This was consistent with the *Great American Dream* - justified on the premise that there were unlimited resources and opportunities for all who were prepared to work hard - but no free lunch!

5 The Development of the Motor Vehicle

Cars built at the turn of the century were hand made and very expensive. Ford first set up his company in 1903 and he saw that American farmers needed a cheap small versatile vehicle for handling produce and tools of the trade. Whereas other car makers employed craftsmanship, Ford's innovation was systems engineering *'know-how'* - he used interchangeable parts (known as *armoury practice*[10]) assembled on a conveyor belt system by interchangeable workers. The main significance was that the company were able to use the moving conveyor belt system to set the pace of the workers. The origins of armoury practice were in early nineteenth century government small arms factories[10] (possibly France), it was used extensively by Eli Whitney in the USA[11] and also known as the *American System*[12]. It is worth noting that Ford is often attributed, quite wrongly, as being the inventor of mass production. Adam Smith described mass production in 1776 and the process is also clearly illustrated in Diderot's *Encyclopedie* of the same period[2].

The significance of Ford's contribution was the simplicity of the parts and his use of the moving conveyor to set the pace of work. Between 1908 and 1927 he produced 15 million 'Model-T's, a car for the masses, and over that period he reduced the construction time to one tenth and the price by 2/3rds whilst doubling the wages of the workers[13]. Pursell[10] reports a 40-fold increase in production between 1909 to 1916 with a price reduction from $950 to $360.

A further significance of his contribution was that his cars were ruggedly built (essential as there were few good roads outside the towns) and were easily maintained (most essential for the remote 'DIY' farmers).

The early development of the motor car led to improved (more comfortable and weatherproof) vehicles with more powerful engines. In Europe the 1920s and 1930s probably represent the peak 'fun' element of motoring as a novelty for the affluent, 3-litre Bentleys, Bugatti's, Brooklands and rallying to Monte Carlo.   Air pollution and noise problems were still not regarded as a serious problem as over here the motoring public were still a minority.

In the USA in the 1930s and 1940s car ownership widened and mass manufacturers produced more useable and refined vehicles. Ford's 'Model-T' was not too different from the original vehicles of the 1890s. However by the 1940s the American sedan bore much more resemblance to the modern day vehicle with flared-in wings which formed part of a 'unitary' car body. These vehicles also gained substantial improvements to the mechanical features particularly regarding engine, suspension and brakes, all of which led to greater reliability and performance. This performance was especially enhanced because of the gradual use of larger engines (particularly in Europe) whereas N.America had always tended to use 'large' engines, as fuel consumption was of little consequence. The typical production family cars reached their largest size during the late 1960s (limousines had always been large!). The next major re-think occurred after the 1973 Oil Crisis when oil supplies to the west were interrupted and the crude oil prices increased four fold[1]. This led to a general trend back towards smaller cars, including a smaller family vehicle.

Following this greater awareness of the fuel costs of private motoring the 1980-1990s would bring even greater awareness of other, hitherto unseen, costs in terms of pollution and damage to the environment. The consequence of this was that manufacturers' attention were directed to producing less polluting vehicles with the introduction of unleaded petrol, catalytic converters and a further general trend towards smaller vehicles. Engine design was to be more important with emphasis on better fuel economy with less pollution gases. But the unique power/weight ratio advantage of gasoline (as identified in 1880's) is yet to be outperformed by any alternative power source.

However one significant change in the political arena was that in the United States' tough legislation against polluting vehicles is now forcing the pace of development and research; rather than the traditional approach of opportunistic, or 'by chance' new technological developments preceding and thus allowing suitable changes in legislation.

Over the years vehicle design has also improved safety, particularly for vehicle occupants, however the current rising popularity of 'off-road' vehicles in the UK presents a greater risk to pedestrians, as well as concern for the countryside through inappropriate use. It is only now that safety consciousness features much more widely in car sales promotions; but performance and style are still often regarded as very significant. For many young and upwardly mobile people the motor car is a very important outward appearance status symbol. Ever since the motor car was generally available to ordinary households then everyone has either wanted a better one, a new one or a second one and the overall demand has ever increased.

6 Transport and the Infrastructure

The early beginnings of the transport infrastructure were trails which became pathways, which in turn became tracks between local settlements. Many early civilisations used paved roads within the towns, but the Romans were the first to build a *designed* major road system (across all of Europe).

In the middle ages the inherited network of tracks and pathways, were used by travellers on foot (most users), riders on horseback, and by bullock or horse drawn carts for trade. It was upon this system that the first stirrings of the 'new age of industrial development' were to rely. In England in 1555 owing to the increased use of the roads and subsequent damage, responsibility for the roads was established with the local parishes[9]. It so happened that wheeled coaches first appeared in Britain at about this time, and as trade and travel increased the roads got worse again! Passenger coach services (the first public transport) commenced in 1605, the effect of the increased volume of wheeled traffic (coaches and carts) was that the rural roads were damaged even more, and congestion in cities became significant[6][9]. In 1663 in order to improve the situation the government initiated the *turnpikes* which allowed toll charges on main roads so that the *users* would contribute to their upkeep. By 1838, some 22,000 miles of routes in England were turnpiked, but in 1895 the turnpike trusts were ended and responsibility handed back to local control[6]. By chance this coincided with the first display of motor cars in Britain.

However back in the eighteenth century things were soon to improve, the first of the new European road builders[9] were Trésaguet (in France) and Phillips (in England) but perhaps more well known here were Telford, Macadam and Metcalf. It was the efforts of such engineers in building a national network of main roads that led to the vital improved communications for easier access across the country for transport and trade. Much of this work was continuing at the same time as the building of canals but because of the bulk carrying capacity of the canals compared to the wider network of roads, the two systems were complementary rather than in competition[6].

In Britain, as elsewhere the role of the canals was quickly overtaken in the nineteenth century by the construction of the railways[6][14], here the main network was constructed between 1825-1850; and development on mainland Europe followed very quickly (particularly in Germany). The development of the railways was particularly significant in that it allowed for speed and it catered for people, as well as goods. In terms of personal travel it allowed the masses, who had flocked to the towns for a living to take a 'day out' to visit the seaside to escape their dreary existence in the factories. The main effect of the railways of the nineteenth century was that it took the long haul off the turnpikes (and canals) but generated extra short haul trips (to get to the railhead from local origins and destinations) but the turnpikes remained very busy wherever there was no parallel railway in direct competition[6].

The completion of the railway infrastructure led to further urban expansion which in turn generated more traffic particularly in major towns and cities. In London where planning regulations prevented the railway routes from crossing the central area, traffic congestion was particularly bad, the local public transport of the day (the horse drawn omnibus) was inadequate but the problem was solved with the very first underground urban railway. The *Metropolitan Railway*, a four mile route constructed in *cut and cover* for steam trains was opened in 1863. The full *inner circle* route to connect all main line stations in central London was completed by 1884[8].

In 1879 at the Berlin Exhibition, Siemens[14] first demonstrated the use of a small electric train, and the world's first electric powered surface railway was developed in Berlin in 1881. By 1887 electric tramways (overground) were expanding everywhere with 10 systems in the USA and 9 in Europe[14], (12,500 miles of operational tramway in the USA by 1895[6]); The world's first use of electric trains in an underground bored tunnel (or *tube*) was in London in 1890, and by 1900 Paris also had started work on its *metro* system. As with steam trains the standardisation of gauges was important, but now this also covered the power supply (DC or AC, voltage and frequency). Such problems are just as common today with the Channel Tunnel trains having to operate over four different signalling systems.

In theory public transport on the roads should have been much simpler. Motor buses (imported) were first operated in the UK from 1899, which led to feeder services to the railways, but not without regular breakdowns. Eventually with improved mechanical reliability the flexibility of the bus system proved very advantageous and was also suitable for small towns and country areas. It is notable that since the 1980s new L.R.T systems are now making a comeback in many larger cities in the UK- they have always been popular in mainland Europe.

The next major change to the infrastructure in the twentieth century was a renewed interest in road building in the inter-war years particularly in USA and Germany. In the early years of the twentieth century the limited capability of the speed of motor vehicles was such that the first needs were to improve the road surface and use improved methods for construction - thus extending the work of nineteenth century engineers. It was not until the late 1930s that *Highway Engineers* were more concerned with route capacity (to determine the required number of traffic lanes) and the *design* of the road alignment using specially determined grades and curvature, with transition curves and carefully applied super-elevation. The so called *curvilinear* alignment of a modern highway was based upon a particular *design speed* suitable for the traffic using each route.

Through the last fifty years of this century the 'motorway' age has certainly provided for the demand for travel for those countries which have been able to afford the cost and space for such infrastructure. However since most journeys start and end in towns and cities it was when the motorway was taken into town that the modern urban transport problems really emerged.

7 Transport and the Environment

Major problems of congestion and air pollution now plague most major cities in all parts of the world - in both the industrialised and the developing world. Athens, Los Angeles and Mexico City are among the world's most congested and polluted cities, some with their particular problems of pollution exacerbated by local terrain and climatic conditions which prevent the dispersal of noxious fumes. But we now know that dispersal through the wider atmosphere is not a solution, it just moves the problem on to the next locality and adds to the overall global problem.

Air pollution is nothing new, London of the 1950s was infamous for its smog but legislation did much to solve the problem in enforcing society to clean up its 'smoky chimneys'. However quite a number of problems of pollution and congestion have been recorded much earlier. In ancient Rome the use of chariots at night was banned because of the noise nuisance and there was also the nuisance of sewage in the streets[15].

In 1635 Charles I issued a royal proclamation to restrict the use of hackney coaches (taxis of the day) because of the nuisance and damage to the roads of London and also because of the effect on prices (extra demand forcing up prices of hay etc); but it would appear the decree was largely ignored[9]. However O'Flaherty comments that two significant points emerge: the public identify with their right to use the public highway (irrespective of environmental conditions); and that if the roads cannot provide the capacity then the traffic should be changed to suit the roads.

Following the road construction era which began in the late eighteenth century one presumed that there was some improvement, at least in the general condition of the roads. However by the end of the nineteenth century every major city in Europe was teeming with traffic (mostly horse drawn) "the noise and stench assaulted the senses and crossing the road could be very hazardous"[13].

The idea of a by-pass to relieve environmental problems of congestion and nuisance of traffic is nothing new. The most recent re-alignment to the A1 trunk road at Durham is reputed to be the fifth successive by-pass to that route since the sixteenth century. The problem is often that once a new by-pass is built, then re-development of land will proceed up to and sometimes beyond that route. In the 1930s in Britain the so called Ribbon Development encouraged development along the new arterial routes radiating from London. This created a mix of local and regional traffic on the routes and also prevented subsequent widening. Thus thirty years or so later a new route was often required (e.g. M4 motorway to replace the A4 trunk road).

The pollution problems of this century and the motor age are often and well reported, but perhaps the main events[1] which stimulated a world wide response were:-

- At Chernobyl in 1986 the explosion of a nuclear power generator.
- In 1989 the Exxon Valdez oil spillage in Prince William Sound, Alaska..
- The burning of the Kuwait Oilfields during the 1991 Gulf war.

There is also the problem of the *greenhouse effect* and global warming, first raised in the mid 1970s but again highlighted by recent reports on climatic changes in Antarctica. (British Antarctic Survey reports).

Whilst on the one hand the rich northern countries have legislated quite substantially regarding most areas of pollution (in industry as well as transport) this has not been the case in the developing world. In the north all new vehicles have to meet stringent pollution standards, but the question of congestion is still to be addressed - except in the *nouveau riche* Singapore where punitive taxes have (unpopularly) priced most motorists off the road, although slightly cheaper motoring may be enjoyed at weekends!

The dilemma for the newly developing countries is that in order to join *the club* they need to exploit their natural resources. In the 1970s developing countries still tended to regard the multi-national oil companies (and other developers) as neo-colonialistic exploiters. However, in the post 1973 OPEC era such countries then took a greater interest and role, including nationalisation of the local assets. Now in the 1990s international companies are again invited in by governments for exploration and development of the resources, recent examples are Vietnam and Siberia[1]. Because of rapidly expanding populations amongst the developing countries it is often seen as particularly important to develop their natural resources in order to provide for the people.

Regarding the major congestion in the world's great cities and its effects, it is nothing new but it is getting worse. In Los Angeles severe restraints are now being applied to the motor car, ironically an investigation into such congestion "The Tide of Traffic" a film made by BP as a contribution to the 1972 'UN Conference on the Human Environment' highlighted many of the problems, so very evident more than twenty years ago. The consequences of *out of town* superstore development and the dereliction of traditional town centres in the USA were also understood more than twenty years ago[16].

8 Urban Transport for the 21st Century - Some Conclusions

All over the world for the past four hundred years or so the rural populations have been migrating to the towns and cities in search of prosperity and a better lifestyle - but in all reality many just exchange one set of difficulties for another. At first the rate of migration was determined by the progress of industrialisation (i.e. the need for labour in the new industries) however a more significant constraint was also the ability of those remaining on the land to support (in food supply) those working in industry. In the twentieth century owing to the vast improvements in agriculture and world food exports this dependency no longer occurs and thus mass migration to the cities in the last 50 years has been dramatic, particularly in the newly industrialised and developing countries. Whether looking at cities of the new world or the old world, many would argue that it is apparent that life in the cities as we know it today is unsustainable as well as inappropriate.

At a time when the *individuals' rights* are often seen by some as vital rather than just desirable, the real political dilemma is where the freedom or 'rights' of the individual conflict with the rights of another or more particularly with the utility (or rights) of society as a whole[17]. The personal use of tobacco, alcohol and drugs as well as allowing dogs in public areas all tend to create such conflict, where inappropriate or over-use by the individual(s) causes severe problems to others or to society as a whole. Excessive use of the motor car in cities and popular areas of countryside cause similar concern of the conflict between individual users and the pollution and loss of amenity to society.

With regard to the problems of air pollution and traffic congestion in our cities, it is very unlikely that there will be a 'magical' technical fix to allow us to carry on using individual cars, in the next century, the same way as we have in the past. Thus surely the question of attitudes to a generally sustainable lifestyle and public utility will be of paramount importance in reaching a balance between freedom of travel for the individual and the problems it causes. This balance will also need to be addressed between the prosperous nations and the poor nations with regard to the consumption and development of resources, as well as a balance for each city according to its own needs.

The new technologies and the information superhighway are expected to give some relief to the traditional transportation networks - but just how much, how quickly, and to whom, seems very uncertain at this moment in time.

References

1.   YERGIN, D. 'The Prize', BBC. Books 1992
2.   GALBRAITH, J.K. 'The Age of Uncertainty', BBC/Andre Deutch, 1977
3.   HOBSBAWM, E.J 'Age of Extremes', Joseph, 1994.
4.   BRONOWSKI, J. 'The Ascent of Man', BBC Books 1973.
5.   LEIBRAND, K. 'Transportation and Town Planning', Hill, 1970.
6.   BARKER T.C. and SAVAGE, C.I. 'Economic History of Transport in Britain' (3rd Edit). Hutchinson, 1974.
7.   BURKE, J. 'The Day the Universe Changed', BBC Books 1985.
8.   SIMMONS, J. 'Transport - 'A Visual History of Modern Britain' Vista. Books, 1962.
9.   O'FLAHERTY, C.A. 'Highways', Vol.1, (3rd Edit), Arnold, 1986
10.   PURSELL, C. 'White Heat - People and Technology', BBC. Books 1994
11.   BRIGGS, A. (Ed), 'The Nineteenth Century' Thames & Hudson, 1985
12.   PARKER, G. (Ed) 'The World an Illustrated History' Times Book, 1988
13.   'Engines of Change', produced by Shell Films Ltd. London, 1993.
14.   ALLEN, G.F. 'Railways Past, Present and Future', Orbis 1982
15.   HALL, P. 'Urban and Regional Planning', Hyman, 1989.
16.   'Traffic in Norwich', Open University Broadcast (GB) 1972
17.   WATSON, P. and BARBER, B. 'The Struggle for Democracy', Dennys, (Toronto), 1988

SECTION 3:
ENVIRONMENTAL ASPECTS

A modelling framework for including environmental impact analysis in transport planning studies: seeking prevention not cure

M.A.P. Taylor, J.E. Woolley, T.M. Young,
S.J. Thompson-Clement
*Transport Systems Centre, University of South Australia,
The Levels, SA 5095, Australia*

This paper considers the development of a method to assess the impacts of transport systems on the urban environment and for investigating plans to ameliorate adverse environmental impacts in a region. The method draws on models for transport network analysis and for fuel consumption and emissions modelling. Models permitting: (1) the examination of alternative policies and broad strategies for metropolitan travel, and (2) alternative vehicle and fuel technologies, are included in the system. The paper indicates how these procedures are being integrated into an environmental impact assessment package, or supermodel, known as IMPAECT (Impact Model for Prediction and Assessment of the Environmental Consequences of Traffic). IMPAECT consists of a set of four PC-based computer models linked through a common data structure. The component models are a traffic network model, a vehicle energy and emissions (air and noise) model, a pollutant dispersion model and a land use impact model. The modular design of the supermodel allows the use of alternative components, to suit local needs and thus enhance flexibility of use.

Transport demand modelling is well established and the models have now devolved to readily available and widely used packages on personal computers. However, the development of these transport demand modelling procedures may not have kept pace with changing community demands, which now insist on the inclusion of environmental factors in the planning, design and construction of transport infrastructure. Traffic on roadways is a significant cause of environmental degradation in urban areas, contributing to air pollution and noise, as well as causing problems of congestion, safety and intrusion. Current practice usually involves an environmental impact assessment for planned works projects. While this procedure is important, and will remain so, particularly in providing ameliorative measures for the worst environmental consequences of any project, its weakness is that it comes too late in the planning process: the important route location decisions having been made many years previously through travel demand modelling. IMPAECT offers one means to include considerations of likely environmental consequences in the transport planning process at the stages when major planning decisions are being made, rather than delaying such considerations until project implementation, when costly decisions may have to be reviewed and/or remedial treatments are necessary.

Brown & Patterson[2] demonstrated how the noise impact of a planned road network could be explicitly included in travel demand modelling and network planning, i.e. when the network is still being developed, modelled and tested, rather than after the preferred route or potential alternative routes have been selected. Taylor & Anderson[6] discussed a combined model for estimating pollutant emissions from traffic streams, based on the extension of a traffic network model to provide information on emissions, by modelling the relationships between traffic congestion, fuel consumption and pollutant emissions, and connecting the traffic model to a pollutant dispersion model.

Estimating the environmental impacts of road traffic

Assessing the relative impacts of alternative transport infrastructure plans is difficult. Survey methods for assessing levels of pollution are available for the study of existing conditions (e.g. Taylor, Young & Bonsall[7]), but these cannot be applied to proposed developments: therefore other means for the appraisal of alternatives are required. This issue was addressed in the 1970s by Wigan[10], who developed the following methodology:

(1)   collate data on a link-by-link basis on road type, width, number of households, amount of activity by category of land use, etc;

(2)   obtain traffic flow data, including traffic composition, travel time and delay;

(3)   develop a database that can provide the required link-by-link data to apply models of fuel consumption, emissions and pollutant dispersion;

(4)   apply a framework that defines the conditions under which the consumption, emissions and dispersion models can be applied;

(5)   generate indices of pollutant loads and environmental impacts (e.g. number of households subjected to a given noise level over a specified time interval);

(6)   prepare tabular and graphical representations of this information as histograms, pollution load maps, etc, and

(7)   indicate levels of individual and community annoyance under different pollution loadings.

Given the logical, 'common-sense' nature of this methodology, it may come as something of a surprise to realise that it has seldom, if ever been fully applied in practice! All too often transport planners and engineers have considered only the generation of pollution at its sources, not where that pollution will end up and who will be affected by it. The IMPAECT package follows Wigan's methodology through the construction of a combined model system, comprising a traffic network model, an emissions and fuel consumption model (or family of models), a pollution dispersion model, and a land use impact model.

The basics of the IMPAECT system are shown in Figure 1. A traffic network model produces the levels of traffic flow and travel conditions on a study area network, under the given traffic management scheme. Models of vehicle fuel consumption and emissions under the modelled traffic conditions then estimate the traffic system fuel usage and the levels and spatial distribution of pollutant emissions. This information, coupled with data on the meteorological conditions, becomes the input to a pollution dispersion model, which estimates the spread of the pollution over the study area, so estimating the levels and spatial distribution of the pollution. The land use impact model superimposes the pollution levels on the land uses and populations in the study area to determine the likely sites and extent of environmental problems.

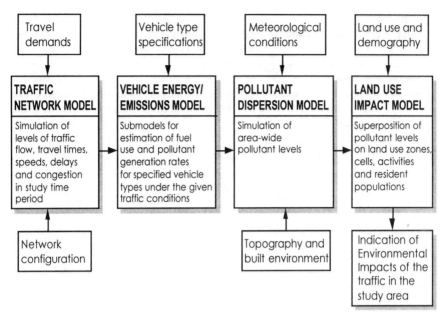

Figure 1: The IMPAECT modelling system for assessing the environmental impacts of road traffic

The application of the modelling system of Figure 1 depends on the accuracy of the traffic model in reproducing travel conditions on the network, and the validity of the vehicle performance models and the pollutant dispersion models. The application to environmental impact analysis is based on the premise that the modelling system can reasonably detect relative differences in levels of pollution between alternative sets of traffic load distributions (e.g. under alternative transport systems management plans or alternative travel demand management schemes). Emission and fuel consumption rates are estimated by aggregating the contributions of the component traffic streams. The network is then treated as a set of line sources of each pollutant. The emissions from these sources may then be spread over the study region using the dispersion model, and the concentrations of pollution at different sites examined. A superposition of the pollutant concentrations on the distribution of land uses in the study area, e.g. through a Geographic Information System (GIS) package, provides the means for assessing the susceptibility of sensitive land uses to the various pollutants.

Traffic network modelling in IMPAECT

Traffic network modelling involves the use of trip matrices (defining the spatial and possibly temporal patterns of travel demand) with a network model that assigns the trips to paths through the network and thus accumulates the link volumes and travel conditions (e.g. congestion levels) on the network. A number of network models are available, these may conveniently be split into two broad types: strategic models which model network flows at the link level, and dense network models which model flows at the turning movement level. The former are most commonly used in transport network planning, the latter in urban traffic control and the evaluation of traffic management schemes. A strategic level model is described here by way of example, but equally a dense network model could also be employed (Taylor & Anderson[6]).

Congestion models
A number of functional forms relating travel conditions to traffic flows at the link level are available (Rose, Taylor & Tisato[3]). One example is the Davidson function, which in its most practical form is

$$
c = \begin{cases} c_0 \left\{ 1 + J \dfrac{\mu}{1 - \mu} \right\} & \mu < \rho \\[2em] c_0 \left\{ 1 + J \dfrac{\rho}{1 - \rho} + \dfrac{J}{(1 - \rho)^2}(\mu - \rho) \right\} & \mu \geq \rho \end{cases} \tag{1}
$$

where c is the link travel time, c_0 is the free-flow link travel time, μ is the volume-capacity ratio and J is an environmental parameter that reflects the road type and abutting land use development (and hence the level of internal friction within the traffic stream). Volume-capacity ratio is the ratio of traffic volume (q) to link capacity (S). The linear extension of the curve for $\mu \geq \rho$ (where $\rho < 1$ is a pre-determined constant) ensures the function is defined for all finite volume-capacity ratios. It also allows for over-saturation of the link (Taylor[4]). This function provides a relationship that can be used to predict the emissions and fuel consumption on that link.

Segmentation of vehicle flows
Changing fleet composition and the contributions of different vehicle types and trip classes to fuel usage and pollution are important in TDM, e.g. to see how such changes might affect pollution levels. The differences in energy and environmental performance between different fuel types is one such issue. Trip class might include different categories of travellers, e.g. through traffic and local traffic, private, commercial and business travel, etc. If q(e) is the total vehicle volume on link e then

$$
q(e) = \sum_k q_k(e) \tag{2}
$$

where $q_k(e)$ is the volume of trip class k vehicles on e. If p_{km} is the proportion of type m vehicles in trip class k, the flow $q_m(e)$ of type m vehicles is given by

$$
q_m(e) = \sum_k p_{km} q_k(e) \tag{3}
$$

If $E_m(X)$ is the mean rate of emission (consumption) of pollutant (fuel) X by a type m vehicle then $TE_e(X)$, the total rate of emission (consumption) is given by equation (4).

$$TE_e(X) \;\;=\;\; \sum_{km} E_m(X)\, p_{km}\, q_k(e) \tag{4}$$

Given models to predict $E_m(X)$ for a range of traffic conditions then total pollution loads and fuel consumption can be estimated. These models can suggest differences in energy and environmental impacts for changes in levels of traffic flow and congestion and for changes in vehicle fleet composition.

Emission/consumption models for traffic streams

Biggs & Akcelik[1] proposed a family of fuel consumption and emissions models, comprising four related models, each at a different level of aggregation:
(1)   an *instantaneous model*, that indicates the rate of fuel usage or pollutant emission of an individual vehicle continuously over time;
(2)   an *elemental model*, that relates fuel use or pollutant emission to traffic variables such as deceleration, acceleration, idling and cruising, etc. over a short road distance (e.g. the approach to an intersection);
(3)   a *running speed model*, that gives emissions or fuel consumption for vehicles travelling over an extended length of road (perhaps representing a network link), and
(4)   an *average speed model*, that indicates level of emissions or fuel consumption over an entire journey.
The instantaneous model is the basic, most detailed model. The other models are aggregations of it (i.e. they use its basic parameters with some simplifying assumptions about vehicle behaviour when accelerating or decelerating), and thus require less information. The running speed model is appropriate for use at the strategic network link level.

Instantaneous model
This model is suitable for the detailed assessment of traffic management schemes for individual intersections or sections of road. The variables in the model include instantaneous values such as speed $v(t)$ and acceleration $a(t)$ at time t. The instantaneous model gives the rate of emission/consumption (E/C) of X, including components for:
(a)   the fuel used or emissions generated in maintaining engine operation, estimated by the idle rate (α);
(b)   the work done by the vehicle engine in moving the vehicle, and
(c)   the product of energy and acceleration during periods of positive acceleration.
The energy consumed in moving the vehicle is further divided into drag, inertial and grade components. Component (c) allows for the inefficient use of fuel during periods of hard acceleration. The model is given by equation (5), where v is speed (ms^{-1}), a is the instantaneous acceleration rate in ms^{-2}, R_T is the total tractive force required to drive the vehicle (the sum of the drag, inertial and grade forces), M is vehicle mass (kg), α is the idling fuel consumption or pollutant emission rate, β_1 is an engine efficiency parameter (mL or g /kJ) (relating E/C to energy provided by the engine), and β_2 is an engine efficiency parameter (mL or g /(kJ.ms^{-2})), (relating E/C during positive acceleration to the product of vehicle mass, energy and acceleration).

$$\frac{dE(X)}{dt} = \alpha + \beta_1 R_T v + \left[\frac{\beta_2 Ma^2 v}{1000}\right]_{a>0} \qquad \text{for } R_T > 0 \tag{5}$$

$$= \alpha \qquad \text{for } R_T \leq 0$$

R_T is given by

$$R_T = b_1 + b_2 v^2 + \frac{Ma}{1000} + g \times 10^{-5} MG \tag{6}$$

where g is gravitational acceleration in ms^{-2}, G is the percentage gradient (negative downhill), b_1 is a drag force parameter relating *mainly* to rolling resistance, and b_2 is a drag force parameter relating *mainly* to aerodynamic resistance: both of these drag force parameters also reflect some component of internal engine drag. The model is accurate to within five per cent. The parameters α, β_1, β_2, b_1 and b_2 are specific to a particular vehicle type, so a knowledge of the vehicle fleet composition is also needed for transport planning purposes (Taylor[5]).

Running speed model
This model may be used for estimation of fuel consumption or emissions along a network link, and is thus suitable for application in a transport network model. The data required to apply the model are travel time c_s (seconds), trip distance x_s (km), and stopped time c_i (seconds) over the route section. The vehicle is then assumed to travel at a constant running speed v_r (km/h), where

$$v_r = \frac{3600 x_s}{c_s - c_i} \tag{7}$$

while moving. The model predicts the mean rate of pollution emission or fuel consumption. It provides estimates of fuel consumption within 10-15 per cent of observed values for travel over road sections of at least 0.7 km. Methods for estimating v_r given overall link speed $v_s = D/c$, where D is link length, are available (Taylor[5]).

A combination of the congestion function defined in equation (1) and the E/C running speed model may then be used to estimate the E/C rate for a link of a given type operating at a given volume-capacity ratio. Taylor[5] provides the necessary parameter values for the generation of specific E/C functions for different road types in terms of one-way link volume/capacity ratios. Figure 2 shows typical functions for emissions of carbon monoxide for dual carriageway arterial roads. These functions can be used in conjunction with a traffic assignment model to predict the impacts of the level of traffic congestion on emissions and, indeed, to determine traffic distribution patterns minimising emission generation over a region (Taylor[5]).

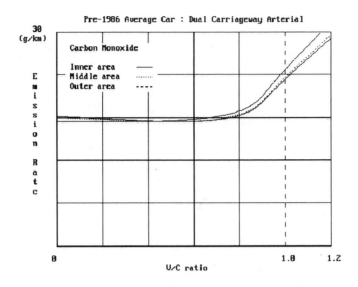

Figure 2: Examples of derived link function for emissions of carbon monoxide

Traffic assignment model

The volume-capacity ratios are determined for links in the study area network using equilibrium assignment models (with either fixed demand or elastic demand, Taylor[5]).

Pollutant dispersion model

Two pollutant dispersion models are incorporated in IMPAECT. These are the NetNoise area-wide noise model, described in Woolley and Young[9] and Thompson-Clement, Woolley and Taylor[8], and a Gaussian plume air pollution dispersion model (Taylor and Anderson[6], Taylor, Young and Bonsall[7]). The inputs to these models are the relevant pollution emission rates from the road network links, which are thus line sources of pollution. The outputs are the concentrations of the pollutants at points over a fine grid covering the study area. These concentrations are used for display and analysis in a GIS (MapInfo or ARC/INFO) and for use in the land use impact model.

Land use impact model

This model is used to predict the levels of pollution to which different land uses and locations in the area will be subject, thus indicating the nature, gravity and extent of any adverse environmental impacts (Woolley & Young[9]). For example, a desired output might be the number of households in an area subjected to traffic noise indices exceeding a given value. It provides information on the rate of *im*mission of pollution by a land use, rather than the rate of *e*mission of that pollutant from its source(s). This is in keeping with the ideas of Wigan[10] and Brown and Patterson[2] that environmental impact assessment analysis should reflect the actual pollutant loads borne by sensitive land uses rather than the emission levels generated by the sources of that pollution.

Common database structure

The IMPAECT supermodel is designed for application at different levels of detail (e.g. to strategic or dense networks). Its component models all require different but related data about network configuration and land use distribution. It thus requires a common database from which the component models can extract their required inputs and to which they can deliver their outputs for use by the other models. The solution has been the development of a comprehensive relational database system, TNRDB (Transport Network Relational Database), as described in Thompson-Clement, Woolley & Taylor[8].

Conclusions

This paper has provided a brief overview into the development of a modelling system for use in transport planning, in which environmental impact and pollution loads can be incorporated into the basic processes of transport planning, rather than being left for consideration until the primary transport infrastructure decisions have been made. If environmental impacts are not considered along with the primary decisions, then the treatment of environmental problems resulting from transport system developments are destined to remain as remedial measures: expensive, frustrating and wasteful for a community. Prevention is better than cure, and a system such as IMPAECT offers transport planners a way to anticipate, resolve or avoid potential environmental problems before they are manifest.

References

1.   Biggs, D.C. & Akcelik, R. Estimation of car fuel consumption in urban traffic. In *Proceedings of the 13th Australian Road Research Board Conf* **13** (7), pp 124-132, Adelaide, 1986, Australian Road Research Board, Melbourne, 1986.
2.   Brown, A.L. & Patterson, N.S. Noise assessment when it matters: environmental evaluation integrated with road network planning. In *Proceedings of the 15th Australian Road Research Board Conf* **15** (7), pp 61-78, Darwin, 1990, Australian Road Research Board, Melbourne, 1990.
3.   Rose, G., Taylor, M.A.P. & Tisato, P. Estimating travel time functions for urban roads: options and issues, *Transportation Planning and Technology*, 1989, **14** (1), 63-82.
4.   Taylor, M.A.P. A note on using Davidson's function in equilibrium assignment, *Transportation Research B*, 1984, **18B** (3), 181-199.
5.   Taylor, M.A.P. Incorporating environmental planning decisions in transport planning: a modelling framework, *Transport, Land Use and the Environment*, ed Y. Hayashi and J.R. Roy, in press, Kluwer, Boston, 1995.
6.   Taylor, M.A.P. & Anderson, M. (1988) Modelling the environmental impacts of urban road traffic with MULATM-POLDIF: a PC-based system with interactive graphics, *Environment and Planning B*, 1988, **15**, 192-200.
7.   Taylor, M.A.P., Young, W. & Bonsall, P.W. *Understanding Traffic Systems: Data, Analysis and Presentation*, Ashgate, Aldershot, 1995.
8.   Thompson-Clement, S.J., Woolley, J.E. & Taylor, M.A.P. Applying the transport network relational database to a turning flows study and a traffic noise model. In *Proceedings of the 7th World Conf on Transport Research*, in press, Sydney, 1995. World Conference on Transport Research Society, Lyon, 1995.
9.   Woolley, J.E. & Young, T.M. Environment: the third dimension of the land-use transport interaction. *Papers of the Australasian Transport Research Forum*, 1994, **19** (1), 223-239.
10. Wigan, M.R. The estimation of environmental impacts for transport policy assessment, *Environment and Planning B*, 1976, **8**, 125-147.

Development and validation of an urban street canyon model based on carbon-monoxide experimental data measured in Firenze

M. Tartaglia,[a] A. Giannone,[b] G. Gualtieri,[a] A. Barbaro,[c]
[a] *Department of Civil Engineering, University of Firenze, Via S. Marta, 3-50139 Firenze, Italy*
[b] *Environmental Physics Unit, Local Health Department 10/A, Firenze, Italy*
[c] *Foundation for Applied Meteorology, Firenze, Italy*

Abstract

An application of a street canyon model was carried out in Firenze. Estimations of carbon-monoxide (CO) concentrations due to road traffic were computed with an integration of traffic, emission, meteorological and dispersion models. Results were compared with hourly mean concentrations measured by one station of the local air quality monitoring network and a calibration procedure was performed. The result of this comparison demonstrates that the whole implemented system is a suitable simulation system for the prediction of CO concentrations in the urban area.

1. Introduction

Street canyons are typical urban structural forms consisting in a road section surrounded by buildings on each side, whose height is greater than or equal to the street width. Some authors have found that, when roof level winds are roughly perpendicular to the street and wind speed is greater than 1.5÷2 m/s, a vortex cell forms within the canyon (e.g. DePaul & Sheih[3]). The following isolated circulation pattern causes the trapping of pollutants into the canyon and the consequent dispersion process can be described by empirical models strictly dependent on local characteristics.

The work presented in this paper was developed in order to validate a system of models able to well explain the pollution process due to traffic in a street canyon of the urban area of Firenze, Italy. The models focused on carbon monoxide (CO), which is one of the most important pollutants emitted by motor vehicles in urban areas. For this purpose, a typical site equipped with a monitoring station was chosen and measurements of significant variables were made. Some models were developed to simulate traffic and atmosphere subsystems on the basis of theory and literature. Due to the influences of specific characteristics of the site and the vehicular fleet, the models obtained needed to be calibrated. Results proved that the final model system could be used in pollution predictions in the studied site.

2. Site and monitoring procedures

In the city of Firenze there is an air pollution monitoring network - made up of 8 stations - that was set up by Provincia di Firenze (the local district administration authority) in 1993 according to the Ministry of Environment Order dated 20th May, 1991 *Criteri per la raccolta dei dati inerenti la qualità dell'aria*. The main purpose of the network is to monitor the air quality in the city and check the observance of the Italian National Air Quality Standards, set down by the President of the Council of Ministers Order dated 28th March, 1983 and, for urban areas only, by the Ministry of Environment Order dated 15th April, 1994.

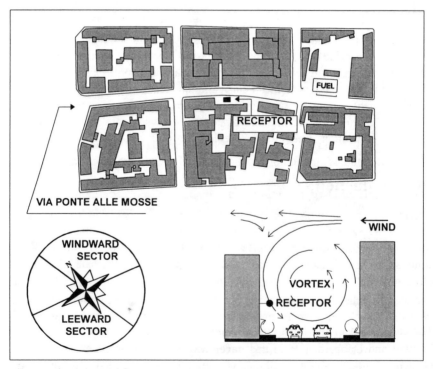

Figure 1: Map and elevation view of the street canyon.

The monitoring station chosen for the experimental procedure is located in Via Ponte alle Mosse, an important one-way urban arterial approaching the city centre (see Figure 1). The street is supplied with a device which can measure and store hourly traffic flow (or volume) and mean speed. The street is flanked with buildings and can be considered a street canyon. The distance between the canyon walls is about 20 m, approximately equal to the mean height of the buildings. The canyon is not properly symmetric since the heights of the buildings are meanly lower on the South-West side. The width of the roadway is divided into two lanes and parking is allowed. The monitoring station is placed 10 m from the axis of the roadway; the sampling inlet is 3 m over the ground level.

The air sample is analyzed to measure the concentration of CO, NO, NO_2, SO_2, and suspended particulate matter. The pollutant chosen for the present modelling application is CO, since it is the substance mainly related to road traffic. Indeed, motor vehicles typically account for 80÷100% of total CO emissions in urban areas (Horowitz[5]). The CO monitor is a PHILIPS gas filter correlation analyzer mod. K50109/00, which uses the U.S.A.-E.P.A. reference method RFGA-0981-054. The instrument is connected with a PHILIPS DMS-5 microprocessor, that collects the CO concentrations data from the monitor, calculates the mean hourly value and sends it to the main computer (VAX 4000) that manages the whole monitoring network. The CO mean hourly concentration is expressed in $mg \cdot m^{-3}$ to enable the comparison with N.A.Q.S. (15 $mg \cdot m^{-3}$ is the lower standard called *attention threshold*).

Hourly mean meteorological data (wind speed and direction at roof level, air temperature, stability class) are measured by the Ximeniano observatory located in the city centre, 25 m above ground level.

3. Models overview

The whole pollution process in the street canyon was simulated by means of a system of models including traffic, emission, atmospheric stability and dispersion algorithms.

The model used to simulate the dispersion process within the street canyon is based on the assumption that total pollutant concentration C is equal to the sum of two components. They are the local contribution C_c, originated from the vehicular emission sources existing inside the canyon, and the area contribution C_a, due to the dispersion of CO from the remaining part of the urban area:

$$C = C_c + C_a \tag{1}$$

The calculation of the local contribution is based on the model proposed by Ludwig and Dabberdt (1972) and developed by Hoydysh and Dabberdt[6] and Dabberdt et al.[2]. The model is related to the kind of urban morphology where the receptor is placed. The mathematical form of the model is different in the following three cases. When the receptor point is on the leeward side of the street, concentrations are given by:

$$C_{c,l} = K \frac{Q}{(u + 0.5) \cdot (L + 2)} \qquad (2)$$

where Q ($g \cdot m^{-1} \cdot s^{-1}$) is the local emission rate, u ($m \cdot s^{-1}$) is wind speed at roof level, L (m) is the euclidean distance between street axis and the receptor, $K=7$ is a nondimensional costant. Eq.(2) holds for wind directions forming an angle θ (°) with the perpendicular to the canyon axis from 0° to $\pm$ 60°. This range of θ is called *leeward sector* (see Figure 1).

When the receptor point is on the windward side of the street, concentrations are equal to:

$$C_{c,w} = K \frac{Q}{(u + 0.5) \cdot W} \frac{H - z}{H} \qquad (3)$$

where W (m) is the canyon width, H (m) the buildings height and z (m) the receptor height. The validity of the above equation is limited to the case of winds blowing from the sector opposite to the leeward one (*windward sector*).

For the remaining wind directions (*intermediate sector*), the local concentration is assumed equal to the mean of those showed above. The application of the described model was conducted with the following values of geometric parameters: $W=20$ m, $H=20$ m, $L=10.44$ m, $z=3$ m according to the characteristics of the site.

Area concentrations at the receptor point were determined using two alternative approaches. One initial model was developed using an eulerian approach under the assumption that there was a stationary atmosphere and istantaneous pollutant dispersion in the whole study area. A simple box model was developed, obtaining that:

$$C_a = \frac{Q_a \cdot D}{u \cdot h} \qquad (4)$$

Where Q_a ($g \cdot m^{-2} \cdot s^{-1}$) is the area mean emission, D (m) is the dimension of the urban extension along wind direction, and h (m) the height of the mixing layer (mixing height).

The alternative approach to the simulation of the area concentration was based on the hypothesis of a gaussian dispersion from a road network source. The model used is a rearrangement of the well-known APRAC3 diffusion algorithm (Simmon et al.[8]).

The two area dispersion models were completed with an algorithm able to simulate mixing height variations depending on time of day, Pasquill stability class, room temperature, wind speed, roughness length, and other boundary layer parameters. This algorithm follows the methodology described by Bellasio et al.[1] and is based on the latest results of the specific literature.

The area models were also connected to a traffic simulation model used to assign a selected origin/destination trips matrix to the main road network of Firenze. The assignment algorithm is based on the user equilibrium method (Sheffi[7]). It gives, for each link i of the network, the simulated flux F_i (vehicle/hour) in the 1-hour time intervals considered.

Local emissions Q_c and area emission Q_a were defined by using an emission model developed from the results showed by Tartaglia[9] and Eggleston et al.[4]. It is based on a set of emission factors expressed as a function of vehicles characteristics and mean operational speed. The model gives the total CO mass emitted hourly from each link starting from calculated vehicle fluxes and speeds (except for the canyon link, where monitored values of these two variables were employed). The mean composition of a vehicular fleet existing in Italy in 1991 (the latest available) was assumed as an input factor, where vehicle types are classified in accordance to EC directives.

4. Models calibration and results

An application of the models was carried out in Firenze in order to validate the estimating procedures and develop, if required, new models. Using eq. (1), we intended to compare the computed pollutant concentrations with the measured ones and make an analysis of the errors (difference between measured and computed data) produced by the models in order to verify their validity. Two sets of computed concentrations were made summing their local contribution to the box model and to the gaussian model respectively. The time period we referred to is given by the first three months of 1994. Although the value of $u = 1.5 \div 2.0$ m/s is the lowest threshold necessary to the onset of the vortical motion within the street canyon and it allows the use of the original algorithms (Hoydysh & Dabberdt[6]), the two models were also applied with lower wind speeds. In fact, the highest pollutants concentrations expecially occur with low wind speeds and this is the most important situation we intended to simulate.

Errors were plotted as a function of all the input variables. We found the greatest errors with high traffic flows, and therefore for low flowing speed, and with low wind speed. A first attempt to improve the models was carried out by fitting them on the basis of the single independent variables behaviours by means of regression analysis, but all efforts failed. So the calibration process went on mantaining the original models structure. The linear regression:

$$C = K_a \cdot C_a + K_c \cdot C_c + K_0 \tag{5}$$

was made for each sector and for each of the two sets of computed data.

From the t-test applied to the K coefficients it turned out that the variable C_a has little relevance in the regression process. This low significance of the area contribution may depend on a low influence of either mixing height or area emissions. In order to verify this statement, the local contribution was fitted to measured concentrations with the same criteria as above, by means of the linear regression:

$$C = K_c \cdot C_c + K_0 \tag{6}$$

in which K_0 can be viewed as a constant area contribution.

Table 1: Coefficients of the (C) model for C and C_c expressed in mg·m^{-3}.

SECTOR:	WINDWARD	LEEWARD	INTERMEDIATE
K_c	5.40	2.75	3.35
K_0	0.05	1.07	0.95

The described procedure led to the realization of three new dispersion models named *Canyon/Box* (CB), *Canyon/Gauss* (CG) and *Canyon* (C). The analysis of residuals showed that the behaviour of the three models is basically equivalent. If the models are applied in the whole range of wind speed the residuals distributions are characterized by negligible means, standard deviations σ between 1.78 and 1.80 mg·m^{-3}, a percentage (Ω) greater than 94% of residuals between ±2 σ (see Table 2).

Table 2: Statistics of the residuals distributions after calibration.

MODEL:	CANYON/BOX	CANYON/GAUSS	CANYON
μ (mg·m^{-3})	1.24	1.25	1.26
σ (mg·m^{-3})	1.78	1.78	1.80
Π (mg·m^{-3})	10.10	10.00	10.00
N (mg·m^{-3})	8.10	7.30	8.10
Ω (%)	94.40	94.00	94.40

The means μ of absolute values of residuals fall in the range 1.24-1.26 mg·m^{-3}. The high frequency of low concentration events found in the set of observed data implies that estimated and measured concentrations differ by an average factor of 0.3÷0.4, corresponding to the above range of absolute residuals. On the whole the models appear to be accurate if compared with similar results reported in literature (e.g. Horowitz[5]).

The application of the models to the classic case of wind speeds greater than 2 m/s reveals only a slight improvement in the distributions of residuals (the ranges of average absolute residuals and standard deviations are only some fractions of mg·m^{-3} narrower).

Modal analysis by wind direction sectors showed that the three models are characterized by the following features: the windward sector is the most reliable one as its residuals have a lower dispersion around the mean value and a lower absolute average; the intermediate and leeward sectors have more substantial errors as their maximum positive (Π) and negative (N) errors increase; the leeward sector has the worst standard deviation.

Once the calibration process has terminated, a validation of the three new models was made by simulating the receptor of Via Ponte alle Mosse for the month of October 1994 (see Figure 2). The errors which the above models produced in this time period fully confirm their validity, since the values of the parameters we characterize the errors with are lower.

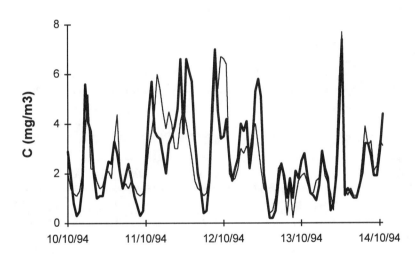

Figure 2: Example of comparison of CO observed concentrations ($\mathbf{|}$) with concentrations computed by the (C) model (|).

Although the three models give comparable results, we can state that the (C) model is the most suitable one to implement. Its advantages are: the fewer code lines number and therefore less computation time; a lower number of input data; only one modelled input datum (local emission) and therefore it is more reliable than the others models.

Conclusions

Three CO dispersion models for the street canyon of Via Ponte alle Mosse were set up. They are supported by a traffic assignment model, an emission model able to characterize vehicular traffic in Firenze and a new algorithm for the evaluation of the mixing height. The latter is necessary to estimate the area contribution by means of two different dispersion models.

The three models provide the same results, but the (C) model reveals the most suitable one for the present application owing to its computational characteristics. Although the behaviour of the three models is more reliable with $u \geq 2.0$ m/s, they were validated in the whole field of wind speed. They give accurate results also in air pollution critical situations such as the ones associated with lower wind speeds.

The (C) model can suitably be used as a CO concentrations prediction model in street canyons such as Via Ponte alle Mosse if supported by an adequate meteorological prediction model.

The present work is the starting point for the realization of a more complex model able to simulate the local air quality monitoring network and to evaluate pollutants concentrations due to traffic in Firenze.

References

1. Bellasio, R. et al. Boundary layer parametrization for atmospheric diffusion models by meteorological measurements at ground level, *Il Nuovo Cimento*, 1994, **2**, pp.163-174.
2. Dabberdt, W.F., et al. Validation and applications of an urban diffusion model for vehicular pollutants, *Atm. Env.*, 1973, **7**, pp.603-618.
3. DePaul, F.T. & Sheih, C.M. Measurements of wind velocities in a street canyon, *Atmospheric Environment*, 1986, **3**, pp.455-459.
4. Eggleston, H.S. et al. *CORINAIR Working Group on Emission Factors for Calculating 1990 Emissions from Road Traffic,* Final Rep. L.A.T.- CEE, 1991.
5. Horowitz, J.L. *Air Quality Analysis for Urban Transportation Planning,* MIT Press, Cambridge Mass., 1982.
6. Hoydysh, W.G. & Dabberdt, W.F. Kinematics and dispersion characteristics of flows in asymmetric street canyons, *Atm. Env.*, 1988, **12**, pp.2677-2689.
7. Sheffi, Y. *Urban Transportation Networks: Equilibrium Analysis with Mathematical Programming Methods*, Prentice-Hall, Englewood Cliffs, 1985.
8. Simmon, P.B., et al. *The APRAC-3/Mobile1 Emission and Diffusion Modeling Package*, Rep.No. EPA 909-9-81-002, San Francisco, 1981.
9. Tartaglia, M. Relazione fra emissioni inquinanti e velocità dei veicoli stradali, accepted for publication in *Ingegneria Ferroviaria*, Roma.

Characterization of construction conditions in a toxic and combustible gas environment for a transit project

B.M. Ghadiali,[a] J.B. Putnam,[b] C.W. Stark,[c] D.J. Sperry[c]

[a] *Engineering Management Consultant, Los Angeles, California 90017, UK*

[b] *Law Engineering and Environmental Services, USA*

[c] *Metropolitan Transportation Authority, USA*

Abstract

Methane gas has frequently been encountered during tunneling for the new Metro Red Line in Los Angeles. Field explorations during final design of the Mid-City Segment identified high concentrations of hydrogen sulfide (H_2S). Like methane, H_2S is flammable. Unlike methane, H_2S is highly toxic at relatively low concentrations and has a noxious odor at extremely low concentrations (2ppb). Additional studies included gas extraction testing; gas reservoir modeling; a data search for other known soil gas occurrences in the future tunnel development area; and a hazard evaluation was performed to analyze the feasibility of tunnel and station construction and operations in the presence of H_2S and other gases.

Introduction

One of the most innovative and technically-advanced mass transportation systems is being constructed in the greater Los Angeles area, including the Metro Red Line subway system. Many segments of the Metro Red Line are designated as gassy (primarily methane) because of their proximity to know active and inactive oil fields. Methane mitigation techniques include ventilation to ensure concentrations well below the lower explosive limit (LEL) and the use of a high density polyethylene (HDPE) membrane between initial and final tunnel liners that doubles as a methane gas cut-off and a waterproofing material.

In July 1993, subsurface investigations for the Mid-City Segment of the Metro Red Line (Figure 1) revealed high concentrations of hydrogen sulfide (H_2S) gas up to 19,000 ppm, in addition to methane (CH_4) as high as 90% by volume.

Figure 1 - Mid-City and other Metro Red Line Segments

Besides being a highly corrosive agent to concrete structures, and ferrous metals, H_2S is extremely toxic and can cause injury or death upon prolonged exposure to moderate concentrations (Table 1). The gas may be called a "one event" hazard, for unlike methane which requires a source and ignition to be hazardous, H_2S only requires a source. Also, the presence of H_2S, even at extremely small concentrations, can be a nuisance and promote ill will on the part of the public during construction and operation.

Project Description

Approximately 3.4km of twin/bored tunnels are planned in soft ground primarily beneath city streets. The tunnels will each have an outside diameter of about 6.4m. The proposed tunnel crowns are expected to vary from approximately 6m to 25m below the existing ground. The stations will be constructed by cut-and-cover methods and will require excavations up to about 23m below the existing ground surface.

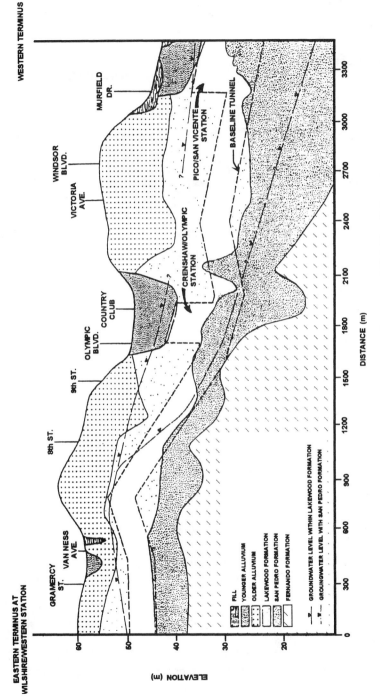

Figure 2 – General Geologic Profile Along Mid-City Segment

Table 1. Human Physiologic Responses to Exposure to Hydrogen Sulfide*

Concentrations of H_2S		Physiological Responses
ppm	mg/m³	
0.003-0.02	0.0042-0.028	Odor Threshold
20 - 30	28 - 42	Strong Offensive Odor ("rotten eggs")
50	70	Conjunctival Irritation
50 - 100	70 - 140	Irritation of Respiratory Tract
100 - 200	140 - 280	Loss of Smell (Olfactory Fatigue)
250 - 500	350 - 700	Pulmonary Edema
500	700	Anxiety, Headache, Unconsciousness
500 - 1000	700 - 1400	Respiratory Paralysis-Death

*After Reiffenstein[1]

Geologic Setting

The alignment is located within the Los Angeles Basin, an elongated northwest-trending structural depression which has been in-filled with sediment up to 4,000m thick since the Middle Miocene[2]. The alignment is in an area of the basin known as the La Brea Plain which slopes gently toward the Pacific Ocean to the south and southwest. Topographically low swale and channel features are present where the alignment crosses former drainages.

The Los Angeles Basin is situated at the convergent boundary between two tectonic plates, the Pacific and the North American. The relative motion of the two plates produces north-south compression and nearly continuous deformation along the boundary resulting in a complex network of seismically active fold and faults. This has produced geologic "traps" within oil-bearing formations, accumulating exploitable quantities of oil and gas. One such oil field traverses a portion of the Mid-City segment[3].

Figure 2 illustrates a geologic profile along the alignment. The sequence of geologic formations encountered over the area of the Mid-City Segment are generally described (in inverse order of disposition) as artificial fill, younger and older alluvium, Lakewood Formation, San Pedro Formation, and the Fernando Formation[4].   The general characteristics of each stratum are described below.

Artificial Fill Commonly found over the entire alignment, this includes utility trench backfill, structural fill, and road base.

Alluvium These deposits consist of layers of sands, silts, and clays with occasional gravel. Perched groundwater was found at varying depths within the primary sand intervals.

Lakewood Formation The Lakewood Formation is composed of late Pleistocene marine and nonmarine silts and silty sand with minor amounts of clay. Generally, the Lakewood acts as a barrier to gas and water flow.

San Pedro Formation This early Pleistocene deposit is typically very dense, fine- to medium-grained sand, with occasional lightly cemented zones and silty zones. Occasional layers of tar sands were found in this formation. A zone of groundwater lies within the San Pedro, perched upon the relatively non-permeable Fernando siltstone below.

Fernando Formation The Fernando Formation consist primarily of massive siltstone with sandstone interbeds. This formation occurs below the depths of most exploratory borings for the Mid-City Segment.

Supplemental Soil-Gas Testing

Basic literature research had established the explosive potential of methane (5% to 15% by volume) and H_2S (4.3% to 45% by volume) as well as the toxicity of H_2S. H_2S is twice as soluble in water as carbon dioxide and is heavier than air, whereas methane is lighter than air.

Various subsurface investigations had identified high concentrations of H_2S and methane gas at the proposed tunnel depth along the Mid-City alignment. These gases were detected particularly in the San Pedro Formation sands, and were reported only occasionally at low concentrations in the overlying Lakewood Formation and older alluvium. To test methods of H_2S mitigation to confirm the presence of H_2S, gas extraction and monitoring wells were installed[5] and a soil-gas survey was performed at various depths along the alignment.

Gas Extraction Testing This study was performed as a preliminary evaluation of in-situ gas pressure reduction and removal or dilution of in-situ hazardous gases. Gas wells were installed for the following tests:
- Type 1 - Passive venting
- Type 2 - Vacuum extraction
- Type 3 - Vacuum extraction with passive air recharge
- Type 4 - Vacuum extraction with air injection

Venting alone was shown to have no effect on soil-gas pressures or concentrations. Similarly, with vacuum extraction there was no indication of H_2S reduction in the soil. Using vacuum extraction with air recharge (active extraction combined with adjacent passive vent wells), the maximum H_2S decrease was on the order of a 20% reduction in concentration.

Vacuum extraction with air injection had a marked effect on measured H_2S concentrations. With fresh-air breakthrough, reductions of over 95% in H_2S concentrations were measured. Initial measurements in the 2,000 to 2,200 ppm range were reduced below 100 ppm in less than one day. These continued to stay low through subsequent readings. Although the H_2S reduction process has not been fully explained, this could be a viable mitigation procedure.

Soil-Gas Survey The field explorations consisted primarily of cone-penetration testing (CPT)/gas-probe soundings to identify soil and groundwater conditions, and to evaluate soil-gas characteristics. The procedure allowed soil-gas and water-level readings to be obtained as deep as 27m, mainly limited by the very dense San Pedro sands.

This investigation confirmed the presence of saturated soil along the northern reach of the alignment and unsaturated San Pedro sands from about Olympic Boulevard south. High levels of H_2S and methane were confirmed in the unsaturated San Pedro sands.

Reassessment Study

The Mid-City Reassessment Study was authorized to further evaluate the alignment's design, construction, and operations, and the feasibility of extending the alignment westward, considering the possible presence of H_2S. Specific field testing and research tasks were conducted. Several construction alternatives were considered for the proposed Mid-City route, including the 1993 bored-tunnel design and several aerial station and cut-and-cover alternatives.

The scope of work focused on evaluating geologic conditions, constructability, operability, and performing an overall system assessment. Five tasks were performed, as highlighted in Table 2.

Task 1—Research of Existing Data Existing data was researched to identify mitigation techniques that have been used successfully in similar projects and to identify geologic conditions conducive to the occurrence of H_2S. Very limited information on construction of subway or similar transit projects in H_2S-prone environments was found. Considerable information was identified on toxicity, odor, and safety threshold levels of H_2S and on related experience in the oil and geothermal industries. However, the oil and geotechnical industry experience had little direct bearing on civil/transit tunnel construction.

Table 2. Mid-City Reassessment Tasks

Task/Description	Purpose
Task 1—Research existing data (geologic, hydrologic, and gas)	To develop a database of existing gas-related information
Task 2a—Additional gas-probe soundings and monitoring wells in western extension area	To provide additional input on geology, hydrogeology, and gases for the western extension area
Task 2b—Additional air injection/ vapor extraction testing	To further evaluate H_2S mitigation techniques
Task 3—Large-diameter boring in known H_2S area	To evaluate reservoir venting and mucking operations
Task 4—Gas reservoir computer modeling	To evaluate gas flow characteristics on construction and operations
Task 5—Performing hazard assessment studies	To identify potential hazards and mitigations for H_2S

Geologic profiles and an overall plan were developed for the western extension area to display geologic conditions, groundwater levels, and incidences of H_2S and methane. Figure 3 shows the Mid-City segment and the geographic area or "envelope" within which alternative routes for the western extension of the Red Line were considered. Figure 4 depicts a simplified example of the northernmost study segment. Travelling westward, the geologic structure and stratigraphy change significantly and the reported gas incidents diminish.

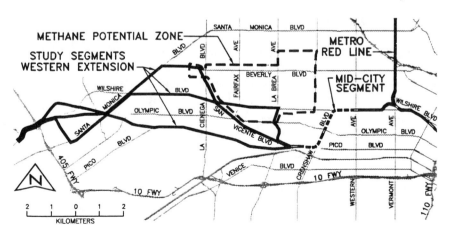

Figure 3: Metro Red Line-Western Los Angeles

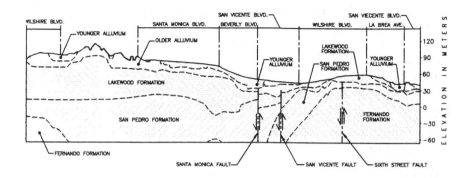

Figure 4: Western Extension Study Segment

Task 2—Field Testing Boring and CPT information was used to fill in the gaps for the western extension data research. These field explorations confirmed the high concentrations of H_2S in the San Pedro sands. Gas recovery tests were undertaken to determine the time required for H_2S to return to previous levels after completion of the extraction. These tests confirmed the inability of passive venting to mitigate the H_2S hazard.

Task 3—Large Diameter Boring/Muck Evaluation A 1m diameter boring, was excavated to a depth of about 25m in a previous gas extraction/air injection test area. Samples of muck collected from the alluvial strata were immediately sealed in $0.03m^3$ containers with headspace gas measured at about 15-minute intervals. H_2S and methane gas were not detected in any of the muck samples. Within the San Pedro Formation, maximum headspace H_2S concentrations of 1 and 4 ppm were recorded from muck samples sealed in 0.2m drums. No gaseous emissions or odors were detected from the large-diameter boring or spoil pile during excavation.

To evaluate an "undisturbed" (not previously vented) sample for "off-gassing" potential, two 20cm diameter borings were completed in areas known to contain high concentrations of H_2S. Samples obtained and transported to a laboratory using stringent protocols did not exhibit H_2S. Apparently, the H_2S either evolved from the soil quickly during sampling or was oxidized by the oxygen-saturated water that was added to the boring during drilling.

Since excavated material could contain odoriferous quantities of H_2S, potential methods of soil treatment were examined in the laboratory. Tests were conducted on synthesized, H_2S-containing, soil samples to evaluate adsorption methods for H_2S-containing muck. The tests included treating the synthesized specimens with calcium hydroxide (lime), iron chloride, and ferrous ammonium sulfate. Results appeared to indicate that H_2S may be efficiently removed from muck by using a saturated lime/water spray.

Task 4—Reservoir Modeling The objective of this task was to develop a reliable mathematical model of the gas reservoir surrounding the proposed construction. Calibration involved matching historical flow data from the gas extraction/air injection tests. Preliminary results indicate that the model can reproduce the rapid decrease in H_2S concentrations resulting from air injection, but the model exhibits a more rapid recovery of H_2S concentration than was actually measured. Apparently, the model does not yet include all processes that affect H_2S movement or development in the subsurface.

Table 3 presents some preliminary results of the gas leak modeling. The results indicate a non-toxic level of H_2S concentrations at the end of each scenario well below the action levels. However, all results are within a nuisance odor range.

Table 3. Summary of Preliminary Results of Gas Leak Modeling

Leak Type	Gas Pressure (kPa)	H_2S Level Outside Tunnel (ppm)	H_2S Inflow Rate (m^3/s)	Ventilation Rate (m^3/s)	Max H_2S Level Inside Tunnel (ppm)
Perimeter	1.2	10,000	2.2×10^{-5}	23.6	0.929
Perimeter	1.2	10,000	2.2×10^{-5}	47	0.466
Perimeter	0.5	400	3.3×10^{-7}	23.6	0.015
Hole	1.2	10,000	6.9×10^{-6}	47	0.142
Hole	1.2	400	2.8×10^{-7}	23.6	0.012
Hole	0.5	10,000	2.8×10^{-6}	9.5	0.297

Task 5—Hazard Evaluation A hazard evaluation was performed to assess overall feasibility of tunnel construction and operations in ground containing H_2S and methane. This methodology provides a systematic approach to identifying potential unsafe conditions or environmental concerns. The hazard evaluation team, composed of an interdisciplinary group of engineers and scientists, reviewed the design and operational issues and developed a fact base and initial set of key questions[6].

A "what-if" checklist procedure[7] in which questions about the design and a checklist of issues or scenarios was developed for the project design team. These discussions served to determine whether the design team had considered all issues raised, as well as the manner in which each was documented or incorporated in design. The hazard evaluation team asked further, if the scenario was not documented, would it be? Issues remaining for further consideration included acceptable safe levels of H_2S, physical characteristics and permeabilities of the various lining systems, and the design life of the project.

Gas Origins/Accumulation

Methane and H_2S can be produced by physical, chemical, or biological action and are commonly encountered in oil production strata. At shallower depths, these gases may be produced by anaerobic bacterial action in an environment rich in sulfates and hydrocarbons. Such an environment can easily exist in the submerged San Pedro marine deposits. Sulfates are readily available in a marine deposit and hydrocarbons are typically available as tar sands and occasionally as man-made contamination.

Isotopic analyses indicate that the H_2S appears to have a biogenic origin (that is, produced by relatively shallow bacterial action), whereas most of the methane appears to be thermogenic (that is, coming from deeper, petroleum-related sources). While the origins of the gases do not affect their health and safety properties, these origins may help predict the mode and intensity of future gas occurrences.

Only specific containment circumstances appear likely to allow significant gas accumulation. In fact, when there are granular soils above the water table and no confinement, there is no detectable H_2S or methane. When there are granular soils above the water table (San Pedro Formation) and an overlying fine-grained confining layer (Lakewood Formation), there appears to be significant gas accumulation.

Remaining Issues

There is no precedent for constructing a mass transportation tunnel project through toxic levels of soil-gas. Although the project is considered technically feasible, special means of construction may be required[8]. Risks still remaining to tunnel construction would include:
- Compressed-air tunneling—gas movement away from tunnel
- Exposure to H_2S and contaminated muck
- Environmental concerns of H_2S mitigation and public perception

Technical questions that still may require additional consideration include:
- At what level or separation from the San Pedro Formation may the threat of H_2S be eliminated, and at what level may it be minimized as a major element affecting design and construction?
- What level of confidence can be given of "no smell" both during construction and throughout the service life of the system

Currently, several alternatives are being considered for future study, including:
- Raised alignment with bored tunnels and cut-and-cover stations
- Bored/cut-and-cover tunnel alignment with cut-and-cover stations
- Bored/cut-and-cover tunnel alignment with aerial stations

The final decision will require preparation of environmental impact reports on the various alternatives and completion of the hazard evaluation for construction and operation.

References

[1] Reiffenstein, R.J., Hulbert, W.C., and Roth, S.H. (1992). "Toxicology of Hydrogen Sulfide, pp. 109-134, *Annual Review Pharmacology & Toxicology, Annual Review, Inc.*, 1992.

[2] Lamar, D.L. Geology of the Elysian Park-Repetto Hills Area, Los Angeles County, California, *California Division of Mines and Geology Special Report 101.* 1994.

[3] California Division of Oil and Gas. *Field Map 118, Las Cienegas, Salt Lake with portion Los Angeles, City, Beverly Hills East Area, San Vicente East Portion, and South Salt Lake*, Scale 1" = 600', 1987.

[4] Law/Crandall, Inc. *Report of Geotechnical Investigation, Proposed Mid-City Segment, Metro Rail Red Line Project, for the Los Angeles County, Metropolitan Transportation Authority, Vols. 1, 2, 3*; 1994.

[5] Enviro-Rail. *Alignment Reassessment for Metro Red Line Segment 3 Mid-City and Western Extension*, 1994.

[6] Law/Crandall, Inc. *Evaluation of Environmental Hazard of H_2S and Methane to Mid-City Segment of Metro Red Line for MTA, An Interim Report*, 1994.

[7] Center for Chemical Process Safety. *Guidelines for Hazard Evaluation Procedures*, American Institute of Chemical Engineers, New York, 1992.

[8] Engineering Management Consultant. *Mid-City Extension, Reassessment Study, Metro Red Line—Segment 3, An Interim Report on Construction Options*, 1994.

Some aspects of environmental problems caused by transport in Dubai: a geographical perspective

J.M. Al-Mehairi

Department of Geography, Faculty of Humanities and Social Sciences, UAE University, PO Box 15551, Al-Ain, United Arab Emirates

Abstract

The aim of this paper is to evaluate the impact of transportation means in Dubai on the environment. This paper mainly focuses on two major problems: **air pollution and noise pollution,** which are the results of increased use of Transports' means. The city of Dubai is a commercial centre and it is the feature that has made this city unique amongst the other emirates. The excessive transportation demand has caused several different problems over the various spatial features of Dubai. There are active factors which also result in an increment in transport. Certainly there are, such as population growth, land use and economical development etc. all these factors naturally processing and result in day by day increased demand for transport. The analysis of this problem will be presented from a the geographical point of view. This significant problem has a great influence on the local community in Dubai. Dubai was and is still recognized as an unpolluted emirate, but how long can it retain its environment with such rapidly growing activities

1. Introduction

Nowadays the issue of economic and social development in any community has become more complicated when and where it is to be copped with the transport system. Movement of people and goods, in urban areas requires more access to the transport facilities. In the other words we can say that the economic and social development cannot go without a well established road network and well managed transport system. On the other hand ' air and noise pollution' generated by the Transportation System is a top list issue in the world's Environment Conferences.

There are very few studies which have examined the relationships between the transport and environment of the Emirates region. Siddiqui, Khan, and Baig (1992), have traced the heavy metallic particles in the soil of Dubai roadsides.[1] Only few attempts were made by the Environmental Protection & Safety Department to monitor some aspects of pollution.

2. Scope of the study

Dubai is the most prominent emirate in the UAE because of its commercial and economical activities. In addition, it is a Gulf's land mark as a trade center or it may be called a 'transit point' for the whole world. Its land use has increased from 530 Hectares in 1960 to 11,000 Hectare in 1985, which shows a rapid development of the infrastructure within a limited period of 25 years. In a city or country, transport plays a very important role for the continued progression of economic activities All three main forms of transport namely air, sea and road, have over pressurized this emirate. For instance, air traffic volume is about 150 flights per day.

3. Major Factors in the problem of pollution

Pollution is the outcome of several different activities in the environment. The main source is human activity. Development of Industries produce a lot of advantages and disadvantages, and at the end a question arises about whether the environment is being improved or destroyed. Industry represented by the factories in the different areas of Dubai is sharing in passive pollution through its transport outcome.

There are also an additional number of noticeable factors that have had an influence on the environment, particularly air pollution, those are:
* The rapid urbanization of the city that started from the mid 1960s to
   date.
* Rapid growth in population.
* Extensive construction of roads, buildings, tunnel, bridges and other
   infrastructures.

After the establishment of the Federal Government in 1971, several policies were made to assist the improvement of infrastructures as stated above. Thus in the course of the past 25 years, a high progress was achieved but at the same time this led to the pollution's problem in the city and now many of its areas are suffering air, noise and other forms of pollution mainly caused by the excessive use of transport means.

3.1 Population

The rapid growth of population in Dubai and its expansion in industrial and commercial activities and the more general activities and urbanization are intensifying the use of vehicles: private cars, buses, and other forms of public transport. Figure 1.1 shows the total population of Dubai between 1975 and 1991 from which the huge increase in car ownership canbe inferred. This leads to a lot of problems and pressure on various services in the city and especially the problems of pollution in the urban areas which covers 43,485 Hectare of area. The annual growth of Dubai's population was estimated at 8.6 percent between 1975 and 1980 known as the 'peak period'.[2]

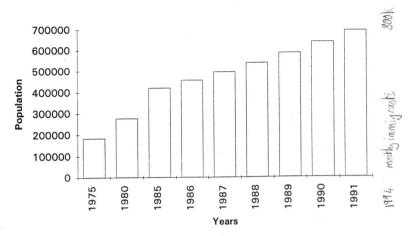

Figure 1.1 Population growth of Dubai Emirate from 1975 to 1991.
(Source: Dubai Municipality, 1992).

The concentration of population as shown in Figure 1.2, through out the areas in the city, is related to the human activities in the fields of industry, commercialization and transport places (creeks and sea ports).

3.2 Car Ownership

The last section gives us some indications on the growth of population and the need for the people to use transport means and the need for improved of mobility. Car ownership has greatly increased with the increase in the population of Dubai. The rate of car ownership in Dubai is 6.2 person per car.[3] The car ownership amongst the Dubai population depends on the nature of the occupational status of individuals. As a commercial function of Dubai, most of the trips carried out are towards the place of work and back. The relationship between the trips and socioeconomic status is a very important point to measure the degree of car use and its effects on the community.[4]

Table 1.1 Trips by transport modes in Dubai Emirate in 1991.

Transport mode	Percent	No. of trips
Private car	54.9	841,958
Taxi	19.5	298,431
Light commercial vehicle	13.9	213,583
Heavy vehicle	0.9	14,164
Non-scheduled bus	6.8	103,590
Scheduled bus	1.2	18,535
Abra (small local ferries)	2.8	43,168
Total	100	1,533,429

Source: DHC,1991

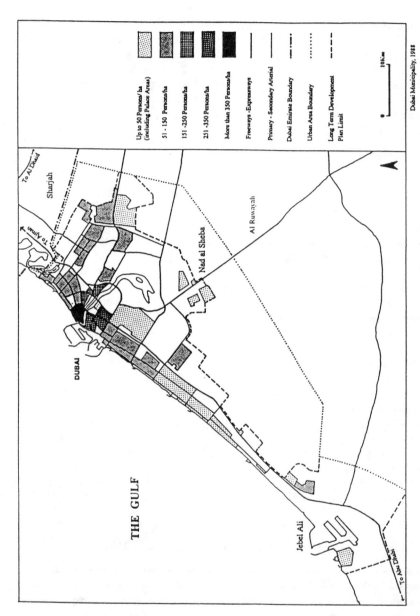

Figure 1.2   Population distribution of Dubai Urban Area. (Net Residential Densties)

The use of private cars has led to congestion on the main roads of Dubai especially in the CBD. Traffic congestion is one of the environmental problems in the urban areas of Dubai. This is related to the use of private cars instead of buses. The problem is well related to the high movement on the road as we will see it in the coming sections. The high traffic, surely produces a lot of the air and noise pollution. The majority of the population uses the private cars followed by the public transport (buses system) as can be seen in table 1.1.

3.3 Land Use

The city has gone through a complex process of planning over many years and by various consultants. This has resulted in CBD evident problems such as parking shortage and a lack of coherent land use planning.

We cannot ignore the fact that the topic of land use/transportation / environment is a very complicated issue.[5] A consequence of human activities as governed by land use and their interaction with transportation has meant increased vehicles emissions especially in areas of leisure and shopping facilities in the city.

Figure 1.3 shows the type of land use patterns in Dubai city. The residential area is estimated at 44.7 per cent, the commercial is 9 per cent and the road network 7.3 per cent of the total.   The policy of land use in Dubai has been changed many times to cope with the fast development of the city. Starting from the first Master Plan in 1960, then the plan of 1970 and then new plans of Dioxides in 1988 and recently a new strategic plan being prepared and expected to be approved soon. These types of plan have created some major problems. For instance, Al Mankhool Road in Bur Dubai that links two major commercial centres Bur Dubai and Satwa passing through residential areas; this movement is classified a **'high movement'** compared to other urban roads which adversely affect the environment residents who are located along this road.

Another significant factor that constitutes part of the problem is the type of land use and its association with the transport system of Dubai. The density of movement is related to the type of land use, commercial, residential or any other. There are some attempts made to link the land use with the volume of traffic through urban roads of Dubai. Day by day, the business and commercial activities such as internal and external trade are developing rapidly. This needs some intervention by the planning authorities to manage the movement of all types of vehicles (trucks or private cars). Otherwise, there will be a significant increase in congestion and roads accidents. Thus, there is a lot of integration to be achieved between these two aspects, that we will describe in the next pages.

4. Environmental problems of transport

The increased awareness from the officials and public, of the environmental problems in Dubai, in particular, and UAE in general has lead to a strategy being formalized to control this issue. As mentioned above, the Dubai is not presented as a polluted city at

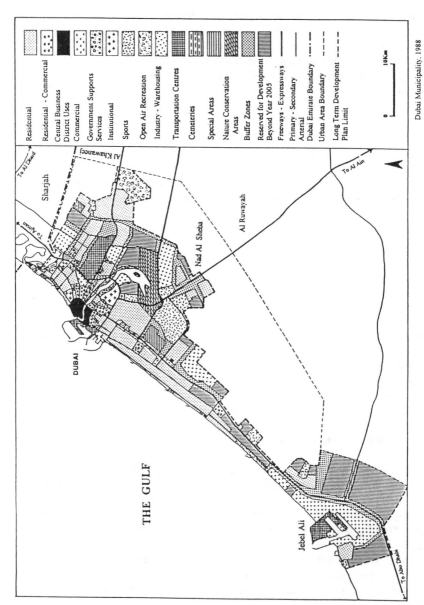

The following legend appears with the figure:

- Residential
- Residential - Commercial
- Central Business District Uses
- Commercial
- Government Supports Services
- Institutional
- Sports
- Open Air Recreation
- Industry - Warehousing
- Transportation Centres
- Cemeteries
- Special Areas
- Nature Conservation Areas
- Buffer Zones
- Reserved for Development Beyond Year 2005
- Freeways - Expressways
- Primary - Secondary Arterial
- Dubai Emirate Boundary
- Urban Area Boundary
- Long Term Development Plan Limit

0 ___ 10Km

Dubai Municipality, 1988

THE GULF

Sharjah

To Al Dhaid

To Ajman

Al Khawaneej

DUBAI

Nad Al Sheba

Al Ruwayah

To Al Ain

Jebel Ali

To Abu Dhabi

Figure 1.3 Land use patterns of Dubai city.

the main time but it is likely to edge towards becoming so, if the significance of hazardous pollution is not realized. Air Pollution Bulletin (1994)[6] has reported that Dubai air quality is good; but there are some pollutants are being released into the air by the different types of activities. The following details will point out some more facts in terms of their relation to " role of transport in the environment".

4.1 Air pollution

Transport is considered a main source of air pollution. The degree or quantity or type of pollutants is related to the odd fuels, density of movement; roads design etc. are also indirect sources of pollution. The pollutants of Carbon Monoxide, Ozone, and Nitrogen Dioxide which are mainly produced by vehicles emissions.

In Dubai the monitoring of air quality has investigated and measured the at various Industrial and densely populated places. If we thoroughly look into the matter we see that we should not ignore the fact that the air pollution is also linked with traffic density on the roads, urban roads, seaports and airports etc.

4.1.1 Road Network

In the CBD area the trips are estimated to be about 16% of total trips which are carried daily in urban areas.[7] 25% of these trips do have movement within the CBD area. The traffic volume in the CBD is high and so is the emission from the vehicles' movement. Carbon Monoxide is the main atmospheric pollutant. Among other pollutants CO_2 is mainly emitted from cars which have high movement along the roads, the incomplete combustion of fuels is also a constituent.

The movement in the urban roads of Dubai. It shows that in Deira, the CBD is highly populated more than the other areas of Dubai. It also show in the figures that the location of commercial activities are in the CBD and together with the densely populated areas which are also located there (Fig.1.2).These are concentrated the main reasons for congestion in the CBD. Moreover, the proximity of transport components like seaports (Rashid Port and the Creek) and the airport attract and encourage the movement of goods and people. See Figure 1.4 that shows the Urban Development Plan of Dubai.

Other pollutants such as Nitrogen Dioxide are concentrated in two major areas of Dubai, Deira and Al Safa, which later recorded higher readings than Deira, with the maximum daily average level 0.036 PPM in Deira and 0.058 PPM in Al Safa. This reflects that Al Safa has industrial activities and high traffic volume. The main road passing along these areas is a link between two major emirates Dubai and Abu Dhabi. A high range of Sulphur Dioxide is recorded in the industrially established areas as mentioned, alongwith Jebel Ali Port and the Free Trade Zone. This emission is the result of refineries and factories located in the area.

Lead is one of the remarkable pollutants emitted from the motor vehicles. It is the element added to petrol to raise its octane value. There are two sites in Deira, one is in the centre of the CBD and the other is out of the CBD, but both of them are located in the urban area of Dubai city; namely: Baniyas Square and Al maktoum street. The

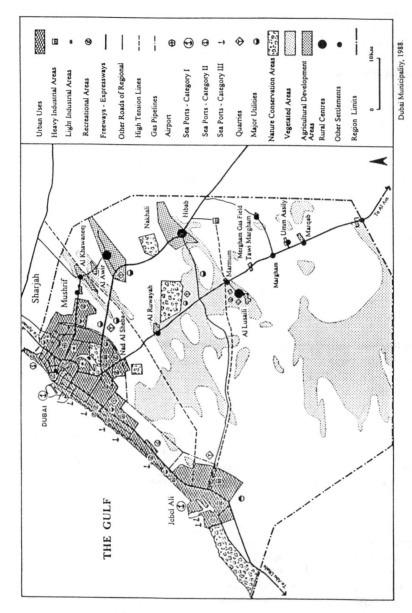

Figure 1.4 Urban Development Plan up to year 2005.

Lead levels range recorded from 0.70-1.22 ug/m3 in Baniyas Square and 0.42-0.69 ug/m3 in Al Maktoom St. Of course, the heavy density of traffic in the CBD is more than that out of it. On the other hand, Siddiqi (1992) has mentioned in his study that the lead concentration in roads is not only related to traffic density but also on the traffic signals where vehicles consume more fuel. Vehicles' fuel consumption is more when it starts, pickup in the top gear and get the speed, however, it consumes less fuel when running on the roads.

4.2 Noise pollution·

The rapid economical growth made this Emirate a major commercial center in the Gulf. As an oil State, development processing creates 'unacceptable noises' for the people who lives in residential areas, and that leads to a lot of health problems. In Dubai, the urbanization development has greatly spread out in all directions and areas.

The main sources of noise are from transportation means: road traffic movement within the road network, which is the outcome of mechanical factors such as the engine, tires, exhaust and the condition of cars. In Dubai city, it might be said that there are two major sources of noise. Mainly the motor vehicles representing the traffic density on the roads, sound of exhaust, engines, hard accelerations; and secondly, the noise caused by the aircraft movement through the Dubai airport. All these comes part of the problem, but here is an attempt to focus the noise problem that comes from the transport means and the geographical dimension of that.

4.2.1 Road network

A survey has been carried out by the Dubai Municipality concerning the noise pollution in the city. It revealed that the noise levels inside the city are higher than those outside the city. This is due to the increased traffic in the city, and that is related to the location of business activities. Figure 1.5 shows the noise levels in the urban areas of Dubai. The movement of vehicles is mostly concentrated on the inner areas of the city (CBD) as highly populated areas.

That was recorded around 64.9 dba in Diera and 55.7 dba in Bur Dubai. On the other hand it is noticed that the areas located far from the major roads' have traffic noise average from 50 dba to 55 dba. In rural areas it has ranged from 44 dba to 49 dba. In terms of vehicles' movement on the urban area roads the highest movement is recorded on major external roads (highways) especially the section linking Dubai with Sharjah. The second heighest movement is on the roads leading into the CBD. Consequently these movements are generating a lot of noise from the cars and heavy vehicles. The main point here is related to the land use specifically along with residential areas (see Figure 1.2 land use). The 'high traffic roads' located among the residential areas represent a significant environmental problem related to transport. For example, Rashid Seaport and the Dry Dock are both located in areas opposite of CBD's areas, the residential areas are located exactly behind the seaport. The traffic movement along the roads linking the seaport with other places cause high noise levels (58.1 dba) in

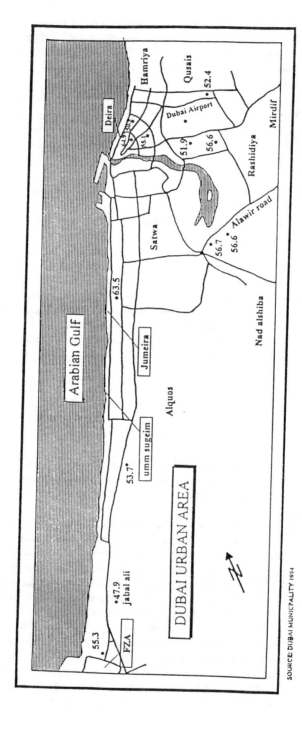

Figure: 1.5   average noise level during daytime, dbA

Karama area. See Figure 1.5. The most distinguished point is the CBD in respect of high level of noise and that is due to high movement of vehicles.

4.2.2 The Airport

We can say that the Airport is the second main source of noise problem in Dubai. As a result of the rapid development of Dubai's infrastructure, the air movement study shows a very high increase in both the passengers and cargo movements on Dubai Airport. The nature of air movement in Dubai is very active. The air traffic becomes more operative in during the night hours especially between 08:00pm to 7:00am.

About 120 aircraft land or take off in these counted hours. Figure 1.4 shows the location of the airport in the middle of the city. The path of the aircraft's' movement passes through many residential areas and that causes a sort of disturbance. there is no precise data which shows that levels of noise. Many interviews have been conducted and they indicate the complains of aircraft noise by affected population.

5. Forecasting of environmental problems in the future

The transport must be given more attention to reduce its environmental problems. The political authorities of many countries in the world have instituted the vehicle emission to control the air pollution caused by the transport. There is no doubt that Dubai is growing day by day, the business activities are increasing and this means more congestion, parking problems and environmental difficulties.

6. Conclusion

The conclusive main points regarding to the environmental problems in Dubai are:

1) As a result, for the long time we did not have a specialized unit or department to monitor environmental problems. Two years ago, the Dubai Municipality established few stations within urban areas of Dubai. the Municipality must set up more stations to monitor the emissions of vehicles particularly in the residential areas.

2) The transport/land use association in the urban areas is a very complicated issue. Dubai Authorities have approved several plans to regulate the development of urban areas in Dubai city. The transport system is one of the integral parts in the development; however, there is more congestion and the inappropriate location of some of commercial centres and a lack of parking the spaces in the very busy areas. Thus, we must be aware of all these issues when studying the plans of urban development.

3) The use of private transport has created a lot of problems in the urban areas such as using 54.9% of all modes of transport. However, public transport has a very tiny use by the community. To improve the environment and keep it clean and share of congestion must encourage the public transport system and make some sort of restriction on areas which face such problems.

Reference

[1]   S.M. Siddiqui, S.A. Khan, Shakeel Ahmad and M.U.Beg. Heavy Metals Concentration In Roadside Soil Of Dubai, paper presented on "Health Fighting Conference" Al Ain, Sept 1992.

[2] Dubai Municipality, *Comprehensive development Plan for Dubai Emirate, Dubai Urban Area Plan,* Report 2, Vol.1, Dubai. P.2/35.

[3] Dubai Municipality, *Comprehensive Development Plan for Dubai Emirate,* Dioxides, 1988.

[4] P.W. Daniels & A.M. Warnes, *Movement in cities,* Methuen, London, 1980. p.36.

[5] Jean-Paul Rodrigue, The utility value of Land use: Theoretical foundations and application to Shanghai, *Journal of Transport Geography,* 1994, 2(1) 41.

[6] Dubai Municipality, environmental Protection & Safety Section; *Annual Air Quality summary,* Dubai, January 1995.

[7] Dubai Municipality, *Comprehensive Development Plan for Dubai Emirate, Dubai Central Business District Plan, Report 7,* Dioxides, 1988.

Procedures for the estimation of vehicle emissions in an urban environment

D. Rayfield, J.W.S. Longhurst, D.E. Conlan, A.F.R. Watson, T. Hewison
Atmospheric Research and Information Centre, Department of Environmental and Geographical Sciences, Manchester Metropolitan University, Chester Street, Manchester M1 5GD, UK

Abstract

Air pollution from road transport is a major environmental problem in urban areas. The steps undertaken in developing an emissions estimation procedure for road traffic in Greater Manchester is presented. This process builds on the existing traffic flow database, by incorporating the facility to estimate current and future emissions from road traffic by entering emission factors, the composition of the vehicle fleet and the daily traffic flow profile. The use of this procedure allied with tools such as Geographical Information Systems, will be important in helping to formulate local air quality management plans and improve the capability of urban transport planning.

Introduction

Pollution from road transport is possibly the major environmental problem of the present day. This is particularly so in urban areas, where the effects of traffic in terms of pollution and congestion are most acutely observed. Consequently much attention is now focused on attempting to alleviate this increasing problem. The recent Royal Commission Report [1] brought together many of the issues that relate to traffic pollution, and has come at a time when there appears to be an acceptance by central government, that current road building programmes cannot continue in their present form [2]. Government policy in the last two decades has been to provide capacity to meet travel demand based on projections of economic growth [3]. This is despite the continuous arguments, expressed as far back as 1977 [4], that estimations of future road traffic were flawed and that procedures to evaluate new roads failed to take proper account of environmental factors. This has been a continuing theme of the Standing Committee on Trunk Road Appraisal (SACTRA) reports [5] and culminated in their most recent report that concluded that the building of more roads was likely to generate more traffic than that which it was supposed to displace [6].

There is an increasing need then, for the effects of road traffic in urban areas and the policies used to reduce the impact that emissions of pollutants have on urban air quality to be re-examined [7]. There has been extensive research into which pollutants from road traffic cause concern. What is needed now are the tools to help policy makers, particularly at the local level, assess the scale of the problem and furthermore how those decisions that they take will effect levels of road traffic and pollution. This research is designed to help local authorities, initially in the Greater Manchester conurbation, do this by estimating emissions from road traffic and then forecasting what effect changing transport parameters have on levels of pollution emitted. The use of emission inventories which incorporate methodological assumptions that limit their final accuracy, are nonetheless useful and can be used for the evaluation of policies aimed at emission regulation and transport management [8].

Emission estimation procedures

The use of emission estimation procedures in providing detailed estimates of vehicle pollution is an ongoing and increasingly complex task. Refinements to the various models that are now used by national and supra-national organisations, such as the EU, will continue to improve their accuracy and reliability. As with any major study involving many parameters and sources of input data, a detailed and logical methodology is required to calculate emissions and estimate the effect of altering traffic parameters in future years [9]. The derivation of emission factors is a particularly difficult task, and studies such as this can only make use of the most current estimates. In calculating emission factors many differing vehicles in terms of age, performance and reliability are tested in the laboratory and on the open road. The resulting pollutant emissions are analysed and compared, to determine an emission factor that is representative of driving cycles on a particular type of road, for different types of vehicles.

Measurements carried out in tunnel studies in California and remote sensing of passing vehicles, indicate that emission levels are higher than those calculated by tests in laboratories on dynamometers. Furthermore as a small percentage of vehicles (20%) were found to contribute to 80% of CO and VOC emissions, and that these high emitters are not generally tested on dynamometers, then their emission levels are either not included in calculating fleet wide average emission factors or are only estimated, thus leading to the under-estimation of vehicle emissions[10]. These high emitters which do not meet emission standards (based on the performance of new vehicles) fail largely due to poor and infrequent maintenance [11]. Engine maintenance has been shown to be the most significant parameter affecting the level of emissions [12].

Traffic flow in Greater Manchester

Information on the volume and type of traffic in the conurbation is collected and used in models to provide forecasts of future road usage and assist in the complex task of planning the areas transport policy [13]. Traffic counts are carried out on motorways, 'A' roads, 'B' roads and some minor roads in the Greater Manchester area. In all there are counts on 70 motorway links, 595 'A' road links and 291 on 'B' road links spread across the conurbation. These are done using a combination of automatic and manual counts. The count is conducted for both directions of the carriageway and whenever a particular count is undertaken it is repeated three years later on the same day of the year. It should be noted that on a given piece of the road network or link the count site may not be in the centre of that link. But the results obtained from that count are considered to be representative of the whole length of the link. The counts themselves consider several classes of vehicle: cars, buses, motor cycles, pedal cycles and three categories of goods vehicles.

The counts of traffic flow for the various types of vehicles can be looked at for many different time periods. The standard twelve hour count which is carried out from 7am to 7pm can be broken down into morning rush hour, off peak and evening rush hour. The flow on the motorway and 'A' road links can be looked at hour by hour for the whole 24 hour period as a sample of these are monitored automatically. By undertaking a small sample of surveys over 16, 18 and 24 hour periods, a set of conversion factors have been derived which enable a traffic flow figure for any of these periods to be calculated from the standard 12 hour count. Similarly there are conversion factors to enable an annual average daily traffic flow to be calculated for a particular day of the week or month of the year [14].

Traffic flow data

The traffic flow data is available for the 956 links of the "Principal road network" of the conurbation. Two forms of data are available, 24 hour annual average weekday traffic (AAWT) and 24 hour annual average daily traffic (AADT). This is presented as follows:-

DoT code number e.g. 6029
Road number e.g. M63
Ordnance survey grid number e.g.
35684020
Duration of count e.g. 12 (Hours)
Day of week count conducted e.g. 1
(1=Monday,....,7=Sunday)
Date of count e.g. 30/9/91
Car flows e.g. 9518

Light Goods Vehicle flows e.g. 2061
Medium Goods Vehicle flows e.g. 1379
Heavy Goods Vehicle 3 axle flows e.g.
154
Heavy Goods Vehicle 4+ axle flows e.g.
972
Bus & coach flows e.g. 90
Motor cycle flows e.g. 52
Total flow e.g. 14226

The transformation of these data is complicated by their collection and storage in a variety of formats. These need to be unified prior to further use in this procedure.

Emission factors

Before applying the relevant emission factors to the different vehicle categories a suitable set of emission factors that correspond to the vehicle data has to be found, so as to maximise the vehicle flow information. Considering the number of organisations that provide emission factors and the different vehicle classifications that they use, a compromise had to be reached in adapting them to suit the traffic data available. Currently, the emission factors that are being used are those provided by the National Atmospheric Emissions Inventory [15], and factors published by the Departments of Transport and Trade and Industry [16]. These comprise emission factors for 12 categories of cars and other vehicles on 4 different driving cycles.

Vehicle fleet information

Within the car category there are further subdivisions to be made. This is into car engine size and the distinction between different fuel types and control technology used. First, the percentage of cars that are petrol or diesel fuelled, use leaded or unleaded petrol, and those that have a catalytic converter fitted needs to be known. So that the total number of cars in each of these groups can be derived from the number of car movements which is given in the traffic flow data as a single total. Secondly the number of cars that are small (<1.4l), medium (1.4-2.0l) and large (>2.0l) was obtained, using information from the Department of Transport [17] and the Department of the Environment [18] to enable the application of more specific emission factors.

Emission calculation

The emission estimation procedure and the process needed to prepare the original traffic flow data for use, which has previously been described, is shown in Fig.1. The box termed "emission estimates" on this diagram, encapsulates the equation for determining the emission totals and is the culmination of all the steps described earlier. The equation for determining estimated emission totals can be given as thus:-

$$T_{s,t} = V_v \times L_r \times EF_{p,v,r} \qquad (1)$$

Where

T=Emission Total (Tonnes)   L=Road Length (km)
V=Vehicle Flow (AAWT, AADT)   EF=Emission Factor (g km^{-1})

and can be given by

s=scale descriptor (road, district, conurbation)   r=road type (motorway, "A", "B")
t=time period (hour, day, week, month, year)   p=pollutant (CO, CO_2, HC, NOx, PTC, SO_2)
v=vehicle type (fuel, control technology,engine size)

The following is an example of the calculations used to obtain the emission total for a section of the M61 in Bolton. This is based on AAWT data and is the estimated amount of NOx emitted in a 24 hour period by the car group (Petrol, No Catalyst, Leaded fuel with engine size less than 1400cc).

$$(V) \ 11566.1 \times (L) \ 0.724 \ km \times (EF) \ 4.21 \ g \ km^{-1} = 0.035 \ Tonnes$$

Output and results

In addition to all of the individual road data, there are totals for all the districts in the conurbation, and for the Greater Manchester area as a whole. These include the total amount of emissions in each of the 19 vehicle groups for each road type within each of the ten districts. The total emissions for all roads in all 10 districts in the base year of 1992 is shown in Fig.2. Additionally the amount of pollutant emitted per kilometre of the road network is given. This is easily calculated by dividing the net totals given above, by the length of the appropriate part of the road network. Calculating this total, enables comparisons to be made between each district and road type, of the amount of pollution emitted by the vehicles on that part of the road network. The emissions per kilometre of NOx on motorways in three of the ten districts is presented with the aid of a Geographical Information System in Fig.3 as an example.

Future modelling

Future estimates of pollutant levels will be the next stage in this research. Referring back to the diagram of the estimation procedure (Fig.1), the effect of changing road traffic forecasts, updated emission factors, a changing road network in the conurbation and the changing composition of the vehicle fleet will be incorporated into the model, and the effect of different scenarios evaluated. Perhaps the most important and interesting aspect of this work will be seeing the effect of strategies to reduce traffic and its related pollution. For example, recommendations made by the Royal Commission [1] and locally by MAPAC [7], to encourage more use of public transport, cycling and restrictions on traffic movement will effect the levels of traffic flow and hence emissions. Furthermore, a procedure will be developed which identifies those roads that pose a pollution "problem", and so can theoretically be targeted with abatement strategies, to see what effect these have on vehicle flows and emission levels.

Conclusion

This paper has detailed the process undertaken in establishing an emissions estimation procedure for road traffic emissions in Greater Manchester. This procedure will be useful in the context of transport planning and local air quality management [19]. The policy advisory tool that this procedure will eventually become, will aid local authorities in trying to assess the implications of their traffic and pollution management policies. For example, the setting of overall targets to be met by urban areas, which may include the definition of maximum emission guide levels for the transport sector that will require appropriate methods to meet them in a defined period [20], would mean that local authorities will need policy advisory tools such as this in order to effectively implement any future strategies.

References

1. Royal Commission on Environmental Pollution (1994) *Transport and the Environment*. H.M.S.O. London.

2. DoT (1989a) *Roads for Prosperity*, H.M.S.O., London.

3. DoT (1989b) *National Road Traffic Forecast (Great Britain)*, H.M.S.O., London.

4. DoT (1977) *Report of the Advisory Committee on Trunk Road Assessment.*, H.M.S.O., London.

5. DoT (1986) *Urban Road Appraisal:Report of the Standing Committee on Trunk Road Appraisal.*, H.M.S.O., London.

6. DoT (1994) *Trunk Roads and the Generation of Traffic:Report of the Standing Committee on Trunk Road Appraisal.*, H.M.S.O., London.

7. Ramsden, P.S., Longhurst, J.W.S., Dinsdale, J.A. and Elliott, R. (eds.) (1993) *A Breathing Space. Vehicle related air pollution in North West England.* MAPAC, Manchester.

8. Joumard R., Zafiris D. and Samaras Z.C. (1994) 'Comparative assessment of two forecasting models for road traffic emissions: a French case study.' *Science of the Total Environment* (146/7) pp351-358.

9. De Vlieger I., Lenaers G. and Craps R. (1994) 'Vehicle emissions estimations and measurements in Belgium.' *Science of the Total Environment* (146/7) pp217-223.

10. Knapp K.T. (1994) 'On-road vehicle emissions: US studies.' *Science of the Total Environment* (146/7) pp209-215.

11. Hickman A.J. (1994) 'Vehicle maintenance and exhaust emissions.' *Science of the Total Environment* (146/7) pp235-243.

12. Pattas K.N., Kyriakis N.A. and Samaras Z.C. (1994) 'Actual emissions of vehicles of the N1 category.' *Science of the Total Environment* (146/7) pp191-199.

13. Greater Manchester Transportation Unit (1993) *Transport Statistics, Greater Manchester 1992*, GMTU report No.265, Manchester.

14. Greater Manchester Transportation Unit (1990) *Transport Statistics, Greater Manchester 1989*, GMTU report No.161, Manchester.

15. Eggleston, H.S. (1992) *Pollution in the Atmosphere: Future Emissions from the UK*, LR888 (AP) Warren Springs Laboratory, Stevenage.

16. ETSU (1994) *U.K. Petrol and diesel demand.* DoT and DTi, London.

17. DoT (1993) *Transport Statistics, Great Britain 1993*, H.M.S.O., London.

18. DoE (1992) *Digest of Environmental Protection and Water Statistics*, No. 14. H.M.S.O., London.

19. Longhurst, J.W.S., Lindley, S.J. and Conlan, D.E. (1994) 'Local Air Quality Management' in Air Pollution II Vol.2, pp525-532, (Ed. Baldasona, J.M., Brebbia, C.A., Power, H. and Zanetti, P.) *Proceedings of the 2nd Int. Conf. Air Pollution 94* Barcelona, Spain, 1994. Computational Mechanics Publications, Southampton.

20. Samaras Z.C. and Zierock K.H. (1994) 'Evolution of road traffic emissions in urban areas of the European Community.' *Science of the Total Environment* (146/7) pp253-261.

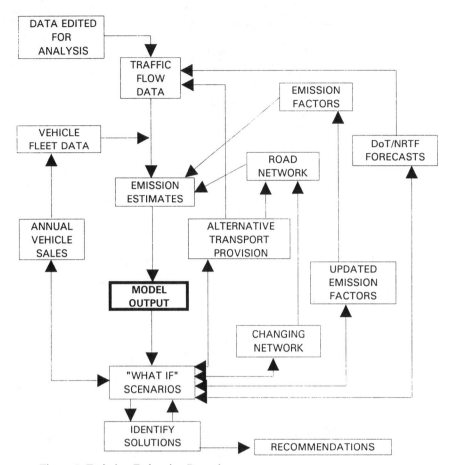

Figure 1. Emission Estimation Procedures

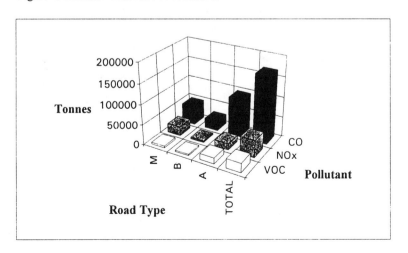

Figure 2. AADT 1992: Greater Manchester Yearly Emissions for All Vehicles

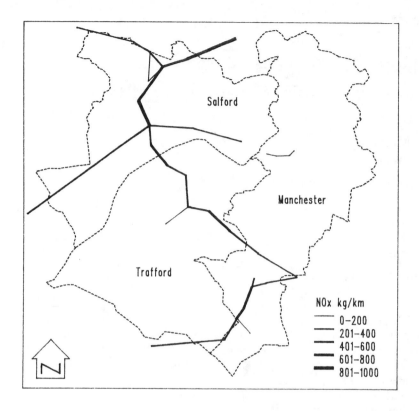

Figure 3. The emissions per kilometre of NOx on motorways in three of the ten districts.

Flexible dynamic scheduling in public transport: environmental benefits of a more efficient system

A. Marqués,[a] M. Torregrosa,[a] A. Camarena,[a]
K. Darby-Dowman,[b] J. Little,[b] S. Moody[b]
[a] *Eletronic Traffic, S.A., Valencia, Spain*
[b] *Department of Mathematics and Statistics, Brunel University, UK*

Abstract

SUPERBUS is a 30 months R&D project funded by the European Union under the ESPRIT programme. The project to develop a Dynamic Scheduling System for public transport (PT) started in November 1993 with an European multidisciplinary consortium involving PT operators. The aim of a conventional PT scheduling system is to produce a schedule consisting of timetables and the associated allocations of buses and crews given a set of available resources (buses, crews) and the desired level of service (bus frequencies). The *SUPERBUS* system will offer additional features of flexibility and integration.

1. Introduction

Urban transport is not only an important economic and social issue but also an increasing source of pollution. In order to avoid excessive environmental damage it is necessary to promote a modal shift from private to public transport (PT). This can only be done if PT is attractive and efficient.

Flexibility is needed to cope with evolving requirements for PT operators. Integration with Automatic Vehicle Location (AVL) systems offers major improvements in the ability to respond to incidents and unexpected events that disrupt a planned schedule. The system can carry out a dynamic or reactive rescheduling process so that the situation may be assessed and actions recommended in real time. The aim is to minimise disruption by returning to an orderly level of service as quickly as possible.

The underlying technology in the *SUPERBUS* system is a combination of advanced optimisation tools, constraints logic programming and the object oriented paradigm.

2. Initial Planing & Scheduling

The initial bus & crew scheduling module of the SuperbuS system provides one of the main modules within the application and is accessed through its user interface. This provides the facility to specify the inputs graphically. The menu items and buttons provide the interface for the user to initiate the processes comprising bus and crew scheduling.

The initial bus & crew scheduling module provides the scheduler with the tools to create a timetable, allocate a set of buses to it, allocate crews to be responsible for the buses and finally create the duty roster for the crews. The problem is defined in terms of a number of specified urban transport characteristics such as, service levels and journey patterns for different periods of the day and types of day. The problem, due to its complexity, is not usually solved as a whole, but broken down into inter-related sub-problems, each with its own characteristic method of solution. These sub-problems are timetabling, bus scheduling, crew scheduling and rostering and are usually solved in a sequential manner.

The initial input for timetabling includes a set of lines with required services levels and journey patterns, from which a timetable is created. The timetabling process should also take into account any synchronisation within or between lines which will take place. This input is available for every different day type (e.g. weekday, Saturday, Sunday, Public Holiday) which requires a different timetable. The timetabling process is carried out using specification techniques from Constraint Logic Programming (CLP). This involves dividing the whole problem into a series of independent sub-problems and then deriving optimal transitions between different time periods of the day. These sub-problems are solved using constraints and combinatorial search techniques. The final timetable is created by placing the pre-computed sections, obtained from the solution of the sub problems, in sequence. From this, sets of vehicle blocks are constructed. Vehicle blocks represent pieces of work one vehicle does between leaving and arriving back at a garage or parking point.

This set of vehicle blocks are then linked together during the bus scheduling process to form a complete work program for a bus on a day. The bus scheduling process allocates (logical) vehicles to one or more vehicle blocks. The maximum number of overlapping vehicle blocks provides an upper limit on the number of vehicles required to cover the timetable. However, more vehicles may be required. For example, if certain lines (and hence vehicle blocks) require particular types of vehicle (e.g. single, double-deckers, mini, articulated) due to physical restrictions on the route (such as low bridges) or due to the estimated demand for that particular time of day then perhaps more buses will be needed. Once these logical vehicles have been allocated to vehicle blocks, then actual buses can be allocated on a daily basis by the depot manager (bus rostering).

The resulting bus schedules provide the basic input to the crew scheduling part of the system and represent the tasks to be covered by the crews i.e. the vehicle blocks represent the times at which a crew must be responsible for a bus. The crew scheduling process involves the generation of a set of feasible duties from the tasks to be covered within the constraints such as legal shift patterns, recommended practices etc. These feasible duties contain information on periods of driving, driver transfers, clocking on & off, cash accounting and breaks. Mathematical Programming (MP) techniques are used to select the necessary duties to cover the set of required tasks at minimum cost. The model used here is a set covering model with under and over cover penalties which provides more flexibility in the types of schedules obtained. Crew rostering is performed by 'fairly' distributing these crew duties amongst a set of real crews.

Throughout the analysis and design phase of the project an Object Oriented approach following the Rumbaugh methodology has provided a framework for the whole system and an OO database will be used to support the system. Combining these advanced technologies of CLP, MP and the OO approach enables more complex problems to be handled. For example synchronization is considered resulting in smoother connections between services and therefore more attractive service for the customer. This approach also enables more flexibility for the evolving needs of the public transport operators.

Initial bus & crew scheduling provides a prescribed schedule which is used at the start of each day as the planned programme of tasks to be carried out. Deviations from this prescribed schedule are monitored by the automatic regulation module of the system. Incidents are reported as soon as they are detected together with guidance to the possible corrective action. Consequently the user is able to take action earlier on without waiting until this incident accumulates into a more severe incident. Therefore many of the problems that arise will be less disruptive to the transport system providing a more efficient and effective service. The major environmental impact however results from the automatic regulation and rescheduling components of the SuperbuS system.

3. Real-Time Control

The real-time control system of SuperbuS complements the planning and scheduling tools presented in section 2. Real-time functionalities such as incident detection and corrective actions are undertaken by each of its two modules: Incident Detection and Automatic Regulation.

The incidents are processed in the Incident Detection module. The consequences on the schedule, the scope and the relation to other incidents are identified. An overall severity evaluation is presented to the operator for validation or cancellation. If the operator decides to cancel the incident it is stored in a historical database. If the operator decides to tackle the incident, then it must be solved by the Automatic Regulation module. This module determines whether the incident can be solved by the Tactical Solver ("soft" incident) or should be attempted at the On-line Rescheduling ("hard" incident). In the first case, a list of tactical solutions will be offered to the operator through the MMI for validation or cancellation. In the second case, the real-time system will request an adjustment of the initial schedule by the Re-scheduling module. The operator may also decide to reschedule if the list of tactical solutions offered is not satisfactory.

The Incident Detection and Automatic Regulation modules of the real-time system provide important tools for sparing the operator from repetitive control actions. The decision-making tasks are simplified but still under the operator responsibility. Within the SuperbuS application, the Incident Detection module represents the interface between the real world and the regulation functions, whereas the Automatic Regulation module alleviates the On-line rescheduling of processing small but probably frequent tasks.

3.1. Automatic Incident Detection
The extent of the automatic incident detection process depends on whether the public transport operator (PTO) has an automatic location system for the buses or not, and whether it is connected to a traffic control system. A monitoring system can provide

SuperbuS automatically with information concerning the position and load of the vehicles. A traffic control system can give information regarding traffic conditions and road work. Comparing these data with the state expected form the planned schedule, the Incident Detection module can detect position and load deviations of buses and predict running time changes due to traffic load changes. Generally, the Incident Detection module will receive incident information manually through the MMI. PTO experience shows that important incidents occur unpredictedly and are transmitted to the operator by radio or other means (telephone, police, etc.).

Four different **incident categories** have been defined according to their causes. Any incident is caused either by the buses, the traffic conditions, the drivers or the load:

B	**Bus:**	the incident is caused by or affects to a bus or set of buses
T	**Traffic:**	the incident is caused by the traffic conditions
D	**Driver:**	the incident is caused by or affects to one or several drivers
L	**Load:**	the incident is caused by or affects to the balance between the offer conditions and the actual demand conditions

Within SuperbuS system there are three methods for detecting or input incidents:

- **Automatic Detection**: Comparing this real-time information (such as buses positions, demand or road traffic status) with the one foreseen in the actual schedule, it is possible to detect discrepancies. These discrepancies are considered incidents that need to be managed.
- **Human Detection**: All the incidents that can not be detected in an automatic way by the system and that therefore must be introduced in the system manually by the human operator.
- **Incident Prediction**: With incident prediction we mean the ability of detecting incidents that will probably occur in the future if the things evolve as expected. SuperbuS will be able to detect these kind of situations because every time a new incident or event is introduced all the causal consequences of this event are calculated according to the information present in the system.

When the incident has been introduced in the system the following step consists in searching the possible consequences produced by the incident. This means to check the logical or causal connections between the disruption caused by the incident and the rest of the schedule for the day. We identify each consequence with one Consequence object, that is associated to the original incident.

SuperbuS system will be able to manage several incidents at the same time. For example, it is possible that while the solver is searching for solutions for an incident a new incident is input to the system. As we can have in our system several incidents at the same time evolving independently, we need to establish mechanisms for relating the incidents that are dependent, and avoid to treat incidents that are related as if they were independent (this could lead to incoherent or contradictory system answers). In order to avoid this the real-time system checks if the incoming incidents are related or not. If the incidents are related, they will be grouped in a single unit and in the future will be treated as a unit.

The analysis of the incident finalizes calculating the severity of the incident and all their related consequences. The severity can be calculated according to different criteria that can be selected by the operator, such as punctuality, regularity, disruption respect the original schedule, etc. This severity will be used by the operator as a help at the moment of deciding if the incident must be passed to the Automatic Regulation module for searching for solutions, or if it must be discarded from the system.

3.2. Automatic Regulation

The approximation taken to make real-time control is based on two methods for solving different kind of problems:

- The **Tactical Solver**: is able to propose standard solutions to standard problems well identified by experienced operators.
- The **On-line Rescheduling:** general procedure for solving big problems not identified by the Tactical Solver (see point 4.2).

The control system will be able to provide automatic solutions to any incident problem presented in real time. Additionally, in order to make the system more reliable and to supervise and validate the proposed solutions, the human intervention is also possible for three aspects:

- To guide the solution search process (deciding strategies, limiting scope, etc.).
- To amend the automatic solutions.
- To validate the solutions.

When an incident group has to be solved the first place where it will look for solutions is in the tactical solver. When the problem is presented, the tactical solver will check if the incident and consequences match one (or more) of the "incident patterns" defined. Each pattern is also associated to a standard solution that can vary depending of certain parameters, available resources, etc. Incident patterns must be defined taking into account not only the original incident but also its consequences. Examples of incident patterns are: general delay in one line, bus gap, bus bundling, etc.

Together with each solution proposed by the system and independently if it is a tactical solution or a rescheduling, it will also be provided a cost-benefit evaluation of the solution. If the controller decides to apply the solution, this will imply to send the corresponding orders to the buses and drivers, and to update the internal data structures to reflect the new situation.

4. Rescheduling

Rescheduling within the SuperbuS application provides tools to the scheduler and network controller to carry out some form of scheduling after an initial timetable, bus schedule and crew schedule have been produced. For the scheduler, the tools allow schedules to be produced, based to some extent on an existing schedule. This allows the scheduler not only to amend an existing schedule, but also to answer 'what-if' questions. For the controller, the rescheduling tools allow different responses to real time incidents on the network to be evaluated and solutions proposed based on the current schedule.

The two types of rescheduling are often called off-line and on-line respectively because of the circumstances under which they take place.

For clarity, the relationship between the initial schedule and current schedule is that the initial schedule is seen as the programme of tasks at the beginning of the day. The current schedule is a reflection of the partially completed set of tasks at a point during the day. The Schedule is defined as being made up of a timetable, bus schedule and crew schedule.

4.1. Off-Line Rescheduling

Off-line rescheduling provides the scheduler with the opportunity to construct a new timetable or crew schedule using, if desired, an already completed one. A relevant scenario for its use is the requirement for rescheduling because of a future 'incident' or problem on the network. The objective is to produce a 'new' schedule trying to minimise the amount of disruption to the passenger timetable and crew schedule, while at the same time ensuring that the service level remains acceptable. Certainly, if incidents are handled inappropriately or not at all, they can lead to major economic and environmental costs. For example, not taking into account increasing running times can result in a decreasing frequency of buses, the passenger timetable unexpectedly becoming invalid, fuller buses, buses becoming 'bunched' together, and reduced layover times affecting crew morale.

Given that there are many common examples of incidents requiring rescheduling, it must be viewed as an essential part of fleet control; making a major contribution to the performance of the company in its service to the community.

The Rescheduling module in SuperbuS provides the scheduler with the tools to reduce the overall effect that a predicted incident might have on the running of the urban transport network.

Four techniques of rescheduling are identified which can be employed for all types of incidents requiring rescheduling. They are:

1. Initial Scheduling means to essentially re-run the timetabling, bus or crew scheduling algorithms either locally on a line, or globally on a set of lines. If buses were scheduled with no interlining, then it is likely that only one line would need to be bus scheduled if changes to the underlying line service timetable were made. Consequently, the amount of rescheduling of the crew would also depend on the level of crew interlining. If both bus and crew scheduling had been done on a per line basis then only those parts of the schedule relating to the line(s) which had been changed should be rescheduled. This same principle is true if sets of lines were bus or crew scheduled together i.e. re-schedule only those parts directly affected. Obviously, if there had been complete interlining of crews and buses, then complete re-initial scheduling would be required under this type of rescheduling.

2. Fix and Schedule means to use some part of the initial timetable or crew schedule as the basis for rescheduling. This can be viewed as freezing part of the schedule and rescheduling using it as a basis. There are two aspects which can be frozen, the timetable and the crew duties. With timetabling a part of the day may be fixed. Since timetabling is done line by line, the rescheduling is similar to the initial timetabling, but with additional synchronizations from the fixed parts of the timetable. Fixing certain duties effectively removes those columns from the allocation matrix in the crew selection/optimisation process. It will also remove other potential duties which also cover those tasks now 'covered'. It then remains to use existing generated duties or generate new ones and use these on the reduced optimisation problem.

3. Editing allows the scheduler to easily change a timetable or schedule graphically. It is often the case that the scheduler can accept, in a limited number of circumstances, certain constraints to be broken or knows of local improvements. These cases are exceptional and are not expected to be predictable from the software.

4. Local Scheduling is concerned with small changes to the schedules made at a an individual vehicle journey level. For example, to compensate for extra driving time required due to some 'incident', it may be possible to use some of the flexibility in the

timetable or crew schedule. This flexibility in timetabling lies in the difference between actual and minimum layovers. It is also present during pauses or waiting times when a crew is responsible for the bus, but it is not actually making any physical progress. For the crew schedule, the flexibility is gained by using time allocated for non-driving tasks.

4.2. On-Line Rescheduling

On-line rescheduling is intended to be a general purpose solving tool for problems arisen in real-time. This kind of rescheduling can of course be minimised, but never removed, by providing robust initial schedules with adequate 'float'. For example, during the layover or waiting time activities, time can be 'gained' in the event of disruption. Therefore a schedule can be produced which needs little controller alteration and still provides the required level of service. This however may use too much resource to achieve a schedule with enough 'float'. Conversely, if layover times are low, greater utilisation of the vehicles is made, but delays to the published timetable are more likely and the quality of the service goes down. The scheduler in practice accepts a certain level of risk within his schedule to accommodate the conflicting goals of minimising resources against providing the expected level of service. Rescheduling in itself can be quite costly in terms of overtime, extra journeys as well as driver morale and customer satisfaction.

The process of on-line rescheduling may appear to be similar to initial scheduling except for four important differences which transform the problem. They are,

1. The time available to perform the rescheduling is very short, of the order of minutes rather than hours.

2. The multi-objective nature of the problem with different objectives such as reduction of disruption, keeping service levels within a temporary acceptable range and minimising cost of crews and vehicles.

3. The schedule has been implemented up to some point in time and only the remainder of the schedule has to be reconsidered in relation to the current status.

4. One of the assumptions on which the original schedule was built is no longer valid. The schedule may need to be altered for the future, as well as resolving the incident at the moment. e.g. durations across some timing links may have changed for the remainder of the day.

The rescheduling process consists of several stages. The operator has control in each of them: he has to decide on the different options, limit the ranges of the parameters, adapt the constraints, etc. The main steps of the process are:

1) Graphical presentation of the related incidents and their consequences.

2) Selection of the solving strategy.

3) Limiting the scope of the possible solution (i.e., defining which part of the schedule can be changed, and which one must remain unaltered).

4) Constraint relaxation or reinforcement. Possibility of tuning constraint parameters to cope with the situation.

5) Start the solution search.

6) When a solution (or a set of them) is found it is presented to the operator together with its cost-benefit analysis. The user has the possibility of graphically amend the solution.

5. Conclusions

The use of the system described in this paper can help to create a more efficient PT system that provides greater customer satisfaction. The result can be one in which there is a reduction in private transport in favour of PT and a corresponding reduction in congestion.

Also, the application of the optimization tools provided with SuperbuS for planification of the public transport services can result in a decreasing of the number of buses needed to cope with a given demand.

Both aspects provide that the potential environmental benefits are significant in most large cities.

References

[1]   **SuperbuS Consortium:** SuperbuS Project Deliverables; R+D ESPRIT Project 8742

[2]   **Blais, J.-Y.; Rousseau J.-M.:** Overview of HASTUS current and future versions; Montreal, Canada

[3]   **Bankovic, Radovan:** Méthodes modernes de détermination des besoins et d'établissemant des horaires dans les services de transport public; Université de Belgrade (Yugoslavie)

[4]   Computer-Aided Transit Scheduling; Proceedings of the Fourth International Workshop on Computer-Aided Scheduling of Public Transport

[5]   **Szelke, Elizabeth; Kerr, Roger M.:** Knowledge-based Reactive Scheduling; Production Planning and Control 1994, Vol5, N° 2, 124-145

Reduction of environmental impact of public transport: DIAMANTE* project

* DIAMANTE: Intelligent Design Applied on Integral Maintenance of Public Transport Fleets

A. Marqués, V. Sebastián, F. Caudet, J.C. de la Rosa
Department of International R&D Projects, Electronic Traffic, S.A.(ETRA), Tres Forques 147, E-46014 Valencia, Spain

Abstract

Breakdowns and malfunctions in Public Transport (PT) vehicles have serious impact in terms of traffic safety, financial profitability, and, very specially, **environmental damage**. Due to these reasons, fleet maintenance is a big share of PT companies' budget.

DIAMANTE is a project that develops a fleet maintenance aid system to improve this task and so a reduction of negative effects derived from badly engine working.

1 Introduction

DIAMANTE (ESPRIT-PASO Programme), a 24 months R&D project started in January 1994, aims to develop an Integral Maintenance System for PT fleets. It is carried out by a multidisciplinary consortium leaded by the company ETRA and including academic partners as well as end users. Part of the project is sponsored by the PASO Special Action that is managed by the Spanish administration (CDTI and MINER) within the ESPRIT II programme of the European Community.

The project execution lasts from January 1994 until December 1995, and its objective is to provide a prototype allowing the supervision and coordination of the maintenance tasks of a public transport fleet, stressing specially the diagnostics of anomalies detected in the vehicle functioning in real time.

DIAMANTE system will provide real time information on vehicles' status (mechanical subsystem, electrical subsystem...) through a set of on-board sensors, automatically reporting any parameter out of its security range. It will also include an expert system (connected by way of radio to the vehicles) that will allow anticipating breakdowns before they actually occur (**predictive maintenance**).

The final DIAMANTE prototype will carry out:

- <u>Preventive Maintenance:</u> It will enable automatic collection, storage and management of each vehicle record (including relevant parameters, past breakdowns, reparations performed on the vehicle so far, etc.) in order to feed the Fleet Maintenance Plan and make its implementation easier.

- <u>Corrective Maintenance:</u> After automatically detecting a breakdown (or upon request), DIAMANTE will make a precise and customised diagnosis of the vehicle, indicating repairing actions to be performed.

- **Predictive Maintenance:** This innovative feature will enable optimising vehicles' performance, by anticipating the appearance of malfunctions through the diagnosis of monitored parameters by an Expert System.

DIAMANTE shows how Advanced Telematics can support PT by:

- Minimising environmental impact: vehicles are maintained in optimal operating conditions, what implies minimising emission of pollutants.

- Increasing quality of service to passengers. This implies promoting PT, what means an additional way of environmental improvement, as private traffic decreases.

2 Product placing

Generally, public transport companies have a maintenance schedule to manage the check-ups and tasks to be completed. The DIAMANTE System is conceived as a two-stage maintenance management tool for transport fleet vehicles: the first maintenance stage in real time, and the second maintenance stage supplying information and statistics referring to the vehicles. The first maintenance stage is represented by the infrastructure accomplishing the tasks needed to maintain the vehicles in correct operating conditions. This stage is formed in some companies by an on-line assistance team and a maintenance team at the depots, accomplishing the relevant tasks during the night to allow the vehicle to operate during the next day. In case a breakdown is too significant to be repaired at the first stage, the vehicle is taken to a company depot, which constitutes the second stage. Bearing in mind the distinction between these two maintenance stages, it is obvious that many more tasks will be carried out at the first stage than at the second stage, although these latter operations will be of greater magnitude. The interest of DIAMANTE is centred in simplifying the management of first stage actions, and providing the second stage with supporting information on the mechanical history of the vehicles and their present status.

The DIAMANTE System monitors the status of vehicles in service by taking parameter measurements at vital points such as the engine, brakes, steering, etc. This monitoring can detect anomalies not noticeable to the driver, at least in the initial phase (i.e. high oil or fuel consumption). The anomaly detection triggers a series of processes in the Coordination Centre of the company so that the Expert Diagnostics System implemented by DIAMANTE may check the vehicle in real time and issue a diagnosis on its state and recommended actions.

3 Description of DIAMANTE

The DIAMANTE System is divided into three modules: the acquisition module (AM), the diagnosis module (DM) and the coordination centre (CC). Figure 1 shows the relationships and information transfers between these modules.

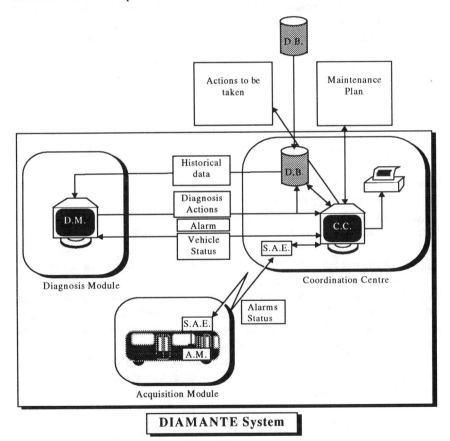

Figure 1: DIAMANTE System

Schematic Acquisition Module

This subsystem measures vehicle parameters and pre-processes the acquired information.

Thanks to a set of sensors, this module periodically determines values of certain parameters from which the vehicle operation status can be deduced. The system carries out these readings and calculates average values after a certain number of them and stores these values in a historical database for future statistical use or to follow up on the operational evolution.

The main function of the *Acquisition Module* is the checking of the stored data. If the module detects values out of a specific range, an alarm is triggered and the *Coordination Centre* is informed of the mechanical state of the vehicle. This communication is established through standard protocols and using the communication infrastructure of the company, if available. If no alarms are produced, the *Coordination Centre* requests the information collected in each vehicle after a maximum time has elapsed (taking advantage of low activity periods in the communication system). This is done to update the historical data-base and free memory in the on-board unit.

Diagnosis Module

An alarm is triggered to start the real time diagnosis process when a deviation in the parameters used to monitor the vehicle is detected.

The *diagnosis module* consists of a rule-based Expert System (ES) which determines the severity of the anomaly by comparing the information describing the present state of the vehicle with the information stored in its knowledge base. If an action on the vehicle is deemed necessary, the ES informs of the severity level and suggests actions to be taken.

The ES knowledge base is composed of historical information such as latest actions undertaken, detected symptoms and the rules needed to infer the diagnostics.

The *diagnosis module* will always be activated from the *coordination centre*, be it due to an alarm or on user request.

Although the greatest innovation of this module is the real-time processing of anomalies, the DIAMANTE System has a wider application: a report on the vehicle status can be requested at any given time. For example, when the monitored parameters of a vehicle are downloaded (at the end of the service or when considered appropriate), the system carries out a global check to verify the status of the vehicles; if the system detects an anomaly or simply a strange tendency of a parameter, informs the operator automatically.

Coordination Centre

The *Coordination Centre* functions as the interface between the system and the user. This module centralises all those functions which allow the integral coordination of the different modules. It acts as coordinator and process manager as well as information server to the system operator.

Two processes run simultaneously in the CC. On one hand, the CC is connected on-line to the DM so that it can communicate incidents to the operator and manage solutions when receiving an alarm. On the other hand, it is used to offer the user any information requested by accessing the historical data-bases.

As the CC is in contact with the fleet management centre there is a common knowledge of the geographical location and mechanical situation of the vehicle which facilitates decision-taking. This characteristic is important because a good anomaly management does not only require a precise mechanical diagnostic, but also information on where the bus is, remaining service time, consequences of stopping the bus, etc. The combination of these two types of information will allow the fleet controller to take the adequate measures.

Since the DIAMANTE System may be another piece in the real-time fleet management system of a company, the CC is designed with a good communication interface with the Operation Aid System (OAS) used. In the prototype implementation, this will be taken into account when connecting the DIAMANTE System to the OAS used by the Public Transport Operator (PTO). Object-oriented technology has been applied to the design and development of the CC in order to obtain a powerful and flexible tool, adaptable to the needs of each company.

4 Real time diagnosis

The on-board module (AM) is constantly processing the values measured by the sensors. When one of these values is off the range, it is compared with those values of other related sensors. An alarm is generated, if the conditions determining anomalous operation are satisfied. The generated alarm is then sent to the *Coordination Centre*, together with the information on vehicle parameters. Once the alarm is received by the CC, information related to the vehicle is gathered (anomaly history, repair history, service status,...) and made available to the diagnosis module. When the ES has completed its diagnosis, the user is presented with a list of possible faults with their certainty percentage, and a recommendation on whether the action should be taken by an on-line assistance team or whether the vehicle should be sent to the depot. It will also generate a list of the corrective actions that should be taken.

5 Conclusions

As described above, DIAMANTE is a tool which can improve the maintenance task for a transport fleet.

The knowledge of the vehicle operative evolution in real-time monitoring, allows to predict future tendencies. Therefore, if values other than expected are detected, the kind of fault can be predicted because the expert system contains very complete information.

Referring to preventive maintenance, a detailed check-up plan can be produced by processing the information on guarantees and life cycles of individual parts, vehicle historical data and information supplied by the diagnosis module.

The optimal working of Public Transport vehicles has important impacts on the environment:

- Minimising emission of pollutants
- Minimising fuel and oil consumption
- Increasing quality of service to passengers. This implies promoting PT, what means an additional way of environmental improvement, as private traffic decreases.

6 Bibliography

Study of Functionalities in Strategic Planning, Maintenance and Management Information Suystem Domains.
Cassiope Project. DRIVE PROGRAMME
May, 1990

Sistema de ayuda a la Explotación - SAE (PTFMS)
De la Rosa, J.C., Nuñez-Flores, J. ETRA
I Simposium of Transport Engineering
Sevilla, 24-26 March 1993.

Optimisation de l'entretien des autobus grace à l'informatique
Mohnhaupot, D; Canal, G.; Feutlinske, H; Flor, L.R.; Pourveuir, G.
UITP 47 Congres International, Lausanne, 1987.

IR remote sensing system for testing urban fleet emission profile

R. Gong, P. Waring
Industrial Research Limited, PO Box 31-310, Lower Hutt, New Zealand

Abstract

An Infrared remote sensing system has been developed at Industrial Research Limited(IRL), New Zealand. This system, which includes an infrared source, a detector with a simple optical system, and a data acquisition component, has a high sensitivity to the detected gases, and a high response speed. It was possible to capture the emissions data from vehicles travelling at up to 100km/h. Laboratory testing and calibrations and preliminary on-road testing have been carried out successfully.The features of the remote sensing system enable us to scan the emission dynamic profiles on road against the type of vehicles, the age of vehicles, and the traffic locations and traffic speeds. With the fleet emission profiles, the urban traffic plan can be examined in terms of environment and safety requirements. Recommendations can be made on reducing emissions of urban fleets and improving energy efficiency for individual vehicles. The overall traffic plan of a city relative to traffic emissions can be drawn.Preliminary on road testing results are encouraging. CO and CO_2 emissions were measured satisfactorily.

Introduction

It is important to investigate the emission profile of an urban fleet for a city transport development plan. Knowing a city's fleet emission situation will provide the basic information for establishing vehicle emission standards and improving energy efficiency particularly in New Zealand, because there are not yet any emission standards. New Zealand is often known as one of the cleanest lands in the world, but the per capita pollution is quite high. Private passenger vehicles and on-road delivery vehicles for commercial goods are the dominant transport method. To investigate the emissions on-road is a priority task for environmental issues.

This investigation requires an emission measurement system, which must be able to collect a great amount of emission information in a short period of time because of the almost complete absence of existing data. Industrial Research Ltd started to develop an infrared remote system almost two years ago in order to be able to carry out this investigation. Infrared remote sensing systems for on-road vehicle emission measurement are a recently developed technology. This type of remote sensing system is very different from ordinary infrared gas analysis systems, inside which a gas sample cell, the infrared source, and the detector are all enclosed. The infrared remote sensing system has an open infrared source and a detector component without a sample cell. It can be set up by a road side to detect the emissions from travelling vehicles, and is able to take a very large number of vehicle measurements at various locations during a single day, which is not possible for the usual stationary measurement systems. The group at Denver University lead by Dr D. Stedman[1] and a General Motors research group[2] started working on remote sensing systems in late 80's and early 90's. Since then Dr Stedman has carried out several on-road emission measurements in California, U.S.A., and in Britain et al. A research group led by Å. Sjödin in Sweden[3][4] monitored on-road emission with a remote sensing system regarding the driving conditions and different traffic locations. And there are other agencies in various countries, which have shown the potential of similar remote sensing systems for active traffic emission measurements. It is clear that the interest in operating infrared remote sensing systems to assist traffic emission monitoring is increasing, particularly in urban areas.

An infrared remote sensing system usually has high response speed and high sensitivity to the emission gases. It is an efficient system for outlining fleet emission profiles in general and can be a diagnostic tool to identify "dirty" cars. However, it would be inappropriate to use the instant reading on the road side from a remote sensing system as a final judgement for whether a vehicle meets emission standards. In reference[5], it is explained that the measurement taken by remote sensing is a time instant value, but the figures in standards are based on stationary measurements, which are time average values.

An Infrared remote sensing system can be structured optically in various ways. For example, it is possible to "split" the infrared beam into separate beams with one or more reflectors. Each beam would go to one single detector. This multi-detector system, similar to that in reference[6], requires well-designed optical elements and relatively complex alignment. Detectors in this system can receive the separate gas emission signals at exactly same time. The IRL remote sensing system adopts a different approach[5] from the multi-detector system, and consists of a single infrared beam and only one detector. An optical chopper with infrared filters rotates in front of the detector to send the signals from the measured exhaust gases sequentially to the detector. This system receives the different gas signals not at exactly the same time, but as the time difference between signals is only a fraction of a millisecond, this is acceptable. It was a simple, low cost and easy to use solution to adopt.

The IRL remote sensing system has been tested with a chassis dynamometer to compare the results with stationary gas analyses. Preliminary on-road tests have followed, and the local Consumers' Association has used the system to carry out a road traffic survey. The results were very satisfactory and the system performance was very encouraging.

Instrumentation

The IRL infrared sensing system adapts the principle of normal stationary gas analyzers. The infrared beam from an emitter crosses a space to a detector. In front of the detector there is a chopper i.e. a spinning disk with optical filters. When emission gases are present in the beam, the detector receives the signals referred to each filter. A signal process unit translates the signals into emission measurement results. The entire IRL remote sensing system comprises an infrared source unit, the detector unit, an electronic and software data processing unit, and the separate power supplies.

Infrared source unit

A small glow bar is used as the infrared beam emitter. Behind the emitter, a parabolic reflector coated with aluminium produces a parallel infrared beam. Its divergance angle is less than 5°. The source is mounted on a frame, which can be adjusted to cope with different levels of the exhaust pipes of various vehicles.

Detector unit

A J10D-InSb infrared detector is used at an operating temperature of 77°K. The detector has high sensitivity, and a response speed of 1 kHz. The detector is located in a metal dewar, which can retain the low temperature for eight hours, and requires one hour to provide a relatively stable signal output. A disk with three filters is placed in front of the infrared detector, as the optical chopper. The chopper turns at over 6000 rpm to produce signal pulses. The three filter wavelengths are 4.0 μm, 4.3 μm and 4.7 μm for reference, CO and CO_2 respectively. Figure 1 is the schematic diagram of the chopper. The holes sited at the opposite sides of the filters are for identification. They act digitally as "01", "10" and "11". At both sides of the identification holes, there is a set of lights and light detectors to produce identifying signals. The signals from the infrared and light detectors are sent to the data processing unit.

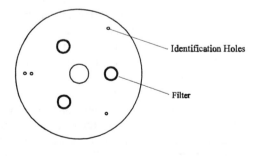

Figure 1 Schematic Diagram of the Chopper

Electronic and software data processing unit

This unit can be triggered to start collecting data automatically from passing vehicles. There are two parts physically in this unit, an electronic circuit component and a portable computer with a DAQ-700 digitizer. The electronic circuit receives and amplifies the signals from the detector unit, and also pre-analyzes the signals. The signals are imported through the digitizer into the computer. A special software programme network is installed in the portable computer. The programme groups the signals, carries out the calculations, and produces the emission level curves of the detected gases. Finally, the data are saved in a specified file.

This data unit is built in such a way that the offset of the system is adjustable, so a certain amount of signal drift can be overcome. The reference signal provides a relative zero point for the specified gases, and the ambient temperature fluctuations and system variations can be isolated. Therefore, the emission signals can be processed more efficiently.

Power supplies

During on-road testing, the source unit is placed at one side of the road, and the detector unit and the remainder of the system are located at the other side. Two power supplies are thus required. A small 600w portable generator is used as the source power for the emitter. Two heavy duty truck batteries can provide power to the electronic and data processing unit for at least two hours.

This remote system is very compact and easy to transport and easy to operate. It allows freedom in choice of the measurement venue because of the portable separate power supplies.

Measurement

Testing

The laboratory tests and the calibration were carried out using an IRL portable chassis dynamometer with a typical standard stationary gas analyzer. The details have been discussed in reference[5]. The results of the tests and calibration are summarized in Figure 2. It was noticed that the difference between the remote sensing measurement and the stationary analyzer reading could be up to 10%.

The preliminary on-road tests were carried out several times based on two venues. The first one was on the main private road of the IRL campus. Twenty five vehicles were measured within one hour. Sixty eight percent were staff private cars, and the remainder were commercial vans and utility vehicles. Nearly fifty percent of the staff cars had higher CO emissions than the commercial vehicles. One reason was that the commercial vehicles were fully warmed up, but most of the staff cars measured had just driven out from the car park. Unfortunately, we were not able to measure the same car out and in again for comparison. Figure 3 and Figure 4 are two typical examples from this testing. The peaks in the records are the readings just after the passage of exhaust pipe, and the following part was where the emissions were diluted with air, as the vehicle moved away.

The second venue was on Oxford Terrace in Lower Hutt City. This road was straight and long (more than 8 km). It was parallel to a railway line, and was one of the faster roads for travel in or out of the city centre. Traffic could flow at a reasonably steady speed, 50 - 70 k/h. The majority of the vehicles on this road would probably have been warmed up. Sixty five vehicles were detected in an hour. Among these vehicles, there were 57 cars, 7 vans and 1 truck.

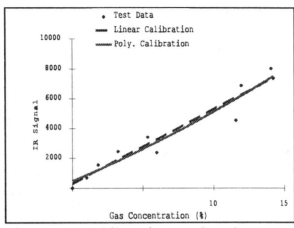

Figure 2 Calibration and Laboratory Tests

Table 1

CO/CO$_2$	Number of Vehicles
< 0.15	9
> 0.2, < 0.4	12
> 0.4, < 0.6	13
> 0.6	14
Invalid	13
too late	4
Total	65

Table 1 above summarises the on-road testing results. Thirteen tests were invalid, and four were collected too late, after the plume had dissipated. Forty-eight records were completed. Nine vehicles were in a good "clean" condition, where their ratios of CO to CO$_2$ were less than 0.15. Twelve had ratios which were greater than 0.2 and less than 0.4, and their condition was uncertain, because the emissions could be indicative of good tuning conditions under load, but could be indicative of poor emission performance if under light load. Fourteen vehicles with ratios of over 0.6 were judged to have poor operating conditions. Several of them had ratios even above unity. From a large number of stationary emission tests, it was recognized that for a vehicle, in any normal driving circumstance, the ratio of CO to CO_2 should not be higher than 0.4, if the vehicle was in a reasonably well tuned condition. If the ratio was too high, that indicated that incomplete combustion was occurring.

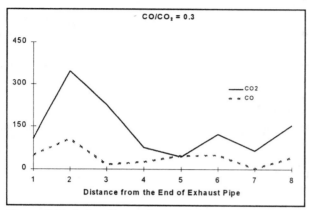

Figure 3 Emission Curves from a Private Car

Analysis
The ratio of CO to CO_2 was taken as a major discussion parameter. There are a number of reasons. Firstly, the level of CO indicated the combustion efficiency of the engines. When the CO level is very high compared to the CO_2 level, there would be a large proportion of incompletely burned fuel in the exhaust pipe, and the engine would be poorly tuned. Normally, for a petrol car, if CO emissions are inceased, HC emission levels would also increase, due to the poor combustion. In other words, changes of CO level for a car can be an indicator of changes of HC. Secondly, the laboratory tests and the calibration showed that the measurement difference between the remote sensing system and the convientional stationary analyzer could be up to 10%. It

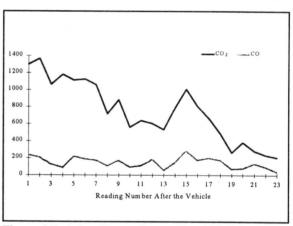

Figure 4 Emission Curves from a Van ($CO/CO_2=0.15$)

was due to "car flippers" explained by reference[7]. There was another important aspect; the remote sensing system took the measurments at a 1 kHz response speed, which was a compatible frequency with an engine firing frequency. So, the remote sensing system could take readings resulting from the emissions of individual cylinders. These readings varied, and could differ from average values, which are measured by stationary gas analyzers. However, the exhaust "cloud" should be a well-stirred gas mixture, and the proportion of each component within it should be relatively stable with an engine running at constant speed. So it would be appropriate to take the ratio of CO to CO_2 as a monitoring parameter.

The ratios of CO to CO_2 were measured from 0.003 up to 2 by both the remote sensing system and the stationary system. According to chassis dynamometer tests, when a car was just started, or the car was idling, the CO/CO_2 value could be high, for example, more than 0.2. For a well-tuned car, it should be less than 0.15(with no catalyst fitted). In other running conditions, the ratio normally would not be less than 0.02 for light load, and should not be larger than 0.4 under full load conditions.

Cars with ratios less than 0.15 could be recognised as well-tuned 'clean' vehicles. At the other extreme were cars where the CO/CO_2 ratios were greater than 0.6, which were gross pollutant emitters. These cars require immediate warning that they should be tuned or have engine check-ups. For vehicles with CO/CO_2 ratios between 0.2 to 0.4, further information would be required to judge their engine condition, such the speed, load situation, the level of engine warm-up, even the road and traffic conditions.

In Table 1, there is one row labled "too late", where manual initiation of data collection was late. The emission peaks shown in Figure 3, and Figure 4, would be missing. There were thirteen disqualifications in the row labled "invalid". Among them, either the measurements suffered interference by another vehicle, or the level of the exhaust pipe on the passing vehicle was too high or too low with regard to the level of the infrared beam. The level of the infrared beam could be adjusted, but for each height, there were a few invalid measurement samples.

The results of the on-road testing showed that nearly 30% of the passing vehicles tested were over polluting vehicles requiring immediate tuning to protect the environment and improve energy consumption to acceptable levels. Their ages varied from three years upwards, and their makes were the popular manufacturers. Clearly, their owners did note accept their responsibility either to the environment or to their own financial benefit. The promolgation and enforcement of emissiom standards is desirable to remedy this situation.

Conclusion

The IRL remote sensing system is a mechanically compact and optically simple infrared remote system for on-road emission testing. It has high response speed and high sensitivity to the testing signals. Electronically, this system has the ability to adjust its offset to overcome inherent signal drifting caused by the ambient environment and system condition changes.

Satisfactory laboratory and calibration tests were carried out using IRL portable chassis dynamometer. Those tests characterised the performance of the remote sensing system, and provided the basic information to assist the road testing analyses.

Preliminary on-road tests have been carried out at varous venues in Lower Hutt City. The remote sensing system worked very efficiently at the rate of one valid sampling in less than two seconds. The ratio of CO to CO_2 has been used as a major on-road testing analysis parameter, which has the necessary stability for fleet emission testing under the complicated conditions that apply on the road. With this system, the on-road fleet emission profile in a city can be investigated effectively and economically. The emission profile can be mapped quickly and relevent recommendations for correction readily proposed

This system involves a variety of technologies. It is still developing. There are many aspects requiring improvement, particularly in measurement accuracy, and the sampling pattern. Overall the remote sensing system is an efficient emission monitoring tool with encouraging testing results.

Acknowledgement

Thanks to Ian Michington for assisting to build the electronic component and to produce the programme software, and Denis Harnett for his mechanical skills and the coordination in the laboratory and on-road tests.

Reference

1.   G. A. Bishop and D. H. Stedman, On-Road Carbon Monoxide Emission Measurement Comparisons for the 1988-1989 Colorado Oxy-Fuels Program, Environ. Sci. Technol.,Vol. 24, No. 6, 1990, 843-847.
2.   R. D. Stephens and S. H. Cadle, Remote Sensing Measurements of Carbon Monoxide Emissions from On-Road Vehicles, ISSN 1047-3289 J. Air Waste Manage. 41:39-46(1991).
3.   Å. Sjödin, Potential of Remote Sensing Technique in Roadside Inspections - Results from a Pilot Study in Sweden,
4.   Å. Sjödin and M. Lenner, On-Road Measurements of Single Vehicle Pollutant Emissions, Speed and Acceleration for Large Fleet of Vehicles in Different Traffic Environments, 3rd Intern. Symposium "Transport and Air Pollution", 6-10 June 1994.
5.   R. Gong and P. Waring, On Road Remote Sensing System, IPENZ, 1994
6.   G. A. Bishop, J. R. Starkey, A. Ihlenfeldt, W. J. Williams and D. H. Stedman, IR Long-Path Photometry: A Remote ensing Tool for Automoble emissims, Analytical Chemistry, Vol. 61, No. 10, May 15, 1989
7.   SAE 940582.

A modelling environment for urban traffic performance evaluation

Q. Delacroix, C. Durandière, M. Gourgand, S. Ruch
Laboratoire d'Informatique, Université Blaise Pascal,
F-63 177 Aubière Cedex, France

Abstract

In this paper we present a modelling methodology and an environment which implement this methodology. This software environment has been designed in order to help the expert of the system in decision making. In fact, the environment is able to support the expert in the building of a model of his system and to evaluate the impact of different configurations (topology and workload) for the given system. Then the experts can make their own decision with full knowledge of the facts. This process can be performed wherever the system exists or not.

1 Introduction

Every urban system has to be seen as a global system which integrate policies based on individual traffic, public transport and goods traffic. Some of the main problems facing urban traffic systems are the measurements, running comprehension, productivity improvement and the performance evaluation. Such studies are made in order to improve the quality (more intelligent use of the urban structure), and to make them closer to the customers attempt. Such studies can be conducted with the help of modelling techniques. In order to make use of such techniques, more or less complicated models of the system to be studied, can be built.

This paper presents the modelling methodology we built in order to study urban systems, and the process named ASDI used to built an environment dedicated to this class of systems: TRASIM. This environment has been build in order to be used by expert of urban systems, who may be non-simulationists experts.

The first part of this paper, presents the objectives of our study, and the assumptions we make on urban systems. The second part is devoted to the ASDI approach. The third part deals with the domain analysis. The fourth part is concerned by the obtention of the specification (attributes and methods) of the different entities. For a given system (a small city like Dieppe in France), performances of different layouts under different workloads are reported as an example in the fifth part. Finally we conclude by giving perspectives for this work.

2   Aims of the study

We define a urban system as a set of entities (cross-roads, streets, traffic lights...), in which flow entities (cars, bus, trucks...) goes through, and all these entities are managed by rules (traffic lights rules, cross-roads crossing, one-way streets...). Such a system sets lots of problems both at the time of its conception and during its exploitation, which are necessary to solve:

- measurement: how many traffic lights, cross-roads need to be foreseen, what size are the parking zone...
- improvement: how can traffic lights be managed (duration) in order to keep traffic most fluent as possible.
- understanding: are there any bottleneck ?, how and why traffic jam appear in the system ?
- unforeseen problems: it is interesting to know how the traffic will evolve if one or more street or cross-roads are unusable (market, accident, road works...)...

Our goal in this types of studies is to give to the system experts informations to help them in decision making. This decision making can be done by hypothesis testing, that is to say by determining the impact of reconfiguration of the urban structures, or increase of the traffic flow on the considered urban system. For example we can test the same urban configuration under different workloads (traffic flow), or by testing different configuration under the same traffic flow, in order to determine the best configuration, or for a given configuration the traffic flow it can support without provoking too many disruptions.

In order to evaluate a solution, experts of the system define indicators, which are representative of the urban system. Therefore testing an hypothesis consist in giving value to these indicators. These indicators reflect one of three aspects of the system: technical aspect (number of vehicles per hour passing the cross-roads), economical aspect (building cost of the urban structure, impact on the trade for the considered town (shopkipping...)), environment aspect: air pollution (vehicle emissions...).

In France, organisms such as INRETS, CETE, CETUR and others research laboratories are leading research from many years in this domain.

Sometimes, many users and political leaders (mayor...) do not agree with these researches that we shortly present in the next section.

3 An overview of some existing studies

Analytic models are used in [4] to evaluate efficiency of planned networks or calculate performances of public facilities [10]. These models require straight hypothesis because they use aggregate data or queueing networks theory. Thus, the results they give back are approximate and they deal only with stationary states. We can not introduce in models traffic light durations or geometric particularities of an intersection. It is not possible to evaluate the effects of these parameters on traffic flows.

Because traffic flows are dynamic -they fluctuate with time- and stationary state is never reached, simulation is able to meet our attempts. [8] and [5] proposed simulation models based on macroscopic descriptions and continuous wave equations. Time is introduced in models, but macroscopic simulation can not integrate priority of emergency services vehicles or length of specific turning lanes. [2] and [1] used discrete events to simulate traffic light control or freeway traffic with microscopic models. They dealled with stochastic models and they considered only few events. We would like to know the effect of car crashes or exit parking lot disturbances. How to evaluate travel times of public transports (if specific lanes are planned) or travel time for emergency vehicles? As mentioned in [3], parameters like traffic light durations, turning lane lengths and density of pedestrian are important features of urban modelling. These values -if unsuitable to the context or misevaluated- can produce very prejudiciable effects on the traffic flow. So, urban system performances are very sensitive to these parameters. But, first of all, *What are the questions the simulation is about to answer to?* and *Which detail level needs the modelling?* thus *Which data are relevant?*

We answer these questions through this paper. Based on manufacturing system modelling experience [7], [9] and [11], we propose a modelling environment for urban traffic simulation called TRASIM. TRASIM is a decision aid tool dedicated to urban infrastructure evaluation. It offers methods and tool-kit required to validate a model and ensure the results of simulation computation are grounded. Using QNAP2 (Queueing Networks Analysis Package), the different entities of urban traffic are considered as objets. This objet oriented approach offers an easy and secure way to build simulation models.

4 The proposed methodology

In order to build a model from a studied system, we adopt a modelling process. The process we adopt includes two models: a knowledge model and an action model [6]. The knowledge model of a system is a normalization in a graphic or a natural language of the structure of the system and its working. The action model is a translation of the knowledge model into a mathematical formalism or into a programming language. It can be put to use directly and supplies the performances of the modelled system without recourse to direct measurement. Using the knowledge model and the action model is called modelling process. This process is generally iterative, and the part of the TRASIM environment is to support this process, and to help the user (expert of the system) to use this process.

In order to build the TRASIM modelling environment, we propose a process named ASDI (Analysis, Specification, Design and Implementation).The two first phases of the process are performed in order to build a generic knowledge model of the domain. We choose to decompose this generic knowledge model into three sub-systems:

- the physical sub-system, which is composed of the physical entities (cross-roads, traffic lights, streets...), their geographical distribution and their logical and physical interconnections,
- the logical sub-system, which describes paths vehicle can follow,
- the decision sub-system specifies the management of the working of the system. It acts both on the physical sub-system (traffic lights managing rules, lane attribution...) and on the logical sub-system (rules for swapping to a replacement path...).

The two next phases (Design and Implementation) are performed, following an object oriented approach, in order to build a software component library. Then, the building of a particular model with TRASIM consists in instanciating elements of this library. Discrete event simulation techniques are used in order to evaluate the performances of the modelled system. A visual animation of the simulated events is also available.

One of the main problems in simulation comes from data. It is of prime necessity to be sure to have reliable data because they are at the source of the simulation. For an urban traffic modelling, there are two kinds of data required: those which concern the physical system (size, width, number of line by road...) and those which concern the vehicles (flow, route...). The first one are easy to obtain but the second one need counting of vehicles and statistic treatments. This method is usable only if the network of roads studied already exists. Problems appear for an non-existing network where counting is obviously impossible. The costs of urban works forbid to do test in live! So, the reaction of users in front of a new local area must be anticipated. The difficulty comes from the behaviour of the human being. An inhabitant can change his uses by the choice of the roads for a moving or by the way of transport. To have an estimation of the movement, the origin point, the destination and the reason of the movement must be known. To obtain these new data and to compute the new traffic, it requires to hold inquires into users hoping that people will do what they say.

First, for the implementation of the model, the area of the system must be defined. The number of strategic points like cross-roads, streets or attractive centers (shopping streets, parking, harbour or railway station...) chosen to be modelled, must be sufficiently important to evaluate the problem globally. To build the model, the system is splitted up in cross-roads of known type (traffic light cross-road, roundabout, priority road). For each type of cross-road, the control rules are always the same. They can easily be integrated in a library of cross-road entities using parameters like number of roads which arrive and leave the intersection, number of line by road, phases and cycle of the traffic lights... So, each intersection of the modelled system is described with the help of this libraryand a QNAP2 code can be generated automatically with object oriented programming. Thus, each intersection is created separately. So, it is easy to add, to delete, or to update parts of the model and testing new configuration, without modifying the whole model.

The relation between each cross-road is done by vehicle routes (transactional approach). The list of the successive roads and intersections visited by each customer permits to link all the cross-roads. For our study, only one kind of vehicle was modelled (particular cars), but it is easy to add trucks or buses by modifying parameters of the customer classes (size, speed...) and by defining particular route for buses.

Each cross-road is modelled using queueing network elements, for instance a four way traffic light cross-road:

- Each road or street is modelled by a queue with a limited size managed by a semaphore and one server. This server permits to stop the vehicles at the end of the street if a rule must be respected.
- The traffic lights are represented by flags (SET=green). There are one traffic light by road arriving at the intersection. If the flag is RESET the customer which is in the server, is waiting for the green light.
- The management of the four traffic lights (phases and cycle) is done by a traffic light controller.
- Inside the cross-road, there are several servers which are used to route customer according to his direction. The access of each server is managed by a semaphore and the waiting queue associated are empty. Four servers are used for the In / Out management, and two servers for vehicles which want to turn left (these vehicles must be stocked while they wait for a space to pass).

In this cross-road, there are twelve classes of customers (four roads and three directions by road). The route of each class is defined by giving the list of queues and servers travelled.

For the animation, the layout of the system must be drawn. The number of strategic points and cross-road displayed must be limited for having a good understanding of the situation. However, the studied system can be larger than the screen, the user can change view and zoom in any parts.

This system permits to have a hierarchical model by views at different levels. The simulation generates a trace file which is used for the animation. The animator needs two files: the layout of the system and the trace of the simulation. The trace file hold data about the evolution of the state of the system (changes of server or queue for each customer, or changes of state for the traffic lights, arrival or departure of a customer,). It can also hold information about indicators. Thus, it is possible to watch simultaneously the evolution of each vehicle and the level of each indicator. This is a powerful help to understand the situation. It confirms with quantitative data the analysis made by watching the animation. Sources of problem can also be found more quickly, and the comparison between two configurations is easier. Indicators can permit to evaluate the traffic jam (occupation rate, flow, average speed...), the environment consequences (pollution, noise, ...) or relevant entities for particular needs (access of shopping streets, time of route for busses...).

5 An example: Dieppe

We present now an example of a French city: Dieppe. The system is composed of the main streets, the shopping streets, the harbour, and the beach access. The aim of this problem is to compare different kinds of configurations of nine cross-roads. For a system of that size, it becomes nearly impossible to count all the route existing and to associate a class to each route. Instead, it exists several routes to join two points. The choice of a route is decided by each driver. It depends of the traffic jam, the driver mood or other parameters which are difficult to evaluate. Moreover, some cars can do loop (when they look for parking for instance). So with TRASIM, the routes of the customers (servers and queues travelled) are defined inside each intersection as described for the traffic light cross-road. The customers change of class between two intersections. With this way of classification the number of classes does not increase exponentially (the classes are added with the intersection instead of being multiplied) and deleting, adding, or updating an intersection in the system does not occur lots of changes for the customer routes (only for the intersection concerned).

In the example of Dieppe, the number of customer classes is thirty. For that model there is a particular class of vehicle which corresponds to the vehicles coming from the car ferries.They do not have particular treatment: when they leave the first intersection, they change of class and become anonymous customer.

The interest of the simulation of Dieppe is to study the reaction of the system to workload due to car ferries and its capacity to solve it. The animation is a powerful way of evaluation for that kind of problem (see figure 1). In fact, it permits to evaluate the evolution of the situation in

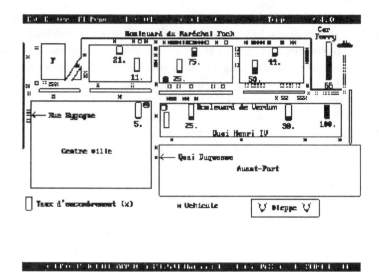

Figure 1: Animation of Dieppe.

real time. It would be difficult, quite impossible, to do same observations with statistic results of a simulation without animation.

6   Conclusion

In this paper we proposed a modelling environment named TRASIM which allows the expert of a urban system (city) to: build a model of their system following the modelling process by instanciating library components from a generic model of the studied system class, and give data about the studied system (traffic lights time, number of vehicle...).

After the code generation phase, TRASIM produces an action model which is simulated by a discrete event simulator (QNAP2). Model running gives statistical results and indicators which allow expert to take a decision. It also produces a visual animation of the simulated events which is a good tool for communication between experts of the system and political leaders (mayors...). This animation can also be used as a dashboard of the system.

As said before, the simulated action model is automatically built by code generation, so the model obtaining time is very short (for Dieppe just a few minutes). Moreover, size of the model (in terms of number of entities, and simulated time) is only bounded by the memory size of the used computer. Results obtention time depends on the performances of the used computer and also on the simulated duration time. We have validated this approach on the French city Dieppe, which is a small city (40 000 inhabitants).

TRASIM help experts of the system in decision making by evaluation of different criteria defined by the experts. These criteria are attributes of the model and can then be changed at will. TRASIM has an open and modular architecture which allow it to be used on a quite wide range of systems (cities). TRASIM manages one kind of vehicle (individual vehicle). As perspectives for this work, we look to incorporate in TRASIM others types of vehicle (trucks, bus, priority vehicle like ambulance, fire-car...). We also look to take into account interactions between different traffic modes (vehicle, railway, ships...), making TRASIM a multimodal modelling environment.

References

1. Bisset, K.R. & Kelsey, R.L. Simulation of Traffic Flow and Control using Conventional, Fuzzy and Adaptative Methods, pp. 331 to 335, *Proceedings of the 1992 European Simulation Multiconference*, York, UK, 1992.

2. Benz, T. The Microscopic Traffic Simulator AS (Autobahn Simulator), pp. 486 to 489, *Proceedings of the 1993 European Simulation Multiconference*, Lyon, France, 1993.

3. Centre d'Etudes des Transports Urbains. *Carrefours à feux*, Bagneux, France, 1988.

4. Centre d'Etudes des Transports Urbains. *Les études de prévision de trafic en milieu urbain*, Bagneux, France, 1990.

5. Cremer, M. & Meissner, F. Traffic Prediction and Optimization using an Efficient Macroscopic Simulation Tool, pp. 515 to 519, *Proceedings of the 1993 European Simulation Multiconference*, Lyon, France, 1993.

6. Gourgand, M. *Outils logiciels pour l'évaluation des performances des systèmes informatiques*, PhD thesis, Université Blaise Pascal, Clermont-Ferrand, France, 1984.

7. Gourgand, M. & Kellert, P. An object-oriented methodology for manufacturing system modelling, pp. 1123 to 1128, *Proceedings of the 1992 Summer Computer Simulation Conference*, Reno, Nevada, 1992.

8. Hilliges, M., Reiner, R. & Weidlich, W. A Simulation Model of Dynamic Traffic Flow in Networks, pp. 505 to 510, *Proceedings of the 1993 European Simulation Multiconference*, Lyon, France, 1993.

9. Kellert, P. Définition et mise en oeuvre d'une méthodologie orientée objets pour la modélisation de systèmes de production, pp. 415 to 436, *Proceedings of the 1992 INFORSID Conference*, Clermont-Ferrand, France, 1992.

10. Larson, R. & Odini, A. *Urban Operations Research*, MIT Press, 1987.

11. Ruch, S. *Un environnement de modélisation multi-domaine pour les systèmes à flux discrets*, PhD thesis, Université Blaise Pascal, Clermont-Ferrand, France, 1994.

Development of tools for the description of urban noise pollution: application to the City of Zaragoza

F.J. Martínez,[a] J. Lladó,[a] J.L. Pelegrín,[a] A. Ibáñez,[b] M.P. Aguerri[b]

[a] *C.P.S.I. University of Zaragoza, Spain*
[b] *Environmental Service of the City of Zaragoza, Spain*

Abstract

As an answer to the problem created by the acoustic pollution in the City of Zaragoza, the Environmental Service of the Town Hall set up the design and realization of a program of anti-noise pollution actions.This program consists of the following types of actions: development of technical tools, civic sensitizing actions and corrective, administrative and legislative actions. In this paper we are going to describe the noise pollution description tools developed as well as a pilot anti-traffic noise action (installation and evaluation of an urban motorway noise barrier).

1 Introduction

Zaragoza is a city of 600.000 inhabitants situated on the Ebro river, in the Northeast of Spain. In view of its strategical situation in the Ebro valley it is the intersection point between basic Spanish axes of communications such as the axis País Vasco-Mediterranean Region, the axis Madrid-Barcelona and the axis Zaragoza-France through the Pyrenees. This situation confers on Zaragoza the character of urban concentration which has suffered a great demographic growth with the resulting rise of all urban activities (transport, commercial, industrial, etc.). All these circumstances have given rise to a series of environmental disorders in its township, including the phenomenon of the urban noise pollution which has been discovered as a very important environmental problem starting from the measurement campaigns carried out by the Municipal Environmental Service.

The analysis of the results of this campaigns shows that the 90% of the population is exposed to levels of traffic noise higher than 58 dB(A), a 50% suffers levels higher than 64 dB(A), a 10% levels higher than 73 dB(A) and lastly a 5% higher than 74.5 dB(A).

2 Development of tools for the description of urban noise pollution in the City of Zaragoza

At this point we are going to describe the tools developed as a consequence of the above mentioned anti-noise pollution plan of actions, which can be classified into two main types: diagnosis tools and noise prediction tools.

2.1 Diagnosis Tools

The diagnosis tools developed were the sonic maps of the City of Zaragoza and a general study of city psico-sociological noise perception.

2.1.1 Development of the sonic maps

As a result of the collaboration between the Department of Mechanical Engineering (D.I.M) of the Superior Polytechnic Center of Engineers (C.P.S.I.) of the Zaragoza University and the Environmental Service of the Town Hall, the day and night sonic maps of the city were worked out.

The realization of these maps pursues the following goals :
-To carry out a general diagnosis of the levels of environmental noise in the municipal area.
-To establish a noise zonification of the municipality, considering the different types of noise sources (road, urban industries, night activities, etc.).
-To act as an objective source of information for urban planning activities.
-Evaluation of the spatial and time distribution of urban noise levels.
-To act as a data base for the modification of the anti-noise by-laws.

The maps were worked out [1] following three formats : iso-L_{eq} lines, iso-L_{eq} outlines, and 3D noise level plots. In the iso-L_{eq} lines format several types of maps have been elaborated (L_{eqd}, L_{eqn}, difference between L_{eqd} and L_{eqn}, etc.) starting from the corresponding data of the L_{eq} noise measurements, these data are represented graphically by means of iso-L_{eq} lines which are obtained when joining points with the same L_{eq} noise level.

The meaning of the abbreviations of the above mentioned noise descriptors are:

$L_{eq\,T}$: equivalent continuous sound level over time T.

L_{eqd} : day equivalent continuous sound level.

L_{eqn} : night equivalent continuous sound level.

In view of the impossibility of a coloured representation in this paper and for a better reproduction, it has been selected the diurnal sonic map for its representation in Figure 1.

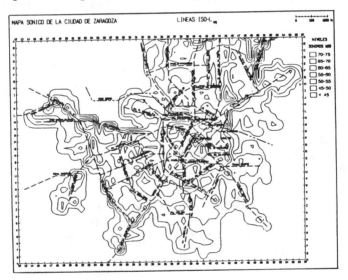

Figure 1: Iso-L_{eqd} sonic map

In the case of graphic outline representations, the different outlines are assigned a colour following the DIN standard 18005, or a codified filling pattern according to the existing noise level inside the outlines. This asignment is carried out according to the value of L_{eq} measured or calculated for the different points. Once all the available data have been proccesed, the program draws a representation of the vial structure of the city to serve as a spatial reference.

In the case of 3D noise map the noise level is assigned to the vertical axis, whereas the horizontal plane corresponds to the streets city plane.

For the drawing of these maps a graphic representation computer program, developed to this end in the D.I.M. of the C.P.S.I.U.Z., was used. The program draws the maps starting from day and night L_{eq} data measured in 486 points of the city.

The city network is made up of 1584 points (34 in North-South direction and 46 in the East-West direction). In urban areas a 200 m. x 200 m. reticle is used, whereas in rural areas the reticle is a 500 m. x 1000 m. one.

Besides these points, others with special noise characteristics, were selected such as hospital and health clinics areas, bus station areas, urban industry areas, sports show areas, educational center areas, amusement areas, commercial areas, park and garden areas and lastly areas of special ecological interest.

2.1.2 Psico-sociological noise perception study

So as to have a global knowledge of the noise urban pollution phenomenon, a psico-sociological survey was made through a standardized questionnaire of 105 variables which includes a scale of attitudes with regard to noise (Likert type) in order to find out how urban noise is perceived by the citizens of Zaragoza.

The aspects analyzed in the investigation [2] are the relationship between noise and quality of life, noise pollution connected social variables and city subjective noise perception.

As a result of the public-opinion poll it is possible to arrive at the conclusion that traffic noise is the most important one for the citizens among all the urban noise sources, qualifying their induced nuisance as "worrying enough", while the rest of the noise sources are situated in the category of "little worrying". As for the variables related to the perception of noise, you can find cultural levels, occupational activities, types of labour (intelectual or manual), without a clear influence of the sex of the polled citizens on the noise perception and a certain increase of the nuisance level according to the age of the polled persons.

As for the attitudes regarding noise, the sensitizing factor is directly related to the degree of the nuisance level, in which the following percentage distribution are obtained: 99% "very sensitized", 57% "sensitized enough" and a surprising 32% "a little sensitized or indifferent to noise", this last result can be explained because important sectors of the population have adopted the noise pollution as a "normal" situation. The detected effects of noise can be summed up in that for a 40% of the population these effects are outstanding (physical and psyquical discomfort) whereas for 25% are slight.

The results of the survey study are represented in a graphical manner by means of noise perception psico-sociological maps. In figure 2 it is shown one of these maps developed starting from the results of the survey study data. The selected map shows the spatial distribution of the noise perception attitudes according to different zones of the city.

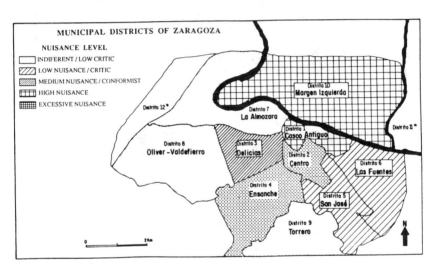

Figure 2: Noise perception psico-sociological map

As a validating conclusion, related to the elaboration of the maps, it is interesting to say that there is an excellent correlation between sonic and noise perception psico-sociological maps.

2.2 Noise prediction tools

Starting from a statistical processing of the noise level data gathered from the measurement campaigns, the Environmental Service in collaboration with the D.I.M of the C.P.S.I.U.Z. developed a set of urban traffic noise prediction models [3] for different areas of the city, whose final formulations are shown in Table 1.

U.Zone	Urban Traffic Noise Prediction Models (Day/Night Leq)
C.V.	Ln Leqd=4.022+0.005%p+0.049 Ln[(VL/h)/D] Leqn=55.249+2.642 Ln[(V/h)/D]
D	Leqd=58.04+0.326%p+2.255 Ln[(VL/h)/D] Leqn=53.451+0.167%p+3.557 Ln[(VL/h)/D]
B.O	Leqd=50.415+2.752 Ln(V/h) Leqn=50.415+2.752 Ln(V/h)
L.F.	Leqd=60.753+1.99 Ln[(VL/h)/D] Leqn=49.884+0.151%p+0.74 [(VL/h)/D]
S.J.	Leqd=53.656+0.416%p+3.577 Ln[(VL/h)/D] Leqn=52.622+2.694 Ln[(V/h)/D]
S.R.	Leqd=58.569+0.258%p+1.761 Ln[(VL/h)/D] Leqn=56.225+2.409 Ln[(V/h)/D]
Z.C.	Leqd=55.574+0.295%p+3.271 Ln[(VL/h)/D] Leqn=56.681+2.67 Ln[(V/h)/D]
T	Leqd=57.465+2.152 Ln[(V/h)/D] Leqn=50.257+1.574Ln[(VL/h)/D]
V	Leqd=51.511+0.23%p+2.275 Ln(VL/h) Leqn=52.52+3.079 Ln[(VL/h)/D]
A	Leqd=58.101+1.585 Ln[(VL/h)/D] Leqn=54.573+1.293Ln[(VL/h)/D]
Z.U.	Leqd=56.781+0.232%p+2.603 Ln[(VL/h)/D] +1.71 Z Leqn=56.729+0.239%p+2.79 Ln[(VL/h)/D]
A.P.	Leqd=53.0879+0.2928%p+2,6237 Ln[(VL/h)/D] Leqn=53.5191+0.1856%p+2,3448 Ln[(VL/h)/D]

Table 1: Urban traffic noise prediction models

The parameters used in the elaboration of the models are: width of the street (D), number of light vehicles (VL), percentage of heavy vehicles (%p), number of light vehicles per hour (VL/h), total number of vehicles per hour(Vh) and a correcting factor related to the commercial character of the zones (Z).

The mathematical models have been developed to be used by the Town Hall Environmental Service as basic tools to:
-Predict the noise impact of new urban transport activities.
-Create and design strategies of noise control.
-Design and realization of specific noise control actions.
-Serve as a data source for the urban planning strategies.

The most important conclusion of the validation process of the mathematical models, made starting from the comparison between predicted and measured data, is that the models work properly for values of total number of vehicles per hour (Vh) between 300 and 500. Out of this interval, some traffic dependent deviations from the measured values have been detected.

3 Description of an anti-noise pilot action: installation and evaluation of an urban motorway noise barrier

In 1993 the MOPTMA (Spanish Ministry of Works and Environment) decided to carry out the pilot experience of installating a noise barrier on the A2 (Madrid-Barcelona) motorway when passing through the township of Zaragoza. The basic aims of the experience are:
-To reduce the noise levels caused by the motorway noise and transmitted to buildings, situated at distances between 55 m. and 67 m. from the motorway hard shoulder, to noise levels below 55 dB(A) for day periods and below 65 dB(A) for night periods.
-To test the performance of different materials used in the construction of the barrier.
-Evaluate the effectiveness of this type of noise protections.
The noise barrier has a surface of 5000 m^2, 3,5 m. in height and 2000 m. in length, for the construction of the barrier different types of materials have been used such as GRC (glass reinforced concrete) panels, transparent PMMA panels, GRC-PMMA hybrid panels and perforated aluminium-mineral wool panels. The main aim of using this variety of panels is to combine the acoustic effectiveness with the aesthetic integration of the barrier in the motorway sorroundings.
The installation process of the barrier has been complemented with a supervision project in charge of the Municipal Environmental Service [4] whose basic aims are:
-To evaluate the noise abatement effect of the barrier by means of the comparison between the preoperational and operational traffic noise level values facing the buildings.
-To evaluate the psico-social effects of the noise barrier by means of pre and postoperational survey studies.
-To promote activities of civic participation with regard to noise pollution aspects (sensitizing campaign)

References

1. Lladó, J., Martínez, F. J. Tratamiento gráfico de las medidas debidas al ruido de tráfico en la Ciudad de Zaragoza, in Tecniacustica/93, (ed M. Arana, J. Salvador, P. Pereda, A.Vela), pp 33-36, *Proceedings of Tecniacustica/92*, Pamplona, Spain, 1992, Spanish Society of Acoustics (SEA) 1992.

2. Ibáñez, A., Aguerri, P. *Estado del ruido en Zaragoza*, Internal Report of the Servicio de Medio Ambiente del Ayuntamiento de Zaragoza, Zaragoza, 1994.

3. Lladó, J., Martínez, F. J. Modelos matemáticos de simulación del ruido debido al tráfico rodado en la Ciudad de Zaragoza, in Tecniacustica/93, (ed M. Arana, J. Salvador, P. Pereda, A. Vela), pp 33-36, *Proceedings of Tecniacustica/92*, Pamplona, Spain, 1992, Spanish Society of Acoustics (SEA) 1992.

4. Ibáñez, A., *Resumen de Actividades de la Sección Protección y Disciplina Ambiental*, Internal Report of the Servicio de Medio Ambiente del Ayuntamiento de Zaragoza, Zaragoza, 1994.

Determination of driving cycles for emission modelling in urban areas: a case study

L. Della Ragione,[a] M. Rapone,[a] V. Luzar[b]

[a] *Istituto Motori, Consiglio Nazionale delle Ricerche, Naples, Italy*

[b] *University of Zagreb, Croatia*

Abstract

An experimental approach has been applied to define driving cycles characterising driving behaviour in urban traffic. Driving cycles are to be used for the evaluation of exhaust emissions from individual vehicles in traffic. Designed trips have been performed by an instrumented car in a highly congested urban area of Naples, vehicle and engine operating conditions have been recorded . The velocity profile of car is analysed in terms of kinematic sequences described by car between two successive stops. Series of successive sequences having homogenous characteristics have been used to define, by cluster analysis, experimental driving cycles representative of different traffic conditions. Results of analyses are summarised in this paper, as well as diagrams of statistically sampled driving cycles.

1 Introduction

In this paper, an application of a methodology for the definition of driving behaviour in urban traffic is presented, that is the first step for the modelling of individual vehicle emissions in traffic. The method widely used to evaluate emissions is to detect car operating conditions on-road, and then measuring emissions in the laboratory using the most representative driving cycles sampled by car in different traffic conditions [1, 2]. Besides, it is well known that the complete characterisation of car kinematics, engine running parameters and gear ratio is required for an accurate evaluation of emissions.

An approach followed to define driving behaviour has been to instrument user driven cars and then to record car velocity and other information during their typical car usage [3, 4]. By this way, a good reproducibility of most diffused car usage is achieved. The alternative approach followed in this study has been to instrument few cars, detecting car, engine and gear operating parameters. In this case, a more complete information is available: statistical information on gear ratio use can be included in the definition of driving cycles, fuel consumption and temperatures can be utilised in lab/road operating conditions correlations. Moreover, trips of car are designed, then analysis can be performed to study relationships between driving behaviour and relevant factors like road typology and more diffused paths, or to study specific situation like car approaching traffic lights, positive and negative trends, etc. The main disadvantage of this approach consists in the scarce information on different users and cars effects on driving cycles. The integration of the two approaches may produce a better traffic characterization.

An Alfa Romeo ALFA 155 catalyst car has been utilised, so far. Using results collected in a preliminary phase of research, [5, 6, 7], trips were designed according to a quasi balanced incomplete factorial plan, considering three drivers, six paths (comprehending centre of town streets and urban highway), two periods of day, namely morning rush hours and afternoon. Trips were performed going from west side of Naples to north (and viceversa), passing through town centre or by highway. Results presented in this paper refer to all trips except those performed in urban highway.

The methodology to define driving cycles is based on the analysis of parts of movements between two successive stops (kinematic sequences), [5]. In most papers only kinematic parameters are used in the definition of kinematic sequences, whereas in the present study sequences are characterised by quantities related to velocity, acceleration and gear ratio.

Sequences have been classified into a number of typical groups using a clustering method. Three larger groups are derived from sequence clusters to identify different situations: slow, fast and neutral gear run (in negative trend streets). Kynematic cycles were then determined by series of successive sequences limited by the passage from one group to another. These were then grouped in clusters related to different traffic levels, the most representative driving cycles sampled from these clusters will be utilised for emission measurement.

2. Definition of sequence clusters

The basic element of driving cycle is sequence. This is defined as the part of movements between two successive stops of car. To analyse sequence pattern, many variables are utilised to describe different aspects related to idle, acceleration, constant speed and deceleration parts of sequence, in this study gear ratio is considered as well. The variables listed in table 1 have been evaluated to characterise each single sequence.

A total of 4007 sequences have been collected, summing 545 km and 43 hours. Morning trips were performed in rush hours (8.30-11.30), afternoon trips (4 p.m. - 6 p.m.) in more variable conditions. Most sequences refer to high congested traffic conditions, with an overall mean velocity of 12.5 km/h and a total of 32 % time at idle, and a 90 % of time at a speed less than 20 km/h.

Table 1.

VMOY (average speed) (km/h)	**DIST** (distance covered) (m)
VMAX (maximum speed) (km/h)	**TRAL** (idling time) (s)
NERV (number of peaks)	**ACC0V** (percentage of time with stable velocity)
V20 (percentage of time velocity is less than 20 km/h)	**GEAR0** (percentage of time in neutral)
V30 (percentage of time velocity is between 20 and 30 km/h)	**GEAR1** (percentage of time in first gear)
V40 (percentage of time velocity is between 30 and 40 km/h)	**GEAR2** (percentage of time in second gear)
V100 (percentage of time velocity is greater than 40 km/h)	**GEAR3** (percentage of time in third gear)
TSEQ (sequence duration) (s)	**GEAR4** (percentage of time in fourth gear)
CONSUMPT (fuel mass rate) (g/s)	**GEAR5** (percentage of time in fifth gear)

The two-stage density linkage clustering method, tested in a preliminary analysis Mc Quitty [9], was used to classify sequences in ten typical groups. To visualise clusters and to point out different characteristics of each cluster, discriminant analysis has been used and the ten clusters plotted in the space of the first two canonical variables CAN1 and CAN2, which are linear combination of the above defined variables. CAN1 is highly and positively correlated to average and max. speed and to percentage of time in second gear, while it is negatively correlated to percent of time spent at speed < 20 km/h and in first gear, thus separating fast from slow sequences. CAN is highly and positively correlated to GEAR0 and negatively to GEAR1, separating sequences with most time in neutral form those in other gears. A plot of CAN1 versus CAN2 for 4007 sequences is shown in figure 1.

Three large groups (more actually clouds) of sequences can be detected by analysing this diagram. The first group(clusters 4,5,6,7,8,: high CAN2, low CAN1) is characterised by high fraction of time in neutral (4,5,6,7 >95%, 8 ≈ 45%), it refers to sequences performed in negative trend parts of trips. The second group (clusters 1,2,3: low CAN2, low CAN1) is characterised by low VMOY and high GEAR1 (>95%), cluster 3 is differentiate by 1 for significantly higher ACC0V and DIST, while cluster 2 is formed by atypical sequences with GEAR1 = 100% and 99% time at idle. Third group (clusters 9,10: low CAN2, high CAN1) presents high VMOY and use of first, second and third gear. Cluster 10 is formed by sequences with significantly longer time and distance.

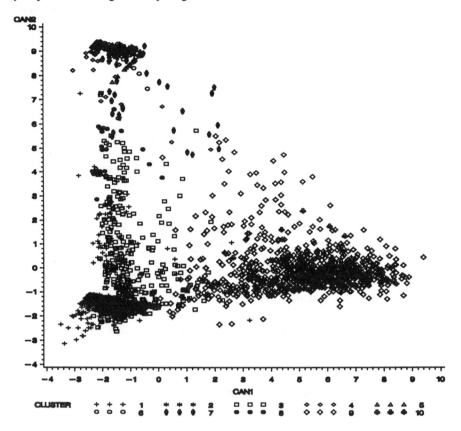

Figure 1: Canonical Variables plot for sequence-clusters

3. Driving cycles

The study of the succession of sequences during different trips gives the basis information for the construction of driving cycles. From the analysis of experimental data resulted that the three groups defined in the previous section well fit different traffic conditions. As a consequence, cycles have been automatically determined by the series of sequences belonging to the same group, starting a new cycle when a sequence of another group starts.

The following variables have been selected to characterise each cycle: **C1MEAN**, **C2MEAN** (the average value computed for each cycle of respectively CAN1 and CAN2 values of sequences belonging to the cycle), **PDR_TIME** (fraction of driving time), **N_SEQ** (number of sequences in a cycle), **TR_SUM** (total idling time of the cycle), **D_SUM** (the distance covered in a cycle).

Eight clusters of cycles have been obtained applying the Ward cluster method to the observations relative to 1184 cycles determined according to the above mentioned method . Cycle clusters are presented in figure 2 in the space of the first two canonical variables.

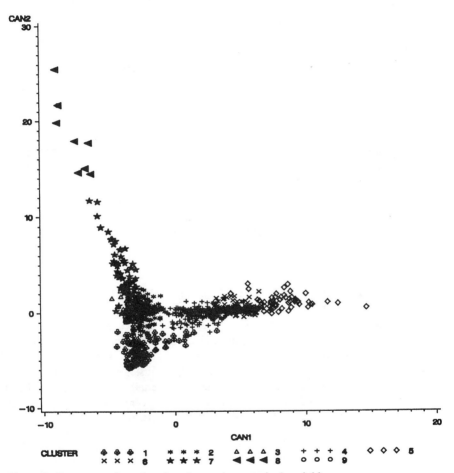

Figure 2: Representation of cycles clusters in canonical variables space

The first canonical variable (CAN1) discriminates clusters in relation to C1MEAN and D_SUM, characterizing cycles respect to velocity and distance. The second canonical variable (CAN2) differentiates, by negative values, cycles with high fraction of time in neutral from the others, for positive values it separates cycles with high idling time (CAN2 is negatively correlated to C2MEAN and positively to TR_SUM). Thus, cluster 1 is composed of cycles mostly performed in neutral, clusters 7 and 8 of cycles with high fraction of idling time, clusters 3, 2, 4, 6, 5 comprehends cycles representing traffic conditions varying from congested to relatively fluent ones. Cycles clusters are summarised in table 2, where cluster averaged values of most relevant variables are reported.

Table 2. Cluster summary by average values

MEAN	CLUSTERS				
	3	2	4	6	5
NSEQ	2.15	2.61	1.34	1.97	4
VMOY (km/h)	3.96	6.77	14	22	25
D_SUM (m)	20	85	241	1091	3504
T_SUM (s)	54	55	70	197	528
TR_SUM (s)	42	18	16	22	46
PDR_TIME (%)	24	68	77	91	91

The most representative cycles of each cluster of cycles, obtained by discriminant analysis on the basis of the estimates of group specific density [10], are shown in figure 3. In each cycle actual gear ratio is reported.

4. Conclusions

An experimental application to determine driving cycles relative to different traffic conditions and a specific urban area has been presented in this paper. Driving cycles have been obtained by classifying kinematic sequences in typical groups, studying succession of sequences groups along trips, and finally segmenting trips into series of sequences having homogenous characteristics. Each segment of trip is defined as a cycle. Cycles are then grouped by a cluster method, each group of cycles can be considered as corresponding to a certain traffic condition. Most representative cycles of each cluster, and thus of a certain level of traffic, are extracted by each cluster by the estimate of group specific density.

5. Acknowledgements

This project was carried out under the contract within the research project "Urban areas and environment - life quality in large urban systems" funded by Environment Committee of National Research Council of Italy. The authors acknowledges the co-operation of ELASYS SpA which supplied the ALFA ROMEO ALFA 155 car.

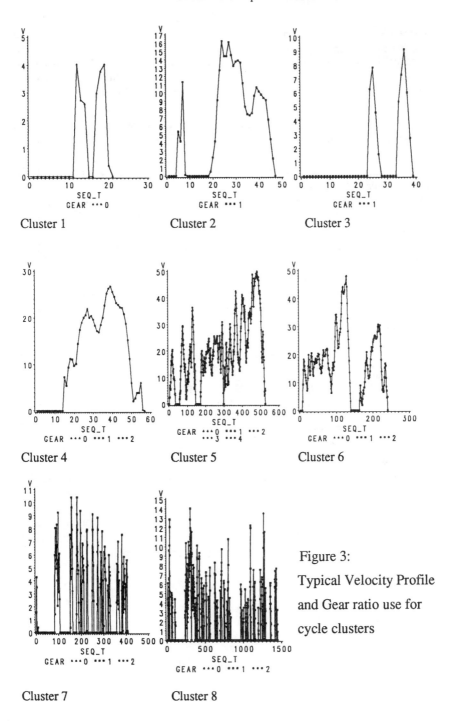

Figure 3:
Typical Velocity Profile
and Gear ratio use for
cycle clusters

References

1 Andre M., A.J. Hickman, T.J. Barlow, D. Hassel, R. Joumard Modelling of emissions and consumption in urban areas: measurements of the driving behaviour and the vehicle operations in actual uses - method. *INRETS Report, NNE 8905.* Bron, France, 1989.

2 Jost P., D. Hassel, F.J. Weber, K.S. Sonnborn Emission and fuel consumption modelling based on continuous measurements. *Report No 7 DRIVE Project V 1053,* 1992.

3 Andre M., R. Joumard, J. Hickman, D. Hassel Realistic driving cycles for passenger cars. *INRETS Report, LEN 9106,* Bron, France, 1991.

4 Andre M., J.P. Roumegoux, J.P. Delsey, R. Vidon Etudes experimentales sur les utilisation reelles des vehicules (EUREV). *Rapport INRETS No 48,* 1987.

5 Maurin M., J.-P. Crauser The kinematic sequences, an atomistic approach to automobile travel and effects of traffic. Recherche Transport Securite, Revue de l'INRETS, English Issue No 5, Arcueil, France, 1990.

6 Della Ragione L., Giglio V., Luzar V., Rapone M. Characterization of actual driving cycles by means of statistical analysis: a preliminary approach, pp.130-136 *Proceedings of 3rd International Symposium Transport and Air Pollution,* Avignon, France, 1994.

7 Della Ragione L., Giglio V., Luzar V., Rapone M. Visualisation and Analysis of Urban Traffic Data, pp.856-866, *Proceedings of the twelfth SEUGI '94,* Strasbourg, France, 1994.

8. Della Ragione L., Giglio V., Luzar V., Rapone M. Urban driving cycles for emissions testing, pp.485-492, *Proceedings of the 27th ISATA Conference,* Aachen, Germany, 1994.

9. Mc Quitty, L.,L. Elementary linkage analysis for isolating orthogonal and oblique types and typal relevancies, *Educational and Psychological Measurement,* 17, 207-229, 1957.

10. SAS/STAT User's Guide Version 6, Fourth Edition, Volume1, 1992.

The potential effects of road pricing on air quality in the Toronto area

K. Helali, B.G. Hutchinson
PMS Limited, Cambridge, Ontario and Department of Civil Engineering, University of Waterloo, Waterloo, Ontario, Canada N2L 3G1

Abstract

This paper describes analyses of the potential impacts of cordon-type road pricing schemes on travel behaviour and automobile emissions in the Greater Toronto Area. The potential influence of road pricing on travel behaviour was analyzed using an incremental logit model and the variable demand automobile assignment feature of EMME/2. Link traffic volumes calculated by EMME/2 were subjected to a post-processor analysis to improve the vehicle speed estimates. MOBILE5C was used to calculate automobile emissions. Five cordon-type road pricing schemes were analyzed and these are shown to have great potential for diverting trip makers to other modes and start times and for improving traffic flow quality. The largest reductions in automobile emissions are shown to be in the central employment area.

1 Introduction

The number of daily work trips in the Greater Toronto Area (GTA) has increased from about 0.5M in 1964 to 1.9M in 1991. This increase in commuting travel has translated into sharp increases in vehicle-kilometres of travel (VkmT) because of the increased number of trips as well as increases in average trip length (9.6 km in 1971 and 13.5 km in 1991) and decreasing use of public transport (22% in 1971 and 19% in 1991). It is expected that this trend in accelerating VkmT will continue into the 21st century unless stringent interventions aimed at reducing the growth in VkmT occur.

This increasing demand for automobile travel is one of the major contributors to the degradation of air quality in the GTA. Automobiles contribute about one-third of the hydrocarbons and about one-fifth of nitrogen oxides, the precursors of ground level ozone. These and other emissions have resulted in the violation of the ozone air quality criteria in the region. For example, recent data have shown that the air quality criteria at monitoring stations in downtown Toronto were exceeded more than 260 times per year.

Vehicle emission control technologies (improved ignition systems, catalytic convertors, low emission engines) and improved fuels are expected to reduce emissions. However, increasing VkmT are expected to overwhelm these improvements and ambient air quality standards are only likely to be achieved through transportation control measures.

The primary objective of the study reported in this paper was to investigate the potential impacts of road pricing on air quality in the GTA. The paper describes the transportation systems analysis method that has been used to analyze the potential impacts of road pricing on travel behaviour as well as the likely impacts of these changes on air quality.

2 The Analysis Framework

Figure 1 illustrates the structure of the analysis procedure. The 1986 peak period trip table for the GTA was used since the 1991 travel survey used very low sampling rates in the developed parts of the GTA. EMME/2 provided the systems analysis framework within which potential travel behaviour responses to road pricing were estimated using an incremental logit model choice model and an equilibrium traffic assignment method. The transport system information calculated by the transport model was then input into the Canadian version of the U.S. EPA MOBILE 5 model. The GTA land use and transport system was represented by a fairly coarse system of 127 zones and 1,050 link nodes and 4,000 directional links.

The Pricing Schemes
Figure 2 shows the pricing cordons that were used in the analyses reported in this paper. One cordon surrounded the central business area and the outer cordon followed mainly the major freeways located about 15-25 km from the central area. Six road pricing scenarios were tested and these consisted of a single outer cordon with three toll levels ($4, $2 and $1) and three multiple cordon pricing schemes ($4 at the outer cordon and $1 at the inner cordon; $2 at the outer cordon and $3 at the inner cordon; $1 at the outer cordon and $4 at the inner cordon).

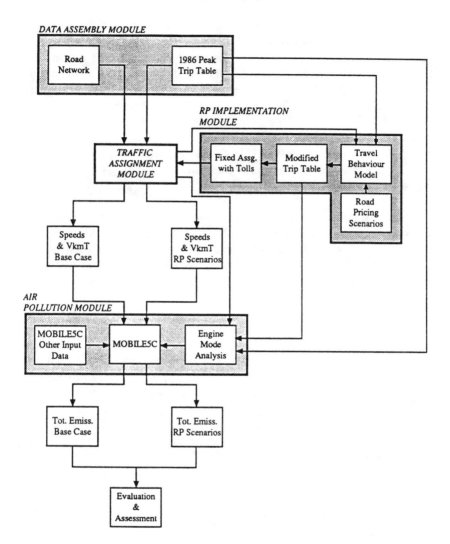

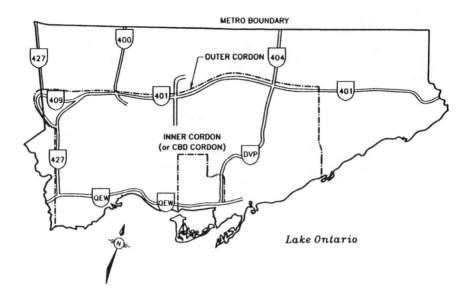

Figure 2: Locations of Pricing Cordons

Influence of Road Pricing on Behaviour

There are three types of response that might occur when congestion pricing schemes are introduced and these are shifts to other modes, shifts of trips to other time periods (peak to shoulder) and route changes. An incremental logit model of the following form was used to estimate modal shifts:

$$p*(i) = \frac{p(i)\exp(dU_i)}{1 - p(i)[1-\exp(dU_i)]} \tag{1}$$

where $p*(i)$ = the new probability of choosing mode i; $p(i)$ = the initial probability of choosing mode i; and dU_i = the change in the utility of mode U.

Some examples of the prior use of the incremental logit model are by Ben-Akiva and Atherton [1] who analyzed car pooling incentives, by Harrison et al [3] who analyzed road pricing in Hong Kong and by Loudon et al [5] who examined the potential impacts of parking management alternatives in Oregon.

The variable demand auto assignment option in EMME/2 provides a powerful tool for incorporating modal split analysis into the traffic assignment step. It is achieved by first calculating a set of shortest paths based on the free flow travel time. Initial demand values were calculated using the modal split model with the shortest path times. In this particular application, the factors that were evaluated are changes in travel times and changes in prices. The resulting demand is assigned to the shortest path and the process repeated until it converges.

Tolls in the variable demand auto assignment were modelled as toll O-D matrices. These matrices consisted of those trips that used the tolled freeway network and were not destined to zones within the priced cordons. Select link analysis was used to identify the origins and destinations of those trips using the tolled freeway network.

The peak hour auto driver trip table provided the input to this analysis and the auto trip table that resulted from the above analysis process reflected the reduction in the number of vehicles on the road network due to the higher prices. The reduction may be due to modal or time of departure shifts.

The modified auto trip table was then assigned to the road network using the fixed demand option of EMME/2, with time penalties representing the tolls, in order to predict the impacts of tolls on route choices. These time penalties were equal to the dollar value of the tolls divided by the estimated value of time ($8/h) and these were then added to the link congestion functions. The output of this assignment provided traffic volumes and travel times that were used as inputs to the post-processor methodology.

Road tolls and changes in travel times were the only two variables considered to influence travel behaviour as a result of the introduction of congestion pricing. The utility function coefficients for in-vehicle travel time and out-of-pocket costs were based on models calibrated for the GTA and those reported in the literature. The magnitudes selected were 0.29 for in-vehicle travel time and 0.0038 for cost which yields a value of travel time of $7.63 which is close to the $8 used for the conversion of tolls to travel time penalties.

Figure 3 illustrates in detail the structure of the traffic assignment module. One of the objectives of the research reported in this paper was to improve the quality of the average speed and VkmT estimates as they are critical input data to the emission model. An important component of this traffic assignment model is the post-processor methodology which improves on the speed estimates output by the equilibrium traffic assignment model.

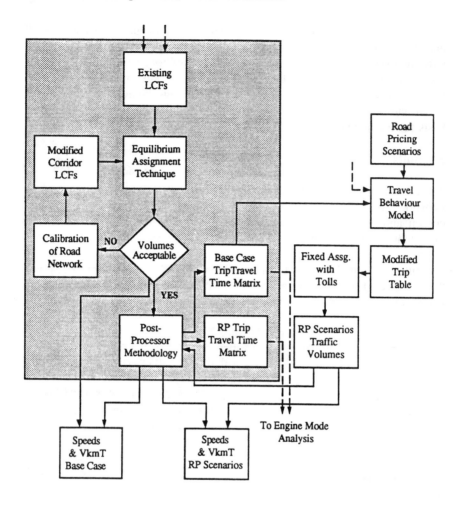

Figure 3: Traffic Assignment Module

The post-processor model combines parts of the procedures developed by
Dowling and Skabardonis [2] and MacDonald et al [7] and is described in
detail by Helali and Hutchinson [4]. The post-processor method consists of an
arterial module and a freeway module. In the arterial module, queues are

formed on links where demand exceeds capacity and queue lengths and speeds are calculated based on a density value for vehicles queuing on an arterial street at a signal. The arterial module uses a set of congestion functions based on the Davidson formulation and calibrated to speed and volume data observed in Toronto. The average travel speed is calculated as the average of the queue speed and uncongested speed. A similar queuing-based approach forms the basis for the freeway module.

3 Results of Road Pricing

Table 1 summarizes the impacts of the fixed pricing schemes on traffic at the network level for all trips, work trips destined to locations within the outer cordon and work trips destined to locations within the inner cordon. The important points to note from Table 1 are the substantial reductions in the number of automobile trips to destinations within the pricing cordons, particularly automobile trips to the central area. This is not surprising, given that a high quality transit system serves the central area and provides a realistic alternative for car drivers.

Table 1. Impacts of Congestion Pricing on Trips

		All Trips	Trips to Zones within Outer Cordon	Trips to Zones within Inner Cordon
Basic Trips		47,620	131,960	37,302
Toll Scenario		**Percent Reduction in Trips**		
Outer	Inner			
$4	---	6.3	18.8	18.1
$2	---	3.2	9.5	9.3
$1	---	1.6	4.7	4.7
$4	$1	7.4	22.5	31.9
$2	$3	6.1	19.6	48.4
$1	$4	5.3	17.5	54.8

A second view of the impacts of road pricing schemes is presented in Table 2 which shows the total VkmT and vehicle hours of travel under the six pricing scenarios. The table entries indicate that the most effective pricing scenarios are those at the outer cordon where average trip lengths are much longer than those focussed on the central employment area. The much larger percentage decrease in vehicle hours is due to the reduction in the number of automobile trips as well as the significant increase in average speeds on freeways within the priced area. For example, the average speeds on the freeways within the pricing cordon were estimated to increase from 73.7 km/h to 82.1 km/h with the $4 toll at the outer cordon and to 76 km/h with a $1 toll.

Table 2. Impacts of Pricing on VkmT and Vehicle Hours

		VkmT	Vehicle Hours
Base Case freeways non-freeways		2,401,300 3,696,200	42,620 101,510
Pricing Scenario		% change	% change
Outer Cordon	**Inner Cordon**		
$4	---	-16.9 -7.3	-33.2 -13.8
$2	---	-8.8 -3.5	-19.9 -8.7
$1	---	-4.8 -1.4	-10.9 -4.8
$4	$1	-17.3 -8.5	-34.2 -15.5
$2	$3	-10.4 -7.1	-24.5 -14.3
$1	$4	-6.8 6.1	-17.4 -12.7

Table 3. Impacts of Pricing on Average Travel Speeds

	Base Case	Toll at Outer Cordon		
		$4	$2	$1
Entire network	52.5	54.3	53.4	52.9
Within Outer Cordon	41.9	46.7	44.5	43.2
Within Inner Cordon	40.9	42.8	41.7	41.2
Freeways for entire network	76.2	83.6	80.1	78.3
Freeways within outer cordon	73.7	82.1	77.9	75.9
Freeways within inner cordon	78.4	80.9	79.4	78.8
Non-freeways for entire network	50.8	52.2	51.5	51.2
Non-freeways within outer cordon	37.4	42.5	40.2	38.8
Non-freeways within inner cordon	36.3	38.5	37.2	36.6

entries are km/h

Table 3 summarizes the estimated average travel speeds on various elements of the road network under the three pricing scenarios at the outer cordon. The table shows that the increases in average speeds for the entire GTA network are rather modest but that the changes in average freeway speeds and in average arterial speeds are quite substantial.

Clearly, the imposition of tolls at any cordon will tend to deflect traffic flows to adjacent non-tolled roads, where the amount of traffic diverted will be a function of the level of service provided by the non-tolled routes. Table 4 provides an example of these traffic volume diversions for two sections of freeways at the outer toll cordon. The second column shows the peak hour traffic volumes for the base case and the third to fifth columns the percentage change in traffic volumes from the base case. The first number shows the total percent reduction while the second number shows the reduction due to route shift where the difference is due to mode and time of departure shifts.

Table 4. Percentage Changes in Diverted Peak Hour Traffic Volumes

	Base Case Volumes	Toll at Outer Cordon		
		$4	$2	$1
freeway	8,410	-25(-13)	-16(-10)	-7(-5)
	6,720	-31(-14)	-19(-11)	-10(-7)
adjacent arterial	460	39	30	5
	210	72	68	36
freeway	11,040	-32(-14)	-15(-7)	-4(-1)
	11,120	-25(-14)	-11(-6)	-3(-1)
adjacent arterial	350	74	68	41
	1,080	21	14	0

The table entries indicate that there are substantial diversions to the adjacent arterials, particularly for the $4 toll at the outer cordon. The table entries also show the significant reduction in automobile trips due to mode and time of departure shifts. Similar effects were observed at other locations around the outer toll cordon. Analyses of traffic diverted to adjacent routes at the inner toll cordon showed traffic increases to be quite high as trips passing through the inner tolled area sought to avoid tolls.

4. Potential Changes in Vehicle Emissions

Total automobile engine emissions are governed by the vehicle operating mode and the vehicle kilometres of travel. Vehicle operating modes are usually classified as the cold start mode, the hot stabilized mode and the hot start mode. Total vehicle emissions, then, are due to engine start emissions (or trip end emissions) and running mode emissions. Trip end emissions typically account for 50 percent of total daily emissions. Figure 4 illustrates the relative magnitudes of hydrocarbon emissions for a prototypical 33 km round trip for a light duty automobile in the Bay Area of California, Loudon and Dagang [6].

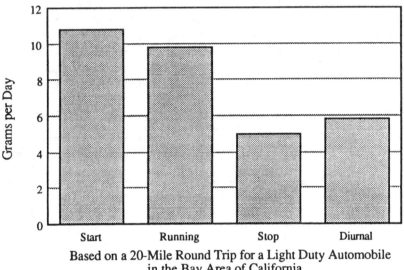

**Based on a 20-Mile Round Trip for a Light Duty Automobile
in the Bay Area of California**

(Source: Loudon and Dagang [6])
Figure 4: Components of Hydrocarbon Emissions

The traffic data provided by EMME/2, which were input into MOBILE5C to calculate running loss emissions were the trip length distributions. Table 5 shows the percentage of automobile trips within the six time intervals used by MOBILE5C for each of the six pricing scenarios.

It was assumed that 90 percent of the peak hour automobile trips involved cold starts which is based on the fact that the percentage of A.M. peak hour home-based trips in the GTA in 1986 was 91 percent. The transient mode analysis was conducted by identifying the number of trips of less than 505 seconds in duration (the running time required for transition to the hot stabilized mode) and summing these to obtain the total trip minutes in the transient mode. For trips greater than 505 seconds, the total trip minutes were divided between the transient and hot stabilized modes. The total transient mode percentage was then calculated by dividing the transient mode by the total duration of all trips. This resulted in slightly higher percentages of vehicle time in the transient mode for the higher toll scenarios because of the shorter trip lengths.

Table 5. Estimated Trip Length Distributions

Pricing Scenario	Percentage of Trips in Time Interval (mins)					
	< 10	11-20	21-30	31-40	41-50	> 51
base case	29	22	17	12	8	12
1	34	25	20	10	5	6
2	32	23	19	12	7	7
3	31	22	18	12	8	9
4	35	26	19	10	5	5
5	34	24	19	10	6	7
6	33	23	18	11	7	8

Table 6 summarizes the percentage change in emissions levels estimated by MOBILE5C for winter conditions from the base case for each of the pricing scenarios for hydrocarbons, carbon monoxide and nitrous oxides. These reductions are shown for arterial streets in the CBD and freeways. The reductions for other arterial streets are rather modest and have not been included. The table entries indicate that the largest potential redirections in automobile emissions are in the CBD, where these reductions reflect the large potential changes in VkmT induced by tolls at the inner cordon around the central employment area. The next largest potential reduction in emissions is on the tolled freeways, where potential reductions of up to 20 percent are indicated. Once again, these potential reductions are due to reductions in VkmT resulting from the potential shifts to other modes and departure times.

Table 6. Percentage in Emissions from the Base Case for Winter Conditions

Pricing Scenario	CBD Non-Freeways			Freeways		
	HC	CO	NOX	HC	CO	NOX
1	-19.3	-19.1	-14.9	-21.1	-20.8	-16.2
2	-9.6	-9.5	-7.9	-11.1	-11.0	-8.8
3	-4.5	-4.2	-3.7	-6.0	-5.9	-4.8
4	-36.8	-36.7	-30.2	-21.3	-21.4	-16.5
5	-53.5	-53.2	-45.9	-13.7	-13.5	-9.9
6	-58.5	-58.4	-51.7	-9.1	-9.2	-6.8

5 Concluding Remarks

This paper has described a methodology for estimating the potential impacts of road pricing schemes on the reduction of automobile emissions in the GTA. The results were obtained within the transport systems analysis framework provided by EMME/2. The variable demand automobile assignment option in EMME/2 was used along with an incremental logit model to estimate shifts from the automobile mode that might be induced by road tolls. The link volumes calculated by the equilibrium traffic assignment were then subjected to a post-processor methodology to improve link speed estimates. The link speed estimates and the travel parameters were then input into MOBILE5C to estimate automobile emissions.

Two toll cordon schemes have been analyzed and these were an outer toll cordon around the freeway system and an inner toll cordon around the central employment area. Tolls of from $1 to $4 were analyzed and the results suggested that reductions in VkmT of as high as 17 percent might be obtained and reductions of up to 30 percent might occur in vehicle hours of travel.

The analysis of changes in automobile emission levels of as high as 50-60 percent in the central employment area might be expected. Reductions in emissions on the freeway system of 20 percent might be expected.

It is clear that the behavioral shifts suggested by these analyses need to be confirmed by empirical information. It is expected that data will become available from various road pricing projects. The first toll road embedded in the Toronto network is expected to be open in about two years.

6 References

1. Ben-Akiva, M. and Atherton, T.J. Methodology for Short-Range Travel Demand Predictions. Analysis of Carpooling Incentives. *Journal of Transport Economics and Policy*, XI, No. 3, pp. 224-262, 1977.

2. Dowling, R. and Skabardonis, A. Improving the Average Travel Speeds Estimated by Planning Models. *Transportation Research Record 1366*, Transportation Research Board, Washington, D.C., pp. 68-74, 1992.

3. Harrison, W.J., Pell, C., Jones, P.M. and Ashton, H. Some Advances in Model Design Developed for the Practical Assignment of Road Pricing in Hong Kong. *Transportation Research*, 20A, No. 2, pp. 135-143, 1986.

4. Helali, K. and Hutchinson, B. Improving Link Speed Estimates for Air Quality Models. *Transportation Research Record 1444*, pp. 71-78, 1994.

5. Loudon,W.R., Coleman, E. and Suhrbier, J.H.   Air Quality Offsets of Parking. *Transportation Research Record 1232*, Transportation Research Board, Washington, D.C.   pp. 68-75, 1989.

6. Loudon,W.R. and Dagang, D.A.   Predicting the Impact of Transportation Control Measures on Travel Behaviour and Pollutant Emissions.   A Paper Presented at the 71st Transportation Research Board Annual Meeting, Washington, D.C., 1992.

7. MacDonald, O.J., Dehgani, Y. and Altan, O.   An Empirical Queuing Analysis for the Central Artery Freeway Complex in the Central Boston Area.   Paper Submitted for the Presentation at the 71st Transportation Research Annual Meeting, Washington, D.C., 1992.

Harmonising transport policy to achieve environmental, social and economic goals

M. Dess
Environment Protection Authority (Victoria), Melbourne, Australia

Abstract

This paper presents estimates, in monetary terms, of the costs of transport noise, the impacts on human health of motor vehicle emissions, and the costs of traffic congestion and accidents in Victoria, Australia. The results indicate that these costs, despite the uncertainty involved in their estimation, are substantial - exceeding \$A6 billion per year. The paper also presents an evaluation of strategies for reducing transport emissions of the greenhouse gas, carbon dioxide (CO_2). It is shown that these emissions can be reduced by around 16% (compared with projected levels in the year 2005), at no net financial cost to the community.

1 Introduction

The Environment Protection Authority (Victoria) (EPA) recently conducted a study of transport externalities in Victoria. That study, which provides the basis of this paper, indicates that the cost of these externalities is substantial. The study also examined the contribution of transport in Victoria to emissions of the greenhouse gas, CO_2, and assessed the cost-effectiveness of measures to reduce those emissions. Based on this assessment, it is apparent that efforts to redress transport externalities need not result in a trade-off with economic well-being. The view that such trade-offs are inevitable fails to account for opportunities to implement policies to tackle transport's environmental and social impacts, while simultaneously generating a *financial return* to the community.

2 Transport Externalities in Victoria

The concept of externalities

The law of supply and demand is central to the study of economics. A basic tenet of this law is that the demand for a product is a function of its price - the higher the price, the lower the demand. A corollary of this is that if a product is *underpriced*, demand for it will be greater than if it were priced 'correctly'. A major cause of underpricing is the lack of accounting for external costs (or externalities). An external cost is a cost which is paid for, not by those who cause it, but by others who have nothing to do with causing it. Because they are 'paid for by others', external costs effectively are *hidden costs*, and are often ignored.

Transport externalities - a cause for concern?
It is difficult to think of any activity that does not generate external costs. The question, therefore, is whether transport externalities should be regarded as a cause for concern. The answer is an unequivocal *yes*. As outlined above, the failure of prices to account for external costs results in the underpricing and over consumption of transport services. In turn, this leads to more resources being used in providing those services, and to higher levels of environmental and social impacts, than would occur if transport users were required to meet the full costs of transport. Furthermore, the level of external costs is likely to vary between modes, resulting in a distortion of competition - modes with high external costs gain an advantage over those with lower external costs, due to the fact that transport prices do not reflect this differential.

Estimates of the monetary value of selected transport externalities in Victoria
A summary of external cost estimates from the Victorian Transport Externalities Study (EPA[1]) is presented in Table 1. A few precautionary comments should be noted. First, because of the uncertainties involved, the estimates are best regarded as indicative. The nature of these uncertainties is well exemplified by Figure 1, which outlines the steps involved in estimating a monetary value for the health effects of motor vehicle emissions.

  Second, while estimates of the costs of road traffic noise and the health effects of motor vehicle-sourced ozone and air toxics are *external* costs, the estimates relating to accidents and congestion represent *total* costs. A proportion of the costs of accidents and congestion are borne by those who cause them - that proportion is, therefore, an *internal*, as opposed to an *external*, cost. A recent report to the OECD (Bouladon[2]) has estimated that 30% of the total cost of accidents is external. However, due to limitations in data and study budget, it was not possible to determine the applicability of this estimate to Victoria, nor to estimate the external component of congestion costs.

  Third, while the cost of accidents is estimated for the whole of Victoria, the estimated costs of congestion, and the health impacts of ozone (photochemical smog) and air toxic emissions from motor vehicles, are for the Melbourne metropolitan area only. In the case of road traffic noise, cost estimates relate only to the arterial road network in Melbourne.

Transport and the "greenhouse externality"
Accumulating evidence indicates that human activity has markedly raised the concentration of greenhouse gases in the atmosphere. The increased concentration of these gases will *enhance* the natural greenhouse effect and is expected to lead to

a change in the earth's climate. Transport, through its consumption of fossil fuels, is a major contributor to the build-up of greenhouse gases - particularly CO_2.

Estimating a monetary value for the "greenhouse externality" is highly problematic. There is general agreement regarding its existence, but considerable uncertainty as to the scale of global climate change, and its likely regional impacts. Therefore, no attempt was made to estimate a monetary value for the external costs associated with transport greenhouse gas emissions. Rather, effort was directed to estimating the scale of transport emissions of CO_2, and to assessing the cost-effectiveness of measures to reduce these emissions (see Section 3).

Table 1. **Estimated monetary value of selected environmental and social impacts of transport in Victoria ($A1992)**

Selected Impact	Estimated Annual Cost ($A million)		Comment
Road Traffic Noise in Melbourne	43 to 86		The estimate relates to the cost of noise levels in excess of 63 dB(A) on arterial roads in Melbourne.
Effects on human health of vehicle-sourced photochemical smog in Melbourne	1988/89	*"low"* 0.8 *"central"* 5.7 *"high"* 10.9	The range of estimates (ie. "low" to "high") reflects uncertainties in estimating health effects associated with air pollution. The variation between years is a consequence of meteorological variability.
	1991/92	*"low"* 0.01 *"central"* 0.08 *"high"* 0.1	
"Excess" cancers due to emissions from vehicles in Melbourne	26 to 45		Estimate relates to 1990 emissions levels.
Road accidents in Victoria	4,000		This estimate represents the *total* cost of accidents - it does not isolate the *external* component.
Traffic congestion in Melbourne	2,000		This estimate represents the *total* cost of congestion - it does not isolate the *external* component.

3   Harmonising Transport Policy - The Case of Greenhouse Gas Emissions Reductions

Targets for reducing external costs - theory and practice
Economic theory suggests that measures to control externalities should be implemented to the economically *optimal* level. This occurs where the marginal (incremental) benefits equal the marginal costs of control. Determining this level in

practice, however, is more difficult than theory might suggest. As discussed above, an important cause of this difficulty is the uncertainty involved in estimating the costs and benefits of externality control measures.

Estimate traffic volumes ↓	Often derived from surveys and transport models. By nature, surveys and models are subject to error and approximation.
Estimate level of emissions from vehicles ↓	The relationship between traffic volumes and total emissions is complex and non-linear. Emissions vary with climatic conditions; vehicle type, age and state of repair; driving conditions; driver behaviour etc.
Estimate the level of pollution resulting from vehicle emissions ↓	Pollution levels are a function not only of emission levels in an area, but also meteorological conditions, local topography, and the rate of formation of secondary pollutants. Complex models are required to produce estimates of ambient pollution levels.
Estimate the impacts of pollution levels on human health ↓	Human health effects are particularly difficult to determine at the relatively low pollution concentrations typical of urban areas. Also, an individual's sensitivity varies according to whether he/she is particularly sensitive to a pollutant; the level of physical activity being undertaken when exposed; the amount of time spent indoors and outdoors etc.
Estimate the monetary value of the human health impacts	Determining appropriate monetary values for human life, pain and suffering, restriction of activity etc. is problematic.

Figure 1   Estimating a monetary value for the health impacts of motor vehicle emissions

In the absence of a precise knowledge of marginal costs and benefits, it is not possible to determine the optimal level of control. Consequently, policy-makers must determine an *appropriate* level of control by reference to a range of information, including scientific assessments of the levels of environmental impact that are ecologically sustainable; public opinion regarding the levels of environmental and social impact that are acceptable; and the costs involved in achieving different levels of control over an externality. As it is not always possible to achieve a consensus, policy-makers often will be required to strike a balance between different views, and between different objectives. The key issue, of course, is the extent to which these different objectives are in conflict.

Following this approach, the Australian government has adopted an interim planning target to reduce greenhouse gas emissions to *20% below 1988 levels by the year 2005* (NGRS[3]). The Victorian Transport Externalities Study estimated that a pro-rata application of this target to land-based transport in Victoria equates to a reduction in CO_2 emissions of *27% compared with projected levels in 2005*.

Complementarities and trade-offs in reducing transport CO_2 emissions

It is often contended that there is an inherent conflict between economic, environmental and social objectives. This view, however, fails to recognise opportunities to implement measures which simultaneously address environmental and social impacts whilst providing a *financial return* to the community.

The existence of such opportunities is demonstrated in Victorian Transport Externalities Study through its assessment of measures to reduce transport emissions of CO_2. The study found that CO_2 emissions could be reduced by around 10% from their projected level in 2005, using measures which yield an estimated *net financial benefit* to the community of \$A973 million. A description of these measures is presented in Table 2, along with estimates of their effectiveness and net financial benefits (shown in the table as a *negative* net cost). The following points regarding the information in Table 2 should be noted:

★   the estimated CO_2 reductions reflect the impact of each measure on *aggregate Victorian* transport emissions of CO_2. They should not be interpreted as showing the reduction in CO_2 emissions for the particular transport segment targeted by the measure. For example, the measure - "reduce car travel in Melbourne by increasing travel costs by 10%" - is estimated to reduce *Victorian* land-based transport emissions by 1.4% in 2005. It would, however, reduce CO_2 emissions from cars operating in *Melbourne* by 4% (EPA[1]). Because car travel in Melbourne is a sub-set of total transport in Victoria, the emissions reduction is adjusted to reflect the impact on state wide emissions.

★   the 10% reduction is more than $1/3$ of the 27% reduction required if a pro-rata share of Australia's interim planning target for greenhouse gas emissions was applied to land-based transport in Victoria.

★   fuel consumption savings are the only benefit considered in the calculation of net benefit - as discussed above, it is not feasible to estimate a monetary value for the effects of global climate change.

★   many of the measures also provide a range of other environmental and social benefits. Depending on the measure, these additional benefits may include a reduction in emissions which adversely affect local air quality; a reduction in traffic congestion; and fewer accidents. The value of these benefits is also excluded from the estimates of net benefit.

★   while each of the measures in Table 2 provide a net financial benefit in addition to a reduction in CO_2 emissions, the *distribution* of the costs and benefits which make up the net result is not identified. As the financial benefits of each strategy result from fuel cost savings, motorists will be the beneficiaries. Costs, however, are borne to a varying degree (depending on the measure) by motorists and the wider community - the latter in providing funds for education, infrastructure improvements etc.

Further measures to reduce CO_2 emissions were considered in the Study. Each of these measures were found to impose a *net cost* on the community. An overview of these additional measures is presented in Table 3.

Figure 2 combines the information in Tables 2 and 3 to show the *cumulative* reduction in emissions and the *cumulative* net cost of measures to reduce CO_2 emissions. It is important to note that the net benefit of $A973 million generated by the measures listed in Table 2, provides a *credit* which "pays for" a further reduction in CO_2 emissions of around 6%. Figure 2 shows that a reduction in emissions of around 16% can be achieved at *zero cumulative net cost*. Because of this "credit", it is only the pursuit of CO_2 reductions in excess of 16% that imposes a net financial burden on the community.

Table 2   Measures which reduce CO_2 emissions from land-based transport in Victoria *and* provide a net financial benefit to the community

Measure[1]	Reduction[2] in CO_2 emissions by 2005 (%)	Net Cost[3] ($A million)
Reduce car[4] travel in Melbourne by increasing travel costs by 10%	1.4	- 233
Reduce travel speeds throughout Victoria by increased education and enforcement	0.8	- 117
Reduce public transport fares by 10% to encourage a shift to public transport	0.3	- 43
Accelerate the introduction of improvements in car technology (eg. lighter materials and improvements in aerodynamics, engine and transmission design and tyres)	5.6	- 460
Encourage telecommuting	1.0	- 75
Reduce travel times on public transport to encourage a shift to public transport	0.5	- 30
Change urban form to promote a second major activity focus in Melbourne, and develop complementary transport systems	0.3	- 15
Total	*9.9*	- 973

Notes   1   Measures are listed in order of *cost-effectiveness*.

2   If measures are introduced concurrently, their effectiveness often will be less than if they were introduced in isolation. These "interaction effects" between measures have been accounted for in the estimates in this table.

3   Net costs are for the period 1995 to 2005, expressed in $A1992 and discounted at 5%. A negative net cost represents a net *benefit*.

4   Cars include cars, station wagons and (passenger) 4 wheel drive vehicles.

Table 3   Measures which reduce CO_2 emissions from land-based transport in Victoria at a net financial cost to the community[1]

Measure	Reduction in CO_2 emissions by 2005 (%)	Net Cost ($A million)
Promote smoother driving in the metropolitan area by providing advice to drivers on optimal travel speed on a given section of road	2.0	105
Improve the technical specification of trucks	1.3	69
Develop new sub-divisions in Melbourne at higher density with mixed land-use and complementary transport systems	1.8	99
Reduce travel by road freight vehicles through modal shift and improved manufacturing, warehouse and distribution systems	0.8	203
Introduce petrol-ethanol blends to capture a 12.5% share of the fuel market for cars	0.2	50
Reduce speed limits	2.1	650
Encourage car pooling for peak period travel in Melbourne	0.1	52
Increase CNG's (compressed natural gas) share of the fuel market for cars from 1% to 11%	1.0	555
Increase LPG's share of the fuel market for cars from 3% to 13%	0.7	467
Regulate to require all cars registered in Melbourne to be subject to annual inspection and maintenance	0.5	493
Increase the market share of smaller cars	1.6	1703

1. See notes to Table 2

4   Conclusion

Does the pursuit of environmental and social objectives involve a trade-off with economic objectives? From the discussion in this paper, it is clear that the answer to this question is likely to be determined by the scale of the environmental and social improvements that are being sought.

The assessment of measures to reduce emissions of CO_2 from land-based transport demonstrates that it *is* possible to tackle transport's environmental and social impacts at the same time as providing a net financial benefit to the community. CO_2 emissions could be reduced by around 10% from projected levels in 2005 by introducing measures which yield a net financial benefit of $A973 million.   Furthermore, the "credit" provided by these measures means that emissions could be reduced by some 16% at zero net cost. It is only the pursuit of reductions in excess of 16% that give rise to a net financial burden.

Significantly, these net cost calculations exclude the monetary value of the environmental and social benefits associated with each of the measures. As part of this paper, we have seen that, despite the uncertainty involved in their estimation, the monetary value of these benefits is significant.

The *distribution* of costs and benefits associated with the measures to achieve environmental and social objectives remains an issue. The financial beneficiaries of measures to reduce transport CO_2 emissions will be motorists, while the costs of the measures often fall on the broader community.

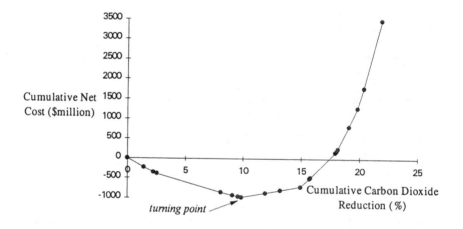

Figure 2   Cumulative CO_2 reductions and cumulative net cost of emissions reduction measures

References

1   EPA.   *Victorian Transport Externalities Study*, Environment Protection Authority - Government of Victoria, Melbourne, 1994.

2   Bouladon, G. 'Mobility in urban areas: learning to conserve transport', Draft paper submitted to the OECD Group on Urban Affairs (restricted), OECD, 1991.

3   National Greenhouse Response Strategy, AGPS, Canberra, 1992.

Dealing with the environmental externalities of urban transport: are we putting the cart before the horse?

L.O.P. Knight

Department of Applied Science, Edith Cowan University, 2 Bradford St, Mt Lawley, WA 6050, Australia

Abstract

Fossil-fuelled motor vehicles are the source of many environmental externalities. In the case of air quality, a range of planning, economic and technical approaches have been applied throughout the world. The usefulness of these mechanisms in controlling motor vehicle emissions in the Australian context is examined before the fundamental assumptions underlying current transport policies are scrutinised.

Introduction

Motor vehicles have entrenched roles in the functioning of western economies and cultures. Cars perform the bulk of the passenger transport task in many cities and entire industries are devoted to servicing motorists' needs. While cars provide considerable utility, their use imposes costs to the community that are not borne by individual motorists. These externalities include air and noise pollution, traffic congestion and accidents.

Estimates can be made of the cost of these transport externalities using a range of economic valuation techniques, such as hedonic pricing and contingent valuation (e.g. Pearce [17]). While these valuation methodologies have acknowledged weaknesses, the Bureau of Transport and Communications Economics [6] estimated the cost of transport externalities in Australia, France, Germany, Netherlands, United Kingdom and United States to be in the range of 2.3 to 3.1 per cent of the gross domestic product (GDP) of their respective economies.

In Australia's case, the Bureau of Transport and Communications Economics [6] estimated the annual cost of motor vehicle emissions to be in the order of eight hundred million dollars ($A) per year, or 0.21% of GDP. This cost includes damage to buildings, crops, forests and human health.

Indeed, motor vehicles are the major source of air pollution in Australian cities. Motor vehicles, for example, contribute approximately 45 - 50% of both volatile organic compounds (VOCs) and airborne particles, 80% of oxides of nitrogen (NO_x) and 90% of carbon monoxide (CO) emissions in the urban air-sheds of Sydney and Melbourne (NSW EPA [14], Hearn [9]).

Historically, the emphasis of air quality management policy in Australia has been on the control of photochemical smog (Eiser [8], Munro [13]). This is mainly in the form of ozone, which is the result of a complex series of reactions involving NO_x and VOCs. The requirement that all new cars from 1986 be fitted with catalytic converters and run on unleaded petrol was aimed at reducing ozone levels.

More recently concern has been raised over benzene, lead and other fine particles (PM_{10}). Motor vehicle emissions are the main source of exposure to benzene for non-smokers (Houghton [10]). Benzene became a political issue in the context of government moves to lower lead levels in leaded petrol and the marketing of 'half-lead' petrol by one oil refiner.

While air pollution standards are occasionally exceeded in Australia's larger cities, overall air quality is relatively good. For example, between 1979 and 1991, ozone concentrations in the Sydney region exceeded the World Health Organisation one hour goal of 0.12 ppm on an average of 5.5 days per year (NSW EPA [13]). This compares to Los Angeles where the 0.12 ppm standard was exceeded on an average of 160.7 days per year (Appleby [1]).

Emission Control Measures

There are many ways to reduce motor vehicle emissions. Mechanical approaches reduce emissions per kilometre travelled through modifications to engine and exhaust designs, cleaner fuels and increased vehicle maintenance. Public transport, land use planning and economic approaches can encourage people to travel by less polluting modes of transport. Alternatively, developments in communications technology can be used to reduce people's need to travel.

Motor Vehicle Standards
This is a regulatory approach that sets emission standards
for new cars. Vehicle manufacturers have complied with
these standards through the development of engine
management systems and catalytic converters (fitted to
vehicle exhaust systems). These measures can reduce
exhaust emissions by up to 90% relative to pre-control
vehicles (e.g. Pearce and Davies [18]).

California's Low Emission Vehicle (LEV) program has
made it a world leader in forcing technological
developments through the application of stringent emissions
standards. The LEV program requires manufacturers to meet
progressively tighter fleet average emission standards and
to start offering zero emission vehicles for sale from 1998
(John et.al. [11]).

Australian Design Rule (ADR) 37 has been tightened to
require all new light vehicles meet the US 1981-93 emission
standards by 1997, and a working party is currently
examining the appropriateness of the US 1994-96 standards
(NSW EPA [14]).

While the implementation of ADR 37 in 1986 has led to
improved air quality in Australian cities (NSW EPA [14]),
several factors limit the benefits of tighter standards.

One is the average age of vehicles on Australian
roads which in 1991 was 10 years (Australian Bureau of
Statistics [2]). It was only in 1994 that sales of
unleaded petrol (mandatory for new cars sold after 1985)
exceeded sales of leaded petrol (Australian Institute of
Petroleum [3]). This indicates that approximately half the
vehicle kilometres travelled (VKT) is by pre-ADR 36
vehicles. It takes the order of a decade or more for
technical improvements to filter through the national
fleet.

The performance of the emission control equipment
fitted to cars declines over time as components are broken
or wear out. Unless older cars are maintained properly,
their emissions will increase and eventually exceed design
standards. With an average vehicle age of 10 years, there
are likely to be many high emitting cars on the road.

Another factor is an ongoing increase in VKT,
reflecting increases in the size of the Australian
population and the distances people travel in motor
vehicles. People are making more and shorter trips, which
is significant since the exhaust emissions at the start of
a trip and the evaporative emissions at the end of a trip
make up a substantial proportion of total emissions for a
typical urban trip.

Inspection/Maintenance Programs

One American response to the decline of emission control effectiveness as vehicles age has been the introduction of inspection/maintenance (I/M) programs. Motorists in air quality 'non attainment' areas are required to present their vehicles for emission testing on a periodic basis. Vehicles that fail an I/M test must be fixed to stay on the road.

Considerable effort (and argument) has gone into the development of a testing regime that can reliably distinguish between cars meeting emission standards and cars exceeding them. The US EPA prefers the 'IM 240', a test cycle using sophisticated sampling systems and inertial dynamometers. This enables the IM 240 to simulate in-use emissions better than cheaper alternatives such as idle-mode testing, which has largely proved to be ineffective (US EPA [19]).

Inspection/Maintenance programs in the US have yet to deliver substantial air quality improvements (e.g. California I/M Review Committee [7]). Test limitations may have a contributing factor, but ultimately faulty vehicles must be repaired before benefits are realised. So far, greater emphasis has been placed on identifying faulty vehicles than on enhancing the capacity of the repair industry to diagnose faults accurately and make cheap and effective repairs.

Several Australian states are investigating the implementation of I/M programs and the development of repair industry skills. Issues such as the choice of test-cycle have been placed on hold pending the outcome of an investigation of emission tests and repair effectiveness, currently overseen by the Federal Office of Road Safety.

Cleaner Fuels

Gasoline is a complex mixture of hydrocarbons whose characteristics have an impact on vehicle emissions. The higher the aromatic content of a fuel, for example, the higher the benzene emissions. Considerable effort has been (and continues to be) put into the 'reformulation' of gasoline to improve vehicle emissions. For example, phase 1 of the US Auto/Oil [4] Air Quality Improvement Research Program (collectively established by oil companies and vehicle manufacturers) conducted over 2200 tests of 29 fuel compositions in 53 vehicles. Across the Atlantic, the European Program on Emissions, Fuels and Engine Technologies is conducting similar investigations.

While improvements in emission performance can be achieved by varying fuel parameters (controlling sulphur content and Reid Vapour Pressure are both quite cost effective) the gains are smaller than those available through vehicle technology. In contrast, the effects are immediate and can vary considerably between vehicles, with both positive and negative consequences.

An alternative is to use fuels with inherently cleaner combustion than gasoline. Standard vehicles can run on gasoline blended with ethanol, methanol or ethers or can be modified to operate on LPG or CNG in addition to gasoline. Unfortunately, the compromises required reduce the benefit achieved. The best performance is achieved with vehicles specifically designed to operate solely on a particular fuel. Dedicated CNG vehicles, for example, have zero evaporative emissions and perform particularly well in terms of particulates and air toxics (e.g. Bureau of Transport and Communications Economics [5]).

In the short term, logistical issues limit the use of alternative fuels to niche areas, such as centrally fuelled fleets. The low energy density of CNG, for example, means large (heavy) cylinders are required to provide an acceptable refuelling range. As such, CNG is better suited to metropolitan bus fleets than private cars.

At some future stage, zero emission vehicles powered by batteries, fuel cells or hydrogen assisted by regenerative braking, and ultra-low emission combustion-electric vehicles will provide low impact transport in sensitive airsheds. The technology-forcing regulations in California will have a significant impact on developments in this area.

Transport Planning
A complementary approach to reducing emissions is a reduction in VKT. This can be done by increasing the use of collective transport, reducing travel distances and encouraging people to walk or cycle.

This approach works well for many areas in Europe and Asia, where population densities facilitate efficient public transport services, pedestrianisation and short trips (Newman & Kenworthy [15]). It has less success in Australia where it must work against cultural and infrastructural currents. Although not as car-dependent as many of their American counterparts, Australian cities have spread with insufficient population densities to support efficient public transport. Travel activities are also decentralising, making centrally oriented public transport less attractive. Even the environmentally conscious are locked into using cars for much of their travel (Knight [12]).

Altering settlement patterns to achieve higher population densities is difficult, particularly in Australia where suburban home-ownership is part of the national psyche and cheaper land is readily available on the metropolitan fringes. Nevertheless, infrastructural developments such as bus lanes can help, as can integrated planning in helping to prevent town planners, public transport managers and road builders working at cross-purposes.

While the judicious use of planning regulations and support for public transport services may be helpful, an alternative is the use of economic instruments to help level the playing field between public and private transport modes. For example, Australian motorists do not have to pay charges each time they use their vehicles (as is the case with public transport). Parking fees only apply in city centres and few roads have tolls.

There has been extensive discussion of policy mechanisms such as road pricing, increased fuel taxes and parking fees in the literature (e.g. John et. al. [11]). Applying road pricing to Australian roads in 1995 would be a politically courageous act. Road tolls in their current form are unpopular, and calls for environmental charges (such as the recent ill-fated carbon tax proposal) do not last long in the public arena.

Are We Putting the Cart Before the Horse?

Each of the approaches discussed so far can make a useful contribution to reducing motor vehicle emissions. They do not, however, exist in a vacuum. A number of preconditions must be met to derive full benefits. The emission control equipment fitted to new cars, for example, must be durable and maintained properly if it is to function effectively throughout the life of the vehicle. Similarly, the repair industry must be able to diagnose faults correctly and make effective repairs to vehicles failing an I/M test if emission reductions are to be achieved.

Attention also needs to be given to the changing nature of urban travel behaviour. Considerable effort has been directed at influencing commuter behaviour through a range of transport control measures (TCMs). However, the travel to work trip is losing its dominance as a generator of VKT as people travel further for other trip purposes, such as social and recreational activities. Work-based TCMs thus have a declining capacity to deliver substantial benefits (Orski [16]). Similarly, people are undertaking a greater number of multiple destination trips which are less suited to public transport services.

There   is clearly a lot of potential for a narrow and an   ad   hoc   approach   to   the   resolution   of   transport externalities   to   result   in   misdirected   efforts.   What   is not so obvious is that our focus on transport could itself represent an example of putting the cart before the horse.

The issue of why people travel in first place is too often taken for granted.   Traditionally, people travelled to get to work and to gain access to goods and services. Developments in computer and communications technology mean that this is no longer necessarily the case.

Existing technologies and services allow people to shop, bank, work, socialise and enjoy live entertainment without having to travel.   As the technology improves, people's   non-travel   options   will   increase   and   social attitudes   will   change.   People's   travel   needs   and subsequent travel patterns will change.   Telecommuting, for example,   has   a   significant   impact   on   people's   weekday travel   activities   (Pendyala   et.   al.   [19]).   Over   time, travel-replacing options could have significant impacts on urban settlement patterns and on the levels and patterns of travel demand.

Ultimately, social and technological changes have the potential to render inflexible transport plans and emission control   strategies   obsolete   very   quickly.   There   is,   for example,   no guarantee that people will continue to travel in boxes on wheels the way they are at present.   It is essential   that   policy-makers   are   sensitive   to   social   and technical developments and able to respond appropriately.

References

1. Appleby, M.R. The US Emission Control Programs pp 175-206, *Proceedings of Wheels 92 Conference*, Sydney, 1992.
2. Australian Bureau of Statistics, *Motor Vehicle Census Australia* (#9309.0), 1992.
3. Australian Institute of Petroleum, *Personal Communication*, Melbourne, 1995.
4. Auto/Oil *Air Quality Improvement Research Program Phase 1 Final Report,* 1993.
5. Bureau of Transport and Communications Economics, *Alternative Fuels in Australian Transport*, AGPS, Canberra, 1994.
6. Bureau of Transport and Communications Economics, *Victorian Transport Externalities Study*, AGPS, Canberra, 1994.
7. California I/M Review Committee, *Evaluation of the California Smog Check Program and Recommendations for Program Improvements, Fourth Report to the Legislature,* 1993.

8. Eiser, C.R. *Personal Communication,* NSW EPA, Sydney, 1994.
9. Hearn, D. Motor Vehicle Emissions in Melbourne, pp 277-296, *Proceedings of the 12th International Conference of the Clean Air Society of Australia and New Zealand,* Perth, 1994.
10. Houghton, J. *Royal Commission on Environmental Pollution, 18th Report Transport and the Environment,* HMSO, London, 1994.
11. John, S.F., Kane, D.N. & Kim, T.J. *Clearing the Air, Choosing the Future,* Illinois Department of Energy and Natural Resources (ILENR/RE-EA-92/09), Springfield, 1992.
12. Knight, L.O.P. Environmentalism, Urban Structure and Transport Choices, *Urban Policy and Research,* 1993, 11, 31-43.
13. Munro, D. *Personal Communication, Vic* EPA, Melbourne, 1994.
14. New South Wales Environment Protection Authority *Submission to the NSW Parliamentary Select Committee Upon Motor Vehicle Emissions,* Sydney, 1994.
15. Newman, P.W.G. & Kenworthy, J.R. Gasoline Consumption and Cities, *Journal of the American Planning Association,* 1989, 1, 24-37.
16. Orski, C.K. Evaluating the Effectiveness of Travel Demand Management, *ITE Journal,* 1991, August, 14-18.
17. Pearce, D., Markandya, A. and Barbier, E.B. *Blueprint for a Green Economy,* Earthscan, London, 1989.
18. Pearce, T.C. and Davies, G.P. *The Efficiency of Automotive Exhaust Catalysts and the Effects of Component Failure,* TRRL Research Report #287, Crowthorne, 1990.
19. Pendyala, R.M., Goulias, K.G. and Kitamura, R. Impact of Telecommuting on Spatial and Temporal Patterns of Household Travel, *Transportation,* 1991, 18, 383-409.
20. US EPA *Inspection/Maintenance Program Requirements Final I/M Preamble: OMB Version,* 1992.

SECTION 4:
PLANNING & DESIGN

Paying for progress: the utility of using roadspace

J. Dinwoodie

Centre for International Shipping and Transport, University of Plymouth, Devon, UK

Abstract

A pragmatic perception survey of 271 motorists in Plymouth is used to explore variations in the willingness to pay for varying levels of road tolls and their behavioural impact on car trips into the city. Frequently stated components of utility, revealed as beliefs associated with such trips, included convenience and time, with expense, comfort and reliability less so, and safety, image and pollution least stated. Studies of the beliefs and utilities of consumers of roadspace are essential if tolls are to be optimised.

1. Background

The technology and economics of road pricing (RP) have been widely discussed [e.g.1,2,3,4] but not so the utilities and beliefs which consumers associate with the use of roadspace. If the right to do so is traded as a scarce commodity, an optimal economic allocation between competing consumers would require the market price (P) for its use to equal the marginal cost (MC) of such consumption. An efficient pricing regime must reflect cases where consumption by one user imposes delay or other costs on other members of society, responding to variations over space and time. RP may satisfy such criteria, but we are less aware of the beliefs and components of utility which underlie road users' willingness to pay (WTP) tolls.

RP may reduce peak vehicle miles by deterring some drivers in lower income groups, but higher income groups may prefer to pay to enjoy higher speeds [1,2]. A few trips may divert to rail, with some re-timing of less essential trips around the shoulders of the peak. Adverse distributional impacts [5] may force trips into the suburbs to avoid toll rings, or extend congested periods beyond the peak, but RP could generate revenue, release roadspace [3] or question our love affair with the car [6].   In Jones'[7] study of attitudes to congestion, RP was not the prime concern. We develop these themes to consider why people would be WTP specific charges for using their cars.   After reviewing the survey methodology, section 3 summarises observed WTP, beliefs and trip utility (TU) are analysed in section 4, before concluding.

2. Survey methodology

Early attitude research in transport [8,9] attempted to reveal the elements of utility inherent in travel by asking individuals to select attributes representing their own beliefs about features of their trips. As recurring beliefs emerged, researchers imposed common choice criteria, typically time-cost tradeoffs, which respondents attempted to evaluate. Here, in assessing the impacts of road tolls on TU, eight locally significant beliefs [10] were evaluated as a compromise between unfettered content analysis of original responses and bivariate tradeoffs. The approach studies the cognitive and affective decision processes in travel choices.

We could conceive an intention to drive as an object, with attitudes towards it as an affect, involving feelings of good or bad. Expectancy value theory [11] postulated that a person's overall attitude towards an object will comprise the sum of the emotive responses to each belief about it, and any associated objects, in a probabilistic belief system. To measure the attitude towards an intention to drive involves individuals identifying their salient beliefs about it, measuring the strength of each belief about the attitude, evaluating the affect about each belief and finally summing the weighted affects for each belief.

Laptop computers were used to survey 271 Plymouth motorists, recalling their usual trip into the city (its origin, destination, mode if not car, time of day, route, trip frequency, need to use a car at the destination, habit, parking type and who would pay for tolls). Remote billing and smart-card systems were outlined as methods of collecting tolls at hypothetical points on all routes into the city, forming a comprehensive cordon. 'Transfer tolls', at which motorists stated they would transfer to other modes were elicited, before studying the effect of additional 50p, 100p and 200p tolls on their behaviour and beliefs associated with making trips into the city by car. With a survey aim to identify beliefs, customised time/cost trade-off decision sets were inappropriate. A pragmatic perception approach [10] reduced noncommitment bias, where stated behavioural intentions may not translate into actual behaviour, by exploring realistic alternative scenarios. Questions covered the effects of not making a trip, other destinations which may be used, social influences on behaviour, and alternative courses of action, including choice of other modes, and even not making the trip, in both the short and long term.

Beliefs were elicited by asking drivers to select the two things which came most readily to mind about making this trip by car, drawn from expense, time, convenience, safety, reliability, image, comfort and pollution [10]. The affect of each belief was evaluated ['Describe on this factor this trip by car as good/bad'] and its probability ['Is this likely/unlikely when making this trip by car ?'] on 7 point Likert scales, converted respectively to affective scores (.9,.6,..,-.9) and probabilities (.8,.7,.,.2). The TU of each trip was found by summing the products of affective score and probability for all beliefs associated with the trip.

Summary tables show sample size (n), and mean WTP for tolls by response group for relevant questions. Null hypotheses of no significant difference between mean WTP for each response were tested using one-way analysis of variance (shown * (**) where rejected with at least 95% (99%) confidence).

3. Willingness to pay tolls

Lower transfer tolls stated by drivers for their most recent trip into Plymouth reflected a specific threat, with 67% >100p and 40% >200p (Table 1). Less immediately, 75% would 'probably' drive at 100p tolls, and 45% at 200p, but 5% not WTP any toll may reflect some policy response bias. Many seemed likely to make pragmatic decisions, based on their perceptions of the prevailing tolling system, traffic, economic and modal conditions. Tempering a 200p toll with a 10 minute car advantage had little impact.

Table 1. The % of motorists stating transfer tolls above levels shown for their most recent trip into Plymouth by car.

Toll	%WTP	Toll	%WTP	Toll	%WTP	
001p	95	075p	70	300p	20	n=271
010p	94	100p	67	400p	10	mean=174p
025p	91	150p	52	500p	7	SD=158p
040p	86	200p	40	1000p	1	
050p	83	250p	28	1001p	0	

The % of motorists stating that they would be likely to take their car into Plymouth at the tolls shown.

Toll:	50p	100p	200p	200p
TIME(mins)	As now	As now	As now	10 less
definitely car	69	49	28	27
Probably car	17	26	17	19
Probably not car	8	12	24	22
definitely NOT car	6	13	31	32

Alternative mode. Beyond their transfer tolls, sampled drivers chose bus, car passenger, train, park and ride, or not to travel (Table 2), but modal availability was not probed. 100p tolls lured 20% of park and riders, with more transfers to bus at 200p, but few chose car passenger. Mean WTP tolls, differing statistically by mode, was higher for those choosing not to travel, or non-tolled modes such as motorcycle or train. Reduced WTP tolls for low cost second choice modes, (walk 89p, bus 130p) may reflect low incomes which affect both WTP tolls, and choice of non-car mode.

Table 2. % of transfers at tolls shown and WTP in response to:

		% transfers at:			Mean transfer
	n		50p 100p 200p		tolls (pence)
How would you make this trip if NOT going by car?					
Bus/coach	102		9 16 36		130**
Car passenger	57		2 2 21		202
Train	39	of	3 10 26		226
Park and Ride	30	whom	7 20 30		192
Other	21		10 19 33		149
I would not bother	11		9 18 45		262
Motor-Cycle	6		0 20 20		244
Walk	5		0 33 67		89
Where did you come from prior to your trip?					
A house	190		6 15 32		170
Work	33	of	3 6 21		208
Place of education	16	whom	0 19 50		95
Rail/bus/air terminus	10		30 40 50		205
Shopping centre	7		0 14 28		246
Place of entertainment	12		0 0 25		177
Hospital/medical centre	3		0 0 0		160
Where is your final destination for this trip?					
A house	57		4 9 28		164
Work	100	of	8 13 33		204
Place of education	36	whom	6 22 42		128
Rail/bus/air terminus	9		11 11 11		239
Shopping centre	49		2 10 29		162
Place of entertainment	16		6 12 25		124
Hospital/medical	4		25 50 50		171

Functions at trip origin and destination. Rising tolls force trips
from houses, (70% of those sampled), to quit cars before those
from work, with highest transfer rates from termini origins
(incurring parking charges) and lowest from entertainment and
medical centres. Few drivers, unwilling to leave cars at work,
would transfer from them, even at 200p tolls, but there were
higher rates for trips to work initially. Work, houses, shopping
and education were popular destination functions, but transfers
from car for trips to houses were less likely than for trips to
work, reflecting trip timing or access to other modes. Personal
income may explain greater (but not statistically so) WTP tolls at
shopping or work origins than for education. Perceived necessity
of trips to work or termini may explain statistically greater WTP
than for education or entertainment trips.

Trip time, frequency and habit. More sampled trips were in the
morning peak and offpeak periods than at other times (Table 3).
WTP differed statistically, with 100p tolls most effective in the
early afternoon, and 200p in the morning peak, with few transfers
at night. WTP was higher in the evening, and morning peak, but
lower in mid-morning and evening peak.

Table 3. % of transfers at tolls shown and WTP in response to:

		% transfers at:			Mean transfer
	n	50p	100p	200p	tolls (pence)
At what time do you enter Plymouth on this trip ?					
0001-0615	3		0	0	0	108 *
0616-0915	106	of	8	14	36	199
0916-1215	65	whom	6	14	32	129
1216-1515	46		4	18	28	174
1516-1815	31		6	13	32	148
1815-2400	20		0	0	15	233
How often do you travel into Plymouth ?				Once every:	
Day	21		10	14	24	223
2-5 days	18	of	6	22	28	186
Week	47	whom	0	6	36	183
2 weeks	109		6	13	34	164
Month	76		9	16	28	166
How long have you been making this trip regularly?					
< 1 year	8		25	38	50	82
1 year	34	of	3	26	29	164
2 years	52	whom	4	13	37	160
3 years	30		3	7	33	201
4 years	28		4	11	25	149
5 years	17		6	12	35	179
6-10 years	68		4	9	28	184
>10 years+	34		12	15	29	198

Many of those sampled travelled into Plymouth every couple of days, or daily, but at 100p tolls, the former were more likely to transfer. At 200p tolls, transfers by weekly travellers became more likely. Frequent travellers, less likely to be retired or low income, were more WTP (but not statistically so). Trips sampled had been made equally from a few months to several years, with habitual trips more (but not statistically so) WTP tolls. At 100p tolls, new trips were more likely to transfer, with established trips less so but at 200p, habit had less effect.

Impacts of destination activity, passengers and parking. Those needing a car while at their destination were statistically more WTP tolls (Table 4), but number of passengers had little impact. Full cars stimulated transfers at 100p tolls, but occupancy had little effect at 200p. Free parkers were marginally less (but not statistically so) WTP for tolls than paying parkers, but those with free parking at work were WTP pay more in tolls. 53% did not pay for parking, 38% did, with 9% 'other'. Free on Street parkers transfer more quickly at 100p tolls; 200p tolls affected paying parkers, but those reclaiming tolls were statistically more WTP.

Consequences of not making trips. At 100p tolls, drivers making 'essential' trips (35% of all trips) were less willing to transfer than those (21%) on inessential trips and short-term, few of those willing to consider other destinations would quit their cars. 200p tolls force 36% of those likely to lose income if not travelling

Table 4. % of transfers at tolls shown and WTP in response to:

.	n	% transfers at: 50p 100p 200p	Mean transfer tolls (pence)

Do you usually need your car in the course of your business while at your destination in Plymouth?

	n		50p	100p	200p	
Yes	206	of	5	14	31	159 **
No	65	whom	8	12	32	222

Enter the number of passengers on this trip (0,1,2..)

			50p	100p	200p	
0	103		6	14	31	185
1	99	of	7	12	32	157
2	50	whom	2	10	30	193
3	14		7	21	29	127
4	3		0	33	67	223
5	2		50	50	50	250

What type of parking do you use ?

			50p	100p	200p	
Pay on street	46		7	9	30	187
Pay off street	56	of	7	16	38	185
Free on street	49	whom	6	18	18	171
Free off street	52		4	10	16	166
Free at work	43		2	9	21	188
Other	25		12	20	40	125

If a toll was charged, would YOU ultimately pay or would it be reclaimed from your employer or some other source ?

			50p	100p	200p	
I would pay	226	of	6	15	36	150**
I would reclaim	45	whom	4	2	7	293

If you did NOT make this trip, IMMEDIATE consequences would be:

			50p	100p	200p	
It would not matter	57		4	21	30	142
Choose another destination	39	of	5	8	31	187
I would lose income	69	whom	7	14	36	161
My health would suffer	10		0	0	30	170
The trip is essential	96		7	11	29	197

If you did NOT make this trip, LONG TERM consequences would be:

			50p	100p	200p	
It would not matter	50		10	20	38	131**
To have to move house	12	of	8	8	33	243
To have to change jobs	20	whom	0	0	0	223
Travel by another means	158		6	16	36	161
Loss of job	31		0	0	16	249

Indicate which route you used on your trip into Plymouth:

			50p	100p	200p	
1. Plymouth Rd/Embankment	83		5	12	28	200
2. Laira Bridge	15		7	7	20	154
3. Eggbuckland Rd	14	of	7	14	50	116
4. Mannamead/Outlands Rd	38	whom	5	16	24	184
5. Honicknowle Lane	18		0	6	28	162
6. Roman Way/Victoria Rd	13		6	23	54	155
7. Pemros Rd from Parkway	16		12	13	44	204
8. Tamar Bridge	44		5	11	32	158
9. Torpoint Ferry	30		20	33	33	149

out of cars, with WTP highest for 'essential' trips and those choosing other destinations. Adverse income or health effects were insufficient to infer any statistically different WTP groupings.

Long term, of 58% of those surveyed who might choose another means of travel, 36% would do so at 200p tolls. 19% of trips were inessential. 100p tolls had little impact on those having to lose or change jobs, or move house.   Predicatably, those able to use another means of travel, or for whom not travelling would have little consequence, were WTP significantly less than those whose job may be affected, or who would have to move house.

Geographical distribution of WTP tolls. The imaginery toll-ring imposed was bordered by the A38 trunk road to the North (sites 3-7 in Table 4), river Plym to the east (sites 1 & 2), sea to the south, and river Tamar to the West (sites 8 & 9).   More sampled trips were via sites 1,4,8 & 9 than elsewhere and drivers from site 9, already paying ferry dues, transferred from cars more quickly with rising tolls.   Small samples and variances on other routes denied inference of statistical differences, but trips via sites 1 & 7 were more WTP tolls than via site 3. Probably a common uniform toll should apply, adjusted to account for existing tolls at sites 8 & 9. The 25% of drivers claiming to be influenced by other people, recorded significantly lower transfer tolls (mean 100p) than those 'considering doing the same' (mean 168p) and the 39% who ignore peers (mean 225p).

4. Beliefs and utilities associated with car travel

In choosing up to 2 beliefs (drawn from 8 known to be important locally [10]) to describe their trip by car, convenience and time were the most stated attributes, with reliability and comfort as secondary beliefs (Table 5).   Expense was stated by only 12%, but increasingly so at higher transfer tolls.   Other beliefs varied little with transfer tolls although comfort and time were weakly related negatively. We can be 99% certain that utility scores were not drawn from a common population, with image and expense rated low and pollution negative, but by an unreliably small subgroup.

Table 5. Stated beliefs and utility associated with car travel.

.	% stating this belief:		Utility scores	
.	First	Second	n	Mean
Expense	13	10	63	19 **
Time	35	20	150	51
Convenience	35	29	172	56
Safety	1	6	19	51
Image	3	2	15	41
Reliability	3	16	53	50
Comfort	9	16	66	52
Pollution	1	1	4	-13

WTP and utility data were calculated for each of 5 time periods on each route, but subgroup samples were too small to reliably infer more general patterns or explanations. Typically, WTP tolls was higher at peak times (eg a mean of 218p 0616-0915 on the Embankment corridor but 173p 0916-1215, 216p & 103p on the Tamar Bridge and 158p & 121p on the Torpoint Ferry respectively), and time and convenience beliefs again predominated in all time periods. Although larger samples would be needed to calibrate models locally, such models might be an adjunct to efficient RP.

5. Conclusion

If asked to pay for the privilege of using road space, motorists in this survey believed that they would be paying for convenience and time. However, in the original content analyses of responses which generated the beliefs evaluated here, 'convenience' included 'door-to-door', 'ease', and 'availability', which may represent several constructs. Income issues, not included here, might reveal more distributional impacts, where deterrence may be linked to ability to pay. Further surveys with larger samples, drawn from different seasons, cities and journey purposes are needed, testing a variety of utility functions, before any attempt to infer any wider applicability of these findings. If the allocative advantages of road-pricing are to be politically achievable and optimised, research along these lines represents an important element in the implementation process.

Bibliography
1. Chartered Institute of Transport, *Paying for Progress*, CIT, London, 1990.
2. Chartered Institute of Transport, *Paying for Progress: Supplementary Report*, CIT, London, March 1992.
3. Goodwin,P. A Balanced Transport Policy: could it be achieved without road pricing ? Lecture 1 in *Practical Possibilities for a Comprehensive Transport Policy with and without Road Pricing*, PTRC Conference Proceedings, December 1990, PTRC, London.
4. Lave,C. The demand curve under road pricing and the problem of political feasibility, *Transportation Research A*,1994,28A,2,83-91.
5. Adams,J. Road pricing in London: diversion or focus? Lecture 8 in PTRC, 1990, *op.cit.*
6. Worksett,D.H. Cars: how to achieve tolerable patterns of use. Lecture 3 in PTRC, 1990, *op.cit.*
7. Jones,P. Public attitudes to options for dealing with traffic congestion in urban areas...What the polsters say, Chapter 1, *Traffic Congestion: Is There a Way Out?*, ed J.Whitelegg, pp.11-29 Leading Edge Publishing, North Yorks, 1992.
8. Thomas K. A reinterpretation of the 'attitude' approach to transport-mode choice and an exploratory empirical test. *Environment and Planning A*, Vol. 8, pp. 793-810, 1976.
9. Henscher D.A., Stopher P.R. *Behavioural Travel Modelling 1. Mathematical models.* Croom Helm, London 1979.
10. Dinwoodie J. Higher fares or fairer hiring of taxis and private hire cars? PTRC, 22nd European Transport Forum, Stream F. *Provision for accessible transport services.* PTRC London. 1994.
11. Fishbein M., Ajzen I. *Beliefs, Attitude, Intention and Behaviour.* Addison Wesley, Phillipines, 1975.

Sustainability and transport: helping ensure policies and infrastructure proposals can be sustainable

C.K. Ferrary

Environmental Resources Management, 8 Cavendish Square, London W1M 0ER, UK

Abstract

Sustainable development is a new principle to guide policy-making at national and international levels. This paper shows how it can guide the development of transport policy and the planning of new transport infrastructure. This paper discusses the principle and its application to transport. The environmental effects of transport influencing sustainability are discussed and how these have helped shape transport policy at EC and national levels examined. A way of examining the extent to which transport policies and proposals are sustainable will then be described by looking at how interactions between transport and the environment may be categorised and related to policy objectives.

1 Sustainable Development and Transport Policy

The most widely accepted definition of sustainable development is:

> *"Development that meets the needs of the present without compromising the ability of future generations to meet their own needs"* [1].

As a means to establish the basis for achieving sustainable development on a global basis, Agenda 21 was adopted at the United Nations Conference on Environment and Development (UNCED) in June 1992. It defines the overall objective for sustainable development as *"improving the social, economic and environmental quality of human settlements and the living and working environments of all people"*.

The document notes that all countries should:

• Minimise environmental damage;

• ensure relevant decisions are preceded by environmental impact assessments;

• integrate land-use and transportation planning to reduce transport demand; and

• adopt urban-transport programmes favouring high-occupancy public transport.

At the European level, an EC common transport policy is evolving [2]. Some of the key issues raised by this are that transport:

• is the biggest consumer of energy and cause of pollution;

• has a permanent and often irreversible impact on the environment through land-take and intrusion;

• requires rationalisation and management of demand by a shift towards environment-friendly modes and collective transport, and a better utilisation of existing capacity; and

• needs to be integrated with land-use and spatial planning.

In elucidating how transport policy will play it's role in it's strategy to promote sustainable development [3], the UK Government note that while it does not see its job as to tell people where and how to travel, it doe aim to develop a transport policy that strikes the right balance between serving economic development and protecting the environment and future ability to sustain quality of life. Serving economic development is an important objective of transport policy in the UK, but this must enable people to enjoy access to goods, services and other people (the reason for travel) while substantially reducing the amount of movement needed to achieve this.

It is also a stated aim of the UK Strategy that CO_2 emissions will be stabilised at 1990 levels by the year 2000. By implication, emissions by transport sources will also need to meet this target. To do this, the Government is:

• increasing fuel duty by at least 5% per year (m real terms)

• allowing local authorities to manage transport demand through land use planning more effectively;

• pursuing the improvement of vehicle standards in the EC; and

• encouraging the proper environmental assessment of transport programmes.

At a more local level, some county councils have attempted to develop "sustainable" transport policies, and the DoT's recently recommended "package approach" to Transport Policy and Programmes submissions give some consideration to environmental issues [4]. Various policy documents have set out a range of recommended measures which could contribute to reduced environmental impacts, including fiscal and market measures to increase the price of transport and reflect wider costs; additional vehicle standards or better speed enforcement; land use changes to improve accessibility and reduce the need to travel; traffic management and public transport improvements. This however only really provides yet another shopping list of policy options. How do we then actually develop, evaluate and implement these? It is to this issue I will turn, but first we must consider what are the features of transport which render it non-sustainable. *and monitor too.*

2 The Effects of Transport on the Environment

Transport policy in recent years has been influenced by the rise in concern about the environment. Environmental protection and improvement are now often explicit aims of transport policy, and strategies which seek to achieve these aims have emerged. However, despite many attempts to categorise them, the interactions between transport and the environment are still generally not well understood by transport planners.

Transport is an inherently unsustainable activity for two main reasons. The provision of transport infrastructure and the operation of vehicles lead to:

- Consumption of non-renewable resources, such as land, aggregates in construction and fossil fuels; and

- Pollution, which may further damage irreplaceable resources or cause long-term environmental changes to occur.

The impact of transport on the environment can be reduced in a number of ways, such as:

- Reducing the number of journeys made;

- Shifting the means by which these journeys are effected to less environmentally-damaging transport modes; and

- Measures to reduce the environmental impacts of those journeys which are made.

However, experience of developing environmentally-orientated transport policy to date has shown that this is still far from becoming a mature science. This is primarily because while environmental issues have influenced transport planning at both the strategic and local levels, they have not become central in the development of transport policy, or properly integrated into the transport planning process. There remains a huge vacuum between the global concerns and the interest in minutiae which have characterised the combining of transport and environmental policies to date. Local initiatives evolve outside of any real regional or national policy framework, and lack cohesion and purpose. Global policies lack realistic or practical means of implementation at a lower level, taking account of the other economic and social aims of national and regional policy. We are left with a set of *"pious hopes"* on the one hand and a shopping list of measures on the other, with no means of justifying the efforts and resources put in to pursuing them or evaluating whether or not they are actually being effective.

At the core of this problem lies a lack of understanding or analysis of what the differential effects of differing transport policies on the environment are likely to be. Very often, it is taken as an article of faith that a new road proposal is bad news for the environment, while a new light rail scheme must necessarily be a good thing. However, there is usually precious little evidence offered up to demonstrate that this is indeed the case. The following sections demonstrate one approach which has been used to help show how particular transport infrastructure proposals accord with the principles of sustainable development, and how different transport strategies may be compared on this basis.

3 Appraisal for Sustainable Development

To provide a full appraisal of whether transport policies and proposals are in line with the principles of sustainable development as defined by the UK Government, it is important to remember that these seek to reconcile economic development and higher living standards with protection and enhancement of the environment. Any approach to appraisal must therefore address both of these. In the past, transport appraisal has tended to concentrate on the economic benefits of providing access to goods and services. More recently, to this has been added assessment of the environmental impacts of transport. However, these have rarely been explicitly linked to allow decision makers to determine where the balance between them lies. While assisting economic development is a primary aim of transport policy, it is not necessary to maximise this at all costs. Similarly, it is not realistic to seek transport policies that never cause significant damage to the environment, if this places a stranglehold on economic development. To provide a workable approach to appraising transport in terms of sustainable development principles, both of these elements should be considered. A practical example of such an approach is described below.

4 Setting Forth: A New Approach to Appraisal

Setting Forth is the collective name applied to a series of proposals being considered by the Scottish Office to provide a transport system in line with the needs of the Scottish economy in the 1990's and beyond. The feasibility studies for Setting Forth [5] included not only the usual transport modelling and economic analysis, but also incorporated strategic environmental assessment as an integral part. An overall approach was adopted to help identify the best strategy to achieve a balance between a number of different objectives, principally those relating to economic development and environmental protection.

The starting points for the approach were the key policy principles for Setting Forth. These had been set at the start of the planning process by the Secretary of State for Scotland, and provided the political framework for the appraisals. The key principles are:

• Ensuring and enhancing accessibility to and from Scotland north of the Forth by the maintenance of effective transport links must be a priority.

• Any new road capacity should be part of a strategy to protect the environment of Edinburgh by helping to improve public transport access to the city centre.

• Any new crossing of the Forth should be environmentally acceptable.

From these, a number of objectives relating to each principles were developed for the purposes of evaluation, together with indicators to asses how packages of proposals performed against them. As well as the three key principles, objectives were developed in relation to the UK Strategy for Sustainable Development and value for money principles which form part of national transport policy in Scotland [6] These are listed in Table 1.

Using this approach, five different Strategy Tests comprising packages of transport proposals were appraised, and advice on this basis was provided to the Secretary of State as regards to the various ways in which the different objectives of the project and other relevant Government policies could be balanced. This highlighted that in some cases there was a direct trade-off between economic benefits and environmental protection, while in others additional costs associated with greater investment in infrastructure provided benefits in both economic and environmental terms although these still provided value for money.

Table 1: Objectives and Performance Indicators Relating to Sustainable Development for the Setting Forth Feasibility Studies

Evaluation Objective

Principle 1: Accessibility
1 Ensure national and local economic development objectives is not hindered by the lack of transport capacity across the Forth.

2 Maintain the level of service for road vehicles (including buses) across the Forth

3 Improve the level of service on public transport across the Forth

4 Ensure that public transport is not disadvantaged in the market for cross-Forth travel.

Principle 2: Protecting the Environment of Edinburgh
5 Maximise the proportion of cross-Forth travel undertaken by public transport.

6 Minimise car travel into Edinburgh city centre, in particular from north of the Forth.

7 Minimise the use of cars in the western areas of Edinburgh and Lothian.

Principle 3: Minimising environmental impact of a new road crossing
8 Minimise impacts on physical and natural features of significance for biodiversity, landscape, agriculture, cultural values or amenity.

9 Minimise impact on local environmental quality and consequent impacts on human health and welfare.

Principle 4: Environmental issues associated with sustainable development
10 Minimise emissions of traffic-related pollutants to the atmosphere.

11 Minimise consumption of non-renewable resources.

Principle 5: Value for Money
12 Maximise the economic value of the transport system in the Study Area.

13 Identify a package of measures which is practicable/implementable in financial terms.

5   Conclusion

The method developed for use in the Setting Forth Feasibility Studies demonstrates how the consideration of sustainable development issues in the appraisal of transport policy and proposals needs to incorporate consideration of both economic development and environmental protection in order to determine the balance between these. Unless both these elements are explicitly considered in a common framework, the principles of sustainable development will never be fully integrated into transport planning.

References

1. World Commission on Environment and Development *Our Common Future (The Bruntland Report)*, Oxford University Press 1987.

2. Commission for the European Communities *The Future Development of the Common Transport Policy: A Global Approach to the Construction of a Community Framework for Sustainable Mobility* 1993.

3. UK Government *Sustainable Development: The UK Strategy* Cmnd 2426, HMSO, London 1994.

4. UK Department of Transport *Transport Policy and Programme Submissions for 1995/96: Supplementary Guidance Notes on the Package Approach* Local Transport Policy Division (*See especially Annex C*) 1994.

5. Environmental Resources Management / The MVA Consultancy / Oscar Faber TPA *Setting Forth: Strategic Assessment Summary Report* The Scottish Office, Industry and Roads Directorate, June 1994.

6. Scottish Office, *Roads, Traffic and Safety*, HMSO, Edinburgh 1992.

Public transport in London – partnership role for local authorities

S. Kearns

Transport Policy Group, Technical Services Department, London Borough of Newham, London, UK

1. INTRODUCTION

This paper will focus on the role played by one local authority, Newham, in London to promote and support public transport and particularly encourage a modal shift from the private car.

Local authorities in London are not generally public transport operators. The major public transport providers are Stagecoach East London and other private bus companies, which provide services on a network planned by London Transport, London Underground Ltd, British Rail and Docklands Light Railway. Local authorities usually are only concerned as direct transport providers through operating their fleets of minibuses that are run by Education and Social Services departments and take children to special schools and people to day centres, lunch clubs etc.

On the surface, therefore, it would appear that local authorities have only a peripheral role to play in public transport policy and provision.

This paper attempts to highlight the fact that this is **not** the case and that a committed local authority can directly influence transport policy at local and regional level.

2. NEWHAM COUNCIL - BACKGROUND INFORMATION

Newham Council is one of 33 local authorities in London - there now being no London-wide democratically elected body since the demise of the Greater London Council in 1986.

Newham is situated approximately 6 miles to the east of Central London. It has a population of 220,000 and covers an area of 3,637 hectares. It is bordered on the west by the River Lee and to the south by the River Thames. It flourished during the industrial revolution and became a centre for the docks and shipbuilding industry.

Since the war the docks have declined and finally closed completely in the 1970's and other traditional industries are no longer major employers of local people. Newham is predominantly a working class area - both due to its traditional industrial heritage and the fact that it has always been a gateway to London and rest of Britain for immigrants from many parts of the world.

Newham has one of the most racially and culturally diverse populations of any area in Britain. In 1991, residents of African, Caribbean, Asian and other ethnic minority groups comprised 42% of the borough's population. This compares to 20% for Greater London as a whole and 4.7% for UK. The Council views this diversity as a positive feature and believes all members of the community can gain from living with one another.

The borough is characterised by many social and economic problems. The Local Conditions Index compiled by the Department of the Environment, which assesses factors such as income, unemployment, housing conditions, general health ranks Newham as **the most deprived of the 366 administrative areas in England**.

The Council consists of 60 elected members, who are elected every 4 years. The last local election (May 1994) resulted in the following Council composition: Labour 59, Liberal Democrat 1, Conservative 0.

3. NEWHAM - PUBLIC TRANSPORT FOCUS OF EAST LONDON

Newham is served by a high density public transport network. The major public transport services located in the borough are:

British Rail
Great Eastern (London - Chelmsford/Southend); North London Line (Richmond - North Woolwich); Gospel Oak - Barking line.

London Underground
Central Line/District Line

Docklands Light Railway/Buses/London City Airport/Riverbus

The diversity of public transport is unrivalled by any other London borough or probably any comparable administrative area in the United Kingdom.

The wide range of public transport services constitutes the framework of the policy of partnership that Newham Council has adopted.

4. FORMATION OF NEWHAM'S TRANSPORT POLICY

My job, as Principal Transport Engineer, is to carry out the decisions taken by Councillors with respect to transport policy. Newham Council's Unitary Development Plan recognises the dependence that local people have on public transport because of low car ownership and because of the need to promote public transport from an environmental and traffic efficiency perspective:

The policy states "The Council supports the development and maintenance of a public transport system which":-

a)   Minimises disruption to the environment
b)   Incorporates measures to ensure the security of every passenger
c)   Is fully accessible for people with mobility difficulties
d)   Offers a frequent and reliable service
e)   Allows convenient interchange between different types of transport
f)   Is within easy reach of all parts of the borough

Newham Council therefore has the political and philosophical commitment, but the problem still existed of the means by which the goals could be attained, given that the Council does not operate public transport.

The method decided on was to develop effective working **Partnerships** with a variety of organisations who operate and have a direct influence on public transport provisions.

Partnerships have been established with:
i)   Transport Operators
ii)   Other Local Authorities
iii)   Central Government
iv)   European Union
v)   Local People

5. PARTNERSHIP WITH TRANSPORT OPERATORS

5.1 Bus operators
The Council liaises regularly with London Transport and local bus operators to identify areas where buses are experiencing particular problems and to jointly formulate possible solutions.

The Council and London Transport have compiled a list of locations within Newham where measures are necessary to improve bus operation.

The volume of traffic in London is such that the average speed of vehicles is now approximately 11mph - the same as 100 years ago. The list compiled by the Council and London Transport was aimed at introducing bus priority measures to alleviate the affects of traffic congestion on buses - such measures include With-Flow Bus Lanes, Contra-Flow Bus Lanes, Bus Only Streets etc.

The Council has also actively worked with London Transport to select traffic signals at major road junctions in the borough where selective vehicle detection can be incorporated to give priority to buses.

The Council is acutely aware that the image of bus travel in London needs to be enhanced to attract more users from private cars. It has, therefore, examined steps that can be taken to bring this about. The Council sees great potential in electronic passenger information at bus stops and is urging London Transport to incorporate such a real-time information system at bus stops in Stratford Town Centre.

5.2 Low floor buses

The Council has worked closely with London Transport and Stagecoach East London to facilitate the introduction of low-floor buses. These buses have kneeling suspension which lowers the floor level of the vehicle to kerb height at bus stops. The principle behind the introduction of such vehicles is to allow all people irrespective of any physical disability to use them. People in wheelchairs will have access to mainstream bus services in London for the first time and people who are ambulantly disabled, those with prams or heavy shopping will be able to use such vehicles much more easily than they can use traditional buses.

The scheme involves low-floor buses being introduced on five bus routes in London in 1994 on a pilot basis. The Council lobbied strongly that one of the five routes should be located in Newham.

When it was decided that Route 101, which operates through almost its entire length in Newham would be chosen as one of the pilot routes for the project, the Council showed its commitment by installing bus boarders at key bus stops along the route to enable the bus to access the stop more efficiently and to discourage inconsiderate and illegal parking. We also participated in familiarisation sessions for passengers and jointly with the bus company produce publicity information about the route.

5.3 Bus stations

The Council, as planning authority is able to influence the design of bus stations being built in the borough. The most significant remit is to ensure that the bus stations are not only user friendly in terms of minimising potential passenger/vehicle conflict, but also convey the image of high quality infrastructure. Accurate and clear passenger information, pleasant waiting areas, toilet facilities, retail and food outlets are crucial elements in this respect. The Council liaised closely with London Transport to achieve these aims for the recently opened bus stations at Stratford and Prince Regent.

5.4 Rail operators

The Docklands Light Railway has recently opened a branch which will link Beckton in the south of the borough to Bank in the City. Newham Council was responsible for providing facilities in or adjacent to the stations such as high quality street lighting, tactile paving, cycle racks etc.

The northern arm of the railway from Stratford - Canary Wharf was constructed in 1986. An act of Parliament was required before the railway could be built. Newham Council, though recognising the benefits that the railway would bring to the area, also perceived some omissions in the parliamentary bill and negotiated the provision of an extra station to serve an important industrial estate, which is not well served by public transport. In return for a capital contribution from the Council, the Docklands Light Railway signed an agreement to construct a station by December 1995. The provision of this station - Pudding Mill Lane - will reduce the public transport journey time between Stratford and the industrial estate for 20 minutes to 2 minutes. The Council also successfully petition for the route to be amended to serve Canning Town.

Newham Council strongly supported construction of London Underground Jubilee Line extension. The Council did, however, petition the parliamentary bill and successfully achieved fully accessible stations along the length of the line and high quality interchanges at stations in the borough.

The Council is pursuing a similar process the CrossRail Project, the new Cross-London regional rail link being promoted by London Transport and British Rail. Despite in-principal support for the project, the Council is petitioning the parliamentary bill to attempt to gain assurances on issues such as fully accessible stations in the borough.

There are two orbital railways in Newham, which are particularly valued by the Council, as vital transport resources. These railways (North Woolwich-Richmond and Gospel Oak-Barking) provide a fast direct link between East and North/South-West London, obviating the need to use radial rail routes and Central London interchanges which are highly congested at peak times. The Council produces publicity and timetable information in conjunction with the operator to raise public awareness of these vital links.

6. PARTNERSHIP WITH OTHER LOCAL AUTHORITIES

Newham Council recognises that peoples's travel patterns are not determined by administrative boundaries. The Council, therefore, works very actively with neighbouring councils to improve cross-borough public transport services. Particular attention is also paid to the authorities in Central London - Westminster and the City - as these represent major travel objectives for Newham residents.

The absence of a London-wide transport planning body has fragmented the public transport planning takes place and made strategic transport planning a very difficult task. This vacuum has been partially filled by initiatives such as the **London Bus Priority Network**.

Each Council in London is participating in this project. London has been divided in to five sectors - Newham is the co-ordinating borough for the North-East Sector on behalf of 8 other boroughs.

The rationale of the network is to identify bus priority measures over major route corridors in each sector. Typical route corridor lengths are 10 - 15 kilometres and traverse two, three or even four boroughs.

A total of £2.5 million was allocated to the five sectors in 1994-95 to identify problem areas for buses and to undertake design work for consequent priority measures. A further £8 million has been allocated primarily for implementation of priority measures in 1995-96, and it is likely that additional funding will be available in subsequent years.

7. PARTNERSHIP WITH CENTRAL GOVERNMENT

Each year Newham Council in common with other highway authorities, submits a Transport Policies and Programme to the Department of Transport. This document outlines the transport policies to be followed by each of the authorities and also acts as a bid for funding to implement the chosen schemes. Until two years ago the schemes which the Department of Transport deemed as being eligible for funding were primarily road based - highway construction schemes and improvements being prime examples. Newham Council has promoted public transport schemes for the past 5 years in the Transport Policies and Programme.

Recently the emphasis on the type of transport scheme being funded by central government appears to have moved from road based to public transport based projects. In 1992/93 the Department of Transport awarded Supplementary Credit Approvals of £500,000 for bus priority measures to four London boroughs, of which £200,000 was awarded to Newham. The funding for public transport schemes in London from central government has risen exponentially since then.

The government has recognised the strategic importance of the Barking-Gospel Oak rail line by granting Newham & the five other boroughs, traversed by the line £200,000 Supplementary Credit Approvals for 1995-96; the funding to go towards station refurbishment and provision of enhanced passenger information.

8. PARTNERSHIP WITH EUROPEAN UNION

Newham Council has long been lobbying for recognition of its problems by the European Union. The Council's efforts were rewarded in February 1994 when it was announced that Newham and five other neighbouring London boroughs would be eligible for European Regional Development Funding.

The Council instigated the East London & Lee Valley Transport Group, which consists of representatives of each of the six recipient boroughs. The ethos of the group was to establish common areas of interest and identify public transport schemes to be submitted for funding. One of the most prominent cross-borough projects to emerge from this exercise is the re-opening of British Rail's Lee Valley Line to passenger services. This line links Stratford in the south to development areas in the Lee Valley and major residential areas in Hertfordshire and Essex.

It is hoped that ultimately a service can be provided to Cambridge and Stansted Airport. The re-opening of this line would aid those people travelling from residential areas north of London, who wish to access Docklands and East London by obviating the need to travel through Central

London.

8.1 Stratford international station
The Council strongly welcomed the government decision that Channel Tunnel Rail Link to St. Pancras would be routed via East London and for the past five years has been pressing for an intermediate international passenger station at Stratford.

The presence of Stratford international station would act as a catalyst for redevelopment of a vast area (120 hectares) of derelict land in Stratford. It would serve as a focus for economic regeneration in East London, which has been particularly badly hit during the most recent recession and has traditionally suffered higher unemployment rates than other areas of London.

In preparing the case for an international station, the Council has drawn heavily on experience of comparable European locations e.g. Lille, Massy, Lyon (Perrache), that have been sites for TGV stations and have enjoyed economic regeneration as a result. The Council has formed a consortium of local and regional interests to progress the bid for an international station. The group - Stratford Promoter Group - consists of landowners, civil engineering companies, finance companies, educational establishments housebuilders etc.

The Promoter group has undertaken discussions with the four Promocos bidding to construct and provide services on the rail link. The sound financial and transport case for Stratford International Station has been put to each of the consortia. We currently await a decision about the station from the Department of Transport.

9. PARTNERSHIP WITH PEOPLE

Lastly, but most importantly - local people. The Council decided that the travel needs and desires of local people must be the basis that underpins the transport polices that it has adopted.

Council Officers maintain regular contact with local people through public meetings, community forums, residents' associations etc. The importance of constant dialogue between council representatives and local people became particularly evident when London Transport undertook a review of all bus services in Newham in the second half of 1993.

The Council was immediately and forcefully able to present the case for new bus services to be introduced to areas previously remote from public transport provision. These included Council estates, an area with a high student population which previously had no direct bus link to University of East London, a new housing development the south of the borough. In accordance with the Council's request the bus service between the two major commercial areas of the borough - East Ham and Stratford - was increased from 3 to 6 buses per hour.

Dialogue with local people also highlighted the needs of people with disabilities who cannot currently easily use existing public transport facilities. In order to meet some of the travel needs of such people, the Council has funded **Newham Community Transport**, which consists of a fleet of 10 minibuses, 8 of which are fitted with passenger lifts to allow people with disabilities to use them.

The vehicles operated by Newham Community Transport are predominantly used by local clubs, residents' associations, youth and children's groups, religious groups, sports clubs. The Council, in funding this organisation has acknowledged the community development facet of the group travel and the relative absence of affordable, accessible transport. The Community Transport vehicles can be taken anywhere in the U.K. and Europe. The only restriction on their usage is that they cannot be used for political or profit making purposes. Newham Community Transport also runs a Woman's Safe Transport scheme which offers a service to women for individual journeys - particularly late at night.

Newham Council in common with all other London boroughs, funds the London Transport Concessionary fares scheme for elderly people and people with disabilities. This allows free travel on buses and underground trains after 9.30am and half price travel on British Rail services in London. This is a financial commitment of nearly £3.5 million per year for the Council. There are 25,000 Newham Residents who have an elderly person's travel permit and 1,650 disabled people with permits.

The Council also recognises the need for door-to-door travel for people who cannot get to bus and train services. It supports the Dial-A-Ride scheme, which is locally managed but administered by London Transport, which provides such a service and the Council itself funds Taxicard, which allows people who are registered disabled to make taxi journeys at a reduced rate of £1.50 up to a maximum taxi fare of £10.80.

10. CONCLUSION

Newham Council, although not a public transport operator has taken active steps to promote and support public transport services. In some ways the Council has felt that it has to assume this role as there has been a vacuum created by the absence of a London-wide democratically elected transport planning body.

The Council asserts that the key to a successful transport policy is to form meaningful and effective relationships with people and organisations at both a **macro** and **micro** level.

The Council is seeking to persuade people living and working in the borough and those visiting that they should use public transport when in Newham. Much more needs to be done but the Council firmly believes that the policy it is adopting will result in an increase in public transport usage and a consequent improvement in the quality of life enjoyed by people in East London.

An integrated transport effects model system (ITEMS)[*]

G. Hitchcock,[a] B. Chateau,[b] J. van Ginkel,[c] J. Bamford,[d]
K. Pedersen[e]

[a] ETSU, Building 156, Harwell Laboratories, Oxfordshire
OX11 0RA, UK
[b] ENERDATA, 2 Avenue de Vignate, 38610 Gieres, France
[c] NEI, PO Box 4175, 3006 AD Rotterdam, The Netherlands
[d] HFA, Vineyard House, Brook Green, Hammersmith,
London W6 7BY, UK
[e] COWIconsult, 15 Parellelvej, DK-2800 Lyngby, Denmark

1. INTRODUCTION

Increasing levels of urban transport are leading to a serious deterioration in
the urban environment. This problem is now a major concern to both local
and national policy makers. It is also becoming clear that a package of
measures, rather than a single measure, is more effective at tackling this
problem. Such packages may include new technologies, public transport
improvements and demand restrictions.

ITEMS is a modelling system designed to assess the effectiveness of a given
package of policy measures at the urban scale. It models transport demand
and evaluates the environmental impacts of this demand, for a range of policy
measures. The types of policy that ITEMS can model includes emissions
legislation, vehicle efficiency improvements, fiscal measures and traffic
management.

This paper discusses the philosophy behind the ITEMS model, outlining the
structure of the model and describing modelling methods used. It also defines
the limitations of the model and concludes that ITEMS is a first but important
step in the development of such modelling tools.

---

[*] This work is co-funded by DGXII of the European Commission under the Joule II
programme

2.   THE ITEMS PHILOSOPHY

The problems caused by increasing urban road traffic relate directly to the traffic itself, through congestion, increased journey time, road accidents and so on, and also indirectly through energy consumption and exhaust emissions. The former problem has always been in the realm of the road traffic planners who aim to optimise the flow of vehicles, reduce queue lengths and identify the need for new infrastructure. The latter problem of vehicle exhaust emissions and fuel consumption is in the field of engineers and environmental scientists. The ITEMS project aims to integrate the knowledge and experience from both of these areas to produce a single tool for assessing urban transport policies.

The project itself is a 'proof-of-concept' project, in other words it is trying to establish the feasibility of integrating the models from these two often diverse fields into a single tool. This will allow the policy maker to assess the likely impact of both fiscal and technical measures on road traffic and emissions. In short it is a tool to aid in the design of an integrated urban transport policy.

Because of the complexity of the urban situation it was decided to construct ITEMS as a strategic model. In other words it will view the urban transport situation in broad brush strokes, not at the street-by-street level of detail. For example the city is represented by simply two zones, inner and outer. Therefore ITEMS can assess the benefits of increase parking fees, new emissions legislation or an overall traffic management plan, but it can not assess a given bus lane or traffic calming scheme.

Also ITEMS does not seek to build a completely new model but to take appropriate models and techniques that already exist and link them together into a single integrated tool. This approach was chosen since ITEMS is intend to demonstrate a principle rather than to develop a completely new suit of models. The use of existing models also reduces the amount of effort required for new model construction and coding.

3.   MODEL STRUCTURE

There are four core models within ITEMS: the Transport Model (TRM), the Economy Model (ECM), the Energy Model (ENM) and the Environment Model (EAM). The transport module as its name suggests generates daily city traffic volumes and speeds. The energy and environment modules generate the energy use, emissions and environmental impacts associated with the traffic activity. The economy module considers the implications for the local economy of different transport policies. Each of these is described in more detail later.

Along with the core modules are communication modules for interaction with the user: the Data Processing Module (DPM) allowing the input of the base city data; the Scenario Processing Module (SPM) for the input of socio-economic scenario data; the Policy Processing Module (PPM) for entering policy options and transforming them into the inputs required for modelling and the Output Processing Module (OPM) providing the end results for user analysis.

The four core models and the communication modules are linked through a central database. This database allows the exchange and control of data between each of the models. So for example the traffic data (vehicle-kms and speeds) is generated by the TRM, fed into the central database and read by the ENM to produce the fuel use and exhaust emissions results. This structure is shown in Figure 1.

Figure 1 ITEMS structure

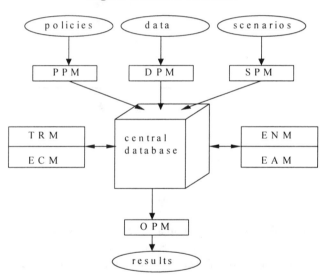

The whole system is controlled by the user through a user shell. The user shell will essentially operate through the four communication modules, but will also allow the launching of each of the individual models. Thus the models may be run consecutively or step by step assessing the results at each stage.

4.   MODELLING METHODOLOGIES

4.1. Transport Demand - TRM
The structure of the transport model is based around the TRL single link model (SLM), used must recently by TRL in a study of five UK cities

(Dasgupta et al. 1994). This approach considers the city as consisting of two zones, connected by a single link, and the rest of the world. Thus it is a very aggregate approach and has no network detail. This simple structure is shown in Figure 2.

Figure 2 SLM model structure

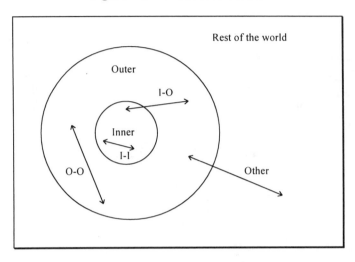

With this representation there are 4 basic trip types:

- Inner to inner trips, I-I;
- Outer to outer trips, O-O;
- Inner to outer trips, I-O;
- trips to and from the outside world, Other.

In terms of time the model operates on a typical weekday, which is split into 4 periods: am peak, pm peak, day off-peak, night off-peak. This gives a basic segmentation of the traffic between two zones and four time segments.

Trip generation assumes 6 trip purposes from and to home: work, school, shopping, business and others. Trip distribution is based on the usual generalised cost function with three basic components:

- Time: access time, waiting time (for public transport only), in-vehicle time, search time (for cars only) and egress time;
- Costs: public transport fares, car costs;
- Others: accounting for factors such as quality of vehicles, safety issues, attractiveness, etc.

The mode split decision process is again modelled with a generalised cost approach using the same set of conditions - time, costs and others. The structure of the mode choice reflects the four modes considered: car, rail based public transport, road based public transport and slow modes.

Freight modelling is considerably less developed than passenger modelling and so is a more difficult problem. An assessment of freight modelling carried out for the ITEMS project identified few developments in the last 10 to 15 years and suggested that a completely new model may need to be constructed.

There were 4 basic approaches to freight modelling suggested: trip modelling, freight volume modelling, aggregate modelling, passenger transport 'add-on'. The first two options being the most sophisticated and the latter options more simple. The final choice of modelling approach will depend on the time available for model construction. Within the limitations of the project this is likely to restrict ITEMS to one of the latter two options.

4.2. Economic modelling - ECM

The main focus of the ITEMS model is the assessment of traffic, energy use and emissions for different policy options. However, it is also important to avoid any policies that could have a serious negative economic impact on the local area. The aim of the economy model is to get an impression of the likely economic impacts of different transport policies.

The ECM is a completely new and relatively simple model. It uses two indicators of economic performance, turnover in the retail sector and employment in the office sector. It also has the assumption that the major economic changes will occur only in the inner zone, as this is the main commercial centre, and so only the inner zone is modelled.

4.3. Energy use and emissions - ENM

The ENM consists of two models, a vehicle stock model and the actual fuel use and emissions model. This is necessary because the transport model only provides vehicle-kms by mode and the emissions model requires information disaggregated by vehicle technology. For example the TRM provides only an estimate of car-km, but the emissions model needs to know how this breaks down between gasoline and diesel cars, and small, medium and large cars, as each of these car types have different fuel consumption and emissions characteristics. The vehicle stock model makes this link by modelling the development of vehicle technologies within the vehicle stock.

The stock model distributes the vehicle-kms generated by the TRM between each of the main vehicle categories and vehicle ages. These main vehicle categories are listed below in Table 1.

Table 1 Vehicle category definitions

Mode	Size	Base Technology	Alternative Technologies
Passenger Car	Large Medium Small	Gasoline non-catalyst, Diesel non-catalyst	Many defined e.g. CNG, LPG, 2-stroke, lean burn, electric and hybrid, but user must choose three.
Light Goods Vehicle	One size	Gasoline non-catalyst, Diesel non-catalyst	Many defined e.g. CNG, LPG, 2-stroke, lean burn, electric and hybrid, but user must choose two.
Bus	Large Mini	Diesel	Many defined e.g. CNG, LPG, electric and hybrid, but user must choose two.
Heavy Goods Vehicle	Large Medium Small	Diesel	Many defined e.g. CNG, LPG, electric and hybrid, but user must choose two.
Rail Vehicle	One size	Electric Diesel	Options provided such as CNG, LPG, fuel cells, but user must choose one.

The total stock is vehicles is modelled through car ownership. The allocation of vehicle size and technology is done through a logit choice function and depends only the relative prices of cars of different sizes and technologies.

The stock model also calculates the age distribution of the vehicle stock, allowing the effects of different emissions legislation and vehicle technologies to be taken into account.

The fuel consumption and emissions model generates fuel consumption and exhaust emissions dependant on the vehicle-kms operated by vehicle category and age. The approach used is similar to that defined in CORINAIR (Eggleston et al. 1991) and builds on work done by ETSU for assessing the impact of a switch from gasoline to diesel in the passenger car fleet (ETSU 1994). The pollutants modelled are: CO_2, CO, HC, NO_X, PM, SOx and evaporative emissions.

The basic method uses average speed-emission functions to calculate the vehicle emissions for each vehicle type, zone and time of day. These basic calculations are then augmented by procedures to account for:

- cold start effects
- driver behaviour and congestion
- future technology improvements and legislation
- fuel quality
- vehicle age and level of maintenance

An important aspect of the ENM is the treatment of new and alternative technologies. The future technologies are considered in two ways, continuous vehicle design improvements and step changes in engine technology. The former improvements include reductions in vehicle aerodynamic drag, reductions in vehicle weight, reduced rolling resistance from new tyres and improvements in transmissions. Step changes in engine technology are essentially the changes that take place to meet emissions legislation, for example the implementation of the three way catalyst. Within the model both of these changes can be driven either by the market or by legislation.

Alternative technologies include alternative uses of conventional gasoline and diesel fuels as well as the alternative fuel vehicles. The main alternatives included are lean burn technology, 2-stroke technology, CNG vehicles, LPG vehicles, and electric and hybrid vehicles (as shown in Table 2). Fuels such as bio-diesel, methanol and ethanol are treated as fuel substitutes and not new technologies.

4.4 Environmental Impact - EAM
This model attempts to quantify the social cost of the transport policies under consideration, i.e. the costs not directly related to the transport system itself. The models has restricted itself to considering the costs of noise, air pollution and congestion and because of the complexity of this subject many simplifying assumptions have been made.

The noise evaluation is based on a Hedonic pricing method, which tries to estimate the cost of noise by relating housing values to the level of noise in a given area. Results from this type of study are taken from the literature, disaggregated to provide factors per vehicle and then applied to each city situation.

For the costing of the impacts of air pollution the greatest problem is the conversion of vehicle exhaust emissions to air quality and pollutant densities. This is traditionally done with dispersion models, but these were much too computing intensive for use within ITEMS. The approach chosen was to develop simple empirical relationships linking vehicle emissions to air quality which would be calibrated using air quality data from the study city.

The costs of congestion will be based on traffic flow information from the TRM and values of time. The time values used in this model are based on results from willingness-to-pay studies and are conceptually different from those used in the generalised costs functions of the TRM.

5.   MODEL APPLICATION

ITEMS is a strategic level model and describes the city in broad brush strokes. Thus its main role is as a decision support tool for the policy makers at an urban and national level. It will allow the initial assessment of a set of policies in a given urban area, indicating options which could be followed up in more detail. The broad nature of the ITEMS approach also allows the assessment at a local level of national policies, landuse changes and longer term scenarios, which most existing transport models cannot provide.

The types of policies that ITEMS could be used to assess are shown below in Table 2. They are broken down into two main categories: transport policies and technology policies. The transport policies are those that relate to the generation of traffic activity and the technology policies are those that relate to the stock of vehicles themselves. The latter policies are a set that most transport models cannot consider.

Table 2 Policies measures that can be assessed by ITEMS

Transport measures		Technology measures	
Pricing	Road pricing Parking fees Public transport fares Car costs	Pricing	Vehicle taxes Fuel taxes
Information	Public transport information Real time driver information	Information	Driver training Public awareness
Restrictions	Parking spaces Changes in PT capacity Changes in road capacity Speed limits	Legislation	Emissions standards Fuel use standards Fuel specifications
Freight efficiency	Loading factors	R&D	Promotion or adoption of new or alternative technologies
Land use	Employment places School places Retail area Population		

The output from ITEMS covers a range of results from allowing a comprehensive assessment of different transport policies. The results can be summaries as follows:

- Transport indicators: vehicle-kms, traffic speeds, transport costs;
- Economy indicators: turnover and employment in the retail and business sectors;
- Energy use and emissions indicators;
- Social costs: noise, air pollution, congestion etc

6.   CONCLUSIONS

ITEMS can provide assessment of a wide range of urban transport polices and produce a wide range of results for this assessment. However, because of its breadth it is necessarily restricted in its level of detail and includes a number of simplifying assumptions. This allows only a strategic view of the urban area, leaving more detailed street-by-street type modelling for other models.

This current project is a proof-of-concept rather that a full model development and as such uses mainly existing models. Thus it is only the *long term view bad data required* first step in building more integrated transport-energy-environment models. The development and use of this model has and will highlight where further developments are required. An initial impression suggests that developments will be needed in the following areas:

- increase the amount of feedback between the different models in an integrated system;
- develop the more sophisticated freight modelling approaches;
- consider including developments in non-average-speed emissions modelling to get a better representation of congestion;
- consider including developments in environmental impact assessment methodologies;

Such improvements, particularly the development of a greater level of feedback within an integrated system, may require a more fundamental remodelling of each of the transport, energy use and environmental components than has been done in ITEMS.

References

Dasgupta, M., R. Oldfield, K Sharman and V Webster (1994) 'Impact of Transport Policies in Five Cities', *Project Report PR107*, Transport Research Laboratory, Crowthorne.

Eggleston H S, D Gaudioso, N Gorisson, R Joumard, R C Rijkeboer, Z Samaras and K-H Zierock (1991), 'CORINAIR Working Group on Emissions Factors for Calculating 1990 Emissions from Road Traffic. Volume I: Methodology and Emissions Factors'. *Final Report Contract No. B4-3045 (91) 10PH*, CEC, Brussels.

ETSU 1994, 'UK Petrol and Diesel Demand - Energy Use and Emissions Effects of a Switch to Diesel', HMSO

A simplified approach to transportation system planning

M. Galaverna, V. Recagno

Dipartimento di Ingegneria Elettrica, University of Genova, Via all'Opera Pia 11a, I-16145 Genova, Italy

Introduction

The increase of passenger and goods transportation demand, both in urban or suburban and in intercity settings, has caused a notable growth of research activities in transportation science; technological, infrastructural, and organisational topics are involved in this field of research. This paper deals with transportation planning, with specific regard to public transport service supply, and it proposes a simplified approach to supply planning, suitable to case studies when no investment in infrastructure is envisaged. The interest in a simplified approach is motivated by the excessive burdensomeness of traditional planning methods, if compared with some particular problems. The proposed methodology is not intended to be opposite to the traditional one when a complete planning problem must be faced, but it can be useful when the cost of planning activities is expected low.

The Traditional Approach

This section resumes the fundamental aspects of traditional approach in transportation planning, as they can be found in literature [1], [2]. According to such an approach, it is firstly necessary to define the transportation system considered, i.e., the set of elements which contribute to producing and consuming transportation supply. Then, the transportation system can be divided into an internal subsystem, that is the subsystem to which planning activities are devoted, and an external subsystem which includes external human activities that give rise to transportation needs; the latter is taken into account only in terms of interactions with the former. The internal subsystem can be divided into the subsystem of transportation demand and the one of supply. There is a correlation between demand and supply, which can modify each other to a great extent; in order to model such a correlation, it is convenient to introduce a system of demand- supply interactions. The logical structure so far described can be represented by Figure 1.

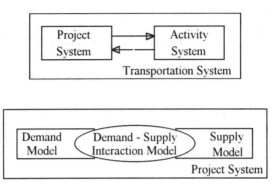

Figure 1: The logical structure of the transportation and project system

Because of their importance in planning activity, the above- mentioned subsystems deserve a precise definition. Transportation supply is defined as the set of physical, organisational, and regulative factors which determine the features of transportation supply. Models of supply systems are usually based on a group of links which describes the topology of the transportation network and on functions which define how traffic flow is affected by level of service and other supply variables.

Transportation demand is defined as the number of passengers which need to travel from a place called Origin to another place called Destination during a fixed time interval. As it can be found in [2], transportation demand for a fixed route does not correspond to the passenger flow of the same route (a route is here intended to be a couple Origin node-Destination node); in fact, it is impossible to estimate transportation demand for a route where no transportation supply is provided. A demand model is defined as a mathematical function that can be applied in order to evaluate the number of passengers which need to travel from an Origin place to a Destination in a fixed time interval; demand models, or functions, may be stochastic or deterministic. As passenger travel demand involves human factors, such as behavioural factors and habits, it is difficult to estimate transportation demand precisely in a deterministic sense. As a consequence, two different approaches have been developed in technical literature to this scope: the deterministic approach yields the number of passengers which travel from A to B as a mean value of a percentage of a population. The stochastic approach yields the probability that a passenger may travel along a route as a function of socio-economic variables related to the passenger and of the level of service. Logit, Nested Logit, and Probit are examples of models based on the stochastic approach.

Models of interactions between transportation demand and supply aim at simulating mutual effects existing between transportation supply and mode or route choice of passengers; choices result from the interactions between the flow of passengers who consume the supply of a transportation system and the effects, both internal and external, that derive from such a consumption [3], [4].

On the basis of the definition of fundamental transportation system elements, it is possible to describe the planning process:

1. a model of transportation supply must be built in order to take into account:
   - topology of transportation network;
   - frequency and schedule of service;
   - infrastructure;
   - operating policies of the system, personnel management;

2. a transportation demand model must be built according to the following procedure:
   - on the basis of the socio-economic variables of the considered geographical context, it is necessary to define zones which produce or attract a flow of passengers; the considered geographical context is therefore subdivided into several zones; for each zone, a node must be defined, connected to other nodes through links corresponding to the flow of passengers;
   - according to the attractiveness of the zones and to their capability of producing transportation needs it is possible to build Origin/Destination matrix, possibly time-variant;

3. for each link between two nodes, the flow of passengers can be estimated through the following procedure:
   - the attractiveness of each mode operated on the considered link can be evaluated by applying choice models;

4. the flow of passengers can be obtained as a product of total transportation demand between the considered nodes, and the probability that a mode be chosen by generic passenger.

5. on the basis of passenger flows, that have been evaluated for each mode and for each route, it is possible to assess revenues and the effectiveness corresponding to alternative decisions concerning transportation planning. Passenger flows may vary as a function of the perceived cost of transportation supply, for instance because of traffic congestion.

The calibration of a mode-choice model represents a critical procedure of the methodology above described. The calibration process needs a statistical analysis to be performed on the considered geographical context. This need may cause some difficulties. A direct statistical analysis makes it necessary:

a) to prepare an adequate questionnaire, with unmistakable, well-focused questions;

b) to select a significant sample;

c) to process the answers, in order to estimate the values of the attractiveness of all the modes.

A well-designed poll must obtain information about different alternative solutions, in order to avoid the need of a second, successive poll in case intervents different from the previous ones should be envisaged. Costs of such a planning process result to be high, and they are economically justified only if transportation planning involves the realisation of new infrastructures, that requires high investments.

The Simplified Approach

As it was suggested in the previous section, the simplified approach is proposed in order to supply a decision support model when a transportation planner, or a general decisor, has to operate in a hard constrained budget framework, i. e. whenever any infrastructural intervention is unwanted. Under that condition, it is authors' opinion that the classic methodology seems to be too expensive to be applied with respect to the revenues that could be collected. Let us take a look at the assumptions of this alternative approach: they are the infrastructure, the fleet, and the number of the employees invariableness. On the other hand, no one supposition about the mode of transport, or about the origin - destination couple is needed. The simplified approach is suggested in order to support decisions on timetables improving, changing the company expenses only in terms of variable costs (energy consumption, worn of rolling-stock). The results of the application of this alternative approach are provided as a list of trips that should be added to the present timetable, in order to satisfy the demand for transportation on a given origin - destination pair, if rolling-stock and employees are available to the transportation company.

The simplified approach aims to evaluate if a mode of transport should attract some of the unsatisfied demand for transportation, by scheduling new trips, given an origin - destination pair, a demand model, and a supply system. In order to make this approach applicable, the distribution function of the demand for transportation (static or time variant) is supposed given for all the modes of transport that provide the transportation supply on the origin - demand pair case study; let $D_{Rf}(t)$ be the mathematical or graphic representation of this distribution function.

In a graphic context, the time is represented on the horizontal axis, whereas on the vertical axis the first order derivative with respect of time of the demand for transportation is drawn. $D_{Rf}(\underline{t})$ represents the first order time derivative of the number of people which intend to act a displacement from O to D (where O and D indicate, respectively, the Origin and the Destination of the trip and R means a path connecting O to D); this number of people is expected to desire to leave from O at time $\underline{t}$. In the next figure, a graphical example of the just exposed hypothesis is shown:

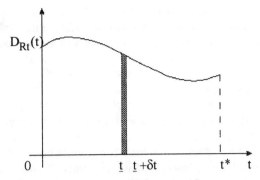

Figure 2: A graphic representation of the demand distribution function $D_{Rt}(t)$

Let us consider the following expression: $\int_{t}^{t+\delta t} D_{Rt}(t)\,dt$; it represents the number of passengers which would like to travel from O to D, and that intend to leave from O during the time interval $[t, t+\delta t]$. Suppose that the transportation mode M is in the supply system; if a trip c, which is performed by the M mode on the R path, leaving from O during the time interval $[0, t^*]$ exists, it will attract some passengers, or better, it could satisfy some of the demand for transportation represented by $D_{Rt}(t)$ according to a relationship $f_{MRc}(t)$ that, from now on, the authors will name the trip fulfilment function; the trip fulfilment function is expected to behave as follows:

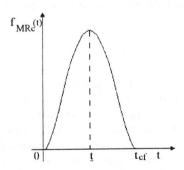

Figure 3: A graphic representation of the trip fulfilment function $f_{MRc}(t)$

The expression $\int_{0}^{+\infty} f_{MRc}(t)\,dt$ represents the number of passengers which travel using the c trip, which belongs to M mode, on the R path. The trip fulfilment function shows how a given trip, which leaves from O at t time, is attractive for both passengers which intend to leave at that time, and for a number of users that would like to leave during the time interval [0, t_{cf}], as it was shown in the previous figure. It is also opinion of the authors that the trip fulfilment function reaches its maximum value in t=$\underline{t}$. $f_{MRc}(t)$ shows, for each time instant t, the first derivative, with respect of time, of the number of people leaving at $\underline{t}$ time; moreover, in its maximum value $f_{MRc}(t)$ means the density function of the demand for transportation of mode M, obviously limited to the path R, if the supply is big enough to satisfy the whole demand for transportation of mode M.

Suppose one has a transportation system which supply provides some trips (e. g.: 3), using means of transportation of M mode, during an assumed time interval (e. g., [0, t*]). Suppose also to plot, on a Cartesian co-ordinate system, both the total demand for transportation and the trip fulfilment functions of all the trips that have been considered.

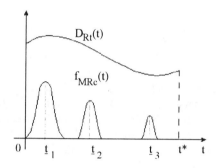

Figure 4: A superimposition of a demand distribution function with 3 trip fulfilment functions

The interpolation of the different values that the trip fulfilment functions reach at time t_1, t_2 and t_3 represents the demand for transportation of the M mode, with respect of R path, during the time interval case study ([0, t*]); from now on, this particular demand function will be named $D_{Rt}^M(t)$. The methodology suggested by the authors proposes to add some more trips, during the time interval case study, in order to fulfil the transportation demand that was not previously satisfied by the M mode supply. Note that this exceeding demand for transportation is travelling from O to D using other modes of transport (i.e., private cars).

<u>NOTE 1</u>: The vehicle, that has to be added into the transportation supply system, has to provide a number of seats which can be estimated taking into account both the definition time interval of the used trip fulfilment function, and the value of the function $D_{Rt}^M(t)$ at instant t_{nc}^*, where nc means the trip number.

NOTE 2: One more consideration is due to the fact that the passengers which catch a means of transport c, to reach D leaving from O, are users of the system that perceive time $\underline{t} \in [0, t_{cf}]$ as the best leaving time. In other words, a user i, having the expected leaving time $t^i \notin [0, t_{cf}]$, will not make use of the means of transport c.

The Operational Procedure

In this paragraph, an operational procedure based on the simplified approach just described is presented. This procedure aims at determining the need of adding a trip on a given path, and, if this need seems to be concrete, it is devoted to estimate the capacity of the vehicle that has to provide this adding supply. The operational procedure can be summarised as follows:

1. to find, for a given path R in a transportation system, the demand for transportation and the parameter set which identifies the trip fulfilment functions $f_{MRc}(t)$ of the mode of transport that has to be upgraded; the parameter set has to be estimated for all trips that leave from O during the time interval $[0, t^*]$;

2. to detect a time interval $[t_1, t_2] \in [0, t^*]$ in which the transportation supply of M mode does not seem to provide a number of seats enough to fulfil the demand for transportation; in other words, the aim of this second procedure is to find the time instants t_1 and t_2 that verify the following equation: where C means the total amount of trips leaving from O during the period case study (i.e., $[0, t^*]$);

3. to evaluate, with the basis of the acknowledge of $D_{Rt}(t)$ and $f_{MRc}(t)$, an interpolation of the $\max_{t} f_{MRc}(t)$ (c = 1, ..., C), as to provide an assessment of the demand for transportation of M mode $D_{Rt}{}^M(t)$;

4. to find a time instant $\underline{t}$ which corresponds to the leaving time of the new trip, that has to be added to the M mode timetable, while evaluating if there is the availability of a means of transport that may fulfil the M mode demand for transportation, as it can be estimated on the basis of the approximate function $D_{Rt}{}^M(\underline{t})$. The choice of the transportation means has obviously to satisfy the constraints imposed by both the number of employees, and the company availability of means of transport;

5. if a time $\underline{t}$, having the features shown in the previous step, has been found, then the decisor has to evaluate the total cost of the adding trip;

6. to assess the total income of the transportation company that derives from the addiction of the new trip in the timetable; this amount obviously depends on the number of people that are expected to use the new trip. If the expected income is considerable enough with respect of the total cost perceived by the company, then the trip is added to the scheduled timetable, otherwise it is suggested to look either for other trip leaving times in the period $[t_1, t_2]$, or for a different time interval.

Conclusions

The simplified approach that had been introduced in this paper aims to be an alternative to the methods that are usually present in the literature, and it is devoted to the organisation of the transportation supply whenever any intervention on the system infrastructure is neglected. This last consideration is very important, in that it allows to underestimate the influence of the transportation supply on the user behaviour, in order to work in a steady demand context. In fact, it is well known that any infrastructure change in the transportation system implies a strong alteration on the demand for transportation, and those variations should not be limited to a new modal division [5]. It is also important to put into evidence the fact that this approach is both transportation mode and trip unconstrained. Further studies are in progress in order to evaluate an analytical form of the trip fulfilment function, and to identify their parameters.

References

1. Cascetta, E. *Metodi Quantitativi per la Pianificazione di Sistemi di Trasporto*, Cedam, Padova, 1990, (in Italian).
2. Kanafani, A. *Transportation Demand Analysis*, Mc Graw-Hill, New York, 1983.
3. Daganzo, C. & Sheffi, Y. On Stochastic Models of Traffic Assignment, *Transportation Science*, 1977, **11**, n° 3.
4. Horowitz J. The Stability of Stochastic Equilibrium in a Two Link Transportation Network, *Transportation Research*, 1984, **18B**, n° 1.
5. Li Donni V. *Manuale di Economia dei Trasporti*, Nuova Italia Scientifica, 1991, (in Italian).

Traffic restraint by SCOOT gating

K. Wood

Transport Research Laboratory, Old Wokingham Road, Crowthorne, Berkshire RG11 6AU, UK

Abstract

SCOOT is the world leading, traffic responsive Urban Traffic Control system developed in the UK. From release 2.4 it has included a traffic restraint tool known as "Gating". To use the facility, the traffic engineer specifies one or more "bottleneck links" where traffic should be limited, and corresponding gated links where the restrained traffic will be held. A Gating saturation is specified for each bottleneck link. When the saturation on that link exceeds the Gating value, the green time on the gated links associated with that bottleneck is reduced to restrain traffic.

TRL now has considerable experience of the practical application of Gating. The Bitterne Road bus priority scheme in Southampton has been converted to operate under SCOOT Gating. In this scheme access to the main road for non-bus traffic is restricted to maintain free-flow conditions on the main road and particularly over a narrow railway bridge at the city end of the scheme. The customised software, fixed-time plans and detectors have been replaced by a standard SCOOT system. Similar systems can now be implemented without the cost of developing special software and signal plans. The traffic engineer simply sets and tunes standard SCOOT parameters to achieve his or her objectives. Kingston-upon-Thames town centre used to become so congested in the morning peak that it could grid-lock. SCOOT Gating has cured the problem by restraining traffic on entries to the town whenever required by conditions in the critical area. Traffic engineers in Nijmegen, Holland, use SCOOT Gating to control the amount of traffic allowed into the town from the major motorway approaches. Gating has also been used to control the entries to a roundabout at a junction of the M25 to prevent traffic queues on the motorway slip-roads locking-up the roundabout.

1. Introduction

The use of the SCOOT "Gating" facility forms part of a TRL research project, on Urban Traffic Control (UTC) strategies for congested conditions, being undertaken for the Driver Information and Traffic Management Division of the Department of Transport.   The objective of Gating is to control the inflow of traffic into sensitive areas to prevent the formation of long queues or congestion. The Gating logic takes "action at a distance" to restrict traffic entering areas susceptible to congestion.   Vehicle queues are redistributed to other roads more suitable for storing traffic. To implement Gating, a user specifies one or more "bottleneck" links and one or more gated links associated with each bottleneck.   When the saturation on the bottleneck exceeds the critical value, traffic is restrained on the gated links. Gating is an uncompromising method of control and so it may be necessary to increase the minimum green time to gated links when Gating is operational.

2. Gating in Southampton

TRL has installed Gating in an area of Southampton known as the Bitterne Road corridor. Gating is currently working in conjunction with an existing bus priority scheme which has been in use for over 20 years (Department of the Environment[1]).

The bus priority scheme is based on fixed-time plans which restrain private traffic in side roads and at gating points on the two main approaches to Southampton that run through the area, see Figure 1.   Buses are given priority by "buses-only" facilities on entry to the corridor, which by-pass the queues of restrained vehicles that occur regularly in the area during the morning peak.

TRL has replaced the fixed-time plans by the SCOOT Gating facility to provide the traffic restraint within SCOOT, but no changes are being made to the bus priority features.   Gating of the side roads and the Bitterne Road is controlled by conditions at junction A in Figure 1 and the main road traffic on Bursledon Road is controlled by Junction B on the figure.

The TRL ASTRID database system (Hounsell and McLeod[2]) was used to monitor the morning peak traffic conditions to compare Gating and the old fixed-time plans. The database automatically collects, stores and processes traffic information for display or analysis.   ASTRID is currently being developed to run on-line and it has been installed in Southampton as part of TRL's work in the DRIVE 2 project, ROMANSE. An on-street survey was undertaken of the effects of Gating on bus journey times.

Figure 1
Schematic plan of Bitterne Road scheme.

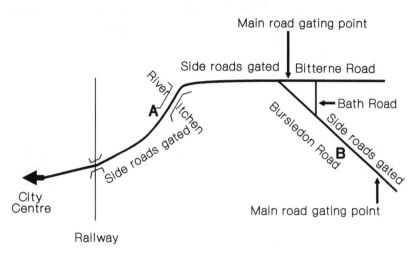

Main road gating point

Side roads gated | Bitterne Road

←Bath Road

A

City
Centre

B

Main road gating point

Railway

Junction A, Northam Road and Princes Street
Junction B, Bursledon Road and Deacon Road

2.1. Assessment of Bitterne Road Gating

Table 1 shows the results of the survey of bus journey times.

Table 1
Results of the bus survey, journey times between timing points (min:s)
Standard errors of the means are shown in brackets.

Bus route	Bursledon Road	Bitterne Road	Combined
Fixed time	15:20 (0:32)	13:07 (0:19)	14:14 (0:20)
SCOOT Gating	16:19 (0:42)	12:15 (0:21)	14:22 (0:34)

The overall impression from the results in Table 1 is that SCOOT Gating slightly improved conditions for buses approaching Southampton on Bitterne Road and slightly worsened conditions for those using Bursledon Road. Similar numbers of buses use the two roads and, as can be seen from the last column of the table, overall, no difference was measured in the bus journey times with the two methods of control. The differences recorded in Table 1 are small and not statistically significant at the 95 per cent level.

In the morning peak buses approaching along Bitterne Road are routed
down Bath Road to join Bursledon Road shortly before its junction with
Bitterne Road. The reason for this route is to avoid the queue of gated traffic
on Bitterne Road; other vehicles cannot use the route as only buses are
allowed to turn right from Bath Road at its junction with Bursledon Road.
Buses approaching Southampton on Bitterne Road gained from the SCOOT
Gating but those approaching on Bursledon Road did not. The most likely
explanation for this difference is that the Gating reduced the journey time on
Bath Road.

The effect of the SCOOT Gating on non-bus traffic was derived from the
SCOOT internal model. The data were collected by the ASTRID database for
convenience and analysed to show the effects on all the gated links and on all
the main road links that should be free-flowing and benefit from the scheme.
Flow-weighting was used to produce the average delay per link. Table 2
summarises the results.

Table 2
Non-bus traffic, flows per link (vehicles/h) and delays per link (veh-h/h).

	Flow per link, Fixed-Time	Flow per link, SCOOT Gating	Delay per link, Fixed-Time	Delay per link, SCOOT Gating
"Free-flow" main road links	929	925	5.5	1.4*
Gated links	239	244	9.9	12.1
All links	570	571	6.5	3.8*

* Statistically significantly different from the Fixed-time value at the 95% level.

There was no overall difference in the flows in the network between
strategies, although there were some differences on individual links. Delay
normally increases with the flow in a network and survey results need to be
corrected for this effect. However, in this survey no flow corrections were
needed to the delays because the overall flows were the same during the
periods when the two strategies were being tested. The delays on each link
were recorded every quarter of an hour by ASTRID. The differences between
the two control strategies were tested for statistical significance using a paired
't' test of the mean values in each quarter hour of the two hour survey period.

All the changes in delay listed in Table 2 are downstream of the relevant
SCOOT detector. Delays upstream of the detectors are indicated by
congestion on the link. Several gated links were considerably more congested

with fixed-time control than with SCOOT Gating, particularly Bitterne Road at its junction with Bursledon Road, the upper main road Gating point in Figure 1. Therefore, the delays on the gated links in Table 2 are underestimates, particularly for fixed-time control. The extra delay, upstream of the detector, was estimated from the degree of congestion and flow and the results are given in Table 3.

Table 3
Estimated delays allowing for congested links (veh-h/h)

	Estimated delay per link, Fixed-Time	Estimated delay per link, SCOOT Gating
Gated links	23.6	15.3[*]
All links	9.3	4.5[*]

[*] Statistically significantly different from the Fixed-time value at the 95% level.

When the results for individual links were examined, it could be seen that the SCOOT Gating had redistributed some of the delays on the gated links. With fixed-time there were large delays on Bitterne Road at its junction with Bursledon Road plus the congestion described above. With SCOOT Gating there was less delay here but at the other main road entry into the system, on Bursledon Road, there was more delay than with fixed-time control. With some effort, the fixed-time plans could have been re-tuned to produce more equal delays over the entry links as the SCOOT Gating has done. It was postulated above, when discussing the bus results, that the journey time along Bath Road was probably less with SCOOT Gating than with the fixed time system. The SCOOT model results supported this hypothesis as it estimated a small increase to the main road traffic at the junction of Bursledon and Bath Roads, implying that extra green time was given to the side road.

There were 25 links in the survey and, therefore, the best estimate of the journey time saving for non-bus traffic is (9.3-4.5) x 25 = 120 vehicle-hours of delay per hour during the two hour survey period. This amounts to a saving of some 60 000 vehicle-hours over a year.

2.2. Conclusions from the Bitterne Road

SCOOT Gating has successfully replaced the Bitterne Road fixed-time control scheme. The bus survey showed a small reduction in journey times for buses approaching the city on Bitterne Road and a similar small increase for those approaching on Bursledon Road. For non-bus traffic, the journey times have reduced and the most severe delay has been reduced at the expense of increasing delays at other entries to the system. The delays at the major entries now appear to be more equal than they were.

The time savings quoted in section 2.1 are equivalent to a saving of approximately £240 000 per annum using the standard value of time for non-working cars.

3. Kingston-upon-Thames

There is a problem in Kingston-upon-Thames caused by queues obstructing the operation of a critical junction in the main one-way system. If the merge area at this junction becomes obstructed by queues of stationary traffic, queues rapidly build up in the rest of the system and can cause gridlock if no action is taken. The normal cause is traffic passing through the town blocking back from the roundabout on the West side of Kingston bridge. A Gating experiment was undertaken to restrict traffic on three main entries to the Kingston one-way system. The police have clearance plans available that restrict these entries, but are not usually aware of the problem until it has become very serious. Gating should be able to take action automatically, as soon as necessary, to store the restrained traffic on the same roads that are used by the police clearance procedures. The effectiveness of Gating was assessed by analysis of video records of traffic queues backing up to the merge area at the critical junction.

Figure 2 shows the length of individual blocking periods. Without Gating there were several cycles where the merge area was continuously blocked for over 30 seconds, a considerable period. The results with gating are quite impressive, the conditions at the merge area were greatly improved. The total period, during which any significant congestion was observed, was reduced from about an hour, without Gating, to between a quarter and half an hour on different days with Gating. With Gating, the longer periods of congestion, of over 30 seconds, were virtually eliminated and the total time that the merge area was blocked by stationary traffic was reduced by nearly an order of magnitude. Without Gating the merge area was blocked for about 20 minutes in each morning peak, but with Gating, it was blocked for only about 2 to 3 minutes.

The Gating experiment was very successful in reducing the level of congestion within the Kingston-upon-Thames one-way system.

Figure 2. Length of individual blocking incidents

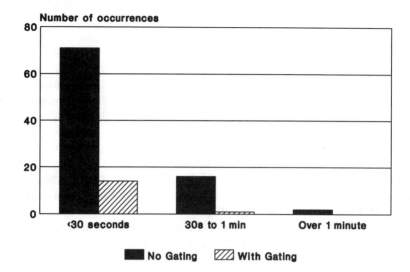

No Gating   With Gating

4. Users' Experience

4.1. Kingston-upon-Thames
Since the TRL experiment in Kingston, Gating has been implemented for the morning peaks on weekdays. Because of the severity of Gating, the Traffic Control Systems Unit, in cooperation with the London Borough of Kingston-upon-Thames, have increased the minimum greens on the gated links, during the Gating hours, to prevent excessive queues.

4.2. M25 junction 10
Surrey County Council are very pleased with the operation of Gating at the roundabout on the A3 at junction 10 of the M25. The motorway is being widened to 4 lanes west of the junction. During the morning peak, westbound traffic wishing to join the motorway at junction 10 backs up onto the roundabout because of the road works Gating has successfully prevented severe lock-up problems and has kept the circulatory carriageway free without creating severe queues on the entries to the roundabout.

4.3. Nijmegen
The SCOOT system in Nijmegen in the Netherlands has been installed by Dutch consultants for the Dutch Ministry of Transport. Gating is an integral part of the scheme. The two main links into the city from the motorway system are gated to prevent overloading the city network. Previously, restricted fixed signal timings were used, particularly in the morning peak. Now, with the SCOOT system, Gating operates throughout the day. In the morning peak periods there are normally large queues at the gating points

because of the amount of traffic approaching the city. At quiet times of day there are no queues, and no restraint, but if there is a sudden influx of traffic, then the Gating logic provides the necessary restraint and holds the excess vehicles at the gating points. Restraint is available throughout the day, but it is only used when justified. The Dutch engineers are happy with the operation of Gating; as in Southampton and Kingston they used minimum stage lengths to prevent excessive restraint and tuned the Gating saturation for their particular circumstances. The Dutch Ministry of Transport are assessing the whole system.

5. Conclusions

SCOOT Gating has been shown to be a useful means of controlling where congestion occurs. It can relocate queues to less critical areas of the network, or to roads where it is possible to give buses priority over the queues of congested traffic. The minimum green to gated links may need to be increased to avoid excessive queues on them.

6. References

1.   DEPARTMENT OF THE ENVIRONMENT. *Bus demonstration project - Summary report NO.8 Southampton.* London, 1975.

2.   HOUNSELL N and McLEOD F. *ASTRID: Automatic SCOOT Traffic Information Database. Department of Transport, TRRL Contractor Report 235.* Transport and Road Research Laboratory, Crowthorne, 1990.

7. Acknowledgements

The work described in this paper was undertaken for the Driver Information and Traffic Management Division of the Department of Transport.
TRL is grateful to the following for their cooperation in providing the Gating data used in this report:

R Morris and J Hammond	-	Southampton City Council, ROMANSE Project Office
J Landles and A Earl	-	Traffic Control , Systems Unit, Corporation of London
K Huggett and P Drummond	-	Royal Borough of Kingston upon Thames
Inspector Dudley and Sergeant Hills	-	Metropolitan Police, New Scotland Yard
Sergeant Upex		Kingston Police, Kingston upon Thames
N Adams	-	Surrey County Council, Epsom

Urban traffic demand management – first findings of the MobilPASS field trial

K. Hug,[a] R. Mock-Hecker,[a] J. Würtenberger[b]

[a] Research Institute for Applied Knowledge Processing
(FAW), PO 2060, D-89010 Ulm, Germany
[b] Ministry of Transport of the State of Baden-Württemberg,
PO 103452, D-70029 Stuttgart, Germany

Introduction

Mobility of persons and goods has a decisive influence on the prosperity of our society, however, a series of problems emerge from this claim for mobility. If the predicted growth rate of traffic comes true (which is to be expected), traffic problems and resulting environmental problems will increase further. Therefore, traffic is in danger of ending in a condition described as "traffic collapse." This is, above all, due to financial and ecological reasons, for which the available infrastructure cannot be extended to an extent as would be necessary to cope with the increasing traffic. Thus, it is vital to develop new approaches in order to meet the critically increasing ecological constraints and, at the same time, to wheigh the demand for mobility against the protection of the environment. In the future we must adapt to a situation of scarcity. Similarly to successfully marking off energy consumption and economic growth, we must mark off increase in road traffic and economic growth. We need a qualitative increase of mobility. Qualitative increase requires a more conscious use of and a more effective managing of the means of transport as well as a fostered use of telecommunications substituting physical traffic.

Combined with collective and individual traffic management, road pricing is a very promising attempt. It enables to realize the effective traffic demand management considering various parameters like traffic density and pollution. It enables to manage traffic dependent both on traffic density and local pollution. Traffic peaks can be smoothed out, road infrastructure can be used more efficiently, which decreases traffic congestions. Simultaneously it is possible to meet ecological constraints (e.g., traffic noise at night or pollution on alternative routes). The implementation of a overall road pricing system requires high investment in technical infrastructure, as well as the generation of a politically acceptable system architecture. This system architecture and particularly the political and social demands on the technology are not discussed in this text (to this [4]). This text deals with the social benefits, i.e., expected effects on traffic, which often have been predicted but seldom proved.

Monetary incentives for intelligent traffic management - the aims of the MobilPASS field trial

In view of the forecast increase in traffic of 20% for passenger traffic and at least 50% for goods traffic by the year 2010, the State of Baden-Württemberg - like most other European regions - is facing a huge challenge in the domain of transport. Often, our transport infrastructure is already congested and traffic-related environmental problems are jeopardizing the function of our cities and the quality of life in them. Baden-Württemberg will accept this challenge and - with a new integrated transport policy - make a substantial contribution to securing mobility in a way that minimizes the environmental impact.

The transport policy in Baden-Württemberg is based on the realization that you cannot solve traffic problems simply by adding more infrastructure. Therefore, the political aim is to improve the efficiency of the transport system and to provide incentives for sensible handling of the scarce resource "mobility." Improving traffic information with telematics systems and applying "market-based" control mechanisms play a central role. In cooperation with European partners, the State of Baden-Württemberg is currently testing the function and effectiveness of such systems in a number of field trials. The aim is to expand these systems to a full-coverage integrated intermodal traffic management system.

Over many years Baden-Württemberg has gathered highly positive experience with conventional traffic management systems. The first automatic congestion warning system was installed on an autobahn nearly 20 years ago. Today, almost 30% of the autobahn network is equipped with fully dynamic route guidance systems and other variable message sign systems.

Currently, the emphasis in Baden-Württemberg is on the establishment of a statewide integrated traffic management system in our metropolitan areas. In preparation for this Baden-Württemberg is currently carrying out several field trials for the provision of intermodal traffic information (STORM, MELYSSA, QUARTET) and a trial - the first of ist kind within Europe - to test changes in road-users' behaviour patterns as the result of variable road pricing (MobilPASS). Other field trials are planned for the coming years. These include testing of a multimode chip card in traffic and the development of guidance strategies for integrated traffic management.

By far the largest field trial with a total cost of about DM 60 million, is currently taking place in the Stuttgart metropolitan area. This project is called STORM (Stuttgart Transport Operation by Regional Management). The State of Baden-Württemberg, the City of Stuttgart, and a number of large industrial partners have joined forces for this project with the aim of testing a global traffic management system for the Stuttgart metropolitan area and introducing it statewide in 1995. Parts of the trial are being funded within the framework of the European Union DRIVE II "QUARTET" project. The field trial is designed not only to demonstrate the technical maturity of the individual subsystems but also to show the effect of global integrated traffic information systems on the overall traffic situation. Subsystems are designed to allow optimal integration of car traffic and public transport and to generally increase the attractiveness of public transport.

The State Government of Baden-Württemberg is not only dedicated to traffic control through information, it is also interested in investigating the impact of road pricing on traffic. Only by telematics has it become possible to apply such market-oriented systems to traffic, particularly in metropolitan areas. In the MobilPASS field trial in southern Stuttgart such a traffic management system with traffic-density-dependent toll collection is tested. Nearly 400 people are taking part in the trial - probably Europe's first attempt to test road users' reactions to variable road pricing. The trial is to show whether automatic toll systems in urban areas lead to a reduction in road traffic, to greater use of public transport, and to avoidance of travel during peak periods. A range of tariff structures is also designed to test how users react to different prices.

For the trial, the southern approach roads to Stuttgart have been equipped with automatic toll collection systems and 400 trial participants have an on-board unit installed in their cars. Participants are offered an attractive alternative by public transportation. Each trial participant has a chip card as a cashless electronic charge system both for both the road toll and public transport fares.

Yet there are many questions to be answered before road charge systems can be actually implemented in urban areas. It is not simply a matter of testing technology and examining its influence. Rather, practical implementation depends on whether such a control mechanism is socially just, whether it is accepted by the general public and whether it does not lead to greater financial burden.

The decisive issue for the introduction of road pricing is acceptance by the general public. The MobilPASS trial was a politically risky venture from the very beginning, given that the subject of road tolls has lead to government crises in other countries. Through extensive public relations work at the beginning of the trial and constant dissemination of information on the content and the results of the trial, a very rational debate of the issue in the public could be accomplished. Whether the introduction of this system will be accepted at a later stage, depends primarily on the perceived motives for introduction. Drivers must see the road tolls as a means to achieve fairer pricing and to improve traffic conditions. It is essential that citizens do not regard road tolls as a kind of tax for the state without any recognizable transport-related benefit.

The MobilPASS trial is intended to show innovative ways to master the traffic problems of the future and to secure economic and social development. First findings can be presented now, final findings cannot be published before autumn 1995.

MobilPASS Field Trial in Stuttgart

The basis of a theoretical consideration of the impacts of road pricing on traffic is the fact that the demand for a good usually decreases when its price increases. However, demand for road infrastructure does not only depend on the price of the road but also on a number of individual factors (e.g., purpose of the trip, its subjective importance, existence of alternatives, and the option to postpone the trip, particularly if time variant charges are applied), which eventually determine a person's choice of transport, time of trip, etc. Figure 1 shows the most important factors, which form the basis of the mobility decision, i.e., the decision if and when a trip is done and which means of transport is used.

It is disputed whether the desired correction of traffic can actually be achieved by road pricing systems. These doubts are mainly due to the lack of empirical data stating a correlation between road pricing and demand for road. The Ministry of Traffic of the State of Baden-Württemberg carries out the road pricing-field trial MobilPASS to obtain better data on impacts of road pricing systems on traffic. The field trial is carried out in cooperation with ANT/Bosch Telecom GmbH, which have taken charge of the installation and management by the technical equipment, and under scientific supervision of the Research Institute for Applied Knowledge Processing (FAW) in Ulm. Other project partners are the City of Stuttgart, Stuttgarter Straßenbahnen AG (SSB) and the market research institute P.+B. Mittag.

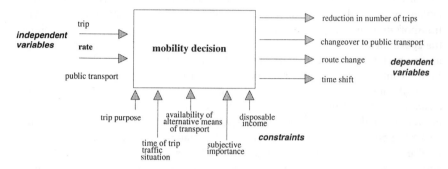

Figure 1: Important Factors of Mobility Decision

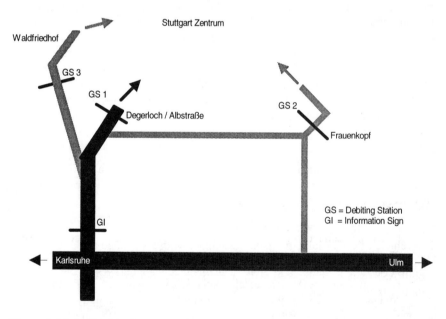

Figure 2: Field Trial in Stuttgart, Trial Region

Goal of the field trial

The main objective of the project is to analyze impacts of road pricing concepts on traffic. The correlation between pricing and mobility behaviour (reduction in the number of trips, changeover to public transport, changes of route, time shift, etc.) belongs to these impacts. Road pricing obtains a global function in conurbations, embracing all means of transport. The car driver's changeover to public transport should be simplified. Necessary requirements can be achieved by a multifunctional system of electronic purses (MobilPASS), which links all means of transport.

The selection of the trial location in a main access road from the southern region into the center of Stuttgart (B27 / Weinsteige) takes these considerations into account. This region distinguishes itself by few alternative routes (which makes recording of evasive reactions easier), efficient connection of public transport with information and transfer nodes of the Stuttgart STORM project, and the possibility of P+R (comfortable transfer). Apart from access to the centre there are two other alternatives: one route along the Waldfriedhof, another along the Frauenkopf. Figure 2 sketches the region.

In all three routes, road-side debiting stations have been set up, thus, almost the entire southern region of Stuttgart is covered. Trial participants using the possibility of P+R receive a combined park and public transport ticket at the car park. The MobilPASS smart-card can be used to pay for this ticket as it can be used to pay for road pricing charges. About 500m ahead of the debiting stations and the P+R car park , trial participants are informed about the current road pricing charges on a variable message sign. In addition, they receive a written monthly information about the month's charges, which vary in the course of a day. The field trial examines, among others, the following questions:

- the price flexibility of the drivers with regard to
  - the modal split,
  - time shift,
  - choice of route,
  - reduction in the number of trips and
  - other kinds of evasive reactions (i.e., combining trips)
- ensuring of the data protection,
- acceptance of the system (handling, pricing, transparency of   charges)

The field trial is intended to find constraints of an intoduction of road pricing concepts in urban centers. Data on long-term effects of road pricing will not be provided since both time and extent of the trial are not sufficient.

Payment of the road pricing charges

The vehicle of each trial participant is equipped with a so-called OBU (On Board Unit). The smart card (MobilPASS) must be inserted in this OBU. The MobilPASS can be compared with a prepaid phone card. Passing a debiting station a trial participant's MobilPASS card is debited with the utilization price. Charged amount and the current credit on the Smartcard are indicated on the display of the OBU.

The trial participants recharge their MobilPASS card at a card recharging station in the center of Stuttgart at the beginning of each month. The amount, which must be paid in cash, is variable depending on the participant's predicted use of the road and on the planned pricing during the following trial phase. The individual use of the road is calculated on basis of the number of trips in the previous month. The charged amounts are reimbursed to the trial participants on their current accounts about three weeks later. The credit remaining at the end of any month remains on the card. The remaining monthly credits can accrue during the trial and are paid out at the end of the trial (up to DM 200). This procedure is intended to impart to trial participants the feeling that they actually spend money although, in effect, they do not pay for the charges from their own pocket. Therefore test conditions are created which simulate an existing MobilPASS system as real as possible and take account of pre-set political and technical standards. In addition, an expense allowance of DM 100 is paid for the participation in the trial

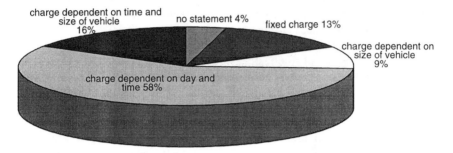

Figure 3: Preferred Price Model

Pricing system and test results

Data is gathered from the trial participants by means of questionnaires. Recording the mobility behaviour in a personal logbook is the most important part. The trial participants record all trips which are undertaken within the trial region. The logbook contains questions on the following issues: trip duration, distance driven, trip purpose, influence of road pricing on choice of transport, subjective estimate of the trip importance. This text does not deal with socio-economic data of trial participants. They are comprehensively presented in [5].

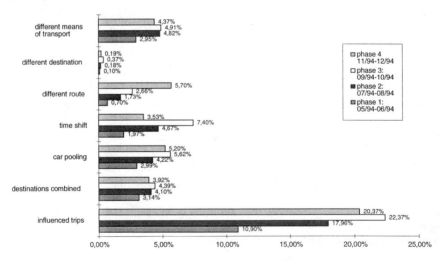

Figure 4: Impacts of Road Pricing

The interviewees should also indicate in an initial survey which charge they assume as a reasonable price for a trip into the centre and and which price model they prefer. The majority of the interviewees think that a charge between DM 1.50 and DM 2.50 is reasonable, which is slightly lower than the fare of a trip to the centre of Stuttgart. According to the interviewees, fee calculation should depend on certain criteria (Fig. 3). Only 13% of the interviewees support a standard charge, 4% are undecided or have no opinion. Almost one out of ten interviewees want a fee purely dependent on the size of vehicle. On the other hand, 60% of the interviewees support a time-variant toll, i.e., day (weekday, Saturday, Sunday) and time of day (rush-hour, normal time). A combination between size of vehicle and time is still supported by 16% of the interviewees.

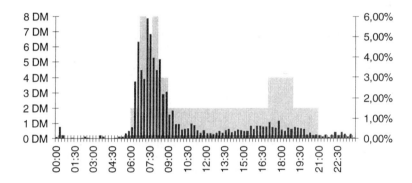

Figure. 5: Number of Trips of Trial Participants into the Centre of Stuttgart Dependent on Time and Respective Road Pricing Charges (Trips in 9/94, B27/Weinsteige).

Trial participants driving into the centre of Stuttgart are charged with time-variant road pricing charges, which are known beforehand. The first findings of the ongoing field trial show an increasing influence of road pricing during the trial time (fig. 4). Particularly in September and October a temporary increased time shift was observed to avoid peak charges in the morning. The corresponding price model is presented in figure 5 together with the number of trips in September. The impacts of road pricing charges on number of trips can be observed very well. The peak charges exactly correspond to the normal time of traffic peaks (i.e., in previous months).

Moreover, in November and December 1995 different charges were introduced for the three debiting stations. Fee for the alternative routes were half as big. The reactions of the trial participants are presented in figure 4: the proportion of participants preferring an alternative route increased (2.66% v. 5.70%), time shift decreased (7.40% v.3.53%). In summary, some participants reorganized their trips, i.e., trips are combined or carpools are formed. First provisional evaluations draw a cautious conclusion that participants tend to change over to public transportation on weekends and holidays while they tend to refrain from using their car less often on weekdays. Further analysis is necessary here. The results are backed by recent studies in other countries (Trondheim, Norway [6]) where correcting effects of road pricing have been proved, too.

Summary

According to these provisional studies the expected correcting effects of time- and route-dependent road pricing charges were proved to be true. In this field trial both time shift and the use of alternative routes were observed. Similar reactions can be assumed in case of a price model, which also includes local environmental factors to realize a traffic management adjusting to the local environmental situation. Changeover to public transport could also be observed; as expected, the effects are strongly correlated to trip purpose. The results are reinforced by recent studies in Norway (Trondheim).

The results of MobilPASS are even more remarkable, since there is no actual paying and a repercussion on total road traffic is not given, due to only 400 trial participants. Additional potential of impact on traffic is achieved if an appropriate pricing system is linked to high-quality traffic information on individual and collective traffic management systems. This is not considered in the trial.

Reference

[1]   Ewers, H.-J.: Dem Verkehrsinfarkt vorbeugen. Zu einer auch ökologisch erträglicheren Alternative der Verkehrspolitik unter veränderten Rahmenbedingungen. Vorträge und Studien aus dem Institut für Verkehrswissenschaft an der Universität Münster, ed. H.-J. Ewers, Heft 26, Vandenhoek und Ruprecht, Göttingen, 1991.

[2]   Straßenbenutzungspreise gegen Verkehrsinfarkt, Deutsche Bank AG, Volkswirtschaftliche Abteilung, 10/1991.

[3]   Verkehr 2000. Europa vor dem Verkehrsinfarkt. Deutsche Bank AG, Volkswirtschaftliche Abteilung, 5/1990.

[4]   Hug, K., Mock-Hecker, R. und Radermacher, F.J.: Anforderungen an die Ausgestaltung von Road Pricing systemen. In Müller, G. und Hohlweg, G. (Hrsg.): Telematik im Straßenverkehr . Initiativen und Gestaltungskonzepte. Springer Verlag, Berlin, 1995.

[5]   Hug, K., Mock-Hecker, R.: MobilPASS Versuchsbeschreibung. FAW-Bericht FAW-TR-94024, FAW Ulm, Dezember 1994.

[6]   Road Pricing in Urban Areas. The Trondheim Toll Ring Results from Panel Travel Surveys. GAUDI-Project, V 2027, 1994.

An integrated multi-discipline dynamic traffic management system, based on information, objects and inter-object communication

D.A. Roozemond

Delft University of Technology, Faculty of Civil Engineering, Stevinweg 1, 2628 CN Delft, The Netherlands

Abstract

The more traffic related problems arise, the better traffic management system is needed by professionals (or the public). Traffic engineers need to design and implement these systems. One of the main objectives of this project is to develop a framework to integrate planning, traffic management, traffic control, information and simulation systems into one multi-user, multi-discipline traffic management system, creating one network integrating all people involved in transportation. Arguably there is no need for totally new and different parts. We require an integrated system, incorporating already operational systems combined with new additional ones.

1 Introduction

This project, which is part of the research program IDEE (Integrated Disciplines Engineering Environment), deals with a preliminary research for a new, integrated and dynamic traffic management system. The reasons for undertaking such a project are plentiful. In the last decades traffic has become both a social and economical problem: traffic congestion, road safety, (im)mobility and environmental implications of traffic are considered important issues. A possible cure is to build more and safer roads, but this is clearly unacceptable as a long term solution due to limits of available space, limited resources and environmental reasons. Transportation is vital to the competitiveness of major cities. The need for better traffic management systems arises from the social and economic dependencies on transportation in our modern world. As traffic is becoming more complex, a better traffic management becomes more vital. Furthermore there seems to be a need for better information towards the public as well as between individuals, dealing with traffic management on the same or different levels. As with all demand-supply problems, solutions made by traffic management can be viewed as one of increasing capacity to meet demand or stretching demand to a level deliverable under curtain conditions.

2 Dynamic traffic management

Dynamic traffic management can be defined as:

"Dynamic traffic management employs technologies for real-time traffic management: the management of traffic flows, traffic adaptive control to respond to changing conditions in the transportation system while improving the efficiency, safety and travel conditions of the overall transport network".

Traffic management can be distinguished in three different levels of decision making each with its own data demands [5]. Firstly, there are decisions to be made concerning short term control. Traffic management with a time-frame of a few minutes, implemented in so-called traffic control systems; in most cases no human actions are required. Secondly there is medium term traffic management (a few hours), normally implemented in traffic management systems. The last level concerns with long term planning (days to years), called traffic planning systems. The different levels of decision making have some consequences for the required data. Long term planning can be done with aggregated, thus semi-dynamic, data and is not used by travellers. Much more detailed data as well as more accuracy, reliability and actuality are required for medium term planning. Highly accurate, up-to-date data is needed for short term planning. To be able to get the necessary data, on-line monitoring the states of traffic is crucial for traffic control.

With the development of faster computers, better and cheaper electronics and telecommunications further research towards new models and applications becomes possible and worthwhile. There has been a great deal of study on the subject of congestion on highways using traffic flow theory. Prigogine & Herman [4] show that flow and kinetic theories are not appropriate ways of modelling traffic in urban areas; even current flow-theoretical traffic models do not sufficiently account for the specific problems in urban traffic. It is suggested that many non-linearities can be expressed in terms of the interactions of traffic participants. Given they are the smallest item in the transportation chain, individual participants play a major role in the process. Usually they can choose between the different modes of transport. Given enough information the chosen mode of transport can differ from the usual thus reducing the overall transportation time (expressed in time/cost ratio). A good multi-modal information forecasting system is essential in this process. By co-ordinating, (re)directing and managing of traffic processes, a substantially higher level of quality and effectiveness of the infrastructure should be achieved.

3 One integrated system

The economical, environmental and social impacts of an integrated system will be significant: more traffic control possibilities, more co-operation between users, lesser unexpected traffic jams and quicker journeys due to better forecasting, better road safety and integration of all traffic, including public transport. The road users, engineers, scientists, as well as those in charge of traffic control and politicians can use such system as their information system. Standardisation is a necessity enabling users to access all information and the simulation models of the system. As it is an integrated, interconnected system, special user groups as traffic engineers, politicians and environmentalists can use each others' models and verify each others' results. It is advantageous to accommodate the new models into one integrated system, thus giving them a testbed and taking care of data collection and aggregation. The different levels of decision making, policy and operational levels, need to be integrated in the system. For policy makers there is the possibility for data exchange, model exchange and communication. The policies to be integrated are social policies (in the interest of the public), traffic policies (politically justifiable) and traffic laws (legally flawless) [9]. Also a large number of organisations have to take part in the design process: not only vehicle manufacturers, electronics industries, public and private telecom providers, but also the public, several different governmental layers, the different road authorities, the police, etc. In this complex setting a change of roles and responsibilities is unavoidable.

Some of the signalled problems can be solved by better co-ordination and information in and between different levels in the transportation sector [7]. In this part of the project the focus is mainly on the information system part. To be able to provide good quality information, an integrated system is needed. The required system is more then existing applications connected to each other; it consists of a network where applications play a role dependent on the situation.

In the case of urban traffic management we can integrate the stream of urban traffic, traffic light systems, re-routing systems, parking management systems and so forth. Integrated inter-urban traffic management focuses on integrated network control, forecasting, incident detection, re-routing systems, tidal flow, etc. There is a need for correct and integral data collection, data processing and traffic control actions as well as travel and traffic information provided for public use. Presentation of such information can in different ways, but preferably it should be provided before and during journeys to improve travel conditions.

4 DTMS

The project described in this paper is part of a DTMS "Dynamic Traffic Management System". Following is a short summary of an overall traffic management strategy based on an object-based model more detailed described by Johanns & Roozemond [1].

We propose a traffic management system, in which intelligent control systems play a prominent role in the management and control of inter- and inner-urban traffic. The proposed overall traffic management system is based on several individual parts working together, thus creating one large system that can easily include other options. The individual and modular parts are chosen to keep information local and to deal with possible introduction of chaotic behaviour, incorrectness or errors of the system. Smaller, intelligent parts can more easily organise themselves. The individual parts of the system should be able to take action, based on the rules implemented in the system and based on actual information gathered by the system. This requires modular systems that can operate within an open architectural framework, consistent with a given standard at each level. For the different levels we support the multi-layer OSI model. An object oriented design enables this integration capability as well as presenting great flexibility; carefully tailored to reflect issues of flexibility, communications bandwidth and other practical aspects. To handle the information requirements (forecasting) for intelligent traffic control, route-guidance and so on, specific models are needed. The processing power requirements of the system become far too big for centralised computing. Therefore, a decentralised, distributed network is needed [1, 9]. A user-centred design is essential to ensure co-operation of the users. For the standardisation of the network, inter-object communication and applications, specific standards should be met.

The system is divided in four large sub-systems on a geographical basis. There is an international level, dealing with information exchange between countries. There is a national level dealing with the national traffic. This information is available in the whole country. There is an inter-urban or regional level; dealing with a specific region. Finally, there is a local or urban level. All levels jointly form the system; sharing information, models, etc. An application or sub-system may belong to more then one level.

5 DTMS/city

DTMS/city is the sub-system dealing with traffic management and traffic control in cities: the most problematic and complicated part of the whole system as well as the most challenging and least researched. Smaller parts of the sub-system, for very specific uses, are still being developed. An implementation of an object-oriented traffic light control system is shown to be a feasible alternative to conventional designs [6]. The next step of this project is to implement several intelligent controlling agents dealing with the specific rules in specific areas. The rules can be implemented in an agent but rules can also be implemented in objects in the control space of that agent. An agent gets its rules from the objects involved and acts accordingly. Arguably this can be implemented in a distributed and co-ordinated way: some information per object and some overall rules per agent. As agents can be objects to agents, a tree-like structure is formed and all rules are available downwards. Developing some kind of voting mechanism is thought of to take care of all requirements. Meta-rules will be included for traffic control situations when operational goals are contradictory.

Designing a good data structure is essential, as each object wants some, but not all, of the available data. As the design is an object oriented one, the data structure should also be object oriented. We are also in need of good on-line monitoring devices for correct data input; for management and control systems, as well as for good dynamic user information. The objects to be integrated in the DTMS/city are at least: monitoring systems, route guiding systems, parking systems, warning systems, traffic light systems, eventually debiting systems and other traffic management systems not limited to public use. A distributed design, based on dynamic locations of traffic participants, is needed to prevent co-ordination problems. It becomes clear that an on-board information transmission device with computing power and database system is essential to prevent the potentially enormous traffic load on the network. To achieve a fully dynamic system, radio data exchange in stead of roadside beacons, is an expensive but essential solution. For remote area's roadside based processing units are expensive and not adequate. A combination of both systems might be a solution to spread the network load and to have some sort of back-up system.

6 Information system approach

One of the main objectives of the project is to design an integrated, multi-user, multi-discipline traffic management system; creating a network connecting all working with or using infrastructure. The travellers, engineers, scientists, as well as politicians can use the system as a general mean for obtaining the required information. The whole system is designed to keep the data as local as possible. Therefore, the monitoring objects can retrieve the historic data. This data is mostly wanted for policy making. Travellers need more dynamic data, as well as forecasts about traffic condition in the near future. Forecasting should be implemented in specific simulation objects getting instructions from users and appropriate data from the monitoring objects. In the information system we try to introduce some fuzzy logic principles. Fuzzy logic seems to be quite promising to deal with some of the rather stiff simulation and information retrieval rules. At this stage it is not certain whether this is a workable solution, but the preliminary results of other applied and operational fuzzy control and management systems seem very promising [8].

Traffic participants who do not have an active system, can be forced to have a passive system as a kind of identification tag, which will include some relevant information. This may contribute to easier data collection. Important aspect of velocity, acceleration and so forth is that they are car-driver dependent as well as depending on the dynamically changing road conditions. An on-board computer will be exchanging the users' data with the DTMS. There are many different kinds of data available and many traffic participants need only a small part of it [3]. Personal tailoring of data depending on needs as well as technical capabilities should be made possible to meet the personal needs as well as lowering traffic load on the network. The effectiveness of systems that provide traffic information, such as route advise to drivers and their potential for reducing congestion, depends heavily on drivers' reaction to additional information. Decisions by drivers made about which road to use and which to avoid during their journeys, are influenced by the purpose of their journey, their personal knowledge of the locality and transportation network, road signs as well as travel information broadcasts. The dynamic capacity of these kinds of information is limited. Benefits of good travel advise can be derived from a study by KLD associates; although completed in 1986 presumably not so different from today's traffic [9]. They found that due to poor navigation skills 6.4 % of distance and 12% of time is wasted, pointing to an arising need for a dynamic traffic advising system.

7 Choosing routes

Fully dynamic route guidance systems offer additional benefits over semi-dynamic ones, in that they can be responsive to random fluctuations of actual traffic conditions. Those random fluctuations may be due to accidents or just some fluctuations in actual traffic conditions. The common feature of those random effects is that there is no way to predict them from historic data alone. In a case of an accident traffic can be redirected to avoid congestion through a new optimum route. One specific function of a dynamic route guidance system, of particular interest here, concerns route choise calculations. The algorithm used to perform this task is the basis of the success of this part of the system; response time, performance, effectiveness and detailedness are all important. Criteria for the "best" route are: shortest, cheapest, fastest, prettiest, etc. Several known principles from the operation research can be used.

When viewing a large road system, every part of the system must be represented. Theoretically even the smallest section can be of importance. Given a road map, the possible roads can be represented by several section-objects, each with their own characteristics. Every section has an entrance and an exit gate; in combination with the distance and the speed the traversing time can be calculated. Every road sub-system has the underlying smaller-road-set that will only be used for transport inside the section and adjoining sections. Several specific road segments can be combined to a traversing link, thus creating a higher level for non local traffic. Example: Travelling from origin to a destination in an other city; the system start using the most detailed network with all routes bottom-up wards, until you are on a tertiary road-network; from there you are directed to travel further upwards until you use the main road-net (highways). Coming close to the destination the system uses the road-networks the other way around (top-down).

If a person can address the travel times on all possible routes and links, one can calculate the overall travel time of a proposed journey. The road segment as an object 'knows' the equations, actual conditions and constraints and, in combination with the actual vehicle/driver information, future situations can be calculated. If the desired information is not in the near future, this can be simulated or calculated as accurate as possible. The kind of simulation proposed is effectively a state prediction model: predicting the states on time t_j, given the state on time t_{j-dt}. Every segment has its travel-prediction at a certain time. Nowadays route choice programs use shortest path algorithms. Faster algorithms, suitable for distributed computers can be useful [2]. As distance and travel time are loosely coupled; quickest, shortest and cheapest routes are not always the same. A route choice calculating algorithm is a necessity as is a hierarchical way of calculating the objective function fast and reliable.

For the several possible routes from origin to destination the chosen objective (time) should be calculated by formula's like:

$$\text{total travel time} = \sum_{\text{All links}} \Delta t_{j,k} \cdot \zeta_{j,k} \quad , \text{ where}$$

$$
\begin{aligned}
j &= \text{Start Node of link } j,k \\
k &= \text{End Node of link } j,k \\
\Delta t_{j,k} &= \text{Traveltime on link } j,k \\
\zeta_{j,k} &= \text{Correctionfactor for link } j,k
\end{aligned}
\tag{1}
$$

Travel times consisting of several adjoining links can be calculated easily by calculating the solely links and adding them to one total trip-time. The travel time of a certain link is calculated on the moment that, real or virtual, car comes from the adjacent link, node or gate and enters the new link. So the correct entering time-state is known or, in case of a virtual car, calculated.

$$
\begin{aligned}
\Delta t_{j,k} &= l_{j,k} / \overline{v_{j,k}} \quad , \text{ where} \\
\overline{l_{j,k}} &= \text{Length of link } j,k \\
\overline{v_{j,k}} &= \text{Mean velocity on link } j,k
\end{aligned}
\tag{2}
$$

$$
\begin{aligned}
\zeta_{j,k} &= \zeta(\chi_{j,k}(t),...) \quad , \text{ where} \\
\chi_{j,k}(t) &= \text{factor for congestion level at time t}
\end{aligned}
\tag{3}
$$

A special zone for traffic control is the interaction zone in which the vehicle's behaviour is restricted by other traffic participants [1, 2]. The presence of vehicles, road edges, road signs, traffic signals, etc.. in the vehicle interaction zone can be calculated by simple and fast algorithms using Cartesian co-ordinates [2] by the on-board processor. In the case of this system the interaction zone is a combination of vehicle and driver as well as the static road properties of the traversing road segment, weather conditions, etc. One important aspect of velocity, acceleration and deceleration limits is that they are partly driver dependent.

8 Benefits of a DTMS

Firstly; a DTMS is no cure for the traffic problems; it may streamline and reduce the traffic load, have more direct routes available, give good information and advises and still there would be a traffic problem. So research on changing attitudes, other ways of transport, etc. are equally important. To give a more explicit overview of the benefits of a DTMS there is a need for categorising the benefits. The comparability between categories, effectiveness and effects is explicitly not addressed here due to different view points; for instance the fact that the government has other goals than individuals. Benefits are not always easy to quantify as they are related to aspects like environment, information, safety and finance. Benefits and costs can be derived from individuals, but are far more difficult to quantify for groups or the whole system. Six categories of benefits can be determined and for each category some measurable effects are listed [5]:

a- *Improved operational efficiency*; throughput, travel speed, travel times, delay times, vehicle occupancy, predictability of travel times.

b- *Improved safety*; number of accidents, number of fatalities, accident costs, incident response time, driver's role in incidents.

c- *Reduced use of energy and environmental impacts*; fuel efficiency, fuel consumption, emissions, noise pollution, land-use.

d- *Increase of productivity*; operating costs, volume of moved goods, JIT delivery.

e- *Improved comfort*; motorists stress, drivers' fatigue, reduction of travel time, better use of transport means.

f- *Improved co-operation between system users*; sharing of information (individual as well as public transport), incident & congestion information, models between agencies and consultation between agencies.

9 Discussion

Finally we still need to introduce a distributed control strategy that can improve efficiency and availability of information. An integrated design that will easily include such options has yet to be developed. Seen from a broader perspective this should be the way and will allow a sensible traffic management strategy to be executed by a network of modular traffic control systems.

Not all traffic participants will participate with the system in the same way. There will be passive users; these occasionally gets data from the system and does not actively transmit data to the system. There will also be really active users gathering relevant data and having a two-way interaction with the system. Several on-board sub-systems should become available from different manufacturer, but they are all part of, and work with, the same system.

There is a certain difference of the required data and the three different levels of decision making. For planning systems there is a need for correct but rather crude aggregated data. Much more detailed, accurate and reliable data is needed for traffic management systems. Control systems need the most accurate data with almost no level of aggregation. Reliability of the control systems should be high as there is almost no time for interventions because no humans are involved. To be able to even partly solve planning, management and control problems, there is a definite need for more suited models and control strategies. The characteristics of these models are that they are capable of realistic, real-time simulations and suitable for calculating the effects of measurements.

Is DTMS a buzzword and will disappear or will it lead to a substantial improvement in our transportation system? Although DTMS might be beneficial for alleviating some congestion and may increase safety, increasing the use of public transport and improve travel conditions, it might be able to relieve congestion in the short term, improve capacity, etc. As seen in the past, the space will attract further travel demands. DTMS won't be a remedy for the real causes of the problem of congestion, real problems like land use, car dependency and so forth are more important and cannot be solved with the aid of intelligent dynamic traffic management systems. Alternative solutions like other transport media are equally important to improve long-term situations.

Despite scepticism on DTMS, there are signs that at least part of this is becoming a fact. In Europe, USA and Japan governments as well as private companies are investing in the establishments of the, to be integrated, technologies to make these systems available. The level of policy making is in those systems not included compared to a DTMS.

Literature

[1] Johanns, R.D. & Roozemond, D.A. (1993), An object based traffic control strategy: a chaos theory approach with an object-oriented implementation; in: *Advanced technologies*; Beheshti, M.R., Zreik, K. (eds.); Elsevier; Amsterdam

[2] Johnson, J.H. (1992), The dynamics of large complex road systems; in: *Mathematics in transport planning and control*, Griffiths, J.D.(ed.); Clarendon press, Oxford

[3] Lotan, T. & Koutsopoulos, H.N. (1994), Modeling route choice behaviour in the presence of traffic information, in: *Cybernetics and systems '94*, Trapple, R. (ed), World scientific, Singapore

[4] Prigogine, I. & Herman, R. (1971), *Kinetic theory of vehicular traffic*, Elsevier, New York

[5] Romph, E. de (1994), *A dynamic traffic assignment model: theory and applications*, DUT-press, Delft

[6] Roozemond, D.A. (1991), *Object-oriented analysis and design of a traffic control system* (Master's degree thesis in Dutch), Delft

[7] RWS; Ministry of transport, public works and watermanagement, DVK (1992), *Dynamic traffic management in the Netherlands*; RWS, Rotterdam

[8] Terano, T., Asai, K. & Sugeno, M. (1994), *Applied fuzzy systems*, Academic press, London

[9] Underwood, G. [at al.] (1994), *Information technology on the move*, John Wiley, Chichester

A new approach for planning and optimisation of urban railway systems

V. Klahn,[a] V. Stölting[b]

[a] *Engineering Office for Railway Operation Systems*
[b] *Institute for Transport, Railway Construction and Operation, University of Hannover, Hannover, Germany*

Abstract

Because of worldwide urbanization and concentration the passenger and freight traffic is increasing rapidly in many large cities of the world. Because of ecological and comercial reasons much more passenger traffic than today has to be handled by public urban railway systems. And although many new lines have been build in the last years, the capacity of the existing lines has to be increased. On the other hand the government must save money and reduce the costs. This makes new methods indispensable in optimization, planning and operations control tasks. For this purpose the simulation model SIMU VII has been developed at the Institute for Transport, Railway Construction and Operation (IVE) at Hannover University.

1 Introduction

In many large cities urban railway systems are the basis for mass transport. There are underground, fast-trains systems or light-rail networks. The advantage of railway systems are, that people can be transported very fast, very ecological and very urban-like. Because of these reasons many cities have increased or are increasing their railway networks. This produces capacity problems especially in the central areas, when several lines use the same infrastructure (e.g. S-Bahn Munich). In other cases few stations with very high number of passengers leaving and entering the trains detemine the frequency on the line.

Simulation methods have been used for years for investigation of railway systems (Klahn [4]). Typical examples are high-speed-lines like Hannover-Würzburg (Hörstel [2]), stations like Bremen main station or complete networks like the railway network of Greater Hannover (Klahn [5]). So it could be shown, that the simulation model SIMU VII permits a very detailed representation of nearly every operational process on railway systems. In the last years also urban railways were examined extensively, founding a new working field for simulation.

2   Simulation components

2.1   SIMU VII

The simulation model SIMU VII was designed as an easy to use simulator with the capability of modelling the full range of railway operations. One of the important features was the ability to display the infrastructure, timetable and operational process in a way that would be familiar to train planners.

SIMU VII runs on UNIX-Workstations (e.g. SUN) with high resolution graphics using the X-Window graphical standard. Actually we are able to handle railway networks which consists of more than 2500 kilometers of track and 2000 trains. This is approximately 5% of the network and the operational process of the whole German Railway.

2.2   Track data and layout

The simulation model uses the graph theorie to depict the infrastructure data. So a schematic diagramm of the represented network can easily be given. Figure 1 shows an example for a graph representing a station with a double track turning unit. All evident additional information like speed, gradients, restrictions are assigned to the graph elements. Also single track lines can be depicted.

The graph can be constructed and altered by interactive programm systems. There are also facilities for panning and zooming and also to cut and paste portions of the track data. By using the modern technique of functional units a network can be separated into different lines.

SIMU VII was designed to model all types of fixed or variable block signals. This includes 2, 3 or more aspect colour light signals, shunting signals and semaphore signals. Moving block and signal less systems can also be depicted. The user can mix different signal types, e.g. to depict a fixed block signals in a central tunnel area and moving block systems outside of tunnel areas. This method was used for simulation of the light rail network of Hannover.

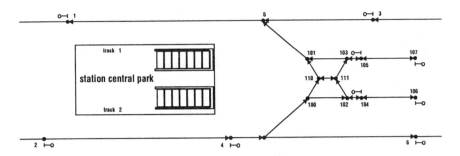

Figure 1: Depiction of the track

2.3   Train performance and timetable

The simulator calculates the train performance of each train with respect to its tractive effort, mass, load, resistances and admissible speed. To get the running times extra-times can be considered and used in the simulation in case of delays.

For each train a timetable can be input, which defines the standard routing, the stopping, the departure and arrival times. This data can also be handled by interactive programms, which allows an on-line check of the timetable data (Hauptmann [3]).

2.4   Connections

Often the turning units are those elements in a urban railway system, which limit its capacity. Therefore in SIMU VII the trains can be connected very extensively. An example is given in figure 2. There train number 1 leave the line into the turning unit, where it stops. The driver can change the cab and after a sufficient stopping time the train enters with a new train number the line in opposite direction. They are connected in the model, so that in case of delay of train number 1 also train number 2 may get an initial delay. Moreover the track keeps occupied until train 2 has left the turning unit.

Other connections are given by correspondence of two or more lines or by shunting movements.

2.5   Simulation

The simulator will run the trains according to the timetable. It uses a mixture of fixed-increment discrete-time and event simulation technique with very small time increment. The maximum speed of the simulation depends on the hardware and is a function of the number of trains and the complexity of the network. Usually it is much faster than reality (200 times or

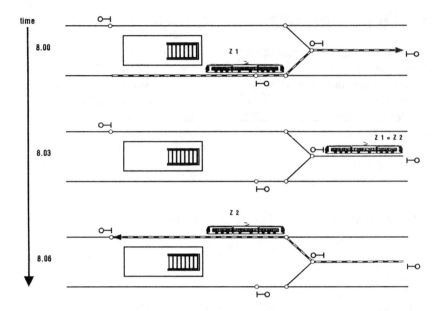

Figure 2: Connection of trains in turning units

more).

During the running of the simulation the occupied tracks and running trains can be visualized on the screen. The user can interrupt the simulation and change interactively train attributes (e.g. change of track, model type, include extra-stops). Delays are printed out, which is a useful way of checking the timetable for errors. Other features are on-line string-line diagramms, track-occupation graphs and extensive protocols.

2.6   Perturbations

By simulation without initial delays the given timetable can be checked for running under ideal conditions. But in reality there occur delays, which can not be avoided and may cause additional delays to other trains. If the robustness of the timetable is insufficient the delays will grow rapidly.

To check the robustness of the timetable, many automatic simulation runs with initial delays based on user-defined distributions are executed. Moreover variations in stopping-times or train characteristics, faults in signaling or traction units can be assigned randomly to train-runs.

After simulation of the perturbed timetables extensivly statistical evaluations are possible. Examples are given by statistics of delays, calculation of electrical systems or detection of hot spots in the system.

3   Depiction of urban railway systems

By using the standard simulation features the track and timetable of nearly every urban railway system can be depicted easliy. Often existing computer-readable track and timetable data can be used to build up the model data automatically. Otherwise a manual import is possible as well.

But there are additional constraints, which are typical for urban railway systems. These constraints have to be taken into consideration. Examples are given by signal-less systems, extensive use of turning-points and high density of traffic. There are model components to depict these constraints (e.g. connection of trains in turning units as seen above).

3.1   Conflicts with individual traffic

A serious problem for light-rails are conflicts with individual traffic like cars, which block the line. Other delays can be caused by traffic lights, which do not prefer public transport systems.

The simulation model SIMU VII is designed for railway systems, which work mainly on separated tracks. Otherwise a model for simulation of individual traffic would be a better choice. However single traffic lights can be simulated by special model algorithms and single conflict points with individual traffic may be depicted by extra stopping times, which can randomly be assigned to the train-runs.

3.2   Stopping times

The stopping-time of a train depends on the passenger flow especially in peak hours. Single train runs with many passengers cause much more delays than other train runs. The effect is described in figure 3.

On a line the trains may run with constant headways t_c. It can be assumed that the passengers come continously on the platforms to enter the next train. If many passengers want to leave or enter the train the planned stopping time is insufficient and will become longer. For train 1 this occurs in one station producing an intial delay t_i. By this delay train 1 arrives the next station later, so that more passengers than normally enter the train again. The delays for this train increase. On the other hand train 2, which follows train 1, keeps empty because all passengers are in train 1. Finally the delay for train 1 accummulates to t_e and the following train 2 will be delayed too.

This effect, called bunching, can be depicted by a special passenger flow algorithms. Then the stopping time can be calculated with respect to the number of passengers in the train, the number of passengers leaving or entering the train and the type of doors or station. This function can be

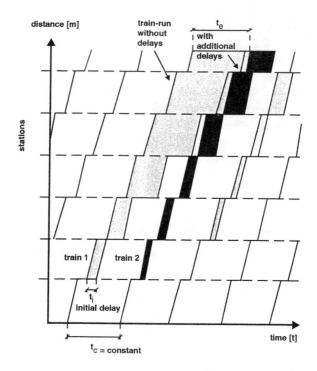

Figure 3: Accumulation of stopping time

applied to compare different train types or to plan extra-traffic after great events (e.g soccer games).

4   Applications

In the past SIMU VII was mostly used for planning of infrastructure and timetables on lines with international or long-distance traffic. Examples are the network of Greater Hannover, the high-speed railway line Hannover-Wuerzburg or main station Bremen. In England the Channel-Tunnel-Rail-Link between the Channel Tunnel and London St. Pancras was studied by our simulation model.

But also extensive studies on urban railway systems have been done in the last years. An example is the underground railway line 1 in Hamburg, where an extra-fast train system was planned in detail (Dannenberg [1]). A similar study about express-trains on the light-rail network of Hannover was carried out last year.

An example for infrastructure planning is given in figure 4. It shows the percentage of delayed trains in different stations along the line. The filled bars show the percentage of trains with delays of 120 seconds or more and the empty bars show the percentage of trains with delay of more than 60 seconds. It can be seen, that in variant 1 between the stations LP and RP the delays increase. This is caused by extra long stopping times in the station RP. In variant 2 an additional signal was installed near RP, which reduces the delays dramatically. By using a second platform in RP (variant 3) no additional delays occur. A similar study was carried out for an urban railway line in a far eastearn country this year.

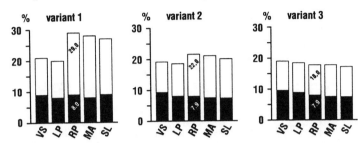

Figure 4: Planning of infrastructure

Figure 5 shows the graph of the future fast-train network of Nürnberg. The existing two lines from Nürnberg to Lauf and Nürnberg to Altdorf will be completed by two new lines to Roth in the south and Forchheim in the north. The lines to Altdorf and Roth are partly single track lines. The line to Forchheim will be used additionally by freight trains, because the planned high-speed line to Berlin is reserved for fast passenger and fast freigth trains. We had to solve the question, which lines should be connected in Nürnberg to guarantee a maxmimum stability of the operational process. It could be proved, that the best way for connection is the -so called- crossing solution, where the line from Forchheim is connected with the line to Altdorf. Otherwise the delays on the single track lines can accumulate.

Actually SIMU VII is used to optimize the S-Bahn system for the EXPO 2000, which will take place in Hannover.

5   Conclusion

It could be shown that by aid of the simulation model SIMU VII a new quality in planning and optimization of urban railway systems can be reached. The infrastructure and timetable of a station, line or complete network can be depicted in detail by a computer based system including those constraints, which are typical for urban railway systems.

This allows extensive studies of the system years before operation. So hot spots in railway systems can be detected and handled a long time before real operation. So future railway systems can be optimized with regard to the costs and operation quality.

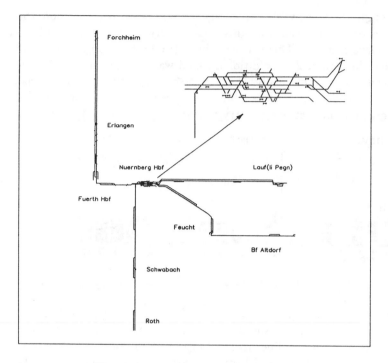

Figure 5: Track layout of S-Bahn Nürnberg

References

[1] H. Dannenberg, V. Klahn und A. Wirsching. Analyse und Bewertungsverfahren von Betriebskonzepten bei Nahverkehrsbahnen. *Eisenbahntechnische Rundschau (ETR)*, 42(12), 1993.

[2] J. Hörstel, V. Klahn und H. Wegel. Planung eines sehr schnellen Güterverkehrs (ICE-G) auf der Schnellfahrstrecke Hannover-Würzburg. *Eisenbahntechnische Rundschau (ETR)*, 42(1/2), 1993.

[3] J. Hörstel, V. Klahn und D. Hauptmann. Interaktive Fahrplankonstruktion mit dem Simulationsmodell SIMU VII. *Eisenbahntechnische Rundschau (ETR)*, 42(9), 1993.

[4] V. Klahn. Die betriebliche Simulation von Eisenbahnstrecken. *Eisenbahntechnische Rundschau (ETR)*, 41(3), 1992.

[5] V. Klahn. Die betriebliche Simulation großer Eisenbahnnetze. *Eisenbahntechnische Rundschau (ETR)*, 43(10), 1994.

A stochastic algorithm for driver scheduling

G. Fleury, M. Gourgand, E. Molimard
Laboratoire d'Informatique, Université Blaise Pascal,
F-63 177 Aubiére Cedex, France

Abstract

Driver scheduling problem in urban transit networks is highly combinatorial and characterized by many constraints sometimes difficult to formalize (feasibility constraints, social rules...). The main purpose is to minimize the number of driver shifts. We present an algorithm inspired by simulated annealing and we explain how it has been adapted to the studied problem. The main interest of our method is that it permits to take into account some constraints that can not be handled by other software products.

1 Introduction

Urban transit companies proceed in three operations in order to satisfy the user transport demand. After the network has been designed, the first operation, called Vehicle Scheduling, consists in assigning at best vehicles to the network lines to satisfy the user demand. The purpose of the second operation, called Driver Scheduling, is to spread over shifts the workload defined by the vehicle schedule. The last operation, called Rotation, consists in namely assigning drivers to the shifts.

Here, we are interested in solving the driver scheduling problem. This is a multicriteria optimization problem characterized by a high combinatoric, many constraints - sometimes difficult to formalize. Moreover, some optimization criteria are more or less explicit. When driver scheduling is computerized, a schedule can either be obtained from an existing solution or be designed overall. Computerization makes it possible to quickly evaluate the impact when some social rules or some network lines are modified. In order to computerize the problem solving, we propose to apply a stochastic algorithm to the driver scheduling problem.

In the first part, we describe the driver scheduling problem. Secondly, we detail difficulties encountered to solve such a problem. In the third part, we propose our formalization and we present the constraints to deal with. We present a stochastic algorithm, called Kangaroo algorithm, in the fourth part and how we have adapted it to the driver scheduling problem in the fifth part. In the last part, we compare our results to those obtained by five driver scheduling software products for the urban transit network of Clermont-Ferrand (France).

2 Description of the problem

For a workday, vehicle scheduling draws up the number of Blocks (workload of a driven vehicle) necessary to cover the user demand. It also gives the dates of vehicle passages in front of Relief Points which are stops where users can get into or off vehicles and where driver changeovers can be performed.

Driver scheduling consists in allocating the vehicle schedule workload among Shifts, respecting social rules. It is a critical operation because it defines the driver workdays and has an important impact on the social atmosphere in the company. Otherwise, its main purpose is to minimize the production costs and the solution has to be suitable for the company.

In order to design a driver schedule, blocks are cut into Tasks. A task is a time interval between two consecutive relief points or between a depot and a relief point. These tasks are assigned to shifts. We call Piece of work an ordered sequence of consecutive tasks of the same block which are assigned to the same shift.

3 Difficulties of the problem

Each urban network purpose is to design a driver schedule which optimizes wage costs (total shift number, bonuses) and which is suitable for drivers (satisfaction of driver scheduling constraints, convenience of the total piece number of each shift). Moreover, a scheduler considers a solution globally and uses his experience to evaluate it. This is difficult to formalize because it is partly intuitive and too proper to the scheduler and the network. So, a rigorous evaluation of a driver schedule seems difficult to be conceived.

The objective function to minimize by driver scheduling is not limited to the previous criteria. Assigning tasks to shifts is progressively done, so the respect of some constraints can only be checked once driver scheduling is completed. A solution consists in integrating those constraints in the objective function as penalties. Some other constraints are not compulsory. Penalizing the objective function is a way to take them into account. Therefore, evaluating this function becomes difficult.

Driver scheduling is a highly combinatorial problem. In fact, the more potential relief times are, the greater the total task number is. This increases the number of possible task combinations (for example, 2100 tasks and 140 shifts). Moreover, driver scheduling is constrained by the work regulations and the trend of the transport offer (peak periods, off-peak periods).

There may be two types of shifts. Line Priority Shifts have to run on a fixed set of lines and are not very constrained about their timetables. Timetable Priority Shifts can run on any line but their starting and ending dates are more constrained. Each task can be assigned to most shifts. So the problem cannot be decomposed and the combinatoric cannot be significantly decreased.

4 Formalization of the problem

To solve the driver scheduling problem, the only wage cost which we take into consideration is the total shift number. We formalize the driver scheduling problem in the following way. Let m be the number of tasks to assign and let n be the maximum number of shifts. We denote the variables x_{is}, $i = 1, \ldots, m$ and $s = 1, \ldots, n$, defined by:

$$x_{is} = \begin{cases} 1 & \text{if task } i \text{ is assigned to shift } s \\ 0 & \text{otherwise} \end{cases} \qquad i = 1, \ldots, m \quad s = 1, \ldots, n.$$

(1)

We call Working Shift a shift s including at least one task. It verifies:

$$\sum_{i=1}^{m} x_{is} \geq 1.$$

(2)

The main purpose is to minimize the total working shift number under the constraint that each task is assigned to exactly one shift:

$$\begin{cases} Min \ Card \{ s/1 \leq s \leq n, \sum_{i=1}^{m} x_{is} \geq 1 \} \\ \sum_{s=1}^{n} x_{is} = 1 \quad i = 1, \ldots, m \\ x_{is} \in \{0; 1\} \quad i = 1, \ldots, m \quad s = 1, \ldots, n. \end{cases}$$

(3)

Shifts have to respect driver scheduling constraints. These constraints represent national and local rules and driver wishes, and they differ from one urban transit network to another.

We call Spell a continuous working period in half a day. It is characterized by an ordered sequence of pieces assigned to the same shift. There are usually two types of shifts: straight shifts and split shifts, and some variants exist. A straight shift includes one spell. A split shift includes two spells which are separated by a gap for the lunch.

Shifts have to respect different driver scheduling constraints which are difficult to handle and to formalize:

- the total number of shifts of each type,
- the starting date and the ending date of shifts,
- the paid breaks and the meal break. A break is an unproductive period between two consecutive pieces of a shift. A break occurring in a spell is paid. A break which splits a workday into two spells is called meal break and is not considered as worked time,
- the length of spells,
- the worked time of shifts (sum of the spell lengths),
- the spread of shifts (duration between the starting and ending dates),
- the allotment of shifts into grids. Shifts sharing the same characteristics may be gathered into a grid.

Driver scheduling is also constrained by the network structure: total vehicle depot number, relief points, travel times between relief points. Drivers generally have to move from a relief point to another when they change pieces. So, the duration of the paid break between two consecutive pieces has to be long enough to allow this moving.

Driver scheduling constraints we have just detailed are compulsory: they are called Hard Constraints. Others are called Soft Constraints and they are usually linked to driver wishes. These constraints are expressed as: "it would be nice that...", "you have to avoid doing...".

5 Solving method: the Kangaroo algorithm

Different methods have been considered to solve the driver scheduling problem: linear programming, branch and bound, constraint logic programming or artificial intelligence. It is difficult to use linear programming or branch and bound on the whole problem because the combinatoric is high and the objective function does not allow a clear characterization of an optimal solution. We have dismissed constraint logic programming on the whole problem because the combinatoric is too high and there are not enough constraints. We have also dismissed artificial intelligence because the knowledge of the scheduler is too specific to a network.

Stochastic algorithms allow to optimize any objective function. They are approximate algorithms and they are especially suitable to optimize a function which is not well defined. Being able to calculate its value for any driver schedule is sufficient. We have chosen to use an algorithm inspired by Simulated Annealing. We present this algorithm, called Kangaroo Algorithm [2] [4].

Let X be a finite set of states and let $H : X \to I\!R$ be the objective function. We use a Stochastic Descent combined with a neighbouring system V. When the cost of the current state x does not change after K iterations using stochastic descent, we make a jump to go out of this local minimum. So, we accept any state in a neighbourhood $W(x)$ of x, provided that it implies a modification of the function H. Otherwise, we make another jump until the state randomly chosen in $W(x)$ modifies the value of the function H (figure 1).

This algorithm is at least as efficient than other stochastic methods. It allows to go out of a local minimum, it does not loose all information related to successive steps and its behaviour depends only on the sign of the difference between the costs of two states. Moreover, adjusting parameters is easier.

```
procedure descent(x, rx, c); / x: current state; rx: record state; c: iteration counter /
begin;
    (randomly) choose y in V(x);
    if H(y) ≤ H(x) then
        if H(y) < H(x) then
            c := 0;
            if H(y) < H(rx) then rx := y; endif;
        endif;
        x := y;
    endif;
    c := c + 1;
end;
procedure jump(x, rx, c); / x: current state; rx: record state; c: iteration counter /
begin;
    randomly choose y in W(x);
    if H(y) ≠ H(x) then
        if H(y) < H(rx) then rx := y; endif;
        c := 0;
    endif;
    c := c + 1; x := y;
end;
program kangaroo;
begin;
    fix K; choose an initial state x; c := 1; rx := x;
    as long as rx is not suitable do
        if c < K then descent(x, rx, c)
                  else jump(x, rx, c);
        endif;
    done;
    return rx;
end;
```

Figure 1: Kangaroo algorithm.

6 Applying Kangaroo algorithm

We present the objective function we have defined, the neighbourhood systems used and the driver scheduling process applied.

In addition to the total shift number, a driver schedule cost takes into account the leftover time (sum of leftover task durations). Some tasks can be leftover. Leftover time is very penalized when it is greater than the authorized leftover task duration; otherwise, it is not heavily penalized. Penalties are proportional to the leftover time. The objective function penalizes breaking constraints which can only be checked once the driver scheduling is completed. Finally, shifts whose productive time is short are also penalized. The soft constraints are not taken into account in the objective function because they would make this function more complex. However, we have noted that they are satisfied for most shifts.

A driver schedule may be slightly better than one other regarding the objective function although its quality is worse from the scheduler point of view. So, we accept any neighbour of the current driver schedule which damages slightly the cost of the current driver schedule.

The quality of the algorithm progress highly depends on the definition of neighbourhood systems V and W. Neighbourhood system V used in stochastic descent disturbs slightly driver scheduling. Neighbourhood system W allows to make a jump and must disturb driver scheduling much more.

Given a driver schedule S_1, the principle used for V is:
- randomly choose two working shifts whose productive time is low and remove tasks assigned to them,
- design a driver schedule S_2 without using these shifts and evaluate it,
- design a driver schedule S_3 using one of these shifts and evaluate it,
- design a driver schedule S_4 using these two shifts and evaluate it,
- retain the best of the four driver schedules S_1, S_2, S_3 and S_4.

Given a driver schedule S, the principle used for W is:
- randomly choose four shifts and remove tasks assigned to them,
- design a driver schedule using <u>all shifts</u>, whether they are working in S or not, and evaluate it,
- retain this driver schedule.

So, the number of working shifts can only decrease during stochastic descent runs. On the contrary, it can increase during a jump.

When we build a neighbour of a driver schedule S, we assign tasks which are leftover in S. We have decided to apply a heuristic to build a driver schedule neighbour. A task i is chosen using an uniform distribution. We respectively denote j and k the block and the line which task i belongs to. We try to assign the leftover tasks in the following order:
- task i and tasks of block j on line k which follow task i,

- tasks of block j on line k which precede task i, beginning with the latest,
- tasks of blocks on line k which follow block j,
- tasks on lines which follow line k,
- tasks on lines which precede line k, beginning with the first,
- tasks of blocks on line k which precede block j, beginning with the first.

While assigning a task to a shift, we try to assign to this shift leftover tasks which belong to the same block than this task, in order to favour grouping tasks of a shift.

7 Results

We have applied Kangaroo algorithm to the driver scheduling problem of T2C which is the urban transit company of Clermont-Ferrand [5]. T2C network includes fifteen lines, one single vehicle depot and four relief points. There are three types of shifts and two of them are split shifts. Some constraints are not linked to the types of shifts. In fact, shifts are allotted into grids. All grids include either line priority shifts or timetable priority shifts, and the total shift number of grids is limited.

Two types of problems have been treated: a moderate size problem upon a part of the network (3 lines, 300 tasks, about 25 shifts), and a large size problem upon the entire network (2100 tasks, about 140 shifts). For these problems, we have to deal with tasks whose durations are very different: some tasks are five minutes long while others have a duration of six hours.

After having solved these problems with Kangaroo algorithm, we compare our results to those obtained with five driver scheduling software products: Busman [6], Habile, Hastus [1], Heures and Matrics. The five criteria used to evaluate a driver schedule are: the total shift number, the leftover task duration, the unproductive worked time, the satisfaction of constraints, the quality of shifts (homogeneity, number of pieces).

Kangaroo algorithm designs solutions of better quality than Busman: the total shift number is lower and driver scheduling constraints are better satisfied (Busman does not fit the problem of T2C very well). The results obtained with Kangaroo algorithm are better than those of Habile: several shifts designed by Habile are not convenient for T2C drivers because they include a lot of pieces, split shifts are not homogeneous enough and the total shift number is sometimes greater. Kangaroo algorithm designs driver schedules of similar or lower quality than Hastus: shifts are of lower quality and their number is sometimes greater. Kangaroo algorithm designs driver schedules which are better than those obtained with Heures: solutions designed by Heures either are made of too many shifts or include too many leftover pieces, the straight shifts are homogeneous but the split shifts sometimes cover too many pieces. Kangaroo algorithm designs similar driver schedules to those obtained by Matrics, but the total shift number is sometimes greater and shifts are of lower quality.

So, the results obtained with Kangaroo algorithm are of good quality for the two types of problems. They are better than the ones designated by the software products Busman, Habile and Heures. Opposite, the software products Hastus and Matrics are more efficient.

8 Conclusion

Applying Kangaroo algorithm to the driver scheduling problem has been proved to be efficient to overcome the high combinatoric and the lack of information about the objective function. The main interest of our method is that it permits to simultaneously handle line constraints and timetable constraints. The study of the different software products has pointed out that it is not the same for every software products. Moreover, our method designs an overall driver schedule without decomposing the problem into sub-problems.

The results obtained with Kangaroo algorithm are of good quality. They can be improved while coupling Kangaroo algorithm with exact algorithms like linear programming [3] or constraint logic programming. Moreover, T2C manages an urban transit network general and significant enough. Therefore, we think that our method can be enlarged to other networks while making minor modifications on constraint handling.

References

1. Blais, J.Y., Lamont, J. & Rousseau, J.M. The HASTUS vehicle and manpower scheduling system at the Société de Transport de la Communauté Urbaine de Montréal, *Interfaces*, 1990, **20**, 26-42.

2. Charpentier, G. & Fleury, G. Stochastic methods for scheduling in manufacturing systems, pp. 159 to 162, *Proceedings of the Pacific Rim International Conference*, Vancouver, Canada, 1992.

3. Djellab, K., Fleury, G., Gourgand, M. & Quilliot, A. Crew scheduling for an urban transit company, pp. 115 to 118, *Proceedings of the 18th Symposium on Operations Research*, Cologne, Germany, 1992.

4. Fleury, G. *Méthodes stochastiques et déterministes pour les problèmes NP-difficiles*, PhD thesis, Université Blaise Pascal, Clermont-Ferrand, France, 1993.

5. Molimard, E. *Etude comparative de logiciels d'habillage de réseaux urbains et application d'une méthode stochastique*, Mémoire de DEA, Université Blaise Pascal, Clermont-Ferrand, France, 1993.

6. Smith, B. & Wren, A. A bus crew scheduling system using a set covering formulation, *Transportation Research*, 1988, **22**. 97-108.

Disaggregation level and variables choice in retail trip: comparison between Italy and England

P. Fadda, G. Fancello
Dipartimento Ingegneria del Terrirorio, sez. Trasporti, Università di Cagliari, Piazza D'Armi, 09100 Cagliari, Italy

Abstract:

Supply charges in the food sector are creating rapid changes in the consumers' behaviour due to the consolidation of new conditions both in the supply and in its support services. The need is felt to formulate behaviour models capable of describing this evolution.

The paper present a methodology, based on multiple corrispondence analysis, that stresses the parameters rapresenting the phenomenon. The results obtained from a comparison between different geographical contexts where the ongoing transformation process is at very different stages (Italy - Great Britain), has pointed out that "Frequency of generator use" is an efficent parameter in structuring the sample only in certain conditions.

1. Introduction

In defining food shopping travel behaviour, factors affecting the choice of shops are associated not only with the location of the shops but also with characteristics of the socio-economic environment of reference.

Thanks to the use of multidimensional statistical procedures for the analysis of the data, we can emphasize the behavioural attitudes related to the reference environment and produce an adequate analytical description of the phenomenon.

In the present paper we have pointed out choice factors in diverse socio-economical contexts. Regarding different territorial contexts our intention was also to point out the possibility of analysing the phenomenon through the self same procedure and if affirmative to distinguish its indispensable requisites.

A poorly efficient transportation system constrains the user to a different shopping frequency, which varies with the user category. Frequency of travel in fact describes how a transport system can affect individual behaviour.

In defining the model's structure in presence of a factor such as frequency, it becomes immediately necessary to organize the sample so that the different behaviour of different user groups may be dealt with together on the basis of homogeneous practice.

2. Survey and data analysis

The survey was carried out in Italy (Cagliari) and in England (London, Winchester, Liss): a total of over 2000 users were interviewed, as well as a few hundred interwies during a pilot investigation.

An English context was chosen in the study because of the sharp differences in habits as compared to Italy and because of the number of published studies available for comparison.

We established fourteen variables representing an individual's behaviour[i] . The Multiple Correspondence Technique (MCT) developed by Benzecri (1973) was used for data analysis. This is the most widely used technique for multidimensional matrices, because it can handle multi-dimensional information and at the same time minimize loss of information due to the complexity of analysed data. By reducing the multidimensional space in which to represent the observed modalities, MCT provides a general view of the phenomenon under study, through factorial plans.

Combined use of MCT and cluster analysis (we used the package SPAD.N) has allowed to organize the variables as a function of one parameter, named "value-test" (v.t.). With this test, at a given level of significativity, we can assess the statistical importance of a determined characteristic in its relation with the factorial axis.[ii]

The higher the value of this parameter the more significative the representation variable of the phenomenon. For this reason it is important to point out in the analysis both the value-test of the most significative variables and their reciprocal position in function of the different partitions in which the data matrix is subdivided.

The analysis was initially carried out on one representative matrix of all the shops in the same size category. The results of this analysis were too aggregated to be significative. By cluster analysis, we therefore obtained a partition according to three different disaggregations of the data matrix:

- 2 clusters (poorly disaggregated matrix);
- 4 clusters (mildly disaggregated matrix);
- 9 clusters (strongly disaggregated matrix).

Our aim was in fact to show that a different disaggregation of data can affect the significativity of the variables, and which disaggregation was the most suitable for a correct representation of the phenomenon (especially for structured samples such as the elderly, housewives, part-time workers, etc.).

This has clarified the role of the variable "Frequency of use of the shop". In fact:

- the frequency is the output, the final result of the user's choice. On the basis of one's own conditions of life and habits, the individual chooses a type of shop and the frequency of use. This can be assumed as the contact element between the behavioural/individual sphere and the observed mobility over the territory;

- in Italy the presence of a non efficient transport system (especially in urban areas) constrains the customer to the use of a shop. In this way frequency affords information on how the transport system affects the behaviour of the individual.

3. The results

3. 1. Medium sized supermarkets in Italy

The significativity of the variable "Frequency" increases on increasing disaggregation level.
However this increase is not proportional to the increase in disaggregation (from 2 to 9 clusters).
This is described well in practice with the partitioning into 4 classes, corresponding to 4 different behavioural clusters, each of which is characterised by a precise frequency modality: daily, many times a week, weekly, occasional or casual.

daily	many...week	weekly	casual
mean of tr.: on foot	Orig=Destin= Home	combined use: ot.shops	use for time saving
use for shop tipology	use for shop quality	mean of tr.: car	Orig=Destin= Other
Orig=Destin= Home	use for habit	Orig=Destin= Work	combined use: other
no combined use	mean of tr: on foot		Mean of tr: Bus

These results are rapresenting in factorial plan on Italian case.

The χ^2 value confirms the indication on the non casual distribution of the variable: in fact the   obtained χ^2 is always greater than at least one or two variables with a higher value-test. This shows that the variable is independently distributed among the four determined classes.
Since the most significative variables in the disaggregation into 4 classes proved to be "Origin" and "Destination ", in order to assess further the significativity of the variable "Frequency", we made an additional subdivision of the matrix as a function of the kind of trip.

	2 clusters		4 clusters		9 clusters	
	V.T.	χ^2	V.T.	χ^2	V.T.	χ^2
Frequency	-1.0	3.11	10.48	150.20	12.68	257.8
Origin	8.8	83.56	10.87	140.36	12.78	218.98
Destination	13.21	181.55	99.99	201.84	12.52	212.08
Combined use	-0.45	1.54	0.24	9.37	176.70	10.31

Three sub-matrices were therefore obtained corresponding to the three different types of trip: HSH (House-Shop-House), WSH (Work-Shop-House), OSH (Other origin-Shop-House). Each of these matrices was subdivided into 4 classes for the reasons explained earlier.
In the HSH trip, Frequency becomes highly significative (the χ^2 value is very high too). This points out the remarkable distance of the distribution of the found variable

from the normal standard one, and therefore in the HSH trip we find travel behaviours significatively described by "Frequency". On the contrary, in the WSH trip, frequency is not significative, and is casually distributed among the four clusters. In fact both the value-test and the χ^2 assume poorly significative values.

The fact that frequency assumes a greater level of significativity on increasing disaggregation (and that the variables relating to the Origin and Destination of the trip are at the front places), means that there are different behavioural categories of users for each kind of trip. In fact, significativity of frequency is very different for the HSH, WSH and OSH trips.

The high v.t. and χ^2 values for HSH show that, for this type of trip, the modalities relating to frequency characterize the single classes obtained by the partition. In Italy in fact for reasons of culture, social customs and organization of work, trips to the shops are so widespread and common that they adequately represent all the modalities of frequency.

On the contrary, on the HSH trip, Frequency was not significative, and therefore caused a totally casual distribution of the variable. It has in fact been observed that due especially to the fact that the working schedule adopted in Italy is non-continuous, inter-connected trips are still not the common run. Even the type of schedule adopted by supermarkets (closing daily at 12.50 pm and at 7.50 pm) obliges those customers returning from work after those times to use smaller sized generators with more flexible times.

	HSH		WSH		OSH	
	V.T.	χ^2	V.T.	χ^2	V.T.	χ^2
Frequency	11.96	185.78	-0.25	7.36	2.48	27.52
Combined use	3.52	31.84	4.04	30.92	5.30	50.12

On the contrary the variable for "Combined Use" is significative only for extreme disaggregations, where the datum of the single generator with respect to the global description of the phenomenon prevails, confirming the poor predisposition of Italian consumers for trips with more than one destination. The variable therefore is significative only if referred to single rather than more aggregated or wider contexts.

In conclusion it can be stated that:

- Frequency is highly significative;
- a disaggregation according to the type of trip faithfully describes the different behavioural approach of the user;
- accessibility is highly significative. This could appear contradictory since the variables relating to accessibility assume low value-test and χ^2. The investigation, however, considered users at their destination, that is users who had already assessed the opportunities of access. The choice of accessibility is in fact directly associated with frequency and therefore with the choice of the type of trip.

3.2. Small shops in Italy

As far as regards the variable for "Frequency" the indications that emerge are stronger than for the preceding variables. In other words highly significative characters are pointed out for numerous disaggregations, thus eliminating components of the casual type. Essentially the found v.t. and the χ^2 are higher than the analogous results obtained for middle-sized supermarkets. This is due to the fact that in Italy small shops still represent a major portion of the general picture of small businesses as far as regards the sales structure, the services offered, and relations with the surrounding social pattern. The customers are mainly people who reside in the neighbourhood, while occasional users, when present, are always related to certain variables. As a matter of fact the characteristics attracting these occasional customers are more flexible opening hours than other shops, the kind of service offered (greater inclination towards interpersonal relations) and the expectation of not having to queue.

	2 clusters		4 clusters		9 clusters	
	V.T.	χ^2	V.T.	χ^2	V.T.	χ^2
Frequency	1.08	6.91	6.95	81.91	9.00	128.72
Origin	8.86	84.70	9.86	118.16	12.78	218.98
Destination	9.47	96.07	8.86	99.04	9.42	137.36
Combined use	0.39	3.29	1.4	15.4	3.34	54.09

In the disaggregation according to the type of trip and partitioning into 4 classes, the most significant datum is the fact that while for middle-sized supermarkets the variable becomes highly significative only in the HSH trip, for small shops this occurs for all kinds of trips. The high χ^2 value for HSH shows that each trip is representative of a particular class of users. The HSH trip is usually made by housewives or people residing in the area, the WSH trip by occasional users along a habitual route, the OSH trip by users attracted by other types of generators. Essentially, for small shops Frequency becomes highly significative because every kind of trip is representative of a specific behavioural category, with practically no casual elements.

It should be pointed out that the three disaggregations have a low value-test and a low χ^2 for the "Combined Use". This confirms that the variable is only significative if it is referred to a local context.

Finally, the role played by the variable for "Means of Transport Used" shows a non-casual distribution among the classes, which proves that partitions according to this variable (and therefore according to the type of trip) represent different approach behaviours to the shop.

	HSH		WSH		OSH	
	V.T.	χ^2	V.T.	χ^2	V.T.	χ^2
Frequency	7.70	94.37	2.61	28.60	3.83	40.25
Combined use	-0.93	5.12	1.63	12.53	1.43	11.44
Mean transport	6.18	55.86	-0.05	5.19	0.68	7.86

3.3. Comparison between English and Italian generators

The foregoing results referred to an Italian middle-sized urban area are functions of typical customs, cultures and attitudes. It will be useful therefore to compare them with results referred to a different socio-economical context in order to find out whether the degree of significativity of the variables changes on changing the contour conditions.

	2 clusters		4 clusters		9 clusters	
	V.T.	χ^2	V.T.	χ^2	V.T.	χ^2
Frequency	3.42	18.68	5.53	54.41	7.59	118.70
Origin	12.36	159.66	99.99	359.70	19.79	458.51
Destination	99.99	288.84	99.99	564.76	22.40	572.20
Combined use	1.96	9.36	7.41	82.02	18.54	442.96

The most interesting fact is the low significativity assumed in England by the "Frequency" variable in the three disaggregations, especially as compared to the results obtained in Italy, as shown by the high value-test and χ^2.
This can be explained by the type of organization of English shops and consequently by the habits of the consumers.
The entry and assertion of the large-scale distribution in England has caused a general upheaval in the field of business as well as substantial changes in the users' habits in the last 10-15 years. In particular with the advent of large-scale distribution, middle-sized supermarkets have lost their characterization as shops for weekly or fortnightly shopping and have reorganized themselves into points of reference for restricted contexts (such as the neighbourhood) and limited daily shopping, to the advantage of the larger hypermarkets or "discount" stores. Essentially middle- sized supermarkets have taken up the role of the small shops for the neighbourhood, or corner- shops, by meeting the individual daily needs of their clients, but partly lost those users who prefer stock shopping, that is from time to time in large quantities. Talking of corner-shops, whose space on the market has been partially occupied by middle-sized supermarkets, they have created themselves a new role in the distribution sector, either by adapting their opening times to the public (e.g. the Seven-Eleven chain open 24 hours a day) or by specializing in particular products (fruit and vegetables, wines and spirits), while others (in truth so many) have had to close shop. Classical corner-shops have resisted in mainly residential areas where together with the pubs they are practically the only shops left in the neighbourhood. In Italy this transformation process is still happening and in most cases shops are still a valid alternative among the business generators available.
As far as regards the "Time Range" variable, in Italy (in spite of the strong tendency towards a strong regular behaviour) the distribution of the time range modalities is casual (due to the greater number of small shops); in England because there are fewer shops (corner-shops are practically inexistent, supermarkets are assuming the function of corner-shops and hypermarkets are present only in the periphery or on important road joints) the users are forced to choose on the basis of access times and habits rather than on the quality of the service or products.

As far as regards the type of trip, the very low "frequency" values of v.t.and χ^2 for the HSH trip in England are evidence of a non-habitual non-stable behaviour and therefore of a clientele that use the shops for immediate momentary needs rather than for big shopping (typical approach towards small shops).

The results referring to WSH and OSH inter-connected trips are substantially similar to the Italian case. Such trips are in fact considered as multipurpose trips and have similar characteristics between Italy and England. They depend on the habitual route, the conditions of the transport network, the location of the services, and the laws regulating the process are substantially the same.

Regarding the "Combined Use" variable, the difference between the English and the Italian case emerges in the HSH trip. In Italy the choice is not conditional upon the presence of support services (that thus hypothesize a combined use of different types of generators), while in England the choice is conditional upon the location of possible services (commercial and non) in the neighbourhood, that allow optimization of the trip time.

	HSH		WSH		OSH	
	V.T.	χ^2	V.T.	χ^2	V.T.	χ^2
Frequency	-0.93	5.11	1.51	16.09	0.53	10.67
Combined use	99.99	331.68	6.54	68.44	1.54	12.00

On the other hand, similar results were obtained for the WSH and OSH trips, where the presence of support services is highly determining.

In conclusion, it can be stated that for the English case:

- frequency is not a significative variable;

- the variables inherent to the type of shop and location in function of the transport system (such as time ranges, location, combined use, etc.) are highly significative;

- there is a sharp difference between Italy and England as far as regards direct trips (HSH), while inter-connected trips are substantially similar (WSH and OSH).

The comparison between the Italian and the English case can also be made for the corner-shops. As in the previous case, though less so, Frequency is not as significative in the England as in Cagliari. The reason being that due to the transformation process described earlier shops in England have lost their role as a local service (which has been taken up by middle-sized supermarkets) and have become points of reference for occasional customers; while stable customer relationships have been formed by shops that have developed a marked specialisation (of goods, services, etc.).

Regarding the type of trip, in the English case Frequency is never significative. This confirms the tendency to a lack of "habit" in trips to a generator, to the advantage of a more *casual* type of approach.

On the basis of the results obtained the most significant variables can be singled out as the origin and destination of the trip , the type of goods sold and the quality of the service offered.

4. Conclusions

The main points emerged by the analysis are:

1) shops in the food sector generate by far the greatest number of trips for reasons other than work or study, and those supported by mechanized means of transport are beginning to assume an increasingly greater role. Moreover, through large scale distribution, the new typologies of generators in the food sector tend to concentrate all mobility on a few poles. The risk here is that of generating strong disequilibria in the urban organization, for which reason adequate dimensioning is the basis of proper town planning;

it is not possible to define descriptive models of the behavioural phenomenon that should be valid for all situations and applicable to different urban contexts. Models that simulate the phenomenon of generation homogeneously, as if all the users could be described by univocally valid relations, are inadequate. The investigations carried out so far have shown that, in choosing shops, there are profound differences among users and that these differences can emerge only through an accurate definition of significative variables. As far as regards Italy frequence is the variable that best describes different forms of behaviour: it is a variable that seems to better define the degree of variation of the users' behaviour in relation to the type and supply level of the transport system. By varying the system of transport that affects frequency of use, we observe a variation in the flow of mobility. Frequency is therefore used as a *spy* variable. Through it we can control the distribution of flow on the transport network and forecast mobility. The results obtained in the data analysis phase have in fact confirmed the necessity of organising the sample, since high v.t. and χ^2 values give evidence that a variable is highly significative and therefore has a strong tendency towards behaviours that should be comparable to the ones described by modalities associated to the variable itself. A proper simulation therefore can not exclude organization through modalities found to be more important.

2) it is not possible to define a priori which variables are significative of the phenomenon and which among them can be used in the structure of the model. In the past the choice of significative variables was made on the basis of either experience or dated references. Here we propose a line of work based on the analyses of multiple correspondences associated with cluster analysis, since the significativity of the variables can vary with respect to the proposed aggregation. In particular, from the combined use of v.t. and χ^2 in data analysis, the potentialities of the variables can be assessed while describing the phenomenon, and therefore the variables that have an information content that can adequately define the simulation process to be adopted can be extracted.

References

1. Barnard, P.O. *Modelling shopping destination choice: a theoretical and empirical investigation*, Australian Road Research Board, Victoria, 1987.

2. Benzécri, J.P. *L'analyse des données*, Dunod, Paris, 1973.

3. Bromley, R.D.F., Thomas, C.J. *Retail change: contemporary issues*, UCL Press, London, 1993.

4. McLHazel, G. The development of a disaggregate trip generation model for a strategic planning control of a large foodstore, *Traffic Engineering and Control*, 1988, 29(1) 33-39; 29(2) 95-105; 29(3) 148-154.

5. SPAD.N users guide, CISIA, Saint-Mandé (Fr), 1991.

6. Vickerman, R.W., Barmby, T.A. The structure of shopping travel. Some developments of the trip generation model, *Journal of Transport Economics and Policy*, 18(3) 109-121.

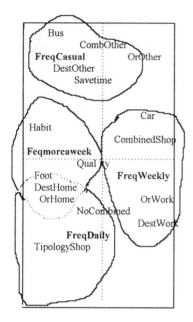

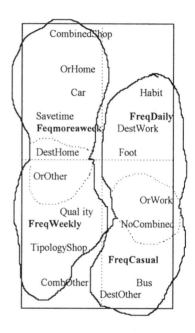

Factorial plan in Italian case   **Factorial plan in English case**

---

[1] Origin fo trip, Destination of trip, Site location, Mean of transport used, Distance home-shop, Trip frequency, Car accessibility, Purchasing goods, Distance carparking-shop, PT accessibility, Shopping time, Combined use, Shop tipology, Pedestian accessibility.

[ii] The value-test is a tool that participates in the explorative and descriptive approach to large numerical tales. It is based on the following principle. Out of a population of n individuals, q nominal variables are observed. A particular group of n_k individuals is determined. How do we classify the variables that best characterize this group by order of importance? A variable does not characterize the group if the found n_k values seem randomly selected among the observed n values. The more uncertain the hypothesis of random extraction, the more significative the variable to characterize the group.

If U_{ij} is the coordinate of modality j on axis at, the value test is:

$$U_{ti} \{ n_j \, [(n-1)/(n-n_j)] \}^{1/2}$$

where n is the number of individuals analysed and n_j the individuals randomly extracted

Trip generation model in urban areas: an activity-based approach for trip chain simulation

I. Meloni, E. Cherchi

Sezione Trasporti, Dipartimento di Ingegneria del Territorio, Facoltà di Ingegneria, Universitá di Cagliari, Italy

Abstract

The paper presents a first summary of the work carried out by the authors on trip generation behavioural analysis. It is divided into two main sections. One concerns behavioural analysis in generation choice with particular reference to the modelling. The advantages and limits of the application of behavioural models to generation are described and the activity-based approach is examined in the light of its potential for better expression and modelling. The second section reports on the first results of a pilot survey with activity diaries carried out on a limited student sample from the University of Cagliari. A few remarks are made on the interrelations among student behaviour, location of the University and related activities and the characteristics of the trips generated.

1 Introduction

The generation of mobility especially in cities has reached very high levels of complexity thanks to the evolution of human (economic, social and technological) activities and life styles in general through an increasingly high and continuous exchange of relations (flows of information, persons and things).

The most obvious effect of these changes has not only been in the quantitative but also in the qualitative development of mobility. The latter can be observed in the change from a commuter pattern of mobility (home-work, home-study) to a so-called "non-systematic" pattern (a trip that may or may not be done). On of the most characteristic aspects of "non-systematic" mobility is the fact that transfers are made by developing a sequence of trips. Because of this "non-systematic" nature of trips and their possible characteristics, activities can be organized in temporal and spatial sequentiality, in such a way as to reduce the negative effects of the trip itself within the limits of the imposed constraints. Some authors have stated that the user behaves like an "urban traveller", in other words he carries out his daily activity through a series of chained trips that arise from "opportunities" of activity that may present from day to day.

What opportunities of activity can present to the user? Which opportunities does the user wish and need to meet? What constraints is he submitted to? How do these constraints affect his wishes/needs? Why does he organize his days in a certain way? How do we want to consider this issue?

It is certainly a "new" phenomenon, considering the number of elements and constraints it depends on, the characteristics with which it is manifest, and the points of view under which it can be studied. In order to analyse, simulate and especially forecast the generation choices, we need to give the answers to these and other issues through a detailed study of behaviour.

2 Behaviour Analysis

To obtain a better understanding of the behaviour underlying the choice of one or another trip, first of all we need to consider the elements that have a bearing on the users' choices and organize them according to their effects.

The first element to be analyzed is the role a trip has in letting people take part in temporally and spatially distinct activities. The trip is not a primary activity but a consequence of movement among activity [4]. Therefore a trip is not only chosen for its singular characteristics, but as part of a programme of intended activities. Activities and trips are therefore two strongly interrelated components of one and the same complex daily behaviour.

If the necessity or pleasure of certain activities induces trips, then we need to examine a person's planned activities or those of his family entirely if we wish to address the phenomenon thoroughly [4].

According to Burns activities may be classified as "non discretional" (work, sleep, etc., and activities relating to married life such as those that a person carries out for other persons and/or insitutions) and "discretional" (recreation, social visits, pleasure, etc.). This distinction relates to whether a person is obliged (non- discretional) or not (discretional) to carry out such and such an activity. Nevertheless, the fact that an activity is necessary does not always imply that it should be carried out at fixed times. For example sleep is an activity that is necessary, but a person is free to choose whether to go to bed at 10 pm or 12 pm, in the latter case with two more hours available for any form of activity, usually pleasure. It is therefore possible to locate a third intermediate category of activity, that we shall call semi-discretional, in other words activities that a person must carry out but is totally free as to the way they are to be carried out. An important point that should be mentioned is that many jobs in Italy can be included among these semi-discretional activities. Though extremely free, these activities have a strong participation priority as compared to discretional activities.

Non-discretional activities are generally stable in time and space, while semi-discretional and discretional activities are more flexible and generally give rise to non-systematic mobility. It is the semi-discretional and discretional activities that generally give rise to chained trips. In fact a person tends to carry out discretional activities within a plan of non-discretional and semi-discretional activity, especially when the semi-discretional activity is one's job.

The fact that people try and carry out a multiplicity of activities is limited by a number of different factors. The urban form, its spatial and temporal organisation, the supply of transport, etc. can be defined *external* constraints since they are objectively present and do not depend on the individual; while interaction with one's family, and with other persons in society, interaction in trip decisions "over time", etc., can be defined *internal* constraints since they depend on the subjective characteristics of the individual. A third category of constraints stems from the interaction between *external* and *internal* constraints, therefore from the individual-structures-roles interaction. These constraints can be defined *behavioural* since they depend on how each person with his own particular characteristics decides to use the available structures when taking part in activities.

It has also been shown that the quantity and quality of the discretional activities is subjected to a person's financial possibilities and therefore to his income from work. Though this cannot strictly be considered a constraint there is a close relationship between leisure activities on the one hand and work activities and needs of the family on the other [1]. Therefore also this factor should be considered when analysing activity programme generation.

The diagram in Figure 1 shows the theoretical structure of a selection process for the set of individual activity. More precisely the diagram shows in what way the constraints affect participation in activities according to whether they are discretional or not. In the former case the user adapts the choice to the constraint, while in the latter the user is submitted and adapts himself to the constraint. It has been said that non-discretional activities are compulsory. Participation in these activities (or planned participation as the user's priority in the case of semi-discretional activities) is therefore in itself a constraint in the choice process of participation in discretional activities.

Given a series of activities available, on the basis of his needs, wishes and constraints, a person locates the single or chained activities in which he has the opportunity of taking part (choice set) and organizes them according to an adequate timetable.

The choice of which activities to carry out, where and at what time of the day, the duration of participation, the frequency, the alternation and chaining of activities, the time, etc., are all closely interrelated elements and present in the decision of choice analysis of a specific programme. It follows that the alternatives available, and therefore the number of activity plans that a person can develop is increased greatly. We have a double complexity. One is referred to the generation of an activity plan and its structure, while the other refers to the interconnection between the two [1].

The diagram in Figure 2 shows the sequence of an activity plan generation process. An activity plan is the result of continuous and dynamic organisation and reorganisation of intended daily activities. Participation in a plan depends firstly on the convenience and feasibility of taking part, secondly on the benefit that can be obtained and finally on their interconnection.

2.1   Trip-based versus Activity-based Approach

In consideration of such a complex phenomenon, we need to face the problem of which techniques are the most suitable to study, model, simulate and forecast the phenomenon. The evolution of mobility demand modelling shows that efforts have always been concentrated on improving the understanding of trip behaviour, because it has been realized that the role human behaviour has become increasingly more important, almost crucial, as is shown above.

The transition from aggregate to disaggregate models was first made because of the need to relate trips to individuals, as subjects that can make subjective though rational decisions concerning the trip. Trip-based models have represented an important turning point in research, because they have shown the importance of behaviour in trips. Nevertheless, both the clarity and simplicity of the basic hypotheses (maximization of utility), originally considered strengths, have been severely criticised, and this gave rise to the activity-based approach [2,5]. By oversimplifying the behaviour of individuals, trip-based models therefore fail to grasp all its important aspects.

The activity-based approach was developed as an alternative to the trip-based approach, in an attempt to explore and understand all those aspects relating to behaviour that were not accounted for by the trip-based approach. The activity-based approach: 1) treats the trip as a demand derived; 2) it concentrates our attention on the sequence or plan of behaviour and overcomes the limits of assuming the discrete trip as a reference element for analysis; 3) it represents trip behaviour as a range of complex constraints, rather than as the result of a real choice process; 4) it accounts for the global organization of time, the duration of the activities and the trip, rather than referring to events that relate to particular times in a day (rush hours or normal hours); 5) it explicitly accounts for the effects of spatial, temporal and interpersonal constraints on trip and localization choices; 6) it specifies the interrelations between trip and participation and scheduling of activity, including the activity links and interpersonal constraints; 7) it points out the alternation of decision strategies that involve family dynamics, levels of information, complexity of choices, discontinuous specification and the formation of habits; 8) it establishes alternative choices available to the decision-maker in a restricted environment; this has led to the mis-specification of individual choice sets. [2,3,4,6]

As reported in the literature the activity-based approach produced a wide range of studies, and at present all researchers are in agreement on the fundamental role of the activity-based approach in understanding trip behaviour. Nevertheless, the activity-based approach still lacks a universal mathematical theory that can be applied to a wide range of planning and policy problems and has had limited practical application. For this reason it is still a controversial point among scholars whether this approach is useful only on a theoretical level or whether it may also have practical advantages as in the case of the behavioural model [2,3]. The debate is still open but research will probably develop along lines such as the development of new methodologies of the activity-based approach, the reorganisation of old ones, and the adaptation of existing methods in order to incorporate the results of research on the activity-based approach.

The authors are at present carrying out a study on the utilization of the results from the activity-based approach in the respecification of individual models, that is in determining new independent and dependent variables.

3 Application of Activity-based Approach: a case study

This section reports on the results of an initial exploration of the factors affecting the trip behaviour of University students. The authors have long been involved in this sector especially with reference to the evaluation of the importance of behavioural analysis in representing the phenomenon. The section is the continuation of a study through an analysis of the activity plans made by the University students and of the links between these plans and the generation choice, with the objective of determining the variables that allow a better expression and representation of the real phenomenon.

University students are an extremely interesting class of users not only because of the extent of daily mobility they produce, but also because their University activity is represented as a semi-discretional activity, as a consequence of the flexibility and freedom in the organization of University tuition in Italy. The analyses include previous studies by the authors. It is pointed out that since in most cases University students are not obliged to attend lessons, they do not perform systematic trips. This freedom is represented by the following two distinct behaviours: 1) the students are free to organize their university activity (that is the number and type of courses to attend) annually, and this does not constitute a constraint; 2) the students can modify and reorganize their activity plans daily in response to new needs/constraints. It is obvious that once the students decide to attend certain courses, the fixed schedules will become a constraint for the students' plans.

A few considerations that have emerged from the daily activity diaries of the University students are presented in the following. Particularly, activity chains and related trips involving University trips will be analysed. The main motivations for making choices and carrying out certain trips (characteristics of the user, the location, the transport, the family, etc.) are examined.

More than 50% of the students perform at least one chained trip during the day, and almost always chained to the University trip. The main discretional activities in which the students take part and for which they perform the chained trip during the day are taking people (friends or family) somewhere, studying at colleagues' homes, work or personal errands (such as photocopying), shopping for food or visiting friends for pleasure.

The students' organisation of their daily activities seems to be affected by the fact that they live with their families (defined as "in family" students) or that they share flats with colleagues or friends (defined as "away from family" students). These two cases present different constraints and needs and consequently the plans made to meet them are also different. For example, it has emerged that "in family" students do not take part in activities such as daily shopping, which is done by other members of the family (usually mothers), while "away from family" students participate in this activity every day.

One of the most interesting aspects concerning the difference between "in family" and "away from family" students is the role of the availability of a car in making out an activity plan. Cars are usually more available to "in family" students. They may have their own personal car, or may share one with their brothers and sisters, or not have a car and use their parents' (though if both parents work, it is the mother who invariably gives up her car), or even benefit from lifts if other members of the family perform the chained trip. Students therefore can choose from a very wide range of alternatives, but at the same time there are heavy constraints on the organization of how to use the car (Figure 3). From an analysis of the activities it has emerged that "in family" students perform many chained trips in order to take a member of the family somewhere and then drive to University.

"Away from family" students on the other hand, do not perform trips of this kind, since they do not have the family constraint. The present of friends sharing the flat is not a constraint in this sense. Moreover cars are less available to "away from family" students - they either have their own personal car or cannot use it.

Participation in activities seems to depend on car availability: non availability reduces the number of participated activities, their territorial extent and the number of chained trips, which are mainly carried out for activities of primary needs such as shopping. Availability of one's own transport seems to play a fundamental role also in the choice of one's residence. Almost invariably students without cars choose their residence at a 10/15 minute walking distance from the University.

An important role in the life of students seems to be represented by fellow students. In Italian Universities, study activities can be considered entirely discretional. Since no such kind of activity (e.g. tutorials) is performed in the lecture rooms, and since the places reserved for study (libraries) are very few, study activity is carried out as, when and where the students choose, generally at home. Study activity has not been defined semidiscretional because unfortunately it often has no priority over others.

The role of constraint substitution between family and colleague is interesting. The colleagues' commitments are constraints to the students. Figure 4 shows an example to explain these complex interrelations: if a colleague cannot use the car because his brother needs it, the student seeks the availability of his own family's car; his family finds a different solution, e.g. his father drives his mother so that the student can use the mother's car. Therefore the needs and desires of the two families can affect each other through the constraint of the two colleagues. Moreover, as the family is a constraint to the parents but also a way of sharing commitments, it is also so between colleagues. An alternative organization is sought for the car, tasks are shared to buy working materials, to make photocopies, or at times even to attend lectures.

Study activity is often chained to the activity of attending lectures: a student studies with his colleague at his house from 9.00 to 11.00, then they attend a lecture together at the University. A chained trip performed quite often is that of picking up the colleague and going together to the lecture. Once again this behaviour has strong links with both territorial and transport characteristics. The need to organize one's activities and chain them to those of the colleague could be not only due to car availability, but could also depend on insufficient parking space at the University, inadequate public transport or the location of University facilities.

Conclusions

Though research is still at the initial phase, a few interesting considerations have emerged for the location of new variables to improve the traditional disaggregate generation models. Trips to reach University cannot be considered single trips, because the students carry them out as part of a daily activity plan. The alternatives available to the student in the generation choice are many (no trip at all, to take part in one activity, in many activities in a certain sequence, etc.). A trip is a function of the activities in which to take part and of their scheduling. The activity programme in turn depends on the user characteristics, the user's needs/desires and on specific constraints relating to family, car availability, and location of the activity. The expression of these elements in (dependent or independent) variables and their testing is the purpose of this research.

References

1. Bath, C.R. & Koppelman, F.S. A conceptual framework of individual activity program generation, *Transportation Research* 27 A, 1993, **6**, 433-446.
2. Carpenter, S. & Jones, P. (ed*). Recent Advances in Travel Demand Analysis*, Pro. 1st Int. Conf. on Travel Demand Analysis: activity-based and new other approaches, Oxford, GOWER Publishing, Aldershot, 1983.
3. Jones, P. (ed). *Developments in Dynamic and Activity-Based Approaches to Travel Analysis*, Pro 2nd Int. Conf. on Travel Demand Analysis, Oxford, Avebury, GOWER Publishing, Aldershot, 1990.
4. Kitamura, R. An evaluation of activity-based travel analysis, *Transportation*, 1988, **15**, 9-34.
5. Mahmassani, H.S. Some comments on activity-based approaches to the analysis and prediction of travel behaviour, *Transportation*, 1988, **15**, 35-40.
6. Recker, W.W., McNally, M.G. & Root, G.S. A Model of Complex Travel Behavior: Part I-Theoretical Development, *Transportation Research* 20 A, 1986, **4**, 307-318.

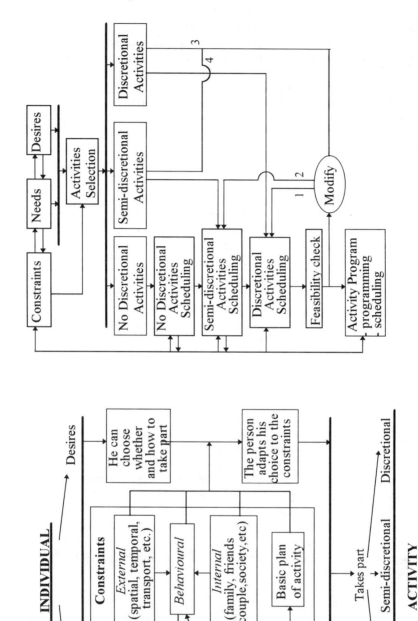

Figure 2

Figure 1

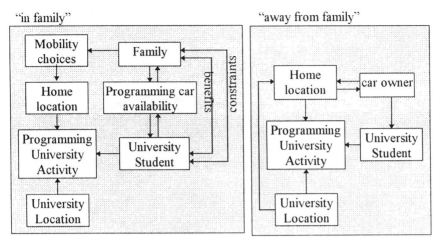

Figure 3

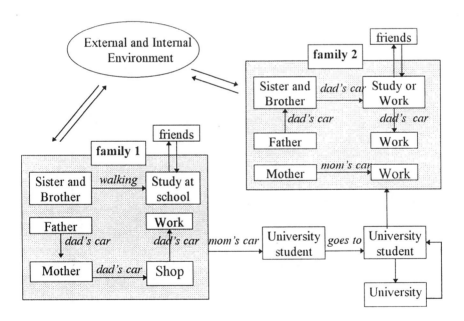

Figure 4

Effectiveness of public transport priorisation

P. Delle Site, F. Filippi
Department 'Idraulica Trasporti Strade', University of Rome, 'La Sapienza', Via Eudossiana, 18 - 00184 Rome, Italy

Abstract

The paper aims at assessing urban transport policies to priorise public transport. A mathematical model is developed to optimise bus operating parameters (average fare, bus size and total bus-kms) under public road transport speed-up measures (bus lanes and signal priority) and car pricing (purchase and fuel taxes, road and parking pricing). The objective is the overall fuel consumption reduction on the road network. Experimentation on the case study of Rome shows negligible effects of policy based on bus operating parameters optimisation alone. This policy proves more effective when joined with car pricing than with public road transport speed-up measures. Optimal bus operating parameters are highly affected by relative sensitivity of bus demand to fare and time costs.

1 Introduction

In the past, transport policies have been "demand" rather than "supply" led, but forecast traffic levels will not cope on the infrastructure in urban areas. A key short-term goal is to improve the competitive position of public transport by priorisation policies able to encourage private car users to switch mode. Such policies envisage an integrated package of different measures, ranging from operational and physical measures directly affecting the service level of public transport ("pull" measures), to legislative measures aimed at making motorised individual transport less attractive or even banned ("push" measures). Notable are measures based on bus operating parameters (frequency, bus size, fare) optimisation and measures aimed at speeding up public road transport (exclusive bus lanes, signal priority) in the former category, and car pricing (purchase and fuel taxes, road and parking pricing) in the latter.

Appraisal approaches followed so far have considered different public transport priorisation measures independently. Assessments based on expert opinions have been produced for a wide range of measures [1], [2]. Computer simulation is commonly used to assess bus line network redesign, according to a "what if" criterion, based on the output of conventional transport planning models. Most recently this approach has been proposed for the assessment of road pricing [3]. Bus service optimisation models produce the optimal policy based on total bus-kms, average fare and average bus size, according to an objective function represented by the total (operator+user) surplus [4], [5] [6], [7].

Here an analytic appraisal is proposed, using a model in which bus service is optimised under different hypotheses of other public transport priorisation measures. The level of treatment is very aggregate, as in the studies on optimal bus service [4], [5] [6], [7]. Unlike these, the objective function is represented by the total (car+bus) fuel consumption, which can be regarded as a proxy for road congestion. A preliminary model, extremely simplified and with solution provided analytically in closed form, had considered bus service optimisation alone [8]. The model was then reformulated to take into account the effects induced by different transport policies on multi-modal equilibrium. The solution is provided numerically due to the more complex structure. A first version of the new model envisages bus service optimisation [9]; a second version adds car pricing [10]. The model presented here includes also public road transport speed up measures.

The model is presented in section 2. The results of the case study of Rome follow in section 3. A comparison of the results with those of previous studies, comments on the implications for practical policy and the potential for further research conclude the paper.

2 The model

The model optimises the following operating parameters of bus service: total bus-kms supplied (which, for a given network extension, depend on the average line frequency), average fare and average bus size, represented by average unit capacity. The objective function is the reduction, with respect to a reference condition, of fuel consumption of the two principal road modes, car and bus.

Public road transport speed-up measures and car pricing are a condition outside the optimisation model. They are represented by, respectively, the following input parameters: the percentage of bus-kms and passenger-kms and the average speed of the bus sub-network on exclusive rights-of-way; the percentage increase of average money cost of individual transport.

The optimisation problem involves two sets of constraint relationships: the first represents the equilibrium of the transport system, and the second the constraints on the bus operator's choices.

The first set of constraints is given by the simultaneous demand and supply equations of the different modes. This set yields, on the demand side, the transfers of users between modes and, on the supply side, the variations of the average road speed in mixed traffic caused by policies under examination. Hence, it is possible to quantify the trade-off between fuel consumption of the two modes, car and bus, caused by modal substitution as well as the variations in consumption caused by variations in average speed. Consumption per vehicle-km decreases with the speed in the interval representative of the average urban conditions (<50 km/h), and therefore a transfer of demand in favour of bus mode is resolved in an energy advantage, partly because of the increased average speed.

The second set of constraints includes the operator financial constraint whereby an assigned limit on the operating (costs to revenues) ratio is imposed, and the constraint on bus capacity, expressed as limitation to the average load factor (ratio of demand to passenger-kms supplied).

The model is formulated according to the following notation, where the indexes "a", "b" and "e" refer, respectively, to car, bus and other modes, the apex "0" to values held in the reference condition.

a^0	bus operating cost per bus-km
c^0	average money cost of car mode
d_a^0, d_b^0	average journey length
D_a^0, D_b^0, D_a, D_b	modal demand
F^0, F	average fare
K^0, K	total bus-kms supplied
P_a^0, P_b^0, P_e^0	modal split
S^0, S	average bus size
t^0	average time delayed at bus stops
u_a^0, u_b^0, u_a, u_b	systematic utility
v_a^0, v_b^0, v_a, v_b	average road speed in mixed traffic
$\overline{v_b}$	average road speed on exclusive rights-of-way
w^0	average waiting time at bus stops
α	bus operating (costs to revenues) ratio
β	average bus load factor
γ_a, γ_b	average fuel consumption per vehicle-km
δ	average car occupancy
$\overline{\Delta c}$	percentage change in average money cost of car mode

$\frac{\Delta\Gamma}{}$ change of total (car+bus) fuel consumption

ε_1 fraction of bus-kms on exclusive rights-of-way

ε_2 fraction of passenger-kms on exclusive rights-of-way

χ fraction of bus operating costs dependent on bus-hours

The problem is:

$$\max_{F,K,S} \Delta\Gamma = \gamma_a(v_a^0) \cdot D_a^0 \cdot \frac{d_a^0}{g^0} - \gamma_a(v_a) \cdot D_a \cdot \frac{d_a^0}{g^0} + \gamma_b(v_b^0, S^0) \cdot K^0 - \gamma_b((1-\overline{\varepsilon_1}) \cdot v_b + \overline{\varepsilon_1} \cdot \overline{v_b}, S) \cdot K$$

subject to:

$$D_a = D_a(v_a, v_b, F, K, \overline{\varepsilon_2}, \overline{v_b}, \overline{\Delta c}) \tag{1}$$

$$D_b = D_b(v_a, v_b, F, K, \overline{\varepsilon_2}, \overline{v_b}, \overline{\Delta c}) \tag{2}$$

$$v_a = v_a(D_a, K, \overline{\varepsilon_1}) \tag{3}$$

$$v_b = v_b(D_a, D_b, K, S, \overline{\varepsilon_1}) \tag{4}$$

$$\frac{a^0 \cdot \left(\chi \cdot \dfrac{v_b^0}{(1-\overline{\varepsilon_1}) \cdot v_b + \overline{\varepsilon_1} \cdot v_b} + 1 - \chi \right) \cdot K}{D_b \cdot F} - \alpha = 0$$

$$\frac{D_b}{K \cdot S} - \beta = 0$$

Function specifications are as follows. Car consumption depends on average road speed according to a function obtained empirically [11]:

$$\gamma_a = \gamma_a(v_a) = \gamma_1 \cdot v_a^{-\gamma_2} \qquad \gamma_2 > 0, \quad 0 \le v_a \le 50 \text{ km} / \text{h}$$

Bus consumption is expressed on the basis of available empirical data as function of bus size alone, yielding, by a linear interpolation:

$$\gamma_b = \gamma_b((1-\overline{\varepsilon_1}) \cdot v_b + \overline{\varepsilon_1} \cdot \overline{v_b}, S) \cong \gamma_b(S) = \gamma_b^0 + m \cdot (S - S^0) \qquad m > 0$$

Demand functions (1) and (2) are expressed according to a Logit model in the incremental form:

$$D_m = D_m(v_a, v_b, F, K, \overline{\varepsilon_2}, \overline{v_b}, \overline{\Delta c}) = \frac{P_m^0 \cdot \exp(u_m - u_m^0)}{P_a^0 \cdot \exp(u_a - u_a^0) + P_b^0 \cdot \exp(u_b - u_b^0) + P_e^0}$$

$$m \in \{a, b\}$$

where the systematic utility variations are given by:

$$u_a - u_a^0 = \vartheta_2 \cdot \left(\frac{d_a^0}{v_a} - \frac{d_a^0}{v_a^0} \right) + \vartheta_3 \cdot \overline{\Delta c}$$

$$u_b - u_b^0 = \vartheta_1 \cdot (w^0 \cdot \frac{K^0}{K} - w^0) + \vartheta_2 \cdot \left(\frac{d_b^0}{(1-\overline{\varepsilon_2}) \cdot v_b + \overline{\varepsilon_2} \cdot \overline{v_b}} - \frac{d_b^0}{v_b^0} \right) + \vartheta_3 \cdot (F - F^0)$$

Supply function of car mode, given in eqn (3), expresses the decreasing relationship between average road speed in mixed traffic and car demand (the number of bus-kms supplied are supposed to affect negligibly average road speed) and is provided by computer simulation. The function is obtained by a linear interpolation of results of a series of assignments of car mode OD matrix to the graph of road network:

$$v_a = v_a(D_a, K, \overline{\varepsilon_1}) \cong v_a(D_a) = v_a^0 + n \cdot (D_a - D_a^0) \quad n < 0$$

Supply function of bus mode, given in eqn (4), expresses the decreasing relationship between average road speed in mixed traffic and car demand (bus demand, bus-kms supplied and average bus size are supposed to affect negligibly average road speed):

$$v_b = v_b(D_a, D_b, K, S, \overline{\varepsilon_1}) \cong v_b(D_a) = \frac{v_a(D_a)}{1 + t^0 \cdot v_a(D_a)} = \frac{v_a^0 + n \cdot (D_a - D_a^0)}{1 + t^0 \cdot (v_a^0 + n \cdot (D_a - D_a^0))}$$

The subset of constraints given in eqns (1), (2), (3) and (4) is solved for modal demand and average road speed in mixed traffic, by a linear approximation of demand and supply functions in the region of the equilibrium state corresponding to the reference condition, as in [12].

The optimisation problem is transformed into a non-constrained optimisation problem by the penalty function method. The solution to the equivalent non-constrained problem is obtained by a global optimisation technique in the class of controlled random search [13].

3 Case study

The model is applied to the case of Rome for the evaluation of four public transport priorisation policies.

Policy A: bus operating parameters optimisation.

Policy B: bus operating parameters optimisation + public road transport speed up measures. The extension of the bus sub-network with exclusive rights-of-way rises to approximately 20%. On this subnetwork, the split, evaluated using simulation, of the trips in both bus-kms and passenger-kms is 44%, the average speed, allowed by measures of bus priority at intersections, is 18 km/h. Individual transport is not penalised if it is assumed that the section of road lost to the public is recovered, for example, with interventions to liberate parking lanes.

Policy C: bus operating parameters + car pricing. The introduction of car pricing measures produces an increment of 20% in the average money cost of car mode.

Policy D: bus operating parameters + public road transport speed up measures + car pricing. In this policy, measures from policy B and policy C are summed.

In the absence of experimental evidence, different demand responses to the measures under examination are tested, by a sensitivity analysis to demand elasticity with respect to travel cost components.

The applications refer to the morning rush hour. The reference condition is that observed in 1989. Both the operating (costs/revenues) ratio and the average bus load factor are kept unchanged from those in reference condition.

Results point up a different sensitivity of variables with respect to the hypotheses that distinguish the cases investigated (policies and demand responses).

A first class of variables depends on the policies and shows negligible sensitivity to demand responses. This includes total (car+bus) fuel saving, modal split and average road speed in mixed traffic (Table 1).

Another class of variables shows negligible sensitivity to policies and is dependent on demand responses. This includes bus operating parameters (total bus-kms, average fare and bus size) and related variables, such as deficit (operating costs minus revenues) (Table 2). The parameter which affects these variables is the relative sensitivity of demand with respect to fare cost and to time cost, represented by the time-to-fare elasticity ratio, of which the interval between 0.5 and 2 is investigated. Negligible sensitivity is shown with respect to absolute values of fare elasticity of bus demand and time cost elasticity of car demand, assumed in all the cases to which the results shown refer, equal to, respectively, -0.3 and -0.56, which fall in the region of observations of a number of European urban areas [14].

As shown in Table 1 (which refers to a time to fare elasticity ratio of bus demand equal to 1), policy A produces negligible effects, policy C proves more effective than policy B. Policy D produces the maximum benefits: total (car+bus) fuel saving of about 16%, modal split in favour of bus rises by 16%, modal split in favour of car decreases by 8%, average road speed (both car and bus) in mixed traffic rises by 18%.

As shown in Table 2 (which refers to policy D), when demand becomes relatively more sensitive to the time cost (increasing values of the time-to-fare elasticity ratio), the optimal service tends towards an increase in the bus-kms supplied and, hence, of the average line frequency, as well as to a reduction of the average bus size and an increase of average fare. The bus deficit increases, operating ratio being equal to that in reference condition. For a value near one of the time-to-fare elasticity ratio, the optimal service is very near to that of the reference condition.

Table 2 also shows car pricing revenues. These hold a value which is in the region of that of bus deficit for a value of the time to fare elasticity ratio equal to one. Solutions that lower the deficit with respect to the reference one and bring it to values lower than car-pricing revenues are obtained when demand is relatively less sensitive to the time cost. These solutions entail lower average fare and bus-kms and higher average bus size.

Table 1. Fuel saving, modal split and average road speed in mixed traffic

	fuel saving %		modal split %			average speed km/h	
	car+bus	car	bus	else		car	bus
ref. cond.	-	57.4	26.4	16.2		22.5	13.9
policy A	0.01	57.4	26.4	16.2		22.5	13.9
" B	3.30	56.5	27.8	15.7		23.3	15.9
" C	13.90	53.4	29.7	16.9		24.3	14.5
" D	15.70	52.8	30.6	16.9		26.5	16.5

Table 2. Optimal bus operating parameters, bus deficit and car pricing revenues

		total bus-kms	average fare Lire/pr	bus size prs/bus	bus deficit Lire million	car pricing revenues Lire million
	ref. cond.	21750	375	110	96	-
time-to-fare	0.5	17000	222	161	66	87
elasticity	1	24000	314	114	93	88
ratio	1.5	30000	377	95	115	88
	2	35000	425	84	135	87

4 Conclusion

Results of the case study are in agreement with other assessments, based on expert opinions, suggesting that strategies based on raising service levels of public transport alone would produce no or small reduction of traffic congestion [1] and of CO_2 emissions [2].

Policies that add car pricing to bus operating parameters optimisation prove more effective. When both car pricing and public road transport speed up measures are added to bus operating parameters optimisation, benefits increase less than proportionally. Optimal bus operating parameters are insensitive to other priorisation measures. Optimal bus service is that in observed conditions for equal elasticities with respect to time and to fare cost. Decrease in bus deficit can be obtained by lower fare and bus-kms and higher bus size when demand is less sensitive to travel time changes than to fare changes, which is hardly found in reality.

The above results hold strictly for the case study and are obtained under the hypothesis that generation effects produced by policies under test are negligible. The issue of transferability of results and the introduction in the model of the generation effects represent potential research lines.

Acknowledgment

The work reported on here has been partially supported by CEC-DGVII under contract A-4/URBAN/1.

References

1. Downs, A. *Stuck in Traffic: Coping with Peak-hour Traffic Congestion.* The Brookings Institution, Washington, DC, and The Lincoln Institute of Land Policy, Cambridge MA, 1992.
2. Tanja, P.T., Clerx, W.C.G., van Ham, J., de Ligt, T.J. & Rijkeboer, R.C. *Possible Community Measures Aiming at Limiting CO_2 Emissions in Transport Sector,* TNO, The Netherlands, 1992.
3. Williams, I.N., & Bates, J. APRIL—a strategic model for road pricing, *Proceedings of the 21st PTRC Summer Annual Meeting,* University of Manchester, September 13-17, 1993.
4. Jansson, J.O. Marginal cost pricing of scheduled transport services, *Journal of Transport Economics and Policy,* 1979, **13**, 268-294.
5. Nash, C.A. Management objectives, fares and service level in bus transport, *Journal of Transport Economics and Policy,* 1978, **12**, 70-85.
6. Nash, C.A. Integration of public transport: an economic assessment, *Bus Deregulation and Privatisation,* eds J.S. Dodgson & N. Topham, Aldershot, Gower Publishing Group, 1988.
7. Oldfield, R.H. & Bly, P.H. An analytic investigation of optimal bus size. *Transportation Research-B,* 1988, **22B**, 319-337.
8. Delle Site, P. & Filippi, F. Saving fuel in urban areas: bus service optimisation, *Proceedings of the 2nd International Congress on Energy, Environment and Technological Innovation,* Rome, October 12-16, 1992.
9. Delle Site, P. & Filippi, F. Saving fuel in urban areas: bus service optimization within multi-modal equilibrium framework, *Proceedings of the 2nd Meeting of the EURO Working Group on Urban Traffic and Transportation,* Paris, September 15-17, 1993.
10. Delle Site, P. & Filippi, F. Bus service optimisation and car pricing policies to save fuel in urban areas, *Transportation Research-A,* forthcoming.
11. ENEA *Progetto CORINAIR: Inventario delle emissioni in Italia nel 1985.* RTI/STUDI VASA (89)8, Roma, 1989.
12. Williams H.C.W.L., Lam, W.M., Austin, J. & Kim, K.S. Transport policy appraisal with equilibrium models III: investment benefits in multi-modal systems, *Transportation Research-B,* 1993, **25B**, 293-316.
13. Brachetti, P., De Felice Ciccoli, M., Di Pillo, G. & Lucidi, S. *A new version of the Price's algorithm for global optimisation,* Università degli Studi di Roma "La Sapienza". Dipartimento di Informatica e Sistemistica, Rap.26.94, 1994.
14. EURONETT *Evaluating user responses of new European transport technologies. A summary of the state of the art.* DRIVE Project EURONETT (V1025). Deliverable 1A, 1989.

The role of the micro/mini buses network in the development of a strategy for the independence of the city centre inhabitants from the private cars – the case of the city of Athens

G. Mintsis, Ch. Taxiltaris, Th. Vlastos
Department of Surveying Engineers, Aristotelion University, 540 06 Thessaloniki & Department of Surveying Engineers, National Technical University of Athens, Athens 157 80, Greece

Abstract

In the heavily populated centres of big European cities it is by now commonly accepted that the only efficient solution is the traffic restrain measures.

However, besides the traffic, there always exist the problem of parking by road. Parking for the residents is still a problem looking for permanent solution and probably the main difficulty in any effort to reform urban road networks. The only solution to reduce road occupancy from parked vehicles is to oblige people to park their car far from their neighbourhood, near the perimeter of the city - centre. For such a measure to be taken, it is necessary to secure a high level of service provided by public transport.

Micro/mini bus networks are the most suitable means to serve the narrow roads of the historic centres. In this paper the results of experiences and studies concerning the establishment of micro/mini bus networks in Athens will be discussed.

1 Introduction

In the beginning of the 21st century the estimations for the rate of the increase of the private car ownership lead the responsible for the city evolution people to take crucial decisions. The existing urban road infrastructure can not any more serve the demand. Every spatial improvement of the traffic conditions operates as a motive for new users of the existing network. The demand for the use of private transport means looks endless since the advantages of the private car can't be offered by any kind of public transport. On the other hand traffic congestion is probably the most discouraging factor for the use of the private car. However it will be highly unrealistic if traffic congestion is to be used as the main tool for defining traffic management strategies because that will decrease the quality of the existing urban road environment. Therefore it seems unavoidable solution the adoption of traffic restraint policies in city centres since the main impact to the networks is the presence of the private car and not the pollution it produces that will soon be controlled.

The private car occupies valuable space of the road network, its movement is dangerous to the pedestrian when they mix creating thus the need for building footways. Under these conditions a more friendly to human being urban design in the cities seems to be a very difficult case.

Traffic restraint policies, that aim only to lessen the traffic volume, as it is the case of alternative use of the vehicle number plate as a criterion for entering controlled areas, that was first introduced in Athens in 1983 and in some Italian cities did not offered the required solutions and proved to be inefficient. And that because the measure leads user to buy a second car as to use taxis or motorbikes. It is also clear that the use of these vehicles leads to the same traffic impact problem in the cities.

It is not also to be overlooked the fact that in countries with developing economies the rapid increase of the private vehicle ownership neutralises all these measures. However the most serious objection to the measures that simply aim to decrease traffic volume is that they do not release road space and also do not allow regeneration.

2 Pedestrian - path policies for the central residence areas and the role of micro/mini buses

The provision of pedestrian - paths seems to be the only suitable solution in order to create friendly city - centre environment. However even the exclusion of private vehicles from Business District Centres and the use only of public transport can be achieved, the transformation of the whole road network to pedestrian - paths in a residential area where off - road parking does not exists is a rather difficult case. And that because the resident is obliged to park its car far away from his residence and definitely out of the restricted to vehicles area. Such a case is the centre of the city of Athens. Any measure that would totally control the use of the private vehicle could possible act as a motive to residents to move from the centre to the suburbs where also the environment is better.

This problem is exactly the same for other densely built up areas in the capital of Greece where there is an obvious absence of parking spaces and no available space for building parking exists.

The introduction of a complete pedestrian - path network will depend upon the ability of public transport authorities and operators to upgrade the role of public transport in Athens. Today the existing public transport network and the frequencies used can not secure for the resident a required level of service that could compete that offered by the private car. However the improvement of the services offered by public transport could be the only argument in an effort to persuade people to use private cars only for long - distance trips and therefore to accept parking far away from his residence.

If public transport wills to compete with the private transport means it has to be more effective and flexible. To supply to the user a dense network with short - distance services that will cover most of the roads, decreasing walking distance to the bus -stop. Also operation has to improve frequencies in order to decrease waiting time at the stops. Thus a resident could easily and quickly reach the heavier and faster transport means for longer urban trips. For such use micro/mini buses would be suitable since they can afford to operate under low demand conditions and in the narrow streets of the residential areas of Athens.

Even more mini - buses could prove to be a useful mean in the arterial street network of the city. The results of various studies that were conducted in Athens, all aiming to assist to the best use of a road network that can not meet the demand, insisted that the use of small size buses could possible allow interventions that otherwise could not be possible. Thus the level of road safety for the motorbikes could be also improved in the centre of Athens since they represent almost the 40 percent of the total traffic volume in the central streets. That is obvious in the main streets where the absence of exclusive to buses lanes leads the bus - drivers to dangerous manoeuvres in their effort to increase speed creating thus unsafe conditions for two - wheeled vehicles. Similar are the problems with the pedestrians who rarely use pedestrian - crossings.

3 Mini - buses in Athens: recent policies and experiences

The use of mini - buses in Athens is a rather new experience. The existing public transport network of the city is complex and difficult to be identified. It consists of buses and trolleys with radial lines, all oriented towards the city centre. Every simple suburban area or small municipality is linked to the centre by an exclusive line. There are few lines that link peripheral municipalities. Also few are the basic axle - lines. There is also an axle - metro line 26 km long that is to be complemented by another two lines which have length of 9.5 and 8.3 km.

Mini - buses, where initially introduced in Athens three years ago in two bus - lines in the historical city centre, the aim was to substitute the large conventional buses and to totally restrict the use of taxis in the historical centre. It is useful to note. Taxis in Athens is probably the main problem to any effort of development in the field of traffic and transport since they operate in huge numbers and competitively to public transport, mainly due to low rates they charge. Finally when mini - buses were put to service neither the taxis or the conventional buses were removed. Thus the role of a mini - bus in the historical city centre of Athens was never realised. Recently a decision was made for the historical centre to be evacuated by any other means of transport apart from mini - buses. However the network will be more attractive to business and less to residence who are few.

All the same, mini - buses are going to operate in Piraeus, the port of Athens, in order primarily to connect the port with the metro station and secondary to serve the residents.

Is also specific the example of the west - Athens area. A number of neighbour municipalities, peripheral to the city centre, are going to install a mini - bus line with main aim to link their Business Centres. Today, these centres are not linked via public transport service although they are adjacent to each other. This solution was selected for two reasons. First because the road network consists of narrow and curvy roads. Second because the demand is low since people are still attracted by the main city centre of Athens. Therefore the challenge for the mini - bus, if it is to succeed, is to alter the every - day habits of the residents of these areas and to divert them to the local market centres.

4 Introduction of a mini - bus network in a main residential area of Athens. - Feasibility

The introduction of dense mini - bus networks in the densely populated areas of Athens of purely residential character was examined in a study that considered all the technical parameters in order to evaluate the feasibility of the system. The aim was to offer to residents a mean of public transport with such characteristics that will allow to be comparable to private cars.

As a pilot site the central district of Kipseli was examined. Kipseli in the last fifteen years, between 1960 and 1975, changed from a residential area with single houses to an area with multi-store buildings, 6 to 7 levels, which were built with no allowance for parking places. In those days the vehicles in use were few but now the pedestrian - paths are occupied by parked vehicles and residents in most cases have to walk on the road pavement. Walking and children playing on the road are habits already disappeared. Today a multi-store building with about fourteen apartments, with at least a vehicle per apartment, takes a road length of about fifteen metres or in other words the respective parking space for every building is only for three cars.

Within the centre of Kipseli, an area of about 115 ha and population of about 56.000 inhabitants and a mean density of 490 inhab/ha was defined for the introduction of a mini - bus service. It is estimated that the mean density, which is already very high, will jump up in ten years time to 550 inhab/ha when all the available space will have been used. If we assume that the private car ownership level will reach 400 veh/1000 inhab. then there will be 26.000 cars corresponding to 65.000 inhabitants. So in ten years even if parking is allowed at both sides of the existing roads the deficit in parking places will be tremendous. Parking at both sides of the road will allow 8.000 places to be given in common use where another 2.000 places exist today inside the buildings. Therefore in ten years time the deficit in parking places will reach 16.000 places which can not be found in the neighbouring districts where the same difficulties exist.

The question is not to identify parking places but to empty the streets from vehicles and to regenerate them if we want them to be given to residents for walking and playing purpose providing thus a more human environment. Knowing that the existing political and social situation does not allow the restructuring of central residential areas in order to secure more off - road parking places it is unavoidable for the residents to move their cars away from the residential areas if they want to improve their living standards. Towards such perspective the role of mini - buses can be fundamental.

Initially the possibility to exclude all large buses and trolleys from the area was examined. That would result to the need for the use of o large number of mini - buses to serve during the peak hours when people move to and from work. It is to be noted that a questionnaire survey revealed that a large number of the home -work trips uses public transport. Daily it reaches 46 percent and every second day 11 percent adds more due to the alternative traffic restraint measure that uses the number plate. These large percentages can be explained by the fact that Kipseli is a district close to the main business centre and it is served rather sufficiently by the public transport network.

The solution that was finally suggested was a compromise that combines during peak hours five mini - bus lines with two existing bus - lines and two trolley - lines. During off - peak hours the five mini - bus lines are to combine with two existing services. Thus instead of the 59 vehicles, large buses and trolleys, that operate today, with the introduction of the mini -buses there will be in operation:

- 34 mini and 41 conventional vehicles during peak - hours
- 34 mini and 20 conventional vehicles during off - peak - hours

The mini - bus service line will have the following functional characteristics (both directions):

	length (km)	travel time (min)
line 1	6.5	40'
line 2	5.9	36'
line 3	4.8	29'
line 4	5.7	35'
line 5	5.6	33'

They will all end to the neighbouring metro station almost at the boundary of the area and there will be connection points with the service lines of buses and trolleys that operate around the perimeter of the area.

It is to be noted that the thirty - four mini - buses will be introduced in the first phase of the project where it is estimated that only the 15 percent of those using the private cars will change transport mode. The fundamental aim of the project is that progressively all residents will move from the private car to public transport. Towards that aim the level of service of the mini - bus especially the frequency of the service has to increased. The need for changing modes that will be obligatory to the residents is not expected to discourage them or to increase their travel time if the system is well organised with high quality standards and well placed within the framework of the public transport means.

Conclusions

The system that is proposed implies an increased capital cost. The problem has not been solved yet. It is also the cost for the regeneration of the road environment that has to be considered.

Necessary presumption for the success of the project will be a strict parking enforcement policy. Also the introduction of the mini - buses has to be complemented by the construction of parking stations at the perimeter of the area where the access priority has to be given to the residents. Also the need for improvement in the level of service for the conventional bus and trolley services is not to be forgot. Finally any regeneration action of the area has to be taken immediately not to discourage people that will no change their confort parking near their home with a better environment and standard of living.

References

1. Taxiltaris, Ch. & Vlastos, Th. La zone protegee du centre d'Athenes: bilan critique et perspectives d' une politique de restriction de la circulation automobile, *Transport -Environnement - Circulation*, 1991, **104**, 22-26.

2. Mintsis, G., Taxiltaris, Ch. & Vlastos, Th. L'organisation des deplacements dans l'Athenes de demain: Solidarite ou Barbarie?, pp. 58-62, *Proceedings of the Congres International Francophone of ATEC "Quels transports pour nos villes de demain?"*, Versailles, France, 1993.

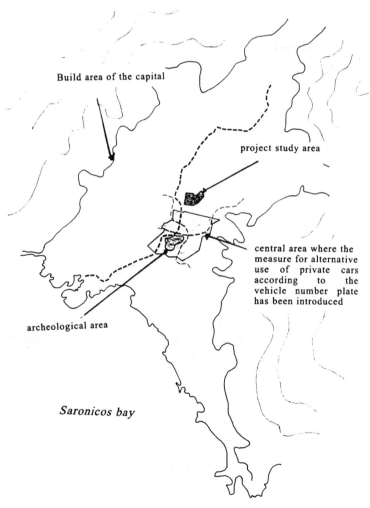

Figure 1

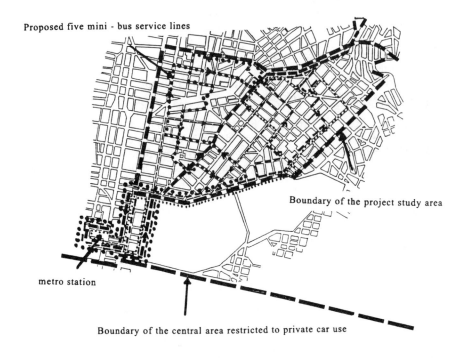

Proposed five mini - bus service lines

Boundary of the project study area

metro station

Boundary of the central area restricted to private car use

Figure 2

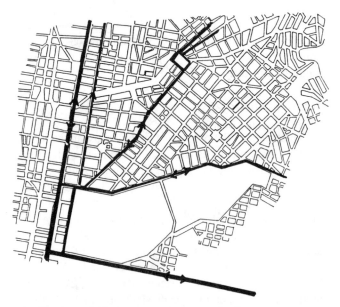

Figure 3: Basic public transport routes in the area

Chapter 4 – The Forgotten modes in UK transport policy

W.F. Prendergast, M.I. Hassounah

Devon County Council Road Safety Unit, & Department of Civil Engineering, University of Southampton, Southampton, UK

Abstract

UK Transport and Land Use Policy has largely ignored the fact that benign modes actually serve our lives unlike the car which governs them, and hence, by emphasising policy geared towards the needs for roads, of cars, and of the car driving minority, unsustainable forms of living are inadvertently supported clearly contrary to the need for energy consumption and reductions in infrastructure's environmental impacts. A national policy to promote benign modes is required if the aims and hopes of the Rio Earth Summit are to be realised in the UK with any significant impact, and the revised PPG13 Land Use Guidance issued in 1994 must be adopted with real conviction by all levels of Government in the UK. These issues are considered with reference to how the plight of the vulnerable road users might be improved.

1. Introduction

The extent of the problems faced by those individuals choosing to use public transport such as late running services, waiting times, overcrowding, vandalised vehicles, and often uncomfortable rides are well documented, but in the car dominated society in which we live today, other benign modes that travellers might adopt including cycling and walking are even more adversely discriminated against, firstly by the presence of large numbers of fast moving vehicles that impose their domination upon all other road users, secondly by antiquated, inaccurate, and stubborn beliefs and attitudes of some senior politicians, planners and decision makers, and thirdly by land use policies that have raised the friction of distance beyond these benign modes' reasonable limits. This third point is specifically associated with the out of town development boom of the last 10 to 15 years and helps highlight the uphill struggle facing planners and politicians alike in promoting such modes' use.

2. Politicians and Benign Modes

The European Charter of Pedestrians' Rights, adopted by the European Parliament in 1988 and to which the British Government has signed, (Tolley[1]) sets out measures designed to improve the plight of pedestrians, and in the context of this paper on vulnerable road users, contains five important statements outlined here. Firstly, the Charter states that a person has the right to live and enjoy a healthy environment 'under conditions that adequately safeguard his physical and psychological well-being.' Secondly persons have the right to 'have amenities within walking or cycling distance.' Thirdly their children have the right to 'expect towns to be places of easy social contact' and not places that exploit their weaknesses. Fourthly, people can expect the fixing of speed limits and modifying of road junctions and layouts to safeguard those vulnerable road users. And finally, people also have the right of complete and unimpeded mobility, via an improved integrated transport network with public transport and bicycle facilities.

Whilst not being the comprehensive set of principals contained within the Charter, these five important statements form the basis of fundamental rights for pedestrians and cyclists, the most vulnerable road using groups in society today, which if were strictly adhered to, would surely see the overwhelming focus of policy, investment, and concern on car orientated transport shift. Yet, as it will be shown throughout this paper, the UK's adherence to the Charter seems rather poor even over 5 years later.

For all too long in the UK cycling and walking have received scant attention and still lack the credible status necessary for them to develop and progress into effective commonly used modes, namely a national policy to promote their rights of movement. Rather than be seen in the mould of a potential solution to urban congestion, these modes are disregarded as little more than recreational and leisure pursuits for adults, and of more particular appropriateness to children as leisure pastimes. In his statement on transport in London in 1989, The Secretary of State dedicated eight paragraphs only to cycling and walking, and then only in Appendix 8! The European Community Ministers for Transport in 1988, meeting on the future needs of transport, gave brief reference to cycling and walking in only one of 15 paragraphs produced; and the 1990 European Commission Green Paper on the Urban Environment acknowledged vehicles' disbenefits, but made no reference to cycling or walking. This blatant disregard compounded with UK transport policy that has concentrated on cars and road building for many years demotes those choosing benign modes to second rate travellers and dictates they must play subordinate roles to the car, supported by its strong, effective, and active lobbying group whose financial muscle and political clout are still far beyond the capabilities of the anti-roads campaigners to date. One merely only has to consider that the largest 10 firms in the world are either oil or car manufacturing companies to realise the position of strength held by the pro-car groups.

3. Why Is It An Uphill Struggle For The Benign Modes?

Transport Policy's Statistical Basis

UK transport policy has been recently criticised because of its theoretical basis, statistics being taken from data within the frequent *National Travel Surveys, Transport Statistics: Great Britain*, (published by the Department of Transport in 1988), and *Social Trends, Section 9*, (published in 1989 by the Central Statistical Office). All three sources of material exclude all those journeys of less than 1 mile, and such trips actually account for a significant proportion of all trips estimated at about one third; of this third, approximately three quarters are by the benign modes of cycling and walking.

Table 1 : 1985/86 All Journeys by Mode, Great Britain

	Journeys		
	Under 1 mile	Over 1 mile	Difference
Walk	34.00%	11.00%	-23.00%
Cycle	3.00%	2.00%	-1.00%
Bus	9.00%	11.00%	+0.02%
Car	51.00%	69.00%	+0.18%
Other	4.00%	7.00%	+3.0%
TOTAL	100.00%	100.00%	

Source : DTp[2]

The net effect of exclusion of short trips is shown in Table 1, where a distorted picture of the UK's travel behaviour is produced which leads to over-emphasising the role and importance of the car; statistics highlight it as the main trend in British transportation journey distances, at the expense of the vulnerable road users and pedestrians. Table 2 shows, however, that nearly 50% of trips by children are less than 1 mile, and three quarters of all trips within a mile are on foot or bicycle.

Table 2 : Journeys Under 1 Mile 1985/86, Great Britain

Age	Under 15	All Groups
Percentage of all journeys	45.00%	33.00%
Percentage of trips on foot/bike	78.00%	76.00%

Source : DTp[2]

As a result of the exclusion of these trips, decision makers themselves highly unlikely to be representative of the pedestrian and cycling groups, being invariably car owners and users themselves as is all too often demonstrated on television news with ministers being ferried in and out of Downing Street in limousines, produce car orientated transport policies based upon an inaccurate assumption that everybody has access to a car. The green modes, being less costly to provide for and less damaging firstly environmentally, in terms of pollution, land-take, severance, and disturbance, secondly socially, in terms of causing less road accidents, and thirdly politically, in terms of not having the strong lobbying influence and pressure compared to the pro-road campaign, are easily shrugged off as less problematic and hence deserving less investment and attention.

The Car and UK Culture

Britain, unlike European countries such as the Netherlands and to an extent even Germany, has missed the fact that these benign modes serve our lives rather than the car that governs them by making our way of life increasingly dependant upon them. Cycling and walking does not inhibit other persons from mobility by either scaring them from making journeys altogether for fear of road danger, or imposing themselves upon remaining road users to the extent that individual's choice of mode, route, or time of travel may be affected. The inequalities rampant in a society geared to wealth accumulation are enlarged by the car and exacerbated in a society already over-orientated to it, as those able to drive do so and impose social costs on the rest of society and especially so on non-car users inhibited from doing likewise by income, age, or some other restriction.

Table 3 : Proportion of Population With Driving Licenses

Age	Male	Female	Total
17-19	41.00%	20.00%	34.00%
20-29	79.00%	60.00%	69.00%
30-39	86.00%	68.00%	77.00%

Source : Dorset County Council[3]

Cleary[4] highlights that while approximately 40% of UK citizens had access to a car in 1992, 90% of these could either walk or cycle, and hence by providing for the majority non-car owners as opposed to the car driving minority, equity issues within society, the need for increasing energy consumption, and reductions in infrastructure's environmental impacts in an increasingly sensitive age, would all be addressed simultaneously giving a far greater social cost benefit return on investments than new road investment.

The Role of Benign Modes

The cost of providing facilities for pedestrians and cyclists such as footpaths, cycle tracks and bicycle racks, is negligible compared to the needs of the roads programme, and this is the crux of the third key factor misleading many, including decision makers, into thinking that their role in the transport programme is insignificant compared to other motorised modes. Between 1984 and 1986, the Department of Transport allocated £160,000 for the cycling budget; the roads investment programme of 1987/88 however received £180 million, (McClintock[5]); purely in terms of levels of funding there is no comparison, but in terms of cost effectiveness, value for money, and sustainable development, the returns on these levels of investment are not so far apart when savings from road casualty reductions are also taken into account, the cost of one fatal road accident being in excess of £750,000.

Statistics support the view that cycling and walking are important modes worthy of proper consideration at the national policy level; 37% of all trips are by foot or bicycle, the average journey time is 25 minutes, or a comfortable 4 or 5 mile cycle ride, and the average journey length is between three and five miles, again comfortable for cyclists to negotiate. It should be stressed, though, that these distances would at least be comfortable were people healthier and used to walking and cycling; for some people the thought of such mileage might on the face of it cause gasps of disbelief in between them gasping for breath as they walk up the stairs in their house with the evening newspaper collected from the corner shop in their car. The fact that the benign modes are most significant at less than one mile and hence excluded from data at the heart of the policy making, means their potential role is hidden and public transport predominates as the apparent only alternative to cars because of the extended journey distances involved . Hillman[6] highlights investment into public transport only increases number of trips rather than alters the modal split, unlike investment into better cycling facilities which could influence some people to leave their cars.

Land Use Policy and The Benign Modes

The car culture gripping the nation has both been served and led by the continued expanding positive feedback of growing demand for it from society itself, namely the growth in out of town developments throughout all sectors of the economy which has certainly been to the detriment of cycling and walking. The car has created a friction of distance too great for all but the most dedicated cyclist, and which cars alone can effectively serve, given the financial difficulty of operating regular bus services to such dispersed low density population areas. Land use policies in the '70's and '80's together with UK Government market led approaches fuelled such decentralisation from urban centres into dispersed, open, greenfield locations without much apparent forethought of the trip generating effects it would predominantly have, of the great inequality disadvantages it would create for the mobility deprived groups, or of the problems for vehicle occupants through commuter congestion that would be caused.

Clearly the benign modes are most effective in urban areas where facilities and amenities are highly accessible to each other and to residential areas, and therefore any meaningful role for them must centre upon them serving the traditional centres and especially the mobility deprived groups. But the economic vitality of inner areas is only now just beginning to recover in many areas from the loss of trade, loss of social interaction, and other subsequent consequences of the car led decentralisation processes including significantly an influx of a new type of inner city resident, namely high income younger people associated with 'yuppiefication', gentrification, and waterfront redevelopment's, and who exhibit very different social behaviour and preferences to the traditional inhabitants of these areas. These processes have affected all aspects of urban area living especially the use of car in preference to public transport and walking, and now with few incentives to the family and person of the '90's to change their 'new' lifestyles by giving up the convenient parking and quick and easy access of out of town superstores and retail parks for the congested, cramped, older and traditional centres, and so necessary to help return economic prosperity and social vitality to such places, measures to promote benign modes will be further hampered unless accompanied by restraint measures as now being finally outlined by the Government in PPG13.

Cities need to be made more attractive and must provide an improved quality and standard of living as part of this process of attracting people back. The degree of success will depend greatly on how the roads can be returned to the majority, who are at present the most vulnerable and most exposed to risk. The little regard and attention they have received was touched on by the Transport 2000 survey[7] carried out in London in advance of its Feet First strategy for the Capital which highlighted problems faced by pedestrians. According to those pedestrians surveyed, 46% referred to poor footway conditions, 37% to the high traffic volumes, 24% to vehicles obstructing the footway, and 23% highlighted the lack of proper crossing points; cyclists themselves are hindered by poor nearside pavement conditions, pot holes in the road, and inconsiderate driving behaviour. The pedestrians and cyclist's rights seem easily compromised to accommodate vehicles, for example by restricting walkway widths with bollards and signs, diverting pedestrians into subways or over bridges, and commonly citing them as at fault when incidents occur. The pollution effects suffered under congested conditions is highlighted by cyclists within large cities like London needing to wear masks, and also by the high smog concentrations that occur in Los Angeles and Athens, for example; the vulnerable road users do not produce the pollution, but are expected or forced to by a lack of suitable alternatives as a result of selfish use of cars, to withstand all the harmful gases. Indeed vehicle exhausts are directed at low level straight towards the cyclists' and pedestrians' locales. By reviving the benign modes and public transport, one can restore areas' vitality and if this includes making more provision for them on roads at the expense of private vehicles, all the better in terms of reducing the effect of severance by heavy volumes of traffic. This is the best way of helping increase traditional centres' retail turnover, productivity, and quality of the living and working environment, (Roberts[8]).

4. Safer Roads - Fact or Fiction

No reference has yet been made to road safety and accident statistics, which will be fully covered in Chapter 5; suffice to say there are approximately 17000 serious and fatal road accidents per year in the UK involving benign mode users, (Whitelegg[9]); in the 20 years from 1970, there were 2 million such accidents, with cyclists and pedestrians accounting for a third, despite these road users only representing approximately $1/14$th of total mileage travelled. Between 1954 and 1988, cycle fatalities in the UK rose 80%, whilst for car occupants, they fell 50%. Whilst technology is making cars ever safer, for example ABS, air bags, better protected crumple zones and safety cages, measures to safeguard those most at risk are relatively simplistic and low cost. As emphasis is placed on the "causers" of most accidents, for example through Road Safety Unit accident cluster reviews, car occupants are becoming potentially too nannied and there is a risk of them being lulled into a false sense of security in their comfortable, warm vehicles. As long as road safety works on the principle that streets are for cars rather than for living, the benign modes will continue to be perceived as dangerous.

Knowing the problems of safety facing the cyclist, walker, or public transport user, it is somewhat surprising to find evidence actually suggesting fewer accidents are occurring in Britain today compared with 20 years ago. However trips involving vulnerable road users, according to the London Area Transport Survey in 1991 by the DoT and London Research Centre, have actually declined at the expense of more car journeys, resulting in less exposure to risk; this may provide one reason for less injury accidents occurring. During the '80's the overall number of journeys in London rose 8%; those by car increased 18%, but by bicycle they fell 30% and by 50% on foot, (Local Transport Today[10]). Accident rates in the same period for cyclists remained static and for pedestrians fell only by 17%, despite a halving of the journeys. Evidence of a change in the modal split can be found at the local, regional, and national level, implying this trend is reflective of the current travel patterns as shown by Table 4 and 5. Leading academics in this field such as Hillman, Adams, Roberts, and Whitelegg all refer to less activity by the benign mode users, and one need only recall from old pictures, films, and memory just how free people were to travel before the onset of mass car occupancy, (Davis[11]).

Table 4. Passenger Transport in Great Britain, 1953 - 1990
Thousand million passenger kilometres (Pax. Kms)

Year	1953		1963		1973	
Mode	Pax. Kms	Share (%)	Pax. Kms	Share (%)	Pax. Kms	Share (%)
Buses & Coaches	82	41.8	64	24.2	53	13.2
Car & Taxi	58	29.6	158	59.6	309	76.7
Bicycle	17	8.7	6	2.3	4	1.0
Rail	39	19.9	36	13.6	35	8.7
Total	196		265		403	
Year	1980		1985		1990	
Mode	Pax. Kms	Share (%)	Pax. Kms	Share (%)	Pax. Kms	Share (%)
Buses & Coaches	45	9.2	42	7.9	41	6.2
Car & Taxi	395	80.1	439	82.1	561	85.0
Bicycle	5	1.0	6	1.1	5	0.7
Rail	35	7.1	36	6.7	41	6.2
Total	491		535		660	

Source : Thorthwaite[12], HMSO[13]

Table 5. Percentage Modal split of Journeys From Southampton
Typical October Weekday, 16:00 - 18:00, 1977 - 1991

Year	1977	1981	1987	1988	1989	1990	1991
Private Vehicle	55.8	65.3	71.0	70.3	71.2	70.7	70.3
Motor Cycle	2.8	2.9	1.7	1.6	1.6	1.5	1.4
Bicycle	1.5	2.3	1.7	1.7	1.9	1.7	2.0
Bus	34.8	24.5	20.8	21.9	20.6	21.4	21.7
Train	4.1	4.2	3.9	3.6	4.0	4.1	4.1
Hythe Ferry	1.0	0.8	0.9	0.9	0.7	0.6	0.5

Source : Southampton City Council[14]

5. Conclusion

To return to the European Charter of Pedestrian Rights and specifically the five points outlined at the start of this Chapter as most significant in the context of this paper on benign modes and the vulnerable road using groups, we can conclude that Central Government Transport Policy of the last two decades which has left a strong legacy of socio-economic, locational, and demographic patterns and trends that have dramatically transformed the way in which UK society leads its life, has become the dominant force behind processes that are infringing upon all five areas within the Charter affecting them.

Continuing need and cultural encouragement to own and drive cars contradicts the first statement; land use policies leading to decentralisation by urban facilities to out of town sites and rationalisation of those remaining behind in the traditional centres to serve the car owning people, contradicts the second. The discrimination against the benign modes of cycling, walking, and public transport by policies favouring car users, such as continued road investment, refusal to fully charge drivers their full social costs, and deregulation of the bus industry contradicts the third. And the continuing placement of vulnerable road users after motorists with for example, people being diverted around, over and under the road space instead of vice-versa, contradicts the final two statements of person's rights. The Government's recent change of heart last year away from complete car orientation demonstrated both by PPG13 and new Transport Policies and Programmes advice, still is not enough and Ministers must travel a long way before any significant penetration of the UK's long established travel and living patterns, notorious for undermining the benign modes for so long, can occur with any significant impact in favour of the non-car modes.

References

1. Tolley, R. *The Greening of Urban Transport : Planning for Walking and Cycling In Western Cities*, Belhaven Press, 1993.
2. Department of Transport, *National Travel Survey*, HMSO, 1985/6.
3. Dorset County Council, *School Traffic and Parking TERI Report 92/2*, Dorsert County Council, 1992.
4. Whitelegg, J, *Traffic Congestion : Is there a way out?*, Leading Edge Press For The IBG/TGSG, 1992.
5. Hillman, M, *Children, Transport And The Quality Of Life*, Policy Studies Institute, 1993.
6. Hillman, M, *Children, Transport And The Quality Of Life*, Policy Studies Institute, 1993.
7. Transport 2000, London casualty fall is due to fewer trips, transport committee told, *Local Transport Today,*1994, Issue 130, 7.

8. Zuckermann, W, *End of the Road : The World Car Crisis and How We Can Solve It*, Lutterworth Press, 1991.

9. Whitelegg, J, *Traffic Congestion : Is there a way out?*, Leading Edge Press For The IBG/TGSG, 1992.

10. London Research Centre, & Department of Transport, Car trips in London rose 18% in last decade, LATS figures reveal, *Local Transport Today,* 1994, Issue 130, 7

11. Davis, R, Road safety needs greater commitment, *Local Transport Today*, 1994, Issue 136, 15

12. Thornthwaite, S, *School Transport : The Comprehensive Guide*, TAS, 1994.

13. HMSO, *Aspects of Britain : Transport and Communications*, HMSO, 1992.

14. Southampton City Council, ,Director of Technical Services, 1992.

Effectiveness of new road investments in metropolitan areas

F. Filippi, N. Papola
*Dipartimento di Idraulica, Trasporti e Strade, Università di
Roma 'La Sapienza', Via Eudossiana 18, 00184 Rome, Italy*

Abstract

A critical examination of the results of Mogridge and Williams clarifies some
theoretical aspects of the Downs-Thomson paradox and the possibilities that
road investment can worsen traffic conditions. The importance that these or
similar cases with little or no effect have in practice is investigated with the data
contained in Newman and Kenworthy's source book. An interesting result is
that the short-term effect on average speed of new road investment in medium-
to high-density areas are modest, but can produce quite considerable increases
in energy consumption. The empirical analysis also shows the inadequacy of the
theoretical framework for long-term effects.

1 Introduction

The rapid motorisation that began in the 1950s was followed in the 1960s by a
series of studies that theorised the need for an ever greater increase in the
supply of infrastructures to meet the growing demand for travel in private cars.
According to this reasoning, the role of public transport services was destined
to become, over time, relatively modest if not marginal.

By the 1970s Hillman et al. [1], Plowden [2] and Schaeffer and Sclar [3],
to name a few, were contesting the technical and economic validity of this
approach, which was, they maintained, self-fulfilling: the policies adopted were
such as to make the predictions come true.

Today no one disputes [4], either the impossibility of increasing the supply
of road infrastructures that can satisfy the demand or the necessity of adopting

provisions that encourage the use of public transport to reduce rush-hour congestion.

The policies of short-term intervention aimed at making best use of the existing infrastructures appear well delineated: it is necessary to combine appropriately public transport priorisation measures with some form of price mechanism to make road users pay a price commensurate with the social cost they generate [5, 6].

As for long-term intervention policies, tending to identify the best endowment of road infrastructures and transport services, things are not so clear cut. This topic will be addressed in the next two sections.

In the first section it will be shown that the Downs-Thomson paradox formulated by Mogridge [7], which would have solved the problem, is based on a hypothesis that does not hold up under analysis. Williams's critical considerations [8] on the same topic show that the Downs-Thomson paradox, put forth by Mogridge as generally valid, occurs in one very particular case, in the hypothesis of a decreasing long-term public transport supply curve. This trend is possible but not usually the case.

To investigate the importance that cases similar to Williams's can have in practice the second section reelaborates the data contained in Newman and Kenworthy's source book [9] (hereafter abbreviated NK).

2 Theoretical analysis

The formulation of the Downs-Thomson paradox is based on three hypotheses: extension of the validity of Wardrop's first principle in bimodal contexts; absence of generation effects; function of supply relative to the public transport reducing as flows increase.

The Downs-Thomson equilibrium is shown in figure 1. The flows are read from left to right for car transport, and from right to left for public transport, and S' and S" are the functions of supply, respectively before and after the intervention, relative to individual transport, index 1, and to public transport, index 2.

In the absence of generation effects ($\Delta Q_G=0$), following the intervention the equilibrium shifts from point M to point N where everybody is worse off than before: this is the Downs-Thomson paradox. The passage from M to N occurs for successive phases: M$\rightarrow$A$\rightarrow$B$\rightarrow$C... $\rightarrow$N, where the variations of the type M$\rightarrow$A, D$\rightarrow$C, ... follow a spontaneous adjustment of the demand to the variations of the supply and the variations of type A$\rightarrow$B, ... represent the adjustment of the public transport supply consequent to a reduction of flow. We will indicate the equilibria as M and N, in the absence of generation effects, as Downs-Thomson equilibria.

The absence of generation effects can be criticised, as a hypothesis of first approximation, on the grounds that with a generation effect the

Downs-Thomson equilibrium does not correspond to the reality. In effect the introduction of a small generation effect provokes the disappearance of the public transport mode.

For this purpose let a generation effect ΔQ_G be introduced and let reference be made to figure 1.

Indicating with Q_1 and Q_2 the flow towards the individual and public transport modes, respectively, before the intervention, we have:

$$Q_1 = Q_M ; \quad Q_1 + Q_2 = Q_{before} ; \quad c_1 = c_2 = c_M \tag{1}$$

After the intervention, in the hypothesis that $\Delta Q_G = 0$, eqn (1) becomes:

$$Q_1 = Q_M + DQ_M = Q_A ; \quad Q_1 + Q_2 = Q_{before} ; \quad c_1 = c_2 = c_M \tag{2}$$

At this stage in the Downs-Thomson process is expected the adjustment of c_2 which goes from c_M to c_B. Eqn (2) thus becomes:

$$Q_1 = Q_M + DQ_G = Q_A ; \quad Q_1 + Q_2 = Q_{before} ; \quad c_1 = c_M < c_2 = c_B \tag{3}$$

From this follows a new variation of the demand, of modal type, which leads from A towards C with c_1 which tends to increase until it again assumes the same value as c_2. Contemporaneously, however, there also occurs a generation effect ΔQ_G and so the new situation becomes:

$$Q_1 = Q_C ; \quad Q_1 + Q_2 = Q_{after} = Q_{before} - \Delta Q_G ; \quad c_1 = c_2 = c_B \tag{4}$$

in which the total flow Q decreases while the flow Q_1 increases.

At this stage, the new intervention of adjustment of the cost to the current value of Q_2 makes c_2 jump from c_B to c_D, situated on the curve s_2' obtained by translation of s_2 towards the left of a quantity equal to ΔQ_G.

At point D the situation is analogous to that in M, with a succession of adjustments of the demand and of the supply that tend towards R, the point at which the condition $c_1 = c_2$. is reached. However, it is not possible to reach R because a new variation of the demand, of generation type, takes place at the same time, involving a further increase of Q_1 and a further reduction of Q_2. The process, once begun, repeats itself indefinitely until Q_2 totally disappears, however small the initial variation ΔQ_G may be. In reality the equilibria are stable. The hypotheses of Downs-Thomson equilibria do not hold up.

Williams et al. [8], in criticising Mogridge, show that the paradox can occur only in a very special and improbable case. Its formulation is unexceptionable from the demand side since both the hypothesis of extension of Wardrop's first principle in bimodal contexts and the absence of generation effects disappear. The hypothesis, however, remains that the long-term supply curve (c_2, Q_2) is decreasing, recalling, in this regard, Mhoring [10]. Mhoring's curves are a completely different thing from those of Williams. The first, in fact, represent the place of the points (c_2, Q_2) as a result of the process of minimisation of the total costs with Q_2 independent variable. Defined $TS \equiv [TS_1; TS_2]$, where in TS_2 are intended included also company policies (frequencies, fares, etc.), the second represent, rather, the place of the points solution of an optimisation problem that can be formulated thus:

$$F(Ts_2; Q_2) = max \tag{5}$$

$$\begin{cases} Q_2 = Q_2(c_1, c_2; LU = \beta) \\ Q_1 = Q_1(c_1, c_2; LU = \beta) \\ c_2 = c_2(Q_1, Q_2; TS_2; TS_1 = \alpha) \\ c_1 = c_1(Q_1, Q_2; TS_2; TS_1 = \alpha) \end{cases} \tag{6}$$

the variables α and β define the *border* of the subsystem relative to public transport. For each specification of α and of β the solution of the problem supplies the best company policy in that context and, therefore, the values of Q_2 and of c_2. In the plan (c_2, Q_2) the curve $c_2 = c_2(Q_2)$, place of the points solution of the system:

$$\begin{cases} c_2 = c_2(\alpha, \beta) \\ Q_2 = Q_2(\alpha, \beta) \end{cases} \tag{7}$$

represents the adjustment of the supply to the demand for public transport services as conditions vary at the border and, therefore, the curve of long-term cost. Around the point of equilibrium there can be any trend, even decreasing, just as both Mogridge and Williams hypothesised. This clarifies the theoretical aspects of the question, but is not reassuring. Theoretically an investment in road infrastructures can worsen the conditions of both modes of transport instead of improving them.

3 Empirical analysis

A first result that emerges from a reading of NK is that in treating the effects of new road investments in cities, land-use characteristics cannot be overlooked. For this reason, the empirical analysis will be made separately for two groups of cities, the first of low density, of the North American type, and the second of medium-high density, of the European type.

For each of the two groups are studied the relations between the average speeds of equilibrium v_1 and v_2 relative, respectively, to the individual and public transport mode, and the relations between each of them and the average fuel consumption per capita y.

From the analysis of the data contained in NK, illustrated in figures 2-6, it emerges, relative, to the first group of cities, that:

1. v_1 and v_2 are both correlated with y with coefficients 0.79 and -0.81 respectively;
2. v_1 and v_2 are not correlated and, generally, rather different from one another while the difference v_1-v_2 is well correlated both with v_1 (coefficient 0.86) and with y (coefficient 0.89).

Relative to the second group of cities it emerges, rather, that:

1. v_1 and v_2 are correlated (coefficient 0.82), and differ little from one another;
2. v_1 and v_2 are not correlated with consumption y; while consumptions can be even very different for practically equal speeds.

Since the state of equilibrium results from the resolution of a system of equations that are considered simultaneously satisfactory, v_1 and v_2 are presumed correlated. Where, as in the low-density cities, that does not happen, individual and public transport do not function as a system and individuals utilise, in substance, the only mode that is concretely accessible to them. When, in fact, the public service is of poor quality, individuals tend to use it only when they have no choice, which explains both the good correlation existing between v_1 and v_1-v_2 and the correlation between v_1 and y, given that the latter increases as car use increases.

As regards the link between v_1 and v_2, the existence of correlation shows that individual transport and public transport behave like a system. Particularly interesting is the fact that the two speeds differ little one from the other. The phenomenon is confirmed all over Rome [11], since along the band of influence of one of the existing metropolitan rail lines, there is, still, $v_1 \cong v_2$, while elsewhere, where public transport is not competitive, the two speeds return to being significantly different.

Let us see now what happens if, starting from any situation of this type, the supply of road infrastructures is improved, leaving unchanged the supply of public transport services.

Functionally to such an investigation, it is useful to differentiate the modes of public transportation on the basis of the average speeds from the flows and to group them in three principal categories, as follows:

1. Speed rapidly decreasing as flows increase (bus and tram in mixed traffic);
2. Speed moderately decreasing as flows increase (bus and tram in reserved lane with possible preferential treatment at intersections)
3. Speed practically independent of the flows (light and heavy metropolitan rails).

In the presence of elevated levels of congestion, the average speed relative to each of the three above categories, taken singly, results in general: very minor (about half), roughly equal, a little greater than the average individual-vehicle speed. The average speed v_2 evaluated on the entire public transport network can result very or slightly different from v_1 according to the degree of reciprocal integration between the different components and of the percent contribution that each of the three components supplied in the execution of the average type trip.

Let $v_{2,1}$ and $v_{2,3}$ be the components of v_2 with respect to such categories.

For the same reason that v_1 is about the double of $v_{2,3}$, Δ_1 is also about the double of $\Delta v_{2,1}$. On the other hand, the fact that v_1 is about twice $v_{2,3}$ conjointly to the condition $v_1 \cong v_2$ implies that the contribution of the component in mixed traffic to the making of the average trip is relatively modest. Overall, therefore, the realisation of new infrastructures involves a modest variation of $v_{2,1}$ and a negligible one of v_1, while it is possible that significant variations occur in average per capita consumption. Still in proportion to the condition $v_1 \cong v_2$ it follows from this that the new equilibrium will not differ greatly from the preceding one, except for consumption y which will be able to vary even significantly in proportion to the size of the intervention. It follows, again, that to improve the characteristics of the point of equilibrium it is necessary to act prevalently on the components of the public transport which depend little or not at all on flow.

4 Conclusions

The theoretical considerations have shown that an investment in road infrastructures can have counterproductive effects in very particular cases.

The empirical analysis has highlighted the necessity of considering the low-density and medium- to high-density areas separately.

In the first, of the North American type, per capita fuel consumption is high because of heavy dependence on the private car, and the marginal role of public transport, highlighted by the non-correlation between the average speeds v_1 and v_2 and by the good correlation of the difference between them both with v_1 and with fuel consumption. In the middle-high density cities, of the European type, public transport is generally competitive. The existence of correlation between the average speeds v_1 and v_2 and the fact that these differ little from one to the other are significant indices of such competitiveness.

A first result of this analysis is the inadequacy of the theoretical framework examined which does not consider land use as an endogenous variable of the model. In this way, the effects of investments in urban road infrastructures on land use are not grasped.

A second result is that in the medium- to high-density cities the investments in infrastructures have modest short-term effects, as far as rush-hour equilibrium speeds are concerned, while they can produce quite considerable increases in energy consumption.

Some questions remain open that require deeper treatment both theoretically and empirically.

The first question regards the possibility that the cities belonging to each of the two groups concretely turn into one another as an effect—desired or not—of investments in the transport sector.

The second question regards the possibility of realising motorway investments in high-density areas, controlling their effects by means of the introduction of road-pricing policies.

These questions can be answered both theoretically—by means of models already available [5] or utilising more complicated integrated transport-territory models—and empirically, following particular field tests such as the new mass transit in low densities cities, e.g. Los Angeles or the motorways in high density cities, e.g. the planned underground motorways in the metropolitan areas of Paris.

References

1. Hillman, M., et al., *Personal Mobility and Transport Policy*, PEP Broadsheet 542, London, 1973.
2. Plowden, S. *Towns Against Traffic*, Andre Deutsch, London, 1973.
3. Schaeffer, K.H. & Sclar, E. *Access for All*, Penguin, London, 1975.
4. Goodwin, P.B. Demographic impacts, social consequences, and the transport debate, *Oxford Review of Economic Policy*, 1990, **6(2)**, 76-90.
5. Delle Site, P., & Filippi, F. Bus service optimization and car pricing policies to save fuel in urban areas, *Transportation Research-A*, forthcoming.
6. Tanjia, P.T., Clerx, W.C.G., Van Ham J., De Ligt T.J & Rijkeboer, R.C. *Possible Community Measures Aiming at Limiting CO$_2$ Emissions in Transport Sector*. TNO, The Netherlands, 1992.
7. Mogridge, M.J.H. *Travel in Towns*, Macmillan, London, 1990.
9. Williams, H.C.W.L., Lam, W.M., Austin, J. & Kim, K.S. Transport policy appraisal with equilibrium models III: investment benefits in multi-modal systems, *Transportation Research-B*, 1991, **25B**, 293-316.
10. Newman, P.W.G. & Kenworthy, J.R. *Cities and Automobile Dependence: a Sourcebook*, Gower Technical, Aldershot, 1989.
11. Mhoring, H. Optimization and scale economies in urban bus transportation, *American Economic Review*, 1972, **62(4)**, 591-604.
12. Filippi, F. L'innovazione tecnologica nel campo dei trasporti urbani, *Atti del convegno: Innovazione tecnologica, trasformazioni territoriali*, Rome, 1989.

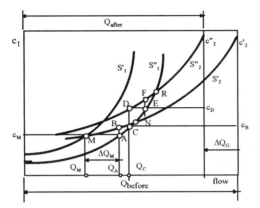

Figure 1: Downs-Thomson like equilibria.

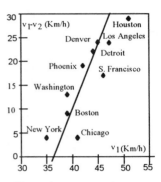

Figure 4: v_1-v_2 vs v_1 in some
North American cities.

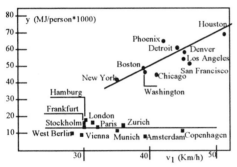

Figure 2: Fuel use per person vs average
speed by private car.

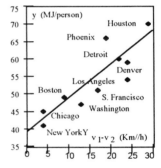

Figure 5: Fuel use per person vs
v_1-v_2 in some N.American cities.

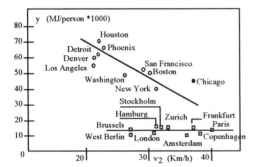

Figure 3: Fuel use per person vs average
speed by public transport.

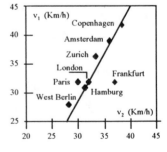

Figure 6: v_1 vs v_2 in some
European cities.

SECTION 5:
URBAN SAFETY

Advanced driver training – its potential role in developing attitudes and skills

D.S. Evans

Transport Research Group, University of Ulster at Jordanstown, Northern Ireland

Abstract

The research aimed to establish whether advanced driver training could be effective in improving road safety. The research focused on a study of the police (basing research on the Essex Police), an organisation which has introduced attitude and belief systems training due to the increasing number of accidents during police pursuits. Attitudes and skill levels of trainees were measured at the beginning and after each phase of training. The stability and longevity of trainees' attitudes were assessed at varying time intervals for each trainee after the training. In addition, an assessment was made of the influence of police driving instructors and police recruitment policy on attitude development. The research concluded that although police driver training (as instructed by the Essex Police) improves driving skills, there is little evidence to suggest that it develops 'safe' attitudes and beliefs towards driving with reference to road safety. If similar training was given to the general public, it is anticipated that such training can only be an effective measure in improving road safety for safety conscious individuals, as opposed to those with 'unsafe' attitudes towards driving.

1 Introduction

Research has shown that the majority of road accidents are primarily caused by human error [1]. One approach to reduce the level of human error in road travel is the development of advanced driver training programmes. However, studies of the effectiveness of advanced driver training programmes so far have produced inconsistent results [2, 3, 4]. Why is this the case if drivers are a major cause of accidents? One explanation is that such training programmes have traditionally focused on improving skills, with far less emphasis being placed on attitude development. The importance of attitude development in addition to skill development can be seen in a study by Parker et al [5] which discovered that drivers who have the most accidents are those who deliberately contravene legal and social norms with regard to driving. This indicates that accidents where drivers are to blame may not only be caused by poor driving skills, but also by driver attitude, which can manifest itself in deliberate violations of codes of road safety. The importance of driver attitude has been recognised by driver training organisations who now emphasise attitude development to a greater degree. However, the effectiveness of such schemes has yet to be established. It is within this context that the research was undertaken.

2 Research Background

The Police in Great Britain adopt an advanced driver training technique known as "The system of car control [6]". It involves the teaching of advanced motor skills and also emphasises forward planning and observation. Most other forms of advanced driver training currently available are based on this technique [7]. However, despite the training given, the number of accidents involving police drivers during police pursuits has increased sharply [8] and has led to growing public concern. Due to these problems, the traffic committee of the Association of Chief Police Officers [ACPO] reviewed police driving [9]. One recommendation of this review was the need to introduce attitude and belief systems training. This has led to police driving schools emphasising attitude development as part of driver training. At present it is not known how effective these changes have been.

The research was conducted at the Essex Police Driving School on their two phase Standard/Response police driver training course, set up following the ACPO report [9] with the aim of training attitudes, beliefs, and skills. Phase one is a four week standard driving course, and phase two is an additional two weeks intensive training in emergency response and containment tactics for those who perform well on the standard course. Phase two of the training also aims to emphasise a calm mental approach towards such driving. This is to ensure that drivers do not become over-excited from the rush of adrenalin which can occur at high speeds, possibly leading to dangerous and irrational driving manoeuvres.

3 Research Design

The primary aim of the research was to discover whether the driver training developed or changed 'safe' or 'unsafe' attitudes towards driving. 'Safe' and 'unsafe' attitudes towards driving were defined in terms of whether the possession of the attitude was deemed to be compatible or incompatible with the objectives of the course. As such, 'safe'/'unsafe' refers to whether responses elicited from attitude statements are consistent ('safe') or inconsistent ('unsafe') with the development of a calm mental approach to driving.

It is possible for an individual to possess numerous different attitudes towards driving. Initial research was therefore undertaken to identify which attitudes were most likely to contribute to unsafe driving to provide the focus for the research. 15 advanced driving instructors were interviewed, and the response training was observed intermittently over a four month period to establish whether there were any 'unsafe' driving attitudes being displayed by driver trainees. From the initial research it was decided to focus upon attitudes towards speed, and attitudes towards using speed to experience thrill and excitement when driving. In addition, if driver training is to be effective, trainees will have to have a positive attitude towards what is being taught, as otherwise there may be a reluctance to apply the skills, and hence change behaviour. Therefore attitudes towards the skills taught on the course were also measured.

Trainees were asked to complete a confidential questionnaire after each phase of the training stating their agreement or disagreement to attitude statements (on scales ranging from 1-7) referring to speed, thrill, excitement, and the skills taught on the course [6]. In addition, trainees were asked to watch several video sequences after each phase of training, and then complete a confidential questionnaire, stating the good and bad points observed in the videos. From the responses, attitudes and beliefs were deduced. The responses were compared to those obtained from Essex Police driving instructors (five instructors) and the 'expert' opinions of individuals from a variety of different advanced driver training and road safety organisations (12 people/organisations). To establish if responses were in accordance with the official police driver training technique, they were also evaluated by referring to the police driver training manual [6]. 78 trainees completed the questionnaires (43 trainees undertook the standard phase, and 33 undertook both phases of the training). The driving instructors who taught the trainees also completed similar questionnaires (to establish the extent to which they also possess 'safe' or 'unsafe' attitudes) and in addition assessed trainees attitudes and skill levels, and were asked what they believed the course aimed to achieve (a total of 18 instructors were used). The longevity of trainees attitudes was evaluated by sending the former trainees a confidential questionnaire (to be returned in a prepaid envelope) at various time intervals (ranging from three to ten months) after the training course. A 72% response rate was achieved. As with the research undertaken during the training course, the former trainees had to state their agreement or disagreement to attitude statements referring to speed, thrill, excitement, and the skills taught on the course [6]. In addition, they were asked which elements of the training they still used, and if this varied during work, or during leisure time. This was asked to determine whether the longevity of attitudes towards the skills taught varied for different elements of the training, and for different types of driving.

The development of 'safe' attitudes towards driving via training may be difficult if the police service attracts and recruits excitement seeking individuals. An assessment of recruitment policy was therefore undertaken to establish the extent to which this may be the case. All recruitment officers for police forces in England, Wales, and Scotland were sent a confidential questionnaire to complete (to be returned in a prepaid envelope). The questionnaire asked what qualities were sought in new police recruits, and whether excitement seeking enhanced recruitment. Only 24% (12) of questionnaires sent to recruitment officers were returned for analysis. Although the response rate was low, some useful insights into recruitment policy have been obtained.

4 Research Findings

Driver Trainees' Attitudes During the Course of Police Driver Training
Before, during, and immediately after the training, the majority of trainees have a positive attitude towards the skills taught on the course (87.9-98.6%, depending upon the scale used and the stage of training). However 44.9-72.7% (depending upon the scale used and the stage of training) also possess 'unsafe' attitudes towards high speed driving. Trainees who undertook the extra two week response phase of training possessed 'unsafe' attitudes towards high speed driving to a greater degree, both before and immediately after training. The differences are not significant at the beginning of training ($p > 0.05$), but become significant on two of the three scales used ($p < 0.01$-0.05) after the standard, and after the response phase of training. The training appeared to exacerbate 'unsafe' attitudes in trainees who undertook the response phase, having the opposite effect on those who only undertook the standard phase.

From analysing the video sequences, it was deduced that trainees in general displayed attitudes and beliefs that were in accordance with the philosophy of the course [6]. However, after each phase of training, it seemed that some trainees possessed 'unsafe' beliefs regarding the use of speed (e.g. "good pace"), although it must be noted that the numbers involved were small.

Overall, it appears that police driver training is ineffective in developing 'safe' attitudes towards speed. In addition, the selection procedure for response training appears to favour trainees with 'unsafe' attitudes. Driving instructors however were unaware of the existence of these problems believing that the majority of trainees generally had 'safe' attitudes towards driving at the end of the standard (83.2%) and response (93.9%) phase of training.

Skill Assessment
Driving instructors rated the majority of trainees positively in terms of overall driving skill after the standard (72.9%) and response phase (88%) of training. Trainees who went on to undertake the response phase of training were rated

significantly more positively (p< 0.001) after each phase of training than trainees who only undertook the standard phase of training. This may display the fact that only trainees with a high standard of driving skill are permitted to undertake the extra two week response phase. It is worth noting that there were no significant increases (p> 0.05) in the rating of overall driving skill for trainees selected for the response phase of training on completion of this phase. A possible explanation for this is that an additional two weeks may not be long enough to further develop overall levels of driving skill. Pursuit and containment skills are usually allocated more time to be developed by other police driving schools (e.g. the Metropolitan Police).

Longevity of Driver Trainees' Attitudes
Three to ten months after the training, attitudes towards speed, thrill, and excitement remained relatively constant. However, attitudes towards the skills taught on the course remained positive, but to a significantly lesser degree (p< 0.000-0.05) than before, during, and immediately after the training. This may explain why several skills taught on the course (the six feature system, the use of speed, gear, and steering techniques) are no longer used by a sizeable number of trainees during their leisure time (23-47%), and a small number (0-17%) during police duty.

Driver Instructor Research
Although attitude development is a key objective of the course, only 21% of instructors explicitly emphasised attitude development as something that the course was trying to achieve. In addition, the skills taught on the response phase of the training were emphasised as something the course was trying to achieve, despite the fact that these skills were only taught on the last third of the course. For example, 47% of instructors stated "safe and alert at high speeds to cope with emergency calls" (a major element of the response phase of training), yet only 10.5% stated "good observation and planning" (a major element of the standard phase of training) as one of the major things the Standard/Response training programme is trying to achieve. As these skills to a large extent involve the use of speed, it might be that speed was over-emphasised.

An assessment of driving instructors attitudes revealed that a large number of instructors possessed 'unsafe' attitudes towards speed, thrill, and excitement. (31.6-57.9%, depending upon which scale was used). If driving instructors display such attitudes in their behaviour, it may affect the way the use of speed is taught and perceived. It is therefore not surprising that little change in trainees' attitudes towards these aspects of driving was discovered.

An analysis of responses to video sequences revealed that there is some evidence to suggest that driving instructors may not be correctly teaching overtaking techniques and the use of speed. For example, the majority of trainees (61% after the standard phase and 71% after the response phase of training), and all the police driving instructors who watched the videos (five instructors) gave positive beliefs regarding the first overtake shown on the video. However, in terms of the police driving technique [9], the overtake was incorrectly undertaken, with the wrong gear chosen (confirmed by the Chief Inspector of the Essex Police Driving School). If the technique was taught correctly, such beliefs would not be stated.

Recruitment Policy Research

The recruitment policy research revealed that excitement seeking is not regarded as a quality recruitment officers believe new recruits should possess. Rather, many of the qualities stated appeared to be compatible with an attitude towards driving which is conducive to road safety; for example, maturity (33%), common sense (33%), and concern for the well being of society (8%). However, the majority of recruitment officers (65%) believed that the enjoyment of exciting situations enhanced recruitment. 50% of the recruitment officers who stated this believed that this was due to the media glamorising and highlighting the more exciting elements of police work. In the 1960's and 1970's, police television series in Great Britain began to emphasise the elements of police work that involved action and excitement, with high speed car chases becoming common occurrences [10]. This portrayal of the work of the police as being of all action and excitement may therefore lead to the service attracting and recruiting some excitement seeking individuals, and could in turn contribute to the development of an occupational culture that emphasises speed and excitement. There is some evidence of this from studies of the police service [11, 12].

5 Discussion

If an individual possesses a high standard of driving skill, it could be argued that 'unsafe' attitudes may not necessarily produce accidents or dangerous driving. However, the Standard/Response course of the Essex Police is essentially only a modified standard police driving course, and is limited in the degree to which advanced skills can be developed. As some former trainees do not always use some of the skills taught, and some skills might have been taught incorrectly, it is possible that 'unsafe' attitudes may be potentially dangerous to possess. In addition, having an 'unsafe' attitude towards speed may cause drivers to drive fast whenever possible, rather than when it is required. This may cause them to take unnecessary risks when driving.

It is possible to drive fast and safely without experiencing thrill and excitement. In such a situation drivers will be in a better state to deal with incidents they are called to when reaching them. From observing several advanced driving instructors at the Essex Police Driving School, a calm and relaxed mental state appeared to be displayed. A study by Pritchard [19] of police drivers who were considered as role models by their peers also discovered this.

6 Conclusions

There seems to be little evidence to suggest that the Standard/Response driver training course of the Essex Police develops 'safe' attitudes and beliefs towards driving, despite introducing changes to driver training. This could be due to a lack of emphasis on attitude development by driving instructors, the driving instructors' attitudes, and the problem of the police service attracting some excitement seeking individuals. Skills (in terms of instructors' assessments) do seem to be developed, although the degree to which the response phase develops pursuit and containment skills is questionable.

The majority of advanced driver training organisations which conduct courses for the general public in the United Kingdom (e.g. the Institute of Advanced Motorists, and the Royal Society for the Prevention of Accidents) adopt the police driving technique [6], although would not teach skills such as pursuit and containment (as these are specialist skills required by a police officer). The degree of emphasis given by these organisations to attitude development is not known. In general, these courses are undertaken voluntarily by people who are prepared to devote time and money to improve their driving ability. Although individuals who opt for such training are likely to be more safety conscious (having a 'safe' attitude towards driving before training), it can be argued that such training programmes can only have a potential role to improve road safety if they have developed techniques that can change attitudes and beliefs towards driving, placing greater emphasis on attitude development than the Standard/Response course of the Essex Police at the time of the research. This could be true, particularly if such training became mandatory for all drivers to undertake, as instruction would possibly have to be given to individuals possessing a range of 'unsafe' attitudes towards driving, many of which would need to be corrected through a programme of attitude development.

References

1.   Sabey B.E. & Taylor, H. The known risks we run: The highway, Transport and Road Research Laboratory, Supplementary Report 567, Crowthorne, 1980

2.   Hoinville, G. Befouled, R. & Mackie, A.M. A study of accident rates among motorists who passed or failed an advanced driving test, Report LR 499, Transport and Road Research Laboratory, Crowthorne, 1972

3. Lund, A.K. & Williams, A.F. A review of the literature evaluating the defensive driving course, Accident Analysis and Prevention, 1985, V 17 (6) pp448-460

4. Sstuckman-Johnson D.L., Lund A.K., Williams A.F. & Osborne D.W. Comparative effects of driver improvement programmes on crashes and violations, Accident Analysis and Prevention, 1989, V21 (3), pp203-215

5. Parker, D., Manstead, A.S.R., Stradling, S.G. & Reason, J.T. Determinants of intentions to commit driving violations, Accident Analysis and Prevention, 1992, V24 (2), pp117-131

6. Roadcraft. The Police Drivers Manual, London, HMSO, 1977.

7. Amey, P. Why the police need to rewrite the rulebook, Autocar and Motor, 1989, 19 July , pp18-19

8. The Daily Telegraph. Car chase code to be adopted by police forces, 16 June, 1989, pp11

9. Association of Chief Police Officers. Working Party Police Driver Training Report, Greater Manchester Police, 1989

10. Clarke, A. Television Police Series and Law and Order, In Politics, Ideology, and Popular Culture 2, the Open University Press, Milton Keynes, 1982, pp37-58

11. Holdaway, S. Inside the British Police: A Force at Work, Basil Blackwell Publisher Ltd, Oxford, 1983

12. Smith, D.J. & Gray, J. The Police and People in London, The PSI Report, Gower Publishing Co Ltd, Aldershot, 1985

13. Pritchard, J. Attitudes of Traffic Police Drivers, A Study of Excellence in the Thames Valley Area to Support the Introduction of Driver Attitude Training to Police Driving Schools, The Driving Business Associates, Oxford, 1993

Effect of driver fatigue on truck accident rates

F.F. Saccomanno, M. Yu, J.H. Shortreed
Department of Civil Engineering, University of Waterloo, Waterloo, Ontario, Canada N2L 3G1

Abstract

A preliminary statistical link is established between truck driver fatigue and truck accident rates, where fatigue could be a contributing factor. Two criteria are used to identify driver fatigue in the police accident report: fatigue reported as a primary cause of the accident, and fatigue as inferred from the report using indirect measures, such as "driver being at-fault in a single vehicle accident". Truck accident rates are estimated for different fatigue criteria and linked to factors such as, hours of driving per day without rest, driving at night, and driving in remote areas. Significantly higher fatigue accident rates were obtained for driving longer than 9.5 hours per day without rest, for driving at night, and for driving in remote areas. These factors were found to have a cumulative effect on fatigue-related truck accident rates.

1   Driver Fatigue as a Safety Concern

Truck accidents typically result in a disproportionately large number of deaths and personal injuries. A major cause of these accidents is driver fatigue. In the 1950's, Prokop and Prokop reported that of 569 truck drivers surveyed 18% acknowledged to having fallen "asleep at the wheel" at one time or another in their careers (cited in McDonald, 1984). In a similar study carried out about two decades later, Tilley reported that of 155 truck drivers surveyed 64% were subject to some form of fatigue on a regular basis, and that about 10% of these drivers actually acknowledged to having been involved in at least one accident while affected by fatigue (cited in McDonald, 1984). A recent American Automobile Association study suggested that driver fatigue occurs on a routine basis on highways in the United States, especially where trucks are considered.

To reduce the incidence of driver fatigue in truck accidents a number of jurisdictions have introduced regulations limiting the hours of continuous driving to a maximum of 10 to 12 hours per day (Yu, 1994). The effectiveness of these types of regulations, however, has not been well established or researched, due in large part to a failure to establish a good empirical link between driver fatigue and accident propensity for different driver attributes and different driving conditions. In the absence of such a link, drivers will inevitably be guided by economic considerations to ignore fatigue-based regulations (Trimac, 1991). A clear and objective understanding of the link between fatigue and accident involvement is necessary, therefore, to develop effective fatigue mitigating strategies, that will be subject to industry-wide compliance and enforcement.

To establish such a link between driver fatigue and truck accident rates three steps need to be taken: 1) gaining a thorough understanding of the nature of driver fatigue and of the conditions under which it arises, 2) establishing objective and reliable methods for measuring fatigue, and 3) establishing a good empirical relationship between fatigue and truck accident involvement. The study reported in this paper applies this three step process to Ontario truck accident and exposure data.

2   Defining and Measuring Driver Fatigue

Grandjean (1988) *defines fatigue* in general terms as a "loss of efficiency or a disinclination to any kind of effort"; this disinclination can be muscular and/or mental in nature. Three types of fatigue are considered to have a special effect on truck driving performance: industrial, cumulative and circadian fatigue.

Industrial fatigue arises from working continuously over an extended period of time without proper rest. This type of fatigue is very likely to be the main cause of fatigue-related truck accidents. In their study of industrial fatigue in truck drivers, Mackie and Miller (1980) found that in over 65% of cases, truck accidents took place during the second half of a trip, regardless of trip length. The changeover from "less than expected" to "more than expected" numbers of accidents was found to take place at about 5 hours of continuous driving. On the basis of this evidence, the authors concluded that truck drivers were more predisposed to experience accidents during the latter stages of each trip and this was due in large part to the onset of industrial fatigue. A similar finding was reported by Matousek (1982), who recommended the scheduling of at least one rest stop for every 8 hour shift of continuous work. To be effective in reducing industrial fatigue, Matousek went on to suggest that each rest stop should be longer than 20 minutes in duration.

Cumulative fatigue arises from working for too many days on any protracted, repetitive task without any prolonged break. This type of fatigue manifests itself most often in a loss of alertness caused mainly by familiarization and boredom. Long distance truck driving, where shipments can take several days to complete, is especially susceptible to the onset of cumulative fatigue. Mackie and Miller (1985) suggested that cumulative fatigue is most problematic in journeys of six or more consecutive days. To reduce the incidence of cumulative fatigue, Matousek (1982) recommended periodic task rotation in order to regain interest in a particular activity such as driving, eg. drivers can be assigned to loading and unloading activities, or to paper work at the shipping depot, etc.

Circadian fatigue, the third type of fatigue affecting truck drivers, is caused by deviations from unique bio-rhythms in the body ... a physiological pre-disposition to work that favours regular daytime schedules over irregular nighttime work. Circadian fatigue is perhaps the most difficult to identify under normal driving conditions, because it is strongly influenced by a wide range of factors, such as, living habits, medical history of the driver, time of day, seasonal factors, availability of sunlight, etc. A survey of truck drivers subject to irregular hours of work found that 50% of accidents involving fatigue took place between midnight and eight in the morning (Mackie and Miller, 1985). Since only 19% of truck shipments were scheduled during this period, fatigue-related accident rates at night were reported to be 7 times higher than the daytime rates for similar road and traffic conditions. The main reason for these differences in accident rates was given as circadian fatigue. In his study of fatigue, Matousek (1982) noted that for many workers morning is the most productive time of the day, and that this productivity drops off sharply by evening and into the early morning hours before dawn.

Any empirical study attempting to establish a link between driver fatigue and truck accidents must first establish acceptable procedures for *measuring fatigue*. The most acceptable procedure for measuring fatigue is to monitor   brain   activity   over   an   extended   period   of   time   using electroencephalography. In this approach, brain waves are classified into different rhythms, each rhythm reflecting a unique pre-disposition to certain types of response. For example, beta rhythms in the range 14-30 Hz reflect increased alertness or arousal reaction. (Grandjean, 1988) Light frequency can also be used to measure fatigue on the basis of subject response (eye flickers).

Using this procedure, researchers have found that perception/reaction time varies with the number of stimuli received. Reaction/perception time in a driving context includes the recognition of danger (for example an obstruction on the roadway ahead), decision on suitable response (whether to apply the brakes or to steer clear of the hazard) and finally, action taken (applying the brakes and coming to a controlled stop before impact).

3   Methodology

The detailed electroencephalography approach was not available for this study. Nevertheless, accident and exposure data were available that could yield indirect measures of driver fatigue, and provide some preliminary statistical evidence concerning the link between driver fatigue and truck accident rates, where fatigue is identified as a possible causal factor.

In this study, three relationships were tested to demonstrate the effect of driver fatigue on fatigue accident rates:

     1.   Regional factors (reflecting industrial and circadian fatigue)
     2.   Hours of driving (night or day) without rest (reflecting industrial fatigue)
and 3.   Driving in night or day conditions (reflecting circadian fatigue)

Large truck accidents (at least one truck involved) were extracted from 1988-89 Ontario police reports for a sample of highway sections. These accidents were classified as fatigue accidents on the basis of two criteria:

a)   Direct evidence on fatigue as reported by the police. Two conditions need to be satisfied: 1) single vehicle truck accidents where the driver was reported as being "at fault", **and** 2) the primary cause of the accident was ascribed by the police to truck driver fatigue. These accidents have been designated as **"fatigue-suspected"** accidents.

b)   Less restrictive evidence that fatigue could be a contributing factor. Only one of two conditions in (a) needs to be satisfied.

Hours of driving profiles for night and day were estimated from the reported hours in the Ontario Commercial Vehicle Survey (CVS,1988) for each highway section containing a survey station. The CVS data provides information on commercial vehicle attributes at 72 representative stations located throughout the provincial highway network (42 southern region and 30 northern region stations). Used in conjunction with information on average annual daily traffic on each CVS section (obtained from the Ontario Traffic Volume Information System database), the procedure yields basic estimates of highway section hours of driving profiles (night and day) for all trucks in the traffic stream, ie. percentage trucks versus hours of driving from last rest stop. From these profiles, the 85th percentile hour was obtained on each CVS section (ie. the hour exceeded by 15% of all trucks in the traffic stream). **In using the CVS data to obtain section-specific 85th percentile hours of driving values, the basic assumption made is that conditions prevalent on the day of the survey at each CVS highway section remain in effect on the same section over the entire year.** Analysis of Variance (ANOVA) and simple linear regression techniques were used to test the significance of the relationship between fatigue truck accident rates (for either of the two fatigue criteria defined above) and factors reflecting both industrial and circadian fatigue. Since the Ontario CVS data does not permit a tracking of shipments over several days, the effect of cumulative fatigue on accidents could not considered in this analysis.

4   Discussion of Results

Northern highway sections in Ontario are characterised by long stretches of remote two lane roads, where traffic volume are low, where trucks comprise a significant share of traffic, and where opportunities for rest along the route are limited. Southern highway sections, on the other hand, are characterised by shorter line haul distances, higher traffic volumes with lower percentage trucks and an increased opportunity for rest along the route. Conditions in the northern region appear to be more conducive to the on-set of industrial fatigue, and higher associated accident rates where fatigue is a contributing factor.

"Fatigue-suspected" accident rates for each CVS highway section were estimated for northern and southern regions. To increase the number of cases for analysis, accident and exposure data for both 1988 and 1989 were combined into a single data base.

The results of a simple one-way ANOVA (fatigue-suspected accident rates by region) are summarised in **Table 1**. An average fatigue-suspected accident rate of 0.237 accidents per million vehicle-kilometres was estimated for the northern region, which can be compared to a value of 0.114 accidents per million vehicle-kilometres in the southern region. These results suggest that conditions prevalent along more remote highway sections (longer distance driving, boredom) could be contributing to higher fatigue-suspected truck accident rates.

Fatigue-suspected accident rates were also estimated province-wide (northern and southern regions combined) for different hours of driving, expressed as the 85th percentile hour on each highway section. Fatigue-suspected truck accident rates do not increase uniformly at all hours of driving. A significant discontinuity (sharp increase) in the accident rate relationship was observed at 9.5 hours. Below the 9.5 hour value, fatigue-suspected truck accident rates were found to be relatively insensitive to changes in the hours of driving. The ANOVA results in **Table 2** suggest that significantly higher accident rates take place on sections where the 85th percentile hours of driving exceeds 9.5 hours. An average fatigue-suspected rate of 0.109 truck accidents per million vehicle-kilometres was obtained for less than 9.5 hours of driving, which can be compared to an average rate of 0.235 accidents per million vehicle-kilometres for hours of driving that exceed 9.5 hours; a difference that was found to be statistically significant at the 1% level.

The combination of geographic region and hours of driving in a two-way ANOVA suggested an additive effect on fatigue-suspected truck accident rates. This result confirms that factors reflecting increased industrial fatigue (in this case remoteness of northern highway sections and increased hours of continuous driving) individually contribute to significantly higher fatigue-suspected accident rates.

The effect of circadian fatigue on truck accident rates was considered by estimating single vehicle accident rates for night and day conditions and for different hours of driving (85th percentile less than or equal to 9.5 hours and greater than 9.5 hours). As indicated in **Figure 1**, significantly higher single vehicle accident rates were obtained for nighttime driving for both hours of driving categories. Introducing both day and night driving and hours of driving together in the ANOVA yielded higher accident rates at night, especially for more than 9.5 hours of continuous driving. These results indicate that circadian fatigue (expressed in terms of day and night conditions) has an additive effect on single vehicle accident rates, when combined with hours of driving (an indicator of industrial fatigue). An average single vehicle accident rate of 0.419 accident per million vehicle-kilometres was obtained for more than 9.5 hours of driving at night, as compared to an average rate of 0.058 accident per million vehicle-kilometres for less than 9.5 hours of continuous driving during the day, a 7 fold increase.

A two-way ANOVA was carried out to assess the sensitivity of the fatigue criteria used in explaining the relationship between accident rates and hours of driving. Fatigue-suspected accident rates were found to differ significantly from single vehicle truck accident rates for the same hour of driving values ($F = 7.94$ for 2 Degrees of Freedom). While the nature of the fatigue criteria was found to affect the accident rate estimates, the choice of fatigue criteria did not alter the basic conclusion that higher accident rates took place at higher hours of driving ($F=5.33$ for 2 DoF). The interaction effect between hours of driving and fatigue criteria was not found to be statistically significant ($F=1.20$ at 4 DoF). Again the largest discontinuity in fatigue accident rates for hours of driving took place at 9.5 hours.

5   Conclusions

The results of this preliminary statistical analysis of Ontario truck accident data support the assertion that higher levels of driver fatigue (both industrial and circadian) result in significantly higher truck accident rates. The effect of both types of fatigue on accident rates appears to be cumulative in nature.

Notwithstanding concerns about limitations in the data and the measures used to reflect fatigue in these data, this study has provided some basic statistical evidence that truck driver fatigue poses a special problems for truck safety, and this issue needs to be addressed in a more in-depth manner.

6   References

Grandjean, E. *Fitting the Task to the Man.* Taylor and Francis. London, UK, 1988.

Mackie, D.H. and Miller, J.C. Effects of Irregular Schedules and Physical Work on Commercial Driver Fatigue and Performance, *Human Factors in Transport Research*, Academic Press Inc. London, UK, 1980.

Matousek, M. *Measures Against Errors in the Building Process*, Swiss Federal Institute of Technology, Zurich, Switzerland, 1982.

McDonald, N. *Fatigue, Safety and the Truck Driver*, Taylor and Francis Inc. Philadelphia, PA, 1984.

Trimac Consulting. *Owner Operator Costs and Earnings Comparison in Canada/US Transborder Trucking.* Final report for Transport Canada, T8080-1-6099, Calgary, Canada, 1991.

Yu, M. *Effect of Driver Fatigue on Commercial Vehicle Accidents*, Unpublished M.A.Sc. Thesis, Department of Civil Engineering, University of Waterloo, Canada, 1994.

Table 1.   **Analysis of Variance of Fatigue-Suspected Accident Rates by Region**

Category	# Sections	Sum	Average	Variance
Northern Region	30	7.112	0.237	0.013
Southern Region	42	4.770	0.114	0.006

ANOVA Summary:				
Source of Variation	SS	df	MS	F (P-value)
Between Groups	0.267	1	0.267	29.6 (0000)
Within Groups	0.631	70	0.009	
Total	0.898	71		

Table 2.   **Analysis of Variance of Fatigue-Suspected Accident Rates by Hours of Driving (85th Percentile)**

Category	# Sections	Sum	Average	Variance
LE 9.5 Hours	40	4.370	0.1093	0.0062
GT 9.5 Hours	32	7.512	0.2347	0.0121

ANOVA Summary:

Source of Variation	SS	df	MS	F (P-value)
Between Groups	0.2800	1	0.2800	31.70 (0.000)
Within Groups	0.6183	70	0.0088	
Total	0.8982	71		

Figure 1.   **Single Vehicle Truck Accident Rates by Night and Day for Different Hours of Driving.**

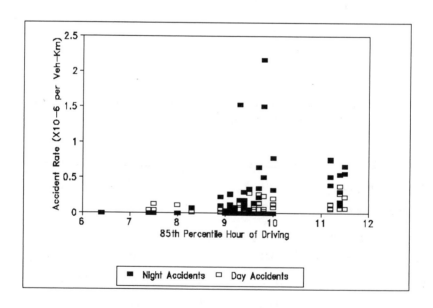

SECTION 6:
EMERGING TECHNOLOGIES

The Bruntel planetary disc extended expansion 2-stroke engine with variable valve control

K. Hall

Bruntel Limited, Maidenhead, Berkshire SL6 3PF, UK

Abstract

A low compression / high expansion ratio spark ignition engine strategy is proposed as a means of achieving ultra low exhaust emission vehicles using a low octane non carcinogenic fuel. Predicted fuel economy is better than a direct injection Diesel engine. Variable capacity capability by means of pulse valve control together with stratified charge mixture control determine the performance output via a fully balanced compact drive mechanism.

1. Introduction

The thermal efficiency of automotive engines has been limited since their inception over a century ago by common compression and expansion ratios of fixed volume. Part load efficiency is limited with the Diesel engine due to friction resulting from high levels of compression work and with the spark ignition engine due to intake throttling. Essential ingredients for an internal combustion engine capable of meeting future emission and fuel consumption requirements are likely to include the following:

1. A high expansion ratio for maximum temperature drop of the working fluid,
        a. to achieve optimum thermal efficiency,
        b. to minimise CO_2 emissions,
        c. to reduce exhaust noise.
2. A low compression ratio,
        a. to minimise negative work   -   friction,
        b. to lower peak temperature   -   reduced NO_x emissions,
        c. to reduce knock sensitivity   -   lower octane number,
                                       -   eliminate fuel carcinogens.

3. Spark ignition to fire the low compression charge.
4. Lean burn stratified charge control,
        a. to minimise NO_x, HC and CO emissions,
        b. to modulate engine output.
5. Variable capacity engine control,
        a. to increase part load efficiency - eliminate intake throttling,
        b. to increase torque back up - driveability.

2. Pulse Valve Solution

Pulse valve control allows the start of compression to be changed in order to vary the effective engine operating capacity whilst retaining the optimum expansion ratio. The Bruntel solution described in this paper (patent pending) uses solenoid activation / control of the exhaust valve in combination with an inlet valve that opens in response to cylinder depression. Hence, the induction phase automatically follows the exhaust phase without the need for camshafts or drive mechanisms. Pulse tuning phenomena are applied to the exhaust process to evacuate the cylinder and reflect the outgoing positive wave back from the expansion box creating the necessary cylinder depression to trigger open the inlet valve and initiate induction. Pulse tuning is also applied to the induction system , with the negative wave being reflected from the intake plenum back into the cylinder as a positive charge. Normally, variable length pipes would be required to optimise the pulse tuning at each speed, but by employing a fixed solenoid pulse period the engine is optimally tuned for all speeds using conventional fixed geometry manifolds.

With such a robust pulse tuned system it is not necessary to employ the extra revolution for induction used by the 4-stroke engine or the crankcase compression of the 2-stroke engine. Instead the expansion phase occupies the power stroke with exhaust, induction and compression phases occupying the return stroke. The intake system may be pressure charged. Such a 2-stroke cycle is only suitable up to half the speed of the typical 4-stroke automotive engine before it runs out of sufficient crank angle to accommodate the three phases in the return stroke, but this simply restricts operation to the quietest most efficient speed range.

Cylinder Head

Figure 1. shows a low compression cylinder head arrangement capable of operating as described. A compact chamber and late fuel admission are selected to enhance the low octane capability. Such a low octane design should allow the fuel scientist to eliminate high octane carcinogenic agents from the fuel. The spark plug is arranged centrally in the cylinder with concentric annular inlet and exhaust valves encircling it. The double seats of the annular valves offer very large areas and rapid rates of opening required to achieve rapid pulse charging. The exhaust valve is outermost and activated by a pair of solenoids. The inlet channel feeds two annular inlet valves which are spring loaded to respond to differential pressure, the innermost valve feeding the fuel rich mixture into the central core of the cylinder under the spark plug, achieving radial segregation from the exhaust port. Guide vanes pressed into the annular inlet ports provide precision turbulence generation for optimum combustion and support the light inlet valves against combustion pressure. Such a pulse valve system is controlled by the exhaust solenoids with fuel quantities adjusted accordingly via port injection.

Variable Capacity
Engine working capacity is decreased by simply retarding the exhaust solenoid timing, or increased by advancing it. As engine speed falls so the capability to increase capacity rises.   Such a characteristic reduces the number of transmission gears required. Figure 2. shows five modulation scenarios across the engine load / speed range.

Urban Economy
The urban mode (low load / low speed / weak stratified mixture) operates most efficiently when the highest peak temperature is generated for a given net cycle work. This implies the lowest charge mass (small engine capacity), lowest engine speed and highest temperature drop for the given work condition. With full expansion approaching atmospheric pressure, and compression capacity / engine speed selected to achieve the highest operating temperature, the pulse valve engine is predicted to offer substantially higher urban economy than the best Diesel. The fully balanced planetary disc drive mechanism described later enables the low engine speeds to be achieved without increased harshness. At low engine speeds and low loads, exhaust, induction and compression account for only a proportion of the return stroke. Similarly, the total swept volume is larger than the full expansion volume required. The solution is to continue expansion to bottom dead centre and then recompress until the pressure has returned to just above atmospheric before opening the exhaust valve. The losses entailed in such a process are small compared to throttling losses or the high compression / friction losses of the Diesel.

The weak stratified mixture combined with the precision concentric combustion process endows the engine with ultra low emission potential. The lower compression ratios (excluding the capacity boosted condition) contribute significantly to the engines ultra low NO_x potential. The engine is also likely to be far more tolerant of spark retard because of the extra expansion volume available.

Cruise Economy
The typical cruise condition of half load / half speed is able to use the large engine expansion capacity to fully expand the combustion products, eliminating the critical exhaust pressure ratio which causes supersonic exhaust flow and high exhaust noise. The extended expansion combined with the advantageous

work ratio as a result of the small amount of compression work (Atkinson cycle) endows the engine with predicted brake thermal efficiency higher than the best direct injection automotive Diesel engine. While full expansion is maintained, efficiency increases as the peak temperature is increased, i.e. as engine load increases.

High Torque

If more torque is required, for example to climb a gradient, the exhaust solenoid timing is advanced by demand from the accelerator pedal, increasing the effective engine capacity and increasing the air / fuel ratio towards stoichiometric. At lower engine speeds a larger effective capacity is achievable because the fixed exhaust and induction phases account for a much smaller proportion of the crankshaft revolution. This characteristic of rising torque with falling speed more closely matches vehicle torque requirements, making the vehicle easier to drive and requiring fewer transmission gears. In high torque mode the efficiency benefits of extended expansion are sacrificed to meet the extra performance requirements. Even so the brake thermal efficiency is predicted to match the highest levels attainable by current spark ignition engines.

The non carcinogenic octane number is likely to determine the level of capacity boosted torque available.

High Power

In the acceleration mode of high power (high load / high speed / stoichiometric mixture) the expansion volume is cut back in order to accommodate a like compression volume. Thermal efficiency is predicted to remain equivalent to current spark ignition engines of similar expansion ratio. With like efficiency and like power strokes per minute as 4-stroke engines maximum performance is predicted as being similar, assuming like volumetric efficiencies.

Downhill

The flexibility of pulse valve control enables the engine to function as a brake for downhill situations. Fuel is cut off and the exhaust timing fully retarded. Now the cylinder itself produces the depression necessary to trigger open the inlet valves and draw in air. The return stroke is used to compress the air and exhaust it. This is a useful additional means of braking.

3. Disc-Yoke Connector

Propulsion system weight and package volume plays a significant role in influencing the overall vehicle efficiency. As a result a disc-yoke mechanism for converting linear to rotary motion is proposed which markedly reduces engine weight and size (Figure 3.). A planetary disc and piston yoke replace the conventional connecting rod. The coupling of a second disc - yoke at 90 degrees to the first on a common crankpin results in a constant radial inertial force through the crankpin and crankshaft axes at all crankshaft angles. This force is equivalent to the reciprocating mass of one cylinder line acting radially at the centre of the crankpin. Inertial torque is completely eliminated because of the radial direction of the inertial force. Complete counterbalancing of primary forces and couples is achieved by lightening holes close to the outer diameter of the flywheel and front pulley.

The throw of the crank and planetary disc are each one quarter of the stroke and counter-rotate at constant angular velocity producing simple harmonic motion. Hence, higher orders of imbalance are eliminated. Yoke guides react side loads in the yoke, eliminating piston side loads for conditions of concentric combustion and thus the requirement for piston skirts. This results in an extremely compact crankcase assembly and eliminates side loads from the removable cylinder barrels. The crankshaft is stiffened by through bolting of the crankpin and this facilitates engine assembly.

Propulsion system smoothness is predicted as better than existing 6 cylinder 4-stroke engines.

Bearing Friction

The oil channels in the planetary discs are also used to control bearing area at each angular position of the crankshaft according to a constant bearing pressure strategy. A small crankpin area results from the stiff short throw crankshaft and long shared bearing length. These factors together with roller main bearings and elimination of piston skirts achieve a quantum reduction in engine rubbing areas which more than offsets the higher side forces experienced by the piston yoke compared to the piston skirt.

Ancillaries

Ancillary drives have been considerably simplified by adopting a concentric flywheel / starter / generator where the rotor is also the flywheel mass (Figure 4.). Such a concept offers the additional potential of regenerative braking to be integrated into the control strategy. It is also proposed to use oil cooling to simplify the vehicle package. The powertrain would be light enough for the vehicle not to require power steering.

Package

The V4 engine shown in Figure 4. easily packages in a front wheel drive vehicle either north / south or east / west and provides a firing pulse every 90 degrees for smoother operation. The power density target is 1kW/kg which exceeds the best volume production performance engines. The energy density of. lead acid battery propulsion systems are typically 40 fold worse than standard spark ignition systems.

Further Bruntel proposals for a safer / lighter vehicle concept are beyond the scope of this paper.

4. Summary

The Bruntel planetary disc extended expansion 2-stroke stratified charge engine with pulse valve variable capacity control offers improved vehicle economy from idle up to the capacity boosted full load performance condition through improved thermodynamics and control strategies.   Urban and cruise modes benefit most. Better matched torque characteristics improve driveability.

The reduced sensitivity to octane number as a result of the low compression ratio regime offers the opportunity to eliminate carcinogenic fuel blends and improve refinery efficiency levels. The low compression regime also implies low NO_x emissions and lean burn stratified charge offers ultra low levels of NO_x, HC and CO. The improved thermal efficiency and low idle speed equates to reduced CO_2 emissions without the particulate emissions associated with Diesels. The emissions signature is of a propulsion system with the potential to meet ultra low emission vehicle standards without resort to expensive package unfriendly after treatment devices.

The disc - yoke connector mechanism offers smoother reciprocating propulsion systems with ultra low idle speed potential and outstanding weight and package reductions.

In comparison a battery propulsion system requires further technological breakthroughs to make its range, performance and efficiency anywhere near comparable.

Such a pulse valve propulsion system merits serious consideration for all forms of urban transportation because its environmental credentials are so attractive and the solution is based on known technological principles.

Internal combustion propulsion systems are unlikely to meet zero emission criteria even if the hydrocarbon fuel were replaced by hydrogen, as such a fuel is still likely to produce NO_x emissions.

A hybrid propulsion system with limited range and performance in the zero emission mode is one solution for densely populated environments. The pulse valve engine with its integral starter / generator and reduced weight / package volume is ideally configured to meet this challenge simply by enlarging the generator and adding the necessary battery power.

The pulse valve engine epitomises simple efficiency, essential ingredients for all transportation systems, from the smallest to the largest.

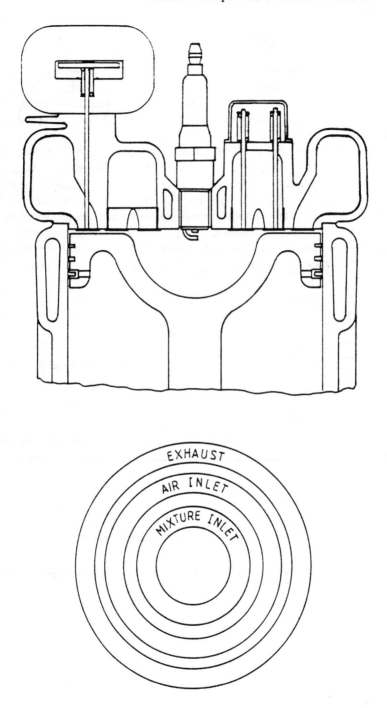

Figure 1: Annular pulse valve low compression cylinder head.

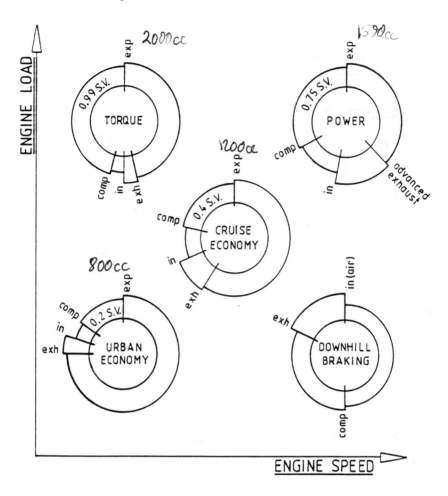

Figure 2: Load - speed effects on valve timing and capacity.

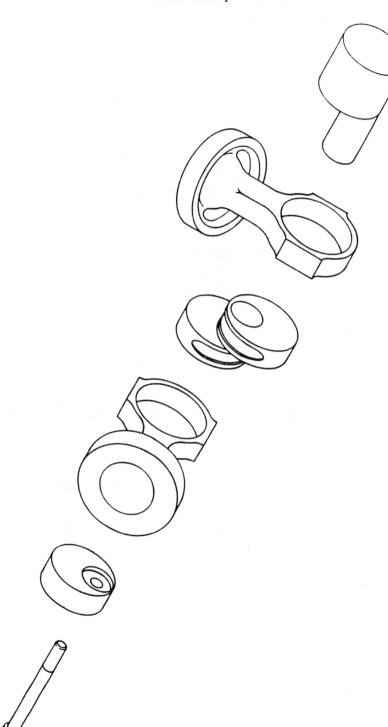

Figure 3: Bruntel disc - yoke connector mechanism.

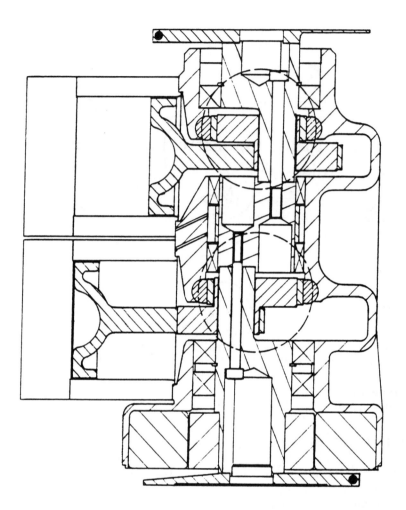

Figure 4: Bruntel V4 disc - yoke engine.

Road tests on the smallest urban vehicle: the electric bike

A. Folchini

Aerospace Engineering Department, Politecnico di Milano, 20133 Milano, Italy

Abstract

In this work we explain the philosophy of the project and the road tests made on a prototype of an electric bike during its normal use in an old and congested town as Milan. Our aim is to show how such a type of little vehicle could help urban designer to resolve some problems correlated with traffic and air pollution.

1 - Introduction

An electric bike is not a new thing among the studies to design an urban vehicle. All the same, we dealt with the project with the purpose of built a very cheap machine using normal products of large diffusion. In fact some market analysis related that the potential buyers of such a vehicle are only a little segment of the whole bike's market, then some other sophisticated projects, which need big investments and equipment's, could be too expensive. Besides, we required that it could be used also as a normal bike pedal pushed to provide in an easy and efficient way for the running out of batteries.

2 - The Bike

So we started from a normal electric motor with worm reduction, studying how to make as fewer changes as possible to a normal city-bike. We chose to design a unisex frame, that could allow an easy mounting of the electric group, with an intrinsic strength to support the heavier loads due to the batteries. Also for the batteries, we chose only those models more used on the market, the Pb ones and the NiCd ones, to restrain the final price of the product.

The same philosophy brought us to avoid the possibility of battery recharge during braking time, as the mechanical and electronic complication doesn't justify the increase in battery operating cycle. On the contrary we resolved to privilege the possibility of an easy insertion of muscular thrust meanwhile the running of the electric motor and vice versa. So we designed only a little special hub (then patented later on) to be

Fig.1 - The hub

assembled with normal bike elements, to mount the electric motor on the rear wheel [fig.1]. A normal PWM electronic control (the same normally used in high quantities for pallet's movers) is mounted under the rear parcel grid [fig. 2] and is piloted from a

Fig.2 - The PWM electronic control

potentiometer housed in a special designed handlebar grip [fig.3].

The batteries, housed in a bag with a fast connection to the electric circuit, can be easily removed [fig.4] and substituted with fully charged ones (for an immediate continuation of the trip) or can be put on charge for a later trip (2 or 3 hours for a fast charge, 6 or 7 hours for a better slow charge).

As result only two things were built on purpose for this bike: the hub and the grip. In fig.5 you can see the prototype of such electric bike.

Fig.3 - The handlebar grip

Fig.4 - The fast connection of the battery bag

3 - The road tests

At first we carried on a short period of laboratory tests on the frame and on the motor. Then we made a fine setting of the electronic control to limit the maximum current to the motor.

Fig.5 - The electric bike

Therefore we decided to test the bike directly "on the road" and to acquire a feeling of its manoeuvrability and real autonomy. We equipped our electric bike with a small data-logger to collect instantaneous information about:
- bike speed
- voltage of the batteries
- current consumption of the motor

(fig.6 shows the bike with another bag housing the data-logger and the signal conditioners). The tests were performed with the help of a motorcycle equipped with a laptop to perform the download of the partial data on floppy disks.

The test trips were chosen at first around the university campus and then across the whole town. This

Fig.6 - The data download

because, even though we stated the theoretical life of the batteries, in fact the total time of use of the electric bike is grown very much during the real road use. We founded that the periods of effective current consumption are much shorter than the time spent waiting for a traffic light or jam, or the time of inertial running of the bike before a stop. So, the entire real period of use of such vehicle without battery re-charging (that for a continuous trip of 20 Km out of the town is only of an hour) became of near an half day, allowing us either to cross a whole town as Milan, either to go forth to downtown and back again.

4 - Test Results

As mentioned in the previous paragraph, during the road tests we collected two kind of information:
- a numerical value of technical parameters.
- a personal feeling of road handling (as manoeuvrability among the traffic - easy parking - time saving for a city crossing).

In fig.7 we show two typical trips of the several ones we made through the city of Milan. The A trip is a crossing one from the University Campus to the S.Siro Stadium. The B trip, named "Turtle Operation" by the Italian Ambient League, was made in comparison with a car, a bus and a motorcycle, starting from Leonardo's Dockyard and ending to the Central Station. The whole distance of about 4 Km, was covered in 10 minutes by the motorcycle, in 13 by the electric bike, in 21 by the car and in 30 by the bus.

In fig.8 you can see two typical plots of the data collected: the speed of the bike and the current to the motor sampled 60 times per second to detect all the peaks during the starting up. We founded a normal current consumption of about 12 A at constant speed, while it could be got a peak of about 40 A for starting the bike from rest. We also founded that the periods of no consumption allow the batteries to recovery a bit, and that, during a normal use of the electric bike in a city, the batteries' voltage remain over 15 V for more than three hours.

5 - Conclusions

All the tests performed show the advantages of the use of an electric bike in a small and congested city as Milan.
You can arrive in time, with no problems of parking and traffic jam, and without having to deep breathe the smog as who ride a

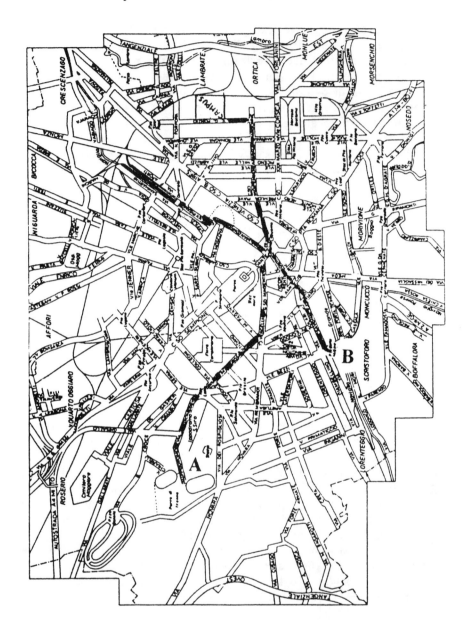

A - A crossing trip from the University Campus to the Stadium
B - The "Turtle Operation" of the Ambient League: a comparative
   test between a car, a bus, a bike and a little motorcycle.

Fig.7

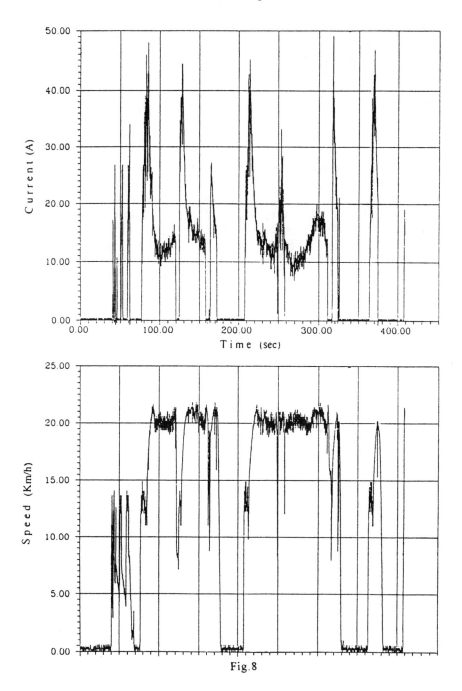

Fig.8

normal bike. Otherwise you can also push sometime on the pedals, with that easiness to slip away the car queues either a motorcycle or a scooter can never afford.

Nevertheless some other problems are yet to be solved before such vehicle could be used in every Italian town. First of all a road traffic rule less restrictive against the electric bike, in Italy classified as a motorcycle, and therefore to be used over 16 years of age with helmet and outside the areas where traffic is restricted (just the best ones for a bike !)

Other problems could be solved by a good urban design providing for guarded parking lots before public offices, areas for batteries recharging, electric bike rental near railway stations.

Last, but not least, it is very important the electric bike could have a cheap retail price, competitive with the little motorcycles' ones. In fact, our little market survey found a big interest in this small electric vehicle, on condition it has a price only a little more expensive than a good city-bike's one, that is about 1,5 millions of Italian liras.

Dynamical analysis of electrodynamically suspended vehicles

V.A. Dzenzersky, N.M. Khatchapuridze, A.L. Manashkin,
N.A. Radchenko, A.A. Zevin
*Transmag Research Institute, Ukraine Academy of Sciences,
Piesarzhevskogo 5, Dniepropetrovsk, 320005, Ukraine*

Abstract

Dynamics of high-speed vehicles using electrodynamic suspension is studied
for both continuous and discrete track structures. New approaches are
developed for determination of electrodynamic forces and stability of the
stationary motion, some numerical results are represented. The problem of
stabilization of an unstable system is discussed.

1 Introduction

The majority of the results relating to the problem of high-speed electrody-
namically suspended transport are devoted to an analysis of various systems
of suspension, propulsion and guidance. The problems of dynamics and stability of the motion were studied less extensively. The detailed investigation
of dynamical forces and types of vibrations as well as the survey of theoretical and experimental results on the dynamics of systems with sheet track
structures were given by F.C.Moon [1]. In the present paper methods and
numerical results of dynamical analysis of some systems (figure 1) are represented (systems consisting of several masses connected to each other by
elastic and dissipative ties were also treated). A comparison of them from
the point of view of stability and safety is carried out.

2 Continuous Track Structure

The equations of motion are obtained under the following main assumptions:
the vehicle may be modelled by a rigid body or a system of connected bod-
ies; the levitation force acting on a superconducting coil may be replaced
by a nonlinear spring (the corresponding characteristic complies with the
force-distance dependence derived by Reitz [2]). Under oscillations additional forces analogous to that of viscous damping appear (a method for
calculating the damping coefficient was developed in [3]). The mechanical

corresponding differential equations are

$$S\frac{\mathrm{d}I}{\mathrm{d}t} + RI = e, \tag{1}$$

$$\frac{\mathrm{d}}{\mathrm{d}t}\left(\frac{\partial L}{\partial \dot{q}}\right) - \frac{\partial L}{\partial q} = Q \tag{2}$$

where S is a matrix of inductances, R is a diagonal matrix of resistances, e and Q are vectors of electromotive and nonconservative forces and L is the Lagrange function. Since the values e depend on q and, conversely, the values Q depend on I, equations (1) and (2) are coupled and have to be solved simultaneously. If the currents in superconducting coils are not considered constant, they should be included in I.

Under the stationary motion q values are constant (vertical oscillations caused by varying levitation force are negligibly small). So the problem is reduced to solving equation (1) in which currents in neighbouring levitation and guidance coils are connected by the relation $i_k(t) = i_{k+1}(t + H/v)$ where H is a pitch of coils and v is a velocity of a vehicle.

As $s_{ii} >> s_{ik}$ in S, a method of successive approximations is found to be very effective for solving equations (1) (an analytical solution corresponding to $s_{ik} = 0$ for $i \neq k$ serves as the first approximation).

Using this algorithm, various levitation systems were analyzed. In particular, it was found that levitation forces F_i acting on neighbouring superconducting coils depend essentially on the distance between them. In figure 2 the function $F_1(\Delta)/F$ and $F_2(\Delta)/F$ are given for two horizontal coils (F is the levitation force of an individual coil; curves 1,2 and 3,4 correspond, respectively, to the same and opposite directions of the coil currents).

A method for investigation of the stability of the stationary motion was worked out. The linearized equation about a stationary solution $x_0(t) = [I_0(t), q_0]$ may be written as follows

$$\dot{y} = A(t)y. \tag{3}$$

The values $y(0)$ and $y(T)$ $(T = H/v)$ are connected by the relations $y(T) = W(T)y(0)$ where $W(t)$ is the matrizant of (3). The system is Lyapunov stable if all $|\rho_i| < 1$ where ρ_i are the eigenvalues of the matrix $V = UW(T)$ (the matrix U is due to the relative shift of the vehicle and the coils on $[0, T]$).

The numerical analysis of various systems shows that the stationary motion is unstable within a large velocity range (note that a simplified analysis not taking into account the coupling of equations (1) and (2) leads to a wrong conclusion on the stability of the system). Analogously to the case of a continuous structure, stabilization can be reached by introducing elastic and dissipative ties between oscillating masses. The use of a dynamical

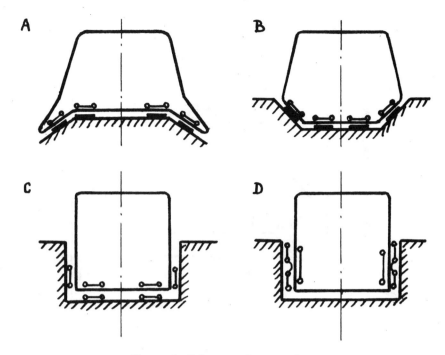

Figure 1: Schemes of suspension

system obtained is described by Lagrange equations.

The stationary motion corresponds to constant values of vehicle's coordinates. Since the damping coefficient mentioned above is negative for a sufficiently large velocity, the motion is unstable. To stabilize it, elastic and dissipative ties between every superconducting coil and the carriage may be introduced. However, it proves out that such a system is very sensitive to switching off a coil that may happen in the case of emergency, so the safety can be ensured only by the use of a large number of coils. From this point of view, the system with coils fixed rigidly on the bogie (or, better, on two hinged bogies) connected with the carriage by means of springs and dampers is preferable.

The comparison of schemes A and B shows that the latter has better guidance properties because here lateral disturbunces decrease faster. In general, lowering of the center of gravity of a vehicle relatively to the longitudinal axis of rotation improves dynamical properties of the system.

3 Discrete Track Structure

A discrete track structure consists of coils generating a levitation force; combined levitation and guidance system [4] composed of two connected coils attached to the side wall (scheme D) was also studied. Let I be a vector of coil currents and q be a vector of vehicle's coordinates. The

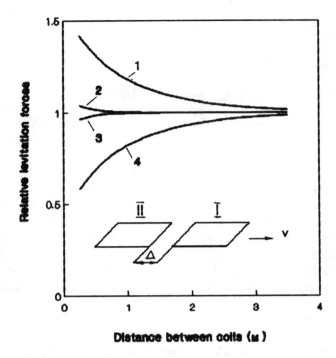

Figure 2: Levitation forces in neighbouring superconducting coils

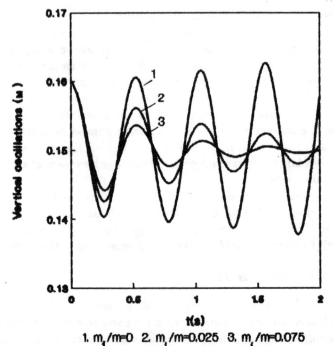

1. $m_1/m=0$ 2. $m_1/m=0.025$ 3. $m_1/m=0.075$

Figure 3: Vertical oscillations of a vehicle with a dynamical absorber

absorber was also examined. In figure 3 vertical oscillations of the vehicle (scheme C) with the absorber are shown m_1 and m are the masses of the absorber and the system). As seen, the initially unstable system ($m_1 = 0$) can be damped using the absorber with a relatively small mass.

4 Simulation of a Linear Synchronous Motor

It is usually supposed that the propulsion of a Maglev (EDS) vehicle is realized via linear synchronous motor (LSM). A mathematical model was worked out for analysis of a vehicle motion with LSM analogous to that of MLU-002 (Japan). The vehicle moves along a U-shape guideway with an arbitrary spatial curvilinear axis.

The electrodynamic levitation and guidance system on the side walls is simulated; the vertical and lateral forces are supposed to be proportional to the corresponding displacements of the superconducting magnets (SCM). The mathematical model includes the equations of the vehicle motion and the equations of magnetic linkages of a stator section. Each side of the section is fed by an independent source of a 3-phase sinusoidal voltage. Their wendings are star-connected, and the voltage frequency is synchronized automatically with the vehicle velocity. The mutual induction of a SCM and a phase is represented in the form $l = M(\Delta y, \Delta z)f(s)$ where s is the path length, $f(s)$ is a periodic function and $M(\Delta y, \Delta z)$ depends on SCM displacements along y and z axes about the equilibrium position. The equations of the magnetic linkages are represented as follows:

$$\frac{d\psi_1}{dt} = U_a \sin\left(\frac{2\pi s}{\lambda_0} + \theta_u\right) - \psi_1 \frac{R_s}{L_s} + \frac{R_s}{L_s} I_{scm}\left(M_{\Sigma 1} f(s) - M_{\Sigma 2} f(s - \lambda_0/2)\right)$$

$$\frac{d\psi_2}{dt} = U_a \sin\left(\frac{2\pi s}{\lambda_0} - 2\pi/3 + \theta_u\right) - \psi_2 \frac{R_s}{L_s} + \frac{R_s}{L_s} I_{scm}\left(M_{\Sigma 1} f(s - \lambda_0/3) - M_{\Sigma 2} f(s - 5\lambda_0/6)\right)$$

$$\frac{d\psi_3}{dt} = U_a \sin\left(\frac{2\pi s}{\lambda_0} + 2\pi/3 + \theta_u\right) - \psi_3 \frac{R_s}{L_s} + \frac{R_s}{L_s} I_{scm}\left(M_{\Sigma 1} f(s + \lambda_0/3) - M_{\Sigma 2} f(s - \lambda_0/6)\right)$$

where U_a is a voltage amplitude, θ_u is an angle of voltage phase shift, λ_0 is a longitudinal distance between stator wendings of the same phase, L_s and R_s are the induction and the resistance of the section phase, $M_{\Sigma 1}$ and

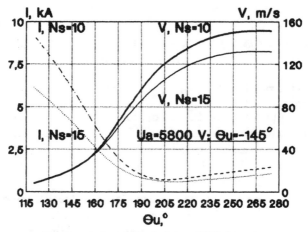

Figure 4: Imax(Θu), kA ; V(Θu), m/s

$M_{\Sigma 2}$ are the sums of the $M(\Delta y, \Delta z)$ values for the SCMs with positive and negative currents, respectively, I_{scm} is the SCM constant current. The equations for the both sides of the section are analogous. Integration of the differential equations enables us to simulate the instantaneous values of the phase currents and, thereby, the forces acting on the SCMs. For the case of the stationary motion an analytical solution of the equations was obtained. In the general case the numerical simulation is used.

Figure 4 shows the dependence of the stationary velocity and the maximal stator current versus the angle of the phase shift of voltage. The curves were obtained for a section including $N_s = 10$ and $N_s = 15$ windings of each phase.

Figure 5 demonstrates the total thrust force and the forces acting on the SCMs with different directions of the current. As seen, the total thrust force varies slightly about its mean value, while the forces acting on an individual SCM oscillate within a broad range. The last is an essential drawback of the single-layer system of stator wendings, because oscillations of the thrust force may cause the SCM vibrations and heating. This effect was noted by J. Fujie and S. Fujiwara when analysing the experiments at Miyazaki Test Track.

Figure 6 represents velocity-time curves under LSM setting to motion. Curve 1 shows the case of non-controlled start; as seen, it results in unacceptable acceleration and currents values. Curve 2 corresponds to the case when U_a increases linearly during 60 s from 5 to 100 per cent of its nominal value. Curve 3 shows the case when θ_s changes linearly from 100^0 to 215^0 during 60 s. The best LSM start regime is in the second case be-

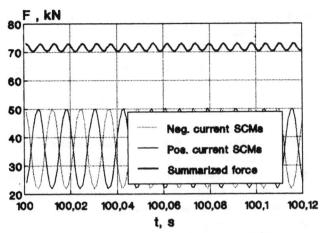

Figure 5: Thrust forces (Θu = -145°)

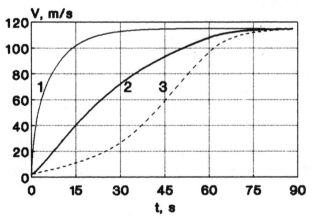

Figure 6: Vehicle velocity-time curves

cause it enables us to reduce the maximal currents and acceleration to any required level. The software designed makes it also possible to study other non-stationary motion regimes (the braking, the abrupt changing of drag force, etc.). The simulation results can be used when choosing the system parameters and the methods of LSM control under various motion regimes.

5 Conclusion

In this paper some approaches to dynamical analysis of suspended vehicles are suggested and the results of a numerical study are represented. The stability and other dynamical properties of a vehicle depend largely on the scheme of the system. As a rule, the stationary motion is unstable, so some stabilization measures are discussed. Reliable conclusions on the system can be obtained only using a sufficiently full mathematical model; e.g., under stability analysis one should take into account the coupling of the equations of motion and the equations of coil currents. A further elaboration of the mathematical model requires, in particular, a detailed examination of aerodynamical forces.

References

[1] Moon, F.C. Vibrations problems in magnetic levitation and propulsion, *Transport Without Wheels*, pp.123-161, London, 1977.

[2] Reitz, J.R. Forces on moving magnets due to eddy currents, *J.Appl.Phys.*, 1970, 41, 2067-2071.

[3] Baiko, A.V., Voevodskii, K.E. and Kochetkov, V.M. Vertical unstable stability of electrodynamic suspension of high-speed ground transport, *CRIOGENICS.*, May 1980, 271-276.

[4] Fujiwara, S and Fujimoto, T. Characteristics of the combined levitation and guidance system using ground coils on the side wall of the guideway, *QR of RTRL*, Aug. 1989, 30, 3, 123-126.

AUTHORS' INDEX

Computational Mechanics Publications

Alternative Engines for Road Vehicles

M.L. POULTON, *Transport Research Laboratory, Crowthorne, UK*

Spark-ignition engines and compression-ignitior diesel engines have been almost unchallenged as power units for road vehicles for the last century. Air pollution problems and poor efficiency in today's typical operating conditions make it essential that alternatives to these engines are explored. This book discusses technologies that presently exist for alternative engines and provides a unique source of information for engineers, scientists and managers involved with vehicle development and planning. For each alternative engine considered, operating principles are discussed, together with primary advantages and disadvantages of the particular technology. Developments of each alternative is noted and current manufacturer research and experimental testing described with results where available. Alternative engines and prospects for further development of conventional engines are discussed and compared with reference to fuel economy and exhaust emissions. Cost issues are made generally, with definitive data where it exists. This book forms part of a programme of study of the contribution of road transport to global warming and air pollution, and investigating ways of reducing it.

ISBN: 1853123005; 1562522248 (US, Canada, Mexico) May 1994 192pp £59.00/$89.00

Alternative Fuels for Road Vehicles

M.L. POULTON, *Transport Research Laboratory, Crowthorne, UK*

Discusses future prospects for conventional and alternative fuels for road vehicle applications. Implications of energy and emissions from the whole fuel cycle are considered, along with vehicular fuel consumption and exhaust emission characteristics. Each chapter describes a particular alternative fuel and is completely self-contained. The reader is able to learn about a particular subject without having to refer to other chapters to gain a full understanding of the fuel's characteristics and notable developments and demonstration programmes underway worldwide. The final chapter provides an overview and inter-comparison of all the fuels discussed. The book will be of interest to mechanical, petrochemical and transportation engineers, and also those with a technical interest in the subject of fuel for the motor vehicle, its development and change in the future.

ISBN: 1853123013; 1562522256 (US, Canada, Mexico) July 1994 232pp £59.00/$89.00

Air Pollution II

Edited by **J. M. BALDASANO,** *Universitat Politecnica de Catalunya, Spain;* **C. A. BREBBIA,** *Wessex Institute of Technology,UK;* **H. POWER,** Wessex Institute of Technology, UK; **P. ZANNETTI,***Failure Analysis Associates Inc.,USA.*

The last decade has shown an increase in public and government concern around environmental issues due to air pollution, in particular those generated by man-made processes seeking the comfort of modern society.

Atmospheric pollution consists of the adverse effects on the environment of a variety of substances (contaminants) emitted into the atmosphere by natural and man-made processes. These phenomena are complicated by the fact that an apparently inert contaminant can be transformed by chemical reaction into an adverse one, during its transport through the atmosphere. Atmospheric pollution is a multifaceted problem that includes phenomena involving the different scales; a near-field phenomena that governs the way in which the contaminant rises, short-range transport in which the ground-effect is predominant, an intermediate transport where chemical reactions become important and a long-range transport where the decay and deposition effects are relevant.

This set of books contains the papers presented at the Second International Air Pollution Conference held in September 1994.

SET ISBN: 1853122718; 1562521950 (US,Canada, Mexico) Sept 1994 1184pp £248.00/$372.00

Computer Simulation - Volume 1

Partial Contents: Meteorological Modelling; Turbulence and Diffusion Modelling; Chemical Transformation; Urban Case Studies.

ISBN: 1853123609; 1562522841 (US, Canada, Mexico) Sept 1994 608pp £140.00/$210.00

Pollution Control and Monitoring - Volume 2

Partial Contents: Global Studies; Emission Inventory and Modelling; Data Analysis and Observation; Monitoring and Laboratory Studies.

ISBN: 1853123617; 156252285X (US, Canada, Mexico) Sept 1994 576pp £133.00/$199.00

All prices correct at time of going to press. All books are available from your bookseller or in case of difficulty direct from the Publisher.

Computational Mechanics Publications
Ashurst Lodge, Ashurst, Southampton,
SO40 7AA, UK.
Tel: 44 (0)1703 293223 Fax: 44 (0) 1703 292853

Computational Mechanics Publications

Computers in Railways

Edited by: **T.K.S. MURTHY,** *Wessex Institute of Technology, UK;* **B. MELLITT,** *London Underground, UK;* **C.A. BREBBIA,** *Wessex Institute of Technology, UK;* **G. SCIUTTO,** *Universita degli Studi di Genova, Italy and* **S. SONE,** *University of Tokyo, Japan*

These two volumes contain the edited proceedings from the Fourth International Conference on Computer Aided Design, Manufacture and Operation in the Railway and other Mass Transit Systems held in September 1994. They discuss how the planners, designers, manufacturers and operators can benefit from the latest developments in the use of computer-based technology in railway and other passenger and freight systems.

SET ISBN: 1853122661; 156252190X (US, Canada, Mexico) Aug 1994 1112pp £255.00/$379.00

Railway Design and Management - Volume 1
Partial Contents: Computer Applications in Toronto's Rapid Transit Expansion Program; Computer-based Planning Techniques and the Appraisal of an Underground Railway Extension; Integration of Power Feeding and Train Dispatching Subsystems to Increase Railway Service Capability;
ISBN: 1853123544; 1562522825 (US, Canada, Mexico) Aug 1994 600pp £151.00/$226.00

Railway Operations - Volume 2
Partial Contents: Improvement in Railway Safety and Train Density by using Continuous Train Control System; Timetable Data Communication to Signal Control Systems; The Problems of Assessing the Safety of ATP Systems which have been Developed under Different National Standards.
ISBN: 1853123595; 1562522833 (US, Canada, Mexico) Aug 1994 512pp £129.00/$193.00

A Constraint Model of Space Planning

K.B. YOON
This book is concerned with the use of constraints in the design process, particularly in architectural space planning tasks. The major aim of this research is to develop a methodology that relates explicitly to the manipulation of constraints in order to discover information about the design space, and to produce design descriptions within the design space.
Contents: Design Constraints; Space Planning; Generative Approaches to Space Planning; Constraint Propagation and Design; Knowledge-based System and Space Planning; Algorithmic Constraint Propagation; Relational Space Planning; A Space Planning System.
Series: Topics in Engineering, Volume 9
ISBN: 1853122033; 1562520075 (US, Canada, Mexico) Aug 1992 240pp £25.00/$45.00

Urban Air Pollution - Volume 1

Edited by: **H. POWER,** *Wessex Institute of Technology, Southampton, UK;* **N. MOUSSIOPOULOS,** *Aristotle University of Thessaloniki, Greece;* **C.A. BREBBIA,** *Wessex Institute of Technology, Southampton, UK*

The last decade has shown an increase in public and government concern about environmental issues due to air pollution, in particular, that generated by man-made processes. The air pollution problem is widespread throughout the world and the elimination of the risks to human health is of paramount importance. Urban areas are one of the major sources of air pollution having characteristic patterns of pollutant emissions, with adverse consequences to the health of their inhabitants. The problem of urban air quality is of international concern, as it applies to cities throughout the world, to a lesser or greater degree. This book is the first volume of a series of publications on *Urban Air Pollution.* It contains a selection of invited review articles covering urban air pollution topics. The nine chapters in the book have been contributed by leading authors in the field.
Contents: Case Studies: Air Pollution in Athens; Air quality study for the city of Graz, Austria; Atmospheric pollution in the Lisbon airshed; Some recent advances on air pollution reactivity in Mexico City; Photochemical modeling of pollution scenarios in Mexico City; Effect of Tokyo Metropolitan Area on the air quality of the Kanto Plain: **Urban Air Pollution Processes:** Landfill emissions of gases to the atmosphere; Reciprocity between the urban heat island effect and air pollution; The ecology of urban emissions.
ISBN: 1853123315; 1562522558 (US, Canada, Mexico) Sept 1994 336pp £95.00/$145.00

Urban Air Pollution
Volume 2

Edited by: **H. POWER,** *Wessex Institute of Technology, Southampton, UK;*
This volume will contain further information, reviews and examples written by leading authors in the field.
ISBN: 1853123722; 1562522965 (US, Canada, Mexico) Sept 1995 apx 330pp apx £95.00/$145.00

All prices correct at time of going to press. All books are available from your bookseller or in case of difficulty direct from the Publisher.

Computational Mechanics Publications
Ashurst Lodge, Ashurst, Southampton,
SO40 7AA, UK.
Tel: 44 (0)1703 293223 Fax: 44 (0) 1703 292853